Bayard Rustin: Troubles I've Seen

ALSO BY JERVIS ANDERSON

This Was Harlem: A Cultural Portrait, 1900–50
A. Philip Randolph: A Biographical Portrait
Guns in American Life

Bayard Rustin: Troubles I've Seen

A Biography

Jervis Anderson

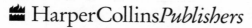 HarperCollins*Publishers*

HarperCollins books may be purchased for educational, business, or sales promotional use. For information please write: Special Markets Department, HarperCollins Publishers, Inc., 10 East 53rd Street, New York, NY 10022.

FIRST EDITION

Designed by Joseph Rutt

Library of Congress Cataloging-in-Publication Data

Anderson, Jervis.
    Bayard Rustin : troubles I've seen : a biography / by Jervis Anderson. —
1st ed.
      p. cm.
    Includes index.
    ISBN 0-06-016702-5
    1. Rustin, Bayard, 1912–1987. 2. Afro-Americans—Biography.
3. Civil rights workers—United States—Biography. 4. Pacifists—United
States—Biography. 5. Afro-Americans—Civil rights. 6. Civil rights
movements—United States—History—20th century. 7. Nonviolence—
United States—History—20th century.   I. Title.
E185.97.R93A53   1997
323'.092
[B]—DC20   96-25003

---

97 98 99 00 01 ❖/RRD 10 9 8 7 6 5 4 3

To the memory of
Janifer Rustin and Julia Davis Rustin

No! I am not Prince Hamlet, nor was meant to be;
Am an attendant lord, one that will do
To swell a progress, start a scene or two,
Advise the prince...
—T. S. Eliot, "The Love Song of J. Alfred Prufrock"

If I am not for myself, who will be for me? But if I am only for
myself, then what am I?
—Rabbi Hillel

The major aspect of the struggle within is determined without. If one
gets out and begins to defend one's rights and the rights of others, spiritual
growth takes place. One becomes in the process of doing, in the purifying
process of action. The proof that one truly believes is in action.
—Bayard Rustin

Bayard represented a new type of leadership. Most people in the racial
struggle represented only themselves and only the racial interest. He covered
the field. He represented a new outlook, a new man.
—Roger Baldwin

Contents

Acknowledgments

For their help and guidance in obtaining documentary material, I am indebted to the curators and employees of these archives and libraries:

The Amistad Research Center; the Chester County Historical Society (West Chester, Pa.); the Columbia University Oral History Collection; the Fisk University Library; the Harry S. Truman Presidential Library; the Haviland Records Room of the New York Friends; the Leslie Pinckney Hill Library (Cheyney University, Pa.); the Library of Congress (Manuscript Division); the Lyndon B. Johnson Presidential Library; the Moorland-Spingarn Manuscript Collection (Howard University); the Mugar Memorial Library (Boston University); the National Archives and Records Administration (Northeast Division); the New York Public Library (Manuscript Division); the Quaker Peace Center, London; the Schomburg Center for Research in Black Culture (New York); the State Historical Society of Wisconsin; the Swarthmore College Peace Collection; the Syracuse University Library; the University of Pennsylvania Sports Information Office; the Wilberforce University Library.

I received generous personal assistance from the following: Charles Bloomstein, C. P. Crow, Tom Donahue, Sandra Feldman, Henry Finder, Carl Gershman, Paula Giddings, Maxine Greene, Hendrik Hertzberg, Watler Naegle, Albert Shanker, Ted Solotaroff, Irwin Suall, and Sondra Wilson—all of whom recommended me for grants-in-aid and foundation fellowships. Tina Brown and Robert Gottlieb, editors of *The New Yorker*, were considerate enough to preserve my position with the magazine during the eight years I devoted myself almost exclusively to this work. Bloomstein and Naegle, of the Bayard Rustin Estate, were indefatigable in making research material available to me, directing me to other sources, and correcting factual errors in my early drafts. (Such errors as may remain are my responsibility, not theirs.) Large portions of the manuscript were written in the serene surroundings of Putney,

Vermont, where I spent many summer months in the homes of Sven and Marya Huseby, Michael and Debbie Valenze Gilmore.

The grants-in-aid and fellowships that supported my eight-year effort were received from the Atran Foundation; the American Federation of Teachers and the United Federation of Teachers; the AFL-CIO; the Phillips Family Fund; Elizabeth Gilmore; the Bayard Rustin Fund; the A. Philip Randolph Education Fund; the Schomburg Center for Research in Black Culture; the Anti-Defamation League; the Communications Workers of America; the Daniel and Joanna Rose Fund; the Echoing Green Foundation; and the National Endowment for the Humanities.

The idea for this book originated with the writer and editor Ted Solotaroff—a friend for many years—who first suggested that I attempt it. Its worth was enhanced by the patient and improving hands of Hugh Van Dusen and Kate Ekrem, my editors at HarperCollins. And its passage from conception to publication was further smoothed by the able and reassuring representations of my literary agent, Robert Lescher.

For interviews, letters, and memoranda, I am grateful to:

Elizabeth Aberman, Louisa Alger, Maya Angelou, Arnold Aronson, Robert Ascher;

Godric Bader, Esmie Bahn, Tim Baker, Judy Bardacke, Paul Barnes, Yetta Barsh, Frances S. Bartholomay, John W. Beale, Richard K. Bennett, Hannah Berman, Paul Berman, Robert Bilheimer, Poynton K. Bishop, Alex Bloomstein, Charles Bloomstein, Steven Bloomstein, Robert Bone, Jonathan Brice, James Bristol, Eileen Brock, Ernest Bromley, Marion Bromley, Thomas R. Brooks, Arthur Brown, Carrol Buchanan, Warren Burton;

Morton Calvert, Stokely Carmichael (Kwame Turé), April Carter, Stephen Cary, Leo Cherne, Katha Chollis, Bronson P. Clark, Derek Clark, Kenneth B. Clark, Moira Clark, Harry Cooper, Maria Rustin Crutchfield, Bernhardt Crystal, Herbert J. Curtis;

Peter Daniels, Charles Darby, Ann Morrisett Davidon, Margaret Davison, Richard Deats, Moshe Dector, David Dellinger, Leonard DePaur, Joseph Derry, Ralph DiGia, Saunders Dixon, Nathan Dodell, James R. Dumpson;

Frances H. Early;

James Farmer, Sandra Feldman, Joseph Felmet, Julie Finch, Roy Finch, Moe Foner, Ted Friedgut, Paul Friedman;

Larry Gara, David Garrow, Herman Gewirtz, Niel Glixon, Edward P. Gottlieb, Adam Green, Ernest Green, Betty Gubert;

Gay Morenus Hammerman, Donald S. Harrington, Joyce Harris, Alfred Hassler, William K. Hefner, Regina Helin, Benjamin Heller, Lorvelle Henry, Nat Hentoff, Hazel Hertzberg, Hendrik Hertzberg, Herbert Hill, Norman Hill, Velma Hill, Marshall Hoagland, Charles D. Hornig, Rachelle Horowitz, Robert Horton, C. Douglas Hostetter, George Houser, Irving Howe, Rascha Hughes, Martha Huset;

Homer Jack, Earl John, Clifton H. Johnson, Eula Johnson, William H. Johnson, Charles Jones, Dorcas Jones;

Tom Kahn, Louis Katlowitz, Abraham Kaufman, Brett Kelver, Eugenia Kemble, Penn Kemble, Maida Spring Kemp, Leonard Kentworthy, Thomas Kilgore, Milton Kramer;

Joan Landis, Ken Landis, Kuno Laren, Kay Lazarus, Eric Lee, Fran Lee, Kenneth Lee, Ernest Lefever, John Lewis, Carolyn Lindquist, Marian Logan; Peter Ludwig, Anna Rustin Luff, DeWitt Luff, Staughton Lynd, Conrad Lynn;

Raymond W. Mack, David McReynolds, John Mecartney, John L. Melton, LuEsther Mertz, Elizabeth Moger, Roger W. Moore, Wilma Mosholder, John Muste;

Walter Naegle, Hermione Nelson, Rosamond Nelson, Wallace Nelson, Marge Nissen;

Laurence Otter;

Marie Palmer, Jack Patterson, Oliver Patterson, Paul Peabody, Mary Pearce, Robert Pickus, Davis Platt, Charles Porter, Seymour Posner, Devi Prasad, Shizu Proctor, Arch Puddington;

Carl Rachlin, Michael Randle, Worth Randle, Joseph L. Rauh,

Richard Ravitch, Catharine Raymond, Curt Regen, Rosalie Regen, Adam Roberts, Cleveland Robinson, James Robinson, John P. Roche, John R. Rodgers, Igal Roodenko, John M. Royall, Jr.;

Scott Sandage, Beverly Sanders, John Anthony Scott, Doris Shamleffer, Albert Shanker, Dorothy Siegal, Andy Simons, Don Slaiman, Glenn Smiley, Tony Smythe, Wesley Sollenberger, Robert Spence, Dorothy Steen, Beverly Stern, E. R. Stewart, Irwin Suall, Sally Sullivan, Leonard Sussman, William Sutherland, Jack Sutters, Helen Suzman, John Swomley;

Nicholas J. Tavani, Jr., Lawrence Templin, Michael Thelwell, Frances S. Thomas, A. C. Thompson, Helen Tompkins, John J. Turner;

Liv Ullmann;

Harry Wachtel, Caroline Wagner, Charles Walker, Howard Wallace, Mrs. Josh White, Denny Wilcher, Sondra Wilson, Harris Wofford, Leon Wofsky, William Worthy, Frank J. Wright.

Part I

Chapter 1

"That Was Bayard"

Some years before he died, in the summer of 1987, Bayard Rustin told Charles Bloomstein—a close friend and political ally of more than four decades—that he would like to be remembered mostly as someone who had great fun in his life. This may not have been surprising to Bloomstein, in view of his long acquaintance with Rustin's personal style and temperament. But others who knew only of Bayard's career in different arenas of serious public activism would have been justified in wondering what had drawn him to so blithe and jovial an epitaph.

After all, in the fifty years of his engagement with public issues, he had been one of the more earnest political intellectuals in American life. Like many young idealists in the late 1930s, he had had a brief and disillusioned dalliance with the communist movement. Shifting his allegiance to democratic socialism (represented by the leadership of Norman Thomas) and to the pacifist Fellowship of Reconciliation (headed by A. J. Muste), he had, at great personal cost, become a militant conscientious objector to service in World War II. He had been a youth organizer in the first March on Washington movement, launched by A. Philip Randolph in 1941. With Randolph, Muste, James Farmer, and George Houser, he had been among the first to promote the

Gandhian method of nonviolent resistance in the civil rights struggle. He had been an original member of the Congress of Racial Equality (CORE), along with Houser and Farmer, its founder. As an adviser to the Reverend Dr. Martin Luther King, Jr., beginning with the Montgomery bus boycott of 1955–56, he had played an influential role in developing the modern stage of the black protest movement. He had helped to inspire some of the young intellectuals who formed the avant garde of the Student Nonviolent Coordinating Committee (SNCC). Long after Black Power radicals in SNCC abandoned Rustin's model of civil rights agitation, he continued to enunciate the principles of nonviolence and interracial cooperation. He had made significant contributions to a number of movements for African freedom and to the global struggle for human rights. At home and abroad, he had been a prominent activist in perhaps the most urgent crusade of his lifetime—the campaign against the building and proliferation of thermonuclear weapons.

For all that, Rustin achieved no significant power in his career. Part of the reason was the breadth and variety of his political involvements. No important black figure of his generation responded to as many causes in which the values of democracy and fair play were at stake. Yet, with rare exceptions, he was a marginal force in the movements he served—though few marginal forces could have made such central contributions to movements led by others.

The complexity of Rustin's personality was also unsuited to the wielding of political power. The details of administration bored him. He much preferred the life of a troubleshooter—an itinerant strategist, tactician, and organizer. Running off here and there, cultivating his interest in art and antiques, was more appealing to him than presiding steadily at an office desk. He took issues seriously, but not himself; the alleviation of social problems was more interesting to him than the exercise of authority.

Essentially, he was a humanitarian. He seldom left his house on a morning, or any other time of day, without putting some extra cash in his pocket, for beggars he might encounter in the streets. Charles

Bloomstein once explained: "While most liberal idealists were wholesale in their concern for the poor and the homeless, Bayard was both wholesale and retail." Nor did Rustin ever reject appeals for financial help from political opponents who had denounced him in the past. "He was all-absorbing, a universal man," said Rachelle Horowitz, who worked closely with Rustin for nearly twenty years. "I don't think he had a racist bone in him. This isn't to say he didn't know he was black; for he had a strong black identity. But he simply viewed all people as human, as soul mates." In Bloomstein's view, Rustin's "essential qualities, the sources that fueled his activities, were his love of life, his compassion, his ability to empathize with the suffering of every human being." To Worth Randle, one of Rustin's fellow peace activists in the 1940s, "Bayard seemed to envelop people with his sense of the oneness of humanity." He was "a thoroughly self-emancipated person," said William Hefner, another of his early colleagues in the pacifist movement.

Rustin's intellectual skills enhanced his attractiveness as a humanitarian. Larry Gara, a conscientious objector who worked with Rustin in the early 1940s, never forgot his "wide vocabulary and extraordinary intelligence." The Reverend Robert Horton—an activist Wesleyan minister in Pennsylvania during the 1940s and 1950s—was to recall: "I don't know what Rustin's IQ was, but it was certainly near the top of the mountain. I never heard him stopped in a debate, discussion, or question period." Charles Bloomstein attributed much of this facility to Rustin's knowledge of black and white history. "Using that knowledge," Bloomstein said, "he was superb in political meetings. He would almost inevitably come up with a resolution that struck everyone as clear, precise, apt, and workable." Others were struck by Rustin's combination of resilience and self-esteem, his ability to recover from painful personal episodes and keep moving forward. "Things that happened to him in his life would have crushed me," Larry Gara said. "But he always bounced back. That was Bayard."

When Rustin said that he wanted to be remembered mostly for having had fun, he was referring to that side of himself which Bloomstein described as "his love of life." Among the forms in which this revealed itself was his wicked sense of humor, his penchant for playing pranks on friends and acquaintances. Gara first met Rustin in 1943, when both worked at the national office of the Fellowship of Reconciliation, in New York City. While Gara found him to be charming and human, "one of the genuine pacifists I had met," he also felt that at times Rustin carried on "like a star." On one such occasion, "I went up to him and asked the meaning of a word. 'Go to the dictionary!' he replied haughtily. '*I've* been there.' And he certainly had been there." Gara felt that he had been put down, but he may really have been put on, victimized by one of the practical jokes Rustin often played with a straight face.

A bon vivant, Rustin loved to dance; was an exhilarating raconteur, who sometimes made things up along the way; an aficionado not only of good wines and whiskeys but also of fine cheeses and elegant cuisine. He was not, however, unfamiliar with cheap delicatessen sandwiches and proletarian dishes. The writer Thomas R. Brooks, a friend, once described him as a gourmet who loved pig knuckles.

Rustin's joie de vivre was almost always in evidence at parties and other informal social gatherings. On a number of those occasions, his brooding political associates—those who did not, or could not, leave their troubles at the front door—regarded him as their antidepressant of choice, even more effective than the libations of an evening. "He had a remarkably cheerful character," Charles Bloomstein said. "Many of his overstatements and exaggerations derived partly from his puckishness and partly from a desire to squeeze the most fun out of every social moment."

Whether or not Rustin carried on at times like a star, he was certainly raised as one. In the small town of West Chester, Pennsylvania—where he was born on Saint Patrick's Day of 1912—he grew up as the youngest and most coddled member of the Rustin household. A circle of older "siblings" adored him; and the heads of his family, Janifer and Julia Davis Rustin, showered him with the lion's share of their attention and affection. Even if he had not been their youngest, the Rustins might still have enthroned him at the center of their stage, for they were all enchanted by his sparkling and entertaining personality. "He was full of life," one of them remembered several decades later. "He always had a joke or a story to tell."

There was yet another reason for their pampering, one they kept hidden from him. Only in his eleventh year did he discover that he was not indeed a sibling of the Rustin children. Earl was not his brother, as he had thought, but his uncle. Five of the girls (Anna, Bessie, Rhetta, Ruth, Vella) were really his aunts. Florence, the sixth and oldest, was in fact his mother. All of this meant, of course, that Janifer and Julia Rustin were not his parents, as he had always believed, but his grandparents. He had been born out of wedlock and was not, in the strict sense, a Rustin—a stunning discovery. And it was the anomaly of his position in the family that helped to gain him the special attention he enjoyed.

But if he was not, legally born, a Rustin, then what was he? He was a Hopkins, fathered by Archie Hopkins, an attractive young man in West Chester, with whom Florence had had an affair. She was seventeen when Bayard was conceived; Archie was twenty-one; and their affair did not survive the birth of their offspring. Janifer and Julia Rustin, feeling that their unwed daughter was unfit for the responsibilities of motherhood, adopted Bayard at an early stage of his infancy and reared him as a child of their own. Anna, one of the Rustin sisters, recalled, "At first my mother said, 'Oh, I'm just going to let Florence raise that baby by herself.' But one day when she looked down at him in his crib, he smiled up sweetly at her. She decided then and there that Florence could not be a suitable parent, that she would take the baby and raise him properly. All of us pitched in and helped Ma and Pa Rustin to rear Bayard."

When Bayard first learned the facts of his parentage, Florence was no longer living in West Chester. She had married a Barbadian immigrant, named William John, and moved with him to Philadelphia, where they soon started a family. Bayard's relationship with the young Johns was never to be as close as the one he had with the young Rustins.

He preferred to regard his half-brothers and half-sisters as his cousins. That was how he described them to schoolmates, thus preventing the more curious and inquisitive ones from wondering how he could be a Rustin if his mother's children were Johns. It was also a way to avoid explaining a personal history that was already complicated enough.

Even in later years, when he had gained recognition as an important national figure, Rustin shared the unpleasant truth of his parentage only with close acquaintances. Extroverted raconteur though he was, he usually kept a stoic silence on matters that pained him deeply. But he was also a gifted and eloquent amateur singer. And whenever he sang—especially such moving Negro spirituals as "Nobody Knows the Trouble I've Seen" and "Sometimes I Feel Like a Motherless Child"—he seemed to be expressing poignant details of his own memory. When the Norwegian actor Liv Ullmann first heard him sing, in the later years of his life, she found his tenor voice "extremely touching." But, she said, "I also didn't find it like singing. It was more like a crying out—'Listen, listen, to my sadness'—like a sharing of the spirit."

Rustin's given names—Bayard Taylor—may or may not have influenced his decision to pursue a career in public life. But he wasn't unaware that he took his naming from an important source. In the spring of 1969, a resident of upstate New York wrote to him: "Seeing your name and picture in this A.M.'s paper reminded me again that I want to ask you where your name, Bayard, came from. Your parents were either steeped in French history, and named you after 'Spotless and Fearless' Bayard, or you may have been named for, or related to, a Bayard in our country."

Probably from a confused memory—or a desire to encourage the romantic Gallic connection—Rustin replied: "One of my aunts was studying French when I was born, and she was very impressed with Chevalier Bayard, who was a pacifist knight. She insisted that I be named after him, and I was." More likely, it was his grandmother Julia had named him for "a Bayard in our country." That would have been Bayard Taylor, a distinguished nineteenth-century Pennsylvania

Quaker—whom Julia, a Quaker herself, would have known about. Born near West Chester, Taylor became a noted writer, artist, and diplomat to Germany. When Rustin had himself become a noted American public figure, Conrad Wilson, director of the Chester County Historical Society (based in West Chester), wrote to remind him that Bayard Taylor was "the most famous man of the 19th century" that Chester County produced. "I think it significant that you bear his name."

Julia Rustin, one of the few black Quakers in eastern Pennsylvania, was undoubtedly an early inspiration. The chief moral and religious influence upon Bayard's upbringing—and indulgent to a fault—she strongly supported the different ambitions he displayed from time to time. According to her daughter Anna, "As a child, Bayard used to say that he wanted to be a minister or a teacher. And when he got to talking, you'd think he *was* a minister." While attending high school in West Chester, he preached an occasional sermon at the local African Methodist Episcopal church, the denomination of his grandfather Janifer. One of the three colleges he entered (graduating from none) was a teacher-training institution. At another college, he excelled as a student of music, regarded by all who heard him as a singer with a brilliant future. It was at a third college that Rustin committed himself wholly to a career in social activism—an idea that had been lurking at the back of his mind ever since high school. Though grandmother Julia had encouraged all his earlier aims, it was his final choice that pleased her most—the one she had always secretly hoped he would make.

But Rustin was such a natural performer—he had also excelled in his high school's drama club—that when he moved to New York City, in the late 1930s, he still harbored thoughts of a career, even part time, on the professional stage. In fact, he joined Actors Equity in 1940, when he played a bit part in the Broadway musical *John Henry,* starring Paul Robeson. Later, when he turned entirely to political activism, friends and critics alike still described his manner, on or off the platform, as "theatrical." James Farmer, one of his earliest colleagues in the pacifist and civil rights movements, was to say, "Very few of the black leaders

with whom I came in contact had the sparkling talent Bayard had, particularly his flair for the dramatic. He could dramatize anything. He
could dramatize a drop of rain falling on the street."

Liv Ullmann was also to be impressed by Rustin's dramatic flair,
but—and she should know—it wasn't "theatrical." Ullmann remembered visits she and Rustin made to refugee camps in Southeast Asia.
"He didn't emote in the presence of other people's misery," she emphasized. "He didn't shed tears when he saw the plight of the refugees. He
would read or sing to the people who were hurting. At times, he would
just walk away, because he was so embarrassed by their suffering. That
was not the behavior of a truly theatrical person. He used the actor in
him for positive purposes."

But partly because of the actor in him, a number of Rustin's friends
and political associates could not at times rely on the factual accuracy of
his reports. A Rustinesque account of an event could be so embroidered
that colleagues sometimes wondered whether it was the same event
they themselves had witnessed. At a point in his fluctuating regard for
Rustin, David Dellinger, the radical pacifist, called him a liar—though
not to his face. Rustin's occasional tendency toward narrative embellishment may have reflected a side of his feeling that found depressing
social details unbearable, so that he probably wished to adjust them
closer to his imagination of what they ought to be—something more
attractive. On the other hand, as in some forms of naturalistic fiction—
a hobby he had practiced in his younger years—Rustin could also exaggerate the seriousness of conditions he had seen, in order to dramatize
the urgent need for social remedy. Finally, as Charles Bloomstein said,
some of Rustin's overstatements sprang from his sheer love of fun, especially when he was among friends.

Still, much as they knew him, some of those friends were presented
with severe challenges to credibility. "Bayard's sense of drama was such
that I could seldom be sure whether the things he said were true or
not," recalled Igal Roodenko, one of his former coworkers at the War
Resisters League headquarters in New York. The New York intellectual
Paul Goodman, once a coeditor with Rustin at *Liberation* magazine,

admired Bayard as "a brilliant tactician." But Goodman could not help also observing in him "a bent for obfuscation" and "slippery truth." The Oxford-educated British pacifist Michael Randle—who worked with Rustin in a number of antinuclear campaigns during the 1950s and early 1960s—was among the colleagues who saw through Rustin's style. Randle formed a strong and high respect for Bayard's "sharp political mind, immense organizational ability," and "conspicuous" qualities of leadership. "You had to admire the panache of Bayard's style," Randle said later, "even when you knew that he was feeding you a line of straightforward bullshit."

Whenever Rustin saw that his friends had caught him in an impish flight of exaggeration, he would explode in laughter—as if to say, "Baby, I was just having some fun." His friends would then laugh along with him, in a show of understanding and forgiveness. Charles Bloomstein once explained what his and Rustin's circle of friends called "the primary and secondary bullshit index." People who "persisted in their bullshitting," he said, "were high on both the primary and secondary index, and they lost respect. To be especially high on the primary index was not at all admirable. But to come off it when challenged was to be low on the secondary index and thus to redeem oneself. Bayard was low on the secondary index. He always chuckled roguishly when he was found out, as though he merely wanted to be challenged."

"We knew that Bayard could sometimes be a bullshit artist," said Ralph DiGia, another former comrade at the head office of the War Resisters League. "But we had an extraordinary faith in him. He was one of the true pacifists in our alliance. We knew that his commitment to our cause was absolute. Furthermore, we were impressed not only by his superb sense of drama but also by the positive political purposes to which he could put it." It was from the example of Rustin's sense of drama—his ability to take "total command of an audience, large or small"—that Igal Roodenko, as he confessed, "learned to be self-confident on the political podium."

Rustin's sense of drama saved him from being silenced by a number of difficult audiences, such as the one he encountered on the evening of

January 19, 1967. He was addressing a hostile gathering in a Newark auditorium, when, by accident or sabotage, all lights went out in the room. After the briefest pause, to assess the nature of his predicament, he went on, "This is the first time I've spoken in the dark. But as long as I'm here, there will be light." He completed his speech without further interruptions from the floor. "He was an excellent soap-box performer," said the teacher and writer Robert Bone, author of *The Negro Novel in America.* "He handled hecklers with great finesse, disarming hostile crowds by the sheer force of his poise and self-confidence, winning audiences over to his most radical positions."

There may have been no more impressive example of Rustin's ability to disarm and convert an audience than the one recalled by his fellow pacifist the Reverend Glenn Smiley: "On one of Bayard's national tours, during the early 1950s, he stopped in Los Angeles, and I arranged a speaking engagement for him at Willowbrook High School. The school superintendent warned me beforehand about the student body. 'They are unruly,' he said, 'and you shouldn't be surprised if they make trouble.' When the students filed into the auditorium, I began to get an idea of what the superintendent meant. They were scuffling; pushing one another around; sitting with their legs crossed over neighboring chairs; throwing objects from one part of the room to another.

"Bayard was introduced, and, standing tall and dignified at the lectern, he began speaking in an upper-class British accent. 'Today,' he said, 'I want to speak to you about the psychological and sociological aspects of a humane society.' The students sent up a loud and heartfelt groan. 'Am I to gather from that sign of disdain,' Rustin asked, 'that you do not care to hear me give a lecture?' There was a chorus of agreement from the youngsters. 'Would you like to hear me sing?' 'Yeah, man, right on,' they shouted. 'Go ahead and sing.' Smiling at them, he said, 'You're crazy. You don't even know whether I can sing.' There was a burst of mocking laughter, followed by more shouts of 'Sing! Sing!'

"Bayard's demeanor then changed from that of a dignified professor to one of pure delight. 'I can't sing without an instrument,' he said, looking from one far corner of the stage to another. 'Oh, here's an orange crate. It's just the right thing; for I'm going to sing you a song from Africa, and I need a drum.' He seated himself on the floor, behind the box; told them the story of the song; then sang it in one of the African languages. Pandemonium broke loose when he finished. Now on a roll, he sprang to his feet and announced a French courting song, which he rendered in fluent French. He did a few more songs, concluding with 'Sometimes I Feel Like a Motherless Child.' The school superintendent was in tears, as were many of the students.

"Then, without giving them a chance to recover, Rustin said, 'Now let me speak to you about nonviolence, self-respect, and human dignity.' For about ten minutes, the kids listened to Bayard in rapt silence. When he closed, with one of his oratorical flourishes, the whole auditorium erupted in a shouting, crying frenzy. I have been a public speaker for sixty years, and I have never seen a hostile audience handled so skillfully."

Beyond the resourceful tactics he employed in silencing and capturing insolent audiences, Rustin was one of the more articulate and engaging public speakers of his time. In the black movement, he lacked the soaring spiritual eloquence of the Reverend Dr. Martin Luther King, Jr. Who didn't? He could not match Roy Wilkins's suave and understated elegance of delivery. He could not ignite an audience with the visceral fire of Malcolm X. Nor, partly because of his high tenor, did his rhetoric possess the deep and rolling resonance of James Farmer's and A. Philip Randolph's. But with his clear and crisp and intellectually sparkling presentations, he had no equal in lucid, instructive extemporaneous oratory.

Disliking the constraints of a prepared text, he almost never read from one—much to the chagrin of assistants who sometimes labored to write him a speech for a special occasion. He would usually organize his remarks at the last moment—scribbling notes on the inside of a matchbook or on the back of a printed program—while awaiting his turn at the microphone. Yet when he began speaking, there was always an extraordinary coherence in the ordering of his ideas.

In 1979, he heard from the president of a university at which he had made a commencement speech: "People were astounded by your ability to deliver so polished an address without an apparent written text." A New York–born coed at Antioch College, in Ohio, had written home to her father in the spring of 1965: "Yesterday was one of the greatest days I've had at Antioch. We had an assembly, and the speaker was Bayard Rustin. I've never heard a man speak with such controlled passion. He's emotional, but the intellectual comes first—so that you can see the arguments with the mind plus the heart." Stephen Cary, an officer of the American Friends Service Committee, felt that "Bayard stood out because of the great clarity of his thought and speech, his bright and penetrating grasp of the issues." Rustin and Norman Thomas, Cary said, "were the best platform people I ever heard."

Rustin's clarity of speech was influenced by the upper-class British delivery and accent he began cultivating at a point in his boyhood. That influence did not come from his grandmother Julia or his grandfather Janifer. It seems to have been planted by Maria Brock, a beloved grade-school instructor, who first taught him literature and elocution. At any rate, Rustin later told the writer Martin Mayer in New York: "I fought for many years against being American—in my speech, in my manner, everything." That effort must have been strengthened by his encounter with English society when, beginning in the early 1950s, he traveled frequently to Britain and made numerous acquaintances among its cultural and political intellectuals. But he could also "get down" into the vernaculars of African American expression whenever he felt like proving that he could talk as black as anyone else.

In Britain, Michael Randle was struck not only by Rustin's brilliant political intellect but also by his joyfully mischievous antics, "his iconoclastic delight in setting the cat among the pigeons." Steven Bloomstein, a son of Rustin's long-standing confidant, saw much of the same in New York. "At dinner parties my parents gave in Greenwich Village," Steven remembered, "Bayard would sometimes advocate views he knew were unpopular with certain guests, then look on zestfully as the sparks flew. On other occasions, he would ignite a squabble, then walk away in amusement as the clamor escalated."

As a coeditor of *Liberation* magazine in the early 1960s, Rustin once assigned Jim Forrest, a young and inexperienced assistant, to edit a piece by James Baldwin—after which Forrest was to call Baldwin and read him the editorial changes. Flattered by his assignment, the young man failed to recognize a hidden or potential danger. He stumbled upon it only when he telephoned the international literary celebrity and began reading the editorial revisions he had made. "Baldwin bawled me out over the phone," Forrest said later, "while Bayard sat by, chuckling to himself." He clearly had known the hornet's nest into which he was sending his innocent assistant.

Yet Rustin could be surprisingly respectful of young people. Perhaps because he had once aspired to become a schoolteacher, he listened tolerantly to their opinions—even when they were very much at odds with his own mature beliefs. In the early 1970s, Steven Bloomstein and his brother, Alex—young family members of what they called "the Bellowing Bloomsteins"—often confronted Rustin with their defiant political views. Alex came of age during the Vietnam War, and as a result, he distrusted all American politicians of an older generation. "I had just graduated from college," he recalled, "and, full of rose-colored radical idealism, I was always on the attack when Bayard visited with our family, as he frequently did. I vehemently denounced his and my father's political positions, showing only enough respect to keep them from giving up on me. I went so far as to accuse them of selling out their radical vision. But Bayard treated me more respectfully than any of his intellectual contemporaries would have done. He listened absorbedly to everything I said. Never patronizing or condescending, he took my arguments seriously, though, as I later saw, many of them were badly flawed. It was in such discussions with Bayard that I learned the way the world truly works. He was good and instructive with the young, although he might have disagreed with everything they said. He was an important part of my education."

•   •   •

Rustin stood just over six feet tall, with broad shoulders and an athletic build, reminders of his high-school years as a track and football star. His heavy growth of hair began graying in the early 1960s and turned spectacularly white in later years. At a meeting with Rustin in the mid-1960s, Robert Penn Warren saw him as "a handsome man . . . with a fine brow under crisp graying hair." His "cleanly molded features" and general appearance suggested "a strong mixture of strength and sensitivity." And his hands, "large and strong-looking," displayed "a delicacy of molding . . . we do not usually associate with that size and strength." From his poet's imagination, Warren added, "He is, I should guess, not unconscious of the beauty of the hands."

Rustin was conscious of beauty in a variety of its forms. He was one of the finer amateur judges of Renaissance painting, statuary, furniture, stringed instruments; African sculpture and the indigenous art of folk societies around the world. An enthusiast of modern dancing, he was, at a late point in his life, among the trustees of Alvin Ailey's dance company. Though homosexual, he had a charmed eye for beautiful women, black and white, and a number of them appraised him with a similar eye. He enjoyed playing classical guitar, piano, and harpsichord. He once said that if he were ever sentenced to live with the music of a single composer, his choice would be the works of Bach. He was an excellent singer not only of Negro spirituals but also of arias by Bach and operatic composers. Many years after he had graduated from high school, an alumna never forgot his rendition of the aria "Una Furtiva Lagrima" (from Donizetti's *L'Elisir d'Amore*). Across the memory of those years, she now wrote to tell him of a high-school experience she still treasured. His Donizetti aria, she said, "was the most beautifully sung piece of music I ever heard." Jonathan Brice, a concert pianist who accompanied Rustin at a few amateur recitals, observed a "fine and finished quality" in his singing "that I wouldn't have associated with the voice of a black man. He sang better than any black tenor of my experience, before I heard the genius of Roland Hayes." At round-table discussions, Rustin often seemed inattentive, though deceptively so, especially when he was absorbed with one of the many doodles he did while listening to every word being said. Most of those drawings were so imaginative that his colleagues saw them as serious works of art. Remarking upon "an incredible piece of drawing" Rustin did at a staff meeting of the War Resisters League, Roy Finch said, "This man really was an artist. But you couldn't ever get him to admit that, because he was so determined to involve himself with things political. He could have been an excellent artist if he had wanted to be, and he might have been happier."

Rustin was generally called a civil rights leader. In the formal sense, he wasn't—at least not until 1965, when he began directing the A. Philip Randolph Institute. Before then, he had headed no black organization, had had no significant following of his own. Such following as he had was mainly among intellectual activists, particularly some of the founding ideologues of the Student Nonviolent Coordinating Committee (SNCC).

"Bayard is not a Negro leader," Whitney Young, of the National Urban League, told a writer for the *Saturday Evening Post* in 1964—some months after Rustin's brilliant orchestration of the 1963 March on Washington. "A Negro leader," he said, "is the head of a Negro organization." Fearing that Rustin may have been stung by the remark, Young wrote him to explain: "One of the qualities I have admired about you has been your willingness . . . to remain in the background, though certainly as an effective, necessary catalyst in the process and in every . . . successful controntation we [the civil rights movement] have had." But Rustin had not been offended at all, for he happened to agree with Young's criterion of black leadership. Besides, he was contented with his status as an intellectual engineer behind the scenes—probably the most adroit tactical aide to almost all the frontline black leaders and organizations. He concurred fully with magazine headlines that labeled him "The Lone Wolf of Civil Rights" and "The Strategist Without a Movement." He belonged, of course, to a movement; he just didn't have a black organization of his own.

Another magazine headline described him as "The Socrates of the

Civil Rights Movement." He surely was a sage adviser to the major black leadership; its shrewdest theoretician; its most sophisticated political analyst; its most talented organizer. Despite his strong beliefs on one question or another, Rustin was also a great reconciler. Sitting, as he often did, among the rival princes of the black movement—each zealously arguing the merits of his own organization and program—Rustin displayed his ability at composing differences, molding disparate contentions into a workable consensus.

From the late 1950s to the early 1960s, he was the most resourceful organizer of civil rights demonstrations, especially those above the Deep South. He had an amazingly quick understanding of the varied tasks needed for the coordination of major public events; and none of the events he organized was as impressive as the March on Washington of August 28, 1963. In putting together the broadest coalition that had yet been assembled for a civil rights demonstration, Rustin had prepared the platform on which Dr. Martin Luther King delivered the great oration for which the march will always be remembered. Although John Lewis, of SNCC, had hoped for a more militant display in the nation's capital, the variety of constituencies that participated, he said later, signified Rustin's "total commitment to the building of an interracial democracy." To Adam Roberts, one of Rustin's political associates in Britain—a professor of international relations at Oxford—the composition of the March on Washington underscored "Bayard's excellence at coalition building, his sense of the need to forge alliances with different organizations."

Rustin's gift at coalition building came in part from his eclectic public attachments and sympathies. His disdain for purely parochial allegiances was nearly as strong as his abhorrence of racial segregation and discrimination. This broad and inclusive outlook did not endear him to certain provinces of the black movement. They felt that he was too wide-ranging in his political itineraries; too ecumenical in his social interests; too popular with white liberals; too close to organized labor; too friendly with the Jewish community. In other words, which side was he really on? But as the historian C. Vann Woodward pointed out in the early 1970s, Rustin was by temperament really a social reformer, responsive to problems of human rights and democracy wherever he saw them. Rustin's "active concern for races and oppressed minorities other than Negro Americans," Vann Woodward said, "is an aspect of his world view."

Not long before he died, Rustin wrote this reply to a critic of his world view: "My activism did not spring from being black. Rather, it is rooted fundamentally in my Quaker upbringing and the values instilled in me by the grandparents who reared me. Those values were based on the concept of a single human family and the belief that all members of that family are equal. The racial injustice that was present in this country during my youth was a challenge to my belief in the oneness of the human family. It demanded my involvement in the struggle to achieve interracial democracy; but it is very likely that I would have been involved had I been a white person with the same philosophy. I worked side-by-side with many white people who held these values, some of whom gave as much, if not more, to the struggle than myself."

Chapter 2

Beginnings

W est Chester, the official seat of Chester County, is one of the many picturesque small towns of southeastern Pennsylvania. Many of its tree-shaded streets and lanes are lined with eighteenth- and nineteenth-century houses, built of brick or of the pale-green serpentine stone that once abounded in the surrounding countryside. Founded by wealthy Quaker farmers and businessmen in 1799, the town is roughly twenty-five square miles in area and lies about twenty-three miles east of Philadelphia. West Chester gradually developed from a rustic trading post into a prosperous commercial and residential center; and at a stage of its growth, its civic leaders stopped regarding it as culturally inferior to Philadelphia. On first visiting the community in 1827, an itinerant chronicler was greatly impressed by its signs of "wealth" and "cultivation." It "possessed more taste, talent, and refinement . . . in proportion to the number of inhabitants" than any other town, "without exception," she had seen. West Chester basked in its confident small-town isolation until late in the nineteenth century, when it was virtually annexed as one of the bedroom satellites of metropolitan Philadelphia. Marking its centenary in 1899, a local historian was obliged to concede: "We are today brought face to face with the fact that we have suddenly, without formal notice, become suburban to the busy and beautiful city of Penn." West Chester's current population, twenty thousand or so, is what remains from nearly two hundred years of in- and out-migration by Quakers, other white Protestants, Catholics, and African Americans.

A number of the latter descended from fugitive slaves, who had paused and later settled there during their flight from the antebellum South. Many of the escapees were rescued and sheltered temporarily by those Quakers—not all—who, honoring the ethics of their religion, had an abhorrence of chattel slavery. Hence West Chester, not very far above the Mason-Dixon line, was one of the earliest and more hospitable "stations" on the Underground Railroad—the clandestine system by which bondsmen and women stole away to relative freedom in the North.

It was there, West Chester, that Bayard Rustin's maternal grandmother, Julia Davis, was born in 1873. Her parents, Samuel and Elizabeth, had moved to the town at an early age—not as fugitive slaves but with the help of a Quaker family in Virginia who bought their freedom and transported them north.

There was a strange, or perhaps not so strange, contradiction in the social morality of early American Quakers—more formally, the Religious Society of Friends. In the majority, they hated slavery and racial oppression; they believed in the oneness of humanity; they almost always tried to convert to their religion the blacks and the Native American tribes—particularly the Delaware Indians—whom they encountered; yet they were averse to worshiping alongside their nonwhite converts.

Quaker Meetings, in Pennsylvania and elsewhere, were virtually lily white. On the occasions when a few blacks were allowed to attend, they sat in a small segregated bunch, usually in the gallery. Thus the humane tradition of Quaker faith did not long survive among most of the African Americans who had been introduced to it. In other Protestant bodies throughout America, where free blacks had been similarly treated, they had eventually left and formed congregations of their own. But so few of them belonged to the Quaker denomination that it was difficult to form or sustain viable groupings of their own color. "At no period in history and in no part of America have Negroes ever become, in large numbers, members of the Society of Friends," the Quaker historian George Cadbury wrote in 1936. He added: "That so few of them became official members is doubtless partly due to the social prejudices which Friends could scarcely escape in entirety."

Samuel and Elizabeth Davis—and later their daughter, Julia— were among the handful of blacks in West Chester who continued to attend Quaker Meetings. At those reticent gatherings, where there was usually no singing, no preaching or scripture reading, individual religious spirit was guided by the truth of "inward" light. And, no doubt, not everyone shared the same inner light. Elizabeth worked in the home of a prominent Quaker family in West Chester, headed by Congressman Thomas S. Butler and his wife, Maud Darlington. Their son, Smedley Darlington Butler, was notable for his departure from the Quaker tradition of nonviolence, or the peaceful resolution of conflict. Following *his* "inward" light, Smedley joined the United States Marines and distinguished himself on a battlefront of the Spanish-American War.

In 1891, Julia Davis—Samuel and Elizabeth's only daughter—met and married Janifer Rustin, a native of La Plata, Maryland, who had recently migrated to West Chester. Janifer's hometown was not far below the Mason-Dixon line, and for some time after the abolition of slavery, blacks from the upper South had continued moving north to neighboring Pennsylvania. There was a conflict in the religious backgrounds of the newly married couple. Julia, who was then eighteen and had been brought up in Quaker Meetings and schools, belonged, of course, to the Society of Friends. Janifer, her senior by nine years, was a member of the African Methodist Episcopal Church, a militant group, founded in late-eighteenth-century Philadelphia, that had revolted against segregated Protestantism in America. Julia resolved the difference in background by joining her husband's denomination, though she would always remain, at heart, a Quaker. The wedding took place in the home of her parents but was officiated by the Reverend J. C. Brock, pastor of the AME chapel, on East Miner Street. One of Julia's more difficult adjustments must surely have been to AME liturgy: the music, the singing, the authoritative sermonizing, alien to the tradition of Quaker worship.

Janifer and Julia lived at various times on Market Street, Matlack Street, Gay Street, and North New Street. While growing up on North New Street, Nicholas Tavani, an Italian American, lived a block away from the Rustins. "They were a fine family in a mixed neighborhood," he remembered. "We all got along very well. They occupied an old two-story house, with a crab apple tree in front. Old Mr. Rustin allowed us kids to come in and pick crab apples. Their house was next to Ricci's ice plant. Later, Mr. Ricci bought the house and made it a part of his ice plant. The site is now [1991] a parking lot for Saint Agnes Church." The Rustins' last and lengthiest tenancy was on East Union Street, also in an old two-story house. Along the way, they produced six daughters and two sons: Anna, Bessie, Earl, Florence, Janifer Junior (who died in 1914, at age sixteen), Rhetta, Ruth, and Vella.

On March 17, 1912—just over a month before the "unsinkable" *Titanic* went down during its maiden transatlantic voyage to New York—Florence bore a son, out of wedlock. She was in her late teens, and Archie Hopkins, the young man-about-town who fathered her child, soon abandoned her. Robert Spence, an older resident of West Chester, remembered Archie as "a member of the Black Stars Social Club, a place where a lot of guys went after work, instead of going home. I don't remember what he did for a living, and I can't say he wasn't any good. But he was very much the happy-go-lucky sort." Florence's parents adopted the infant, named him Bayard Taylor Rustin, and raised him as a son of their own. Bayard grew up as the youngest member of the Rustin household and his grandmother's favorite.

Bayard Rustin would remember growing up in a close-knit family, over which his grandmother Julia was the chief moral and religious influence—imparting values she had learned as a young Quaker. "We were told," Bayard said, "that we should never discuss an issue when we were wrought up, but only when we were calm. We were taught that it was too tiresome to hate, and that we should never go to sleep without first reconciling differences that had occurred during the day. We should never raise the question as to who had caused a dispute, for nothing constructive was to be gained by arguing over who started what." Julia Rustin also emphasized the "simple idea" that no one was unimportant, that it was "our duty to treat each person as a complete human being." When she learned that Bayard, with a group of his high-spirited schoolmates, had taunted the owner of a Chinese laundry, she ordered him to spend the next two weeks of his after-school hours washing and ironing in the laundry. A former nurse and civic activist, Julia cofounded such black organizations as the Nurses Association, Day Nursery, Garden Club, Summer Bible School, and the Community Center—established for the nonwhites who were barred from the local YMCA/YWCA. She was a charter member of the National Association for the Advancement of Colored People, founded in 1910. And, as there were no black hotels or guesthouses in West Chester, she often hosted such visiting NAACP leaders as W. E. B. Du Bois and James Weldon Johnson. Janifer Rustin was an accomplished caterer for the Elks Club and a number of wealthy families in West Chester. Bayard's earliest memories included helping to make mayonnaise and piling and counting dishes and flatware for the various affairs Janifer catered. He would also remember occasions when the family dined in fine style on turtle soup, lobster Newburg, and pâté de foie gras—leftovers from the banquets of the well-to-do.

Bayard was educated first at the Gay Street elementary school; and graduated from the West Chester Junior High School in 1929. Both were all-black, for segregation was still the order of life at almost all public institutions in West Chester—a notable exception being the town's senior high school. "Other than Bayard's Quaker grandmother and her husband," one of his schoolmates recalled, "the Gay Street school faculty and the AME church played an important part in his early development. Though segregated, the school had a faculty of master teachers and an outstanding principal, named Joseph R. Fugett. The school and the church addressed many of the urgent topics of the day having to do with the advancement of race relations."

Bayard's progress at Gay Street was slow at first, inhibited by the insistence of a few teachers on changing his natural left-handed penmanship into orthodox right-handedness. Joining him in resisting this imposition, Julia Rustin marched to the school, lodged a vigorous complaint with Joseph R. Fugett, and demanded that her grandson be left alone to write as he pleased. Fugett instructed his staff accordingly, and freed to write as he pleased, Bayard recovered from his shaky academic start and went on to become an outstanding product of the school.

The teachers who impressed and influenced him most at Gay Street were Warren Burton (mathematics and music); Helena Robinson (history); and Maria Brock (English and elocution). Under Burton's tutelage, he learned the fluent reading of music; and it was Robinson who introduced him to African history and the postabolitionist struggle of blacks in the United States. But his favorite by far was Maria Brock, a daughter of the clergyman who had presided at his grandparents' wedding. To some of the classes she taught Brock invited literary luminaries of the Harlem Renaissance movement, including the Philadelphian Arthur Huff Fauset—whose sister, the novelist Jessie Fauset, worked closely with W. E. B. Du Bois in editing the NAACP's monthly journal *The Crisis*. Brock was the first to teach Bayard the fundamentals of essay writing, debating, and public speaking; and her refined speech is believed to have been the example on which he modeled the aristocratic British accent he developed. "Bayard started coming on with what some of us described as funny language," Charles Porter, a classmate at the Gay Street school, remembered. "He would always be saying 'cahn't' when the rest of us were saying 'cain't.' I think he was picking up his new way of speaking from Miss Brock. Coming from a very educated background, she wanted to raise us above the ordinary cultural standards to which we were accustomed." Decades later, in an address to the United Federation of Teachers in New York, Rustin paid this tribute to

Maria Brock: "She not only stimulated in me a great desire to learn but also introduced me to the possibilities that education had for liberating one from the prison of inherited circumstances."

In 1930, Rustin entered West Chester Senior High School, later renamed for its principal in those years, B. Reed Henderson. At the school, with an enrollment of nearly six hundred, Rustin was one in a small minority of blacks and, of those, among the few who ever stayed on long enough to graduate. "In the 1920s and '30s, when we grew up in segregated West Chester," Oliver Patterson, one of the dropouts, later explained, since "the best you could hope to become was a black schoolteacher or a black nurse, you saw no point in preparing yourself for a college education, or for some profession you couldn't attain in the life of [West Chester]. You may have been ambitious, but you didn't feel the future had much to offer you. Consequently, most of the black students who went to high school dropped out during the first year or two. Bayard Rustin was different. He had ambition and a great feeling about possibility. His determination was extraordinary. He had to prove that he was inferior to no one. He had to do what anybody said he couldn't do. If he fell down six flights of stairs, he would get up and tell you how good it felt landing six flights down. And you would almost believe him. That is why he excelled at so many things in high school."

In the judgment of John Rodgers, class of 1933, "Bayard had no equal in academic subjects. He was also our best athlete, and he took part in more extracurricular activities than anyone in the history of West Chester High School. He was very mature, very much in love with life, quite knowledgeable, very poetic, with the unusual ability to laugh even while performing the most serious and exacting tasks." The 1932 edition of *Garnet and White,* the school's yearbook, recorded his participation in the history, French, science, and drama clubs; in the chorus and the glee club; in basketball, track athletics, tennis, and football.

At home, Rustin's family called him "Bye." At school, his black friends called him "Pin-Head." One of them, John Melton, later said, "'Pin-Head' was an excellent tennis player, the school's singles champion. But when you played tennis in those days, people called you a sissy. So we said to Bayard one afternoon, 'Look, why don't you go out for football?' And he did." He soon became the school's best offensive lineman. "He never came out for a substitute," John Rodgers said, "and he was never flagged for a penalty. In scrimmages, I found it impossible to get by him. Sometimes, after knocking me down on my face, he would gently help me to my feet and recite a line or two of poetry." Oliver Patterson, who played the guard position alongside Rustin, at tackle, remembered that "he simply couldn't be overpowered. He was the toughest hitter on the front line. I wouldn't have expected that of a young man whose grandmother was raising him to be nonviolent. There wasn't an ounce of nonviolence in me, yet I could never hit as hard as he did." In the football season of 1931, Rustin led his varsity squad, the Warriors, through an undefeated ten-game schedule, the first such achievement in the school's history. And as the dominant 220-yard sprinter at West Chester High, he represented its track team at the Penn Relay Carnivals of 1931 and 1932, held at Philadelphia's Franklin Field.

But Rustin's academic and athletic excellence earned him no exemption from the segregated embarrassments of West Chester society. Like all other blacks, he was barred from the YMCA. He could neither eat in white-owned restaurants nor shop in major department stores. His white friends at West Chester High—including Jean Cessna, Pascela DuBondo, and Barney Hool—were cordially received in Julia Rustin's home, but their homes were closed to Bayard. At movie theaters like the Warner and the Rialto, he and other blacks were directed to the balcony—"Nigger Heaven," as that section used to be called in big cities like New York. He was arrested at the Warner, on South High Street, for refusing his "reserved" place in the balcony and daring to sit in the white section—the first of more than twenty-five arrests he was to log in a near lifetime of social protest. The night before his West Chester football Warriors were to engage a high school team in neighboring Media, Rustin instigated a revolt among his black teammates. They would not participate in the contest, he warned his head coach, unless they were pulled out of their Jim Crow accommodations and moved into those shared by the white players. The warning was heeded.

Impressed by Rustin's determination to resist the segregated status of blacks in West Chester, a number of his classmates rallied behind his progressive leadership—a rare phenomenon in the town's African American community, except among braver spirits in the NAACP. The young Rustinites followed him into restaurants, soda fountains, movie houses, department stores, and the YMCA; they were usually intercepted and thrown out into the street. Not even the local NAACP risked itself in such militant direct action. Nor, certainly, did the quieter elements of the black middle class. "They were hands-off, don't-rock-the-boat types" was how Charles Porter, one of the Rustinites, saw them. "They couldn't afford to get fired from their jobs as teachers and nurses. Where else could they go? In those days, people called you something worse than radical for taking the stands Bayard did. They called you crazy. In fact, those of us following Bayard did wonder at times whether he wasn't a bit crazy."

To Oliver Patterson, another of the young Rustinites, "Bayard's determination was frightening. But we looked up to him as our leader. He was persuasive. He could sell you anything. He was the most progressive person of his age in West Chester. We used to sit for hours and hours discussing what we saw as a blight upon the whole town of West Chester. We often sat outside Spriggs Restaurant, on Market Street, and Bayard always had a group around him. Some of us were ready to give up the fight and accept the status quo, but he never would. He had a strong inner spirit. He was determined to be better than West Chester said he could be. He didn't want to step on anyone, but he didn't want anyone to step on him either.

"Yet for all the leadership he gave us, it never crossed my mind that his future career would be that of a social activist. I expected him to become a great black singer, like a Roland Hayes or a Paul Robeson. Bayard was the finest singer in all of West Chester. Our high school chorus, with Rustin as tenor soloist, once competed at Temple University for all-state honors. We won. But the Temple music department held up our award. They said Bayard's voice was so good that he had to be older than the age limit. They said they would have to check his age before deciding whether or not to release our award. They thought there was no way in the world Bayard could have so excellent a voice unless he was older than all the other competing students."

Rustin's early development as a singer and a player of the piano and harpsichord took place under the tutelage of Floyd Hart, perhaps the most renowned high-school music teacher in West Chester's history. Hart's students included Samuel Barber, who, graduating two years ahead of Rustin, entered the Curtis Institute of Music in Philadelphia, where he launched his career as a distinguished American composer. Barber's "Adagio for Strings" was to become one of Bayard Rustin's favorite pieces of instrumental music—although he was much fonder of Baroque than of modern compositions.

Floyd Hart, a demanding but inspiring teacher of vocal and instrumental music, was the school's choirmaster as well. Partly because of that, Rustin was not at first fond of singing Negro spirituals, which were chiefly what audiences expected of black soloists. He felt, or was made to feel, that they would inhibit his development in sophisticated vocal technique. "Mr. Hart was an enthusiast of early music," Rustin said later. "So we did a lot of Bach, Buxtehude, Corelli, and other classical composers. He introduced us to Wagner's use of the leitmotif, what it meant in composition and appreciation. Quite frankly, I then regarded spirituals as being rather simplistic. Much more study was required when you were doing Bach, Brahms, Schubert, Donizetti, and the others." Ironically, though Rustin sang well from the classical repertoire, it was the rendition of spirituals for which, in later years, he would be most highly regarded.

In the West Chester of his boyhood there were at least two cultural figures of national status, whose achievements local youngsters could emulate. One was the primitive painter Horace Pippin—an acquaintance of the Rustin family—whose works were to be among the finer black contributions to American art. The other was Joseph Hergesheimer, judged by H. L. Mencken—who happened to be his close friend—as being second only to Theodore Dreiser on the list of major American novelists. There was a slight professional resemblance between Pippin and Hergesheimer: the latter had failed as a painter before he turned to the writing of fiction. Hergesheimer was also an avid collector of antiques, which he often wrote about in the *Saturday Evening Post.* The Pippin-Hergesheimer connection may have figured in the passion Rustin later developed for the collecting of international art objects and antiques.

In June of 1932, Rustin graduated with honors from West Chester High School—nineteenth in a class of one hundred. Among other distinctions, he was the first African American to win the D. Webster Meredith Prize, that school's highest award for excellence in public speaking. Not surprisingly, he was the class valedictorian. And he also contributed these farewell stanzas to *Garnet and White,* the school's yearbook:

> *Long shadows linger on the wall*
> *As purple tints adorn the sky;*
> *Oh! Now I hear the swallows call,*
> *And we must part, must say good-bye.*
>
> *Yet parting, moving as one must,*
> *We feel no tears, no grief, no fears,*
> *For in our hearts there lies a trust—*
> *A bond made strong by joyful years.*
>
> *Together we did learn to live,*
> *To do our best, to fight the wrong.*
> *We found that they succeed who give.*
> *Life is a chorus; each has his song.*
>
> *So let us leave on dancing toe,*
> *With faces upturned to the sky,*

Remembering as we gladly go—
In each bare field some riches lie.

"I don't think any of us in the black community reached the academic heights Bayard reached," Robert Spence said. "His high-school achievement was publicized throughout the community, because it was a rarity. Not too many blacks ever graduated from high school, so the colored families in town were proud when one of us graduated, no matter whose child it was." When B. Reed Henderson High School inaugurated a hall of fame, in 1990, Rustin was the first inductee; a roadside marker, erected in 1995, now announces West Chester as the birthplace of Bayard Rustin; and in 1993, the town's *Daily Local News* named him among the ten famous figures born in Chester County. The list included Bayard Taylor (1825–1878), Smedley Darlington Butler (1881–1940), Horace Pippin (1888–1946), and Samuel Barber (1910–1981).

Rustin had hoped—not unreasonably, in view of his excellent scholastic and athletic record—that his graduation would be crowned with the award of a college scholarship. He was bitterly disappointed when the local school authorities did not recommend him for one. On a visit to West Chester more than thirty years later—now recognized as a prominent national figure—he told an admiring hometown audience, "I got not one penny when scholarships were handed out. I was told in the Dramatics Club that there was no place for black boys in American drama. Guidance counselors were still dispensing negative counseling to Negro youths. I wish that officials in every school in the nation could be black for one week. It would be un-Christian of me to put such a burden on them for eight days."

In the summer of 1932, Julia Rustin put on her hat and went out to meet with influential persons and organizations in the community. Campaigning on behalf of her disillusioned grandson, she argued that no recent graduate of the high school could have been more deserving of a scholarship. She was granted respectful hearings, but in the end, her appeals were to little or no avail. The Rotary Club promised the contribution of a hundred dollars toward Bayard's college education—hardly enough to pay tuition and board for a semester. It was when Julia turned to Bishop R. R. Wright, an AME clergyman in Philadelphia, that she got the assistance she sought. Wright, a trustee of Wilberforce University, near Xenia, Ohio, used his influence to obtain Bayard a scholarship at the AME-sponsored institution.

Wilberforce, where Rustin registered on September 14, 1932, is among the oldest black colleges in the United States. Founded by white Methodists in 1856 (for the benefit of the African race in America), it was named after William Wilberforce, the great English abolitionist and parliamentarian—a member of London's evangelical Clapham Sect. The African Methodist Episcopal Church acquired the school in 1863, mainly through the initiative of Daniel A. Payne, one of the distinguished bishops in the history of that organization. "Many regard the purchase of Wilberforce by Payne as his most outstanding contribution to the Church," wrote the Reverend George Singleton, an AME historian. "For years it stood as a towering monument to the genius and capability of African Methodists to educate themselves. It was the pride of the race, a star of hope for the descendants of slaves."

It was at Wilberforce, in 1894, that W. E. B. Du Bois, the black intellectual leader, began his career—teaching English, German, Greek, and Latin. He had been lured there, he said, by the AME Church's reputation as "the greatest social institution" in African American life; and he "wanted to help build a great university." But the teaching of languages was not his preferred means of achieving that end. He desired mostly to establish a department of sociology, in which he would design and direct pioneering programs in black social research. That was not to be. Du Bois encountered two insuperable obstacles: the poor finances of the school and the intransigence of its ruling clergymen. Frustrated, he resigned in 1896 and took a more appealing position with the University of Pennsylvania.

As a music major at Wilberforce, Bayard Rustin formed a greater respect and affection for Negro spirituals than he had felt when he studied with Floyd Hart. This was partly because of their prominence in the curriculum and because Wilberforce was among the black colleges—like Fisk, Hampton, and Tuskegee—that celebrated them as proud expressions of African American cultural heritage and had helped to gain them a wide acceptance in America.

"I had never known southern blacks until I went to Wilberforce," Rustin recalled many years later, in a discussion with the black musicologist Carroll Buchanan. "And I was amazed by the degree to which black schools had steeped their students in African American cultural history. All of that spurred me to study in greater depth what the spirituals truly meant and what other forms of black music meant as well. So at times when we sang the spirituals at Wilberforce, we introduced other forms of music, like work songs and the blues. The church leadership of the school didn't appreciate that aspect of our work. But we were rebellious. Although we were scholarship students, we said to the church leadership, 'You may be paying our way, but we're still independent.' We wanted to recognize the modern developments in black music. We wanted to show the churchmen who led Wilberforce that the old spirituals had helped to create the idiom of twentieth-century blues and the idiom of black work songs as well."

Rustin's "we" referred chiefly to the Wilberforce Quartet, in which he was the first tenor and principal soloist. His supporting cast were Eddie Jackson (baritone), George Hall (bass), and Ira Williams (second tenor). George Hall recalled, "Rustin had excellent training in harmony, piano, and voice. He was so much more advanced than the rest of us, not only in art and music but also in general education. And his high tenor voice was as beautiful as any we had heard. That's why we latched onto him."

The quartet traveled widely, partly as cultural ambassadors and partly as fund-raisers for Wilberforce—a form of compensation for their free tuition, housing, and board. A typical two-week tour on behalf of the university would take them through Ohio, to the Deep South, to Pennsylvania, and even to New York City. They appeared occasionally on radio and more frequently in the larger AME congregations. At such churches, they were careful to sing mostly spirituals and art songs, for—despite their own convictions about the value of black music—they feared that work songs and blues might alienate the pious gatherings upon whose support Wilberforce depended. "At the end of our performances," Rustin said, "the powerful bishops would rise and harangue their regional preachers, demanding an increase in their annual pledge to the financial upkeep of Wilberforce University, the major educational institution in the African Methodist Episcopal Church. Those preachers would send their church money to the bishops, and the bishops would send it on to Wilberforce. At other times, key AME bishops and congregations would request our appearance, virtually threatening a cutback in financial support unless the Wilberforce Quartet were sent to enliven church conventions."

The quartet always had to be well dressed, and accounts differ regarding the members' financing of their formal attire. "None of us had any money," Rustin said. "I went to Wilberforce with no money, and I got none from home." According to George Hall, "Members of the Kiwanis Club or the Rotary Club would give us their old suits." Rustin added, "The university supplied you with suits if you couldn't provide them yourself. I cannot state with any certainty that other members of our group had their suits paid for. But mine was paid for. That was something you worked out quietly with the president of the university, to spare yourself the embarrassment of everyone knowing that you couldn't afford to buy your own suits."

Between official appearances on behalf of the university, the quartet hired themselves out for private engagements, responding to any call within four or five miles of Wilberforce. "We sometimes sang in three or four little churches on one Sunday," Rustin recalled. "But these little churches were very poor. They had lots of spirit and hardly any money. Sometimes they paid us a few dollars. Sometimes they just gave us supper."

It was only in retrospect that he recognized how much his work with the Wilberforce Quartet contributed to his career in public activism. "As we traveled doing these concerts, making these appearances," he recalled, "one or another of us would have to explain to an audience the meaning of what we were going to sing. That job usually fell to me. I was young and fairly dumb when I arrived at Wilberforce. I had a feeling of unease, as anyone would, being poor and not knowing where the next penny was coming from to pay my personal expenses on campus. But while explaining and describing the songs we were going to sing, I developed a considerable aplomb, a great sense of how to present myself as a speaker. The Wilberforce Quartet gave me status and a greater self-assurance." That was a significant step forward by a young man who as a student in West Chester had already made an impression with his self-assurance.

Rustin spent just over a year—from the fall of 1932 to the end of 1933—at Wilberforce University. Perhaps following a policy of protecting the privacy of its alumni, Wilberforce would not later disclose the reason for his premature departure. One might conjecture on the basis of a report by a classmate, who remembered that Bayard fell in love with a son of the college president. If so, nothing was more likely to foreshorten his stay at an institution run by fiercely religious clergymen. Rustin's own explanation was political. He later said that he lost his scholarship when he not only refused to join the ROTC but also organized and led a strike against the poor quality of meals served in the dormitories. Evidence supports part of his account. One of his friends at Wilberforce—John M. Royall, Jr., the son of a wealthy black realtor in early black Harlem—was to recall, "I tasted the food a few times, and I called home. I told my father that I didn't want to stay in a dormitory, that I wanted to live off campus. The food was so bad."

Early in 1934, Rustin enrolled at Cheyney State Teachers College (now Cheyney University), not far from his home in West Chester. Founded by Philadelphia Quakers in 1837, it remained in that city for the next sixty-five years. The school came into being as the Institute for Colored Youth; its early curriculum emphasized manual and agricultural training; and that continued to be its policy until 1902, when it moved to Cheyney—where it began evolving into a college for the education of black teachers.

Its president when Rustin arrived was Leslie Pinckney Hill, one of the nation's notable black intellectuals. Hill's first teaching position, after graduating from Harvard in 1904, was with Booker T. Washington's Tuskegee Institute, in Alabama—the most prominent exemplar of the idea that a program of agricultural and industrial training was the one most urgently needed by the recent descendants of ex-slaves. Washington's advocacy of this practical program versus W. E. B. Du Bois's call for an equal emphasis on higher education—the building of an intelligentsia to aid the struggle for political and intellectual progress—was an issue that split early black leadership into two camps: pro-Washington conservatives and pro–Du Bois radicals. Leslie Pinckney Hill was at first torn between both factions. His training in the humanities at Harvard—where Du Bois himself had been educated—did not prevent him from believing that industrial *and* academic education could coexist harmoniously and productively at Tuskegee. But Hill, as he later discovered, was mistaken. He resigned in 1907, feeling that the Tuskegee leadership had undermined the token academic program he was hired to develop.

After teaching at another industrial school, in Virginia, Hill joined the faculty of Cheyney State Teachers College in 1913 and became its president in 1931. An able poet and prose writer, a lover of music as well, Hill quickly stamped the school with his cultural enthusiasms. Rosamond Nelson, one of Bayard Rustin's classmates at Cheyney State, said of Hill, "He was a marvelous orator. He had been a member of Harvard's debating team, and he influenced the development of a similar activity at Cheyney. He was versed in classical music. And he also promoted the singing of Negro spirituals, as a means of emphasizing the history and background of African Americans."

Rustin's decision to enter a teachers college suggests that he may still have been searching for a sure sense of the vocation he wished to pursue—singing, teaching, or social activism. At Cheyney State, he displayed abilities in each of those areas, excelling in music, student teaching, sociology, world civilization, and American government.

He was not only the best performer in the Debating Society but also chief soloist in the chorus, codirected by the artist Laura Wheeler Waring and Leslie Pinckney Hill. With Rosamond Nelson and Elmer Calloway (a brother of the jazz musician Cab Calloway), Rustin formed a singing group that toured small towns in southeastern Pennsylvania and nearby New Jersey. And, as at Wilberforce University, he was the featured vocalist in the Cheyney State Quartet: Rustin, first tenor; Joseph P. Smith, second tenor; Lewis Comegys, baritone; Rosamond Nelson, bass. The quartet was accompanied at the piano by James R. Dumpson, a future commissioner of welfare and human resources in New York City; and the chorus often sang over the radio in Philadelphia.

The school's newspaper (the *Cheyney Record*) reported in February 1935:

> The third successful broadcast of the Cheyney Chorus was given over station KYW on Sunday, January 20. . . . As a result of the delight and satisfaction which these programs have given the radio public, the Chorus has been invited to give a monthly broadcast. . . . The featuring of Bayard Rustin, gifted and popular tenor soloist, in these radio programs has resulted in an invitation from the broadcasting company for him to sing with the organ program on Sunday afternoon, February 3.

Later that year, when the quartet won an amateur contest—sponsored by WFIL, the local CBS affiliate—each member received a gold medal. "But we weren't so proud of those medals," Rosamond Nelson said, "because they were inscribed to the effect that we had won them on the Feenamint Radio Hour. We didn't think awards from Feenamint, a producer of laxatives, were flattering things to display. So we put the medals in hock. We needed the money anyway, for we were all struggling students."

Leslie Pinckney Hill's acquaintances included several prominent classical musicians, whom he often invited to appear on campus. One was the coloratura Lillian Evanti, probably the first African American to have performed on a European opera stage. Another was Leopold Stokowski, conductor of the Philadelphia Orchestra, who occasionally invited the Cheyney Chorus to appear at his youth concerts. "Dr. Hill wanted Stokowski to hear me sing individually," Rustin recalled, "and he arranged for me to visit Stokowski's home in Rittenhouse Square. It was a very elegant house. I had never seen anything quite so beautiful. After my audition, Stokowski urged me to become more interested in the classics. At that point I decided to drop out of the Cheyney Quartet, so that I might devote more time to the classics. But then something happened."

It is not clear exactly what that "something" was, but it had to do with a form of misconduct that was severely disappointing to Leslie Pinckney Hill. In any case, as at Wilberforce University, Rustin was asked to leave Cheyney in the winter of 1936. He himself admitted later that he had been "naughty," that he had "misbehaved," that "in a moment of youthful carelessness" he had "made a mistake." He told an interviewer in 1985, "I ran into some difficulties at Cheyney because I was quite obstreperous. And Dr. Hill, whom I greatly admired, called me in and told me I had to get the hell out of there. I was dismissed. Dr. Hill was right and I was wrong." In 1951, shortly before Hill retired as president of the school, Rustin, who had moved to New York fourteen years earlier, wrote to him: "In some sense I look upon my personal experiences at Cheyney with some regret. . . . I suppose that there were many students like me who are somewhat responsible for the grey hairs you received earlier than you should have."

Whatever the cause of Rustin's dismissal, a number of influential admirers retained their belief in his great musical promise. Roland Hayes, the internationally acclaimed black tenor of those years, offered to coach him during the spring and summer of 1937. And, Rosamond Nelson recalled, "a rich white lady, either in Delaware or southeastern Pennsylvania—she might have been a Du Pont—offered to guarantee Bayard's musical education as far as Juilliard or beyond." When Rustin declined those and similar offers, Nelson said, "Roland Hayes told my father he suspected that Bayard was lacking in the self-discipline required for serious musical study." That was probably true. Unlike Hayes, who remembered that his mother had raised him "to be single-eyed, to concentrate on a task and finish it without diversion," Rustin tended to be restless, impatient with extended periods of regimentation.

Just as likely, the mysterious incident that ended his collegiate life at Cheyney might have played a part in turning his mind decisively to a profession in social action rather than one in teaching or the arts. To Rosamond Nelson, "That was most unfortunate, for Bayard had a marvelous tenor voice. If he had been born thirty years later, he could have become an internationally known singer or an outstanding tenor at the Metropolitan Opera. He had the talent and he had the intellect. The young Bayard was a genius." But at least one student at Cheyney, James R. Dumpson, was not surprised when Rustin chose to pursue a career in political activism. Dumpson had always suspected that "singing wasn't the principal medium through which he desired to express his life. I felt that the righting of wrongs was mainly what consumed him. At Cheyney, he was always looking around for social causes in which to involve himself." William Sutherland, with whom Rustin later worked in the pacifist, civil rights, and African freedom movements, thought that Bayard was "simply a political animal." Sutherland was convinced that "the give-and-take of the public arena was much more exciting to him than the idea of standing up there on a stage, in full dress and white gloves, singing 'Swing Low, Sweet Chariot' in an Oxford tone."

Chapter 3

Toward New York

In the late spring of 1937, Rustin returned to the campus of Cheyney State Teachers College to undergo a two-week training program as a peace volunteer—a prelude to his formal entry into the arena of public activism. This was under the auspices of the Emergency Peace Campaign, organized by the American Friends Service Committee (AFSC) and a number of other pacifist groupings—all of which saw the rise of fascist movements in Germany, Italy, and Spain as omens of a new world war. The campaign was designed to help build popular American opposition to such a conflict; and Rustin was among the three hundred young people, mostly college students, whom Harold Chance, an officer of the AFSC, invited to volunteer their services to that effort. Recently turned twenty-five, Rustin was no longer a student; but he qualified as a young intellectual, well known (by AFSC headquarters in Philadelphia) for his firm Quaker-pacifist convictions.

He met the requirements Harold Chance had enumerated for work in the Emergency Peace Campaign. Volunteers, Chance said, should be "physically strong, mentally alert, idealistic, and adventurous." They should "have a factual background in . . . world affairs and social problems, coupled with leadership ability." They were also expected to "exemplify the spirit of reconciliation and tolerance"; to "meet with courage and goodwill any criticism or opposition which might develop"; to be "resourceful enough to adapt themselves to complex and changing conditions." And they should "possess the initiative which will permit them to seek out the key peace-minded individuals of a community and with them develop" needed educational programs. Cheyney State was one of five colleges at which the peace volunteers were trained before being dispatched, in teams of three and four, to towns and cities across the United States. It was during the orientation sessions that Rustin first met the inspiring British pacifist Muriel Lester—an international ambassador for the Fellowship of Reconciliation and a friend of Mahatma Gandhi—with whom he was to work closely in later years.

At the end of the training program, Rustin was the only black in a group of four assigned to a summertime of peace activism in Auburn, in upstate New York. His colleagues, all leftists of one stripe or another, were Carl Rachlin, a recent graduate of New York University, who would be entering Harvard Law School in the fall; Kenneth Cuthbertson, a radical member of the Christian Student Movement; and Robert Bilheimer, a sophomore at Yale, who planned to do post-graduate work in theology. The foursome were not particularly impressed with Auburn. Rachlin saw it as "a very small and very ordinary town," with only two distinctions: "its proximity to a state prison" and its identity as the birthplace of William H. Seward, Abraham Lincoln's secretary of state. Still, they all enjoyed the summer's work in Auburn—though their enjoyment, extreme at times, was on the whole counterproductive to the task they had been assigned.

In the small town and its vicinities, the four-man team addressed social clubs, Sunday school and YMCA/YWCA classes, farmer and labor organizations. At times, they even conducted church services: Rustin would lead the choir; Rachlin, a trained musician, would play the organ; Bilheimer would deliver the biblical message; after which Rachlin would deliver the political sermon—"for Bayard always wanted me to preach the social gospel." That was because Rachlin was the most sophisticated leftist in the gang of four. But on occasions

Rustin took over the role of political spokesman. Rachlin remembered a church garden party, attended by "nice old ladies and gentlemen," at which Rustin, "taking one look at those nice people," launched joyously into a speech about revolution. "I couldn't believe my ears," Rachlin said later. "I think Bayard had recently heard a speech in Philadelphia espousing the Trotskyist point of view and decided to try that stuff on the old folks. He nearly scared them out of their wits. But it was really one of the antics he liked to play on people."

Antic or not, it wasn't the thing to do on a mission of peace among an ideologically conventional people. Thus, while Rustin and his comrades were a harmonious grouping, they seemed unsuited for political work in a predominantly conservative community. Nothing exemplified this more than another event Rachlin recollected:

"All four of us once approached the manager of a radio station, requesting some weekly time to broadcast our message of peace and social justice. We were persuasive youngsters, and the manager agreed to give us a program of one hour a week. Bayard directed the program. Sometimes he made the main speech. Sometimes Bob Bilheimer and Ken Cuthbertson did. At other times Bayard had me read a program of poetry. And of course, he always sang. There came a point when we felt the need for a piece of theme music to introduce our weekly broadcast; and, with youthful exuberance, we chose the 'Internationale' to be that piece of music. But we didn't want to have it sung in English. That would have been too much for our conservative audience. So I called up a friend in New York City and asked him to send us a recording of the 'Internationale' with words in Polish. He did, and for several weeks the radio station announced our program with that anthem. We didn't think anyone in Auburn had ever heard it, let alone knew what it meant.

"But there was at least one man in the community who eventually caught on. He called up the radio station and complained bitterly about the piece of revolutionary music he was hearing. The next day, as Bayard and I were strolling down Main Street, we ran into the station manager. He was furious. How, he asked, could we have done a thing like that to him? Bayard looked at me and chuckled in his roguish manner. Of course, that all put an end to our weekly radio program."

It was also the virtual end of their summer in Auburn—more spirited and less successful than their peace sponsors had hoped it would be. "I have often wondered," Robert Bilheimer said later, "why the Friends Service Committee sent such a left-oriented group into such a citadel of upper New York State conservatism. There was to be no doubt in my mind that we exhibited no little immaturity in administering the shock treatment we did."

Politically, Carl Rachlin was more knowledgeable than his three colleagues, better versed than they were in some of the major international issues of the mid and late 1930s. He belonged to the radical movement in Manhattan, where clever and slashing sectarian debates were common; where leftist ideologues argued over Stalin's bloody purges and show trials in the Soviet Union; where France's Édouard Daladier was pilloried for adding his compromising signature to the Munich Pact; where the Hitler-Mussolini alliance was closely scrutinized and loudly denounced; where the Italian seizure of Ethiopia— with the dethronement of Emperor Haile Selassie—was a cause célèbre among liberals and radicals; where progressive young women stopped wearing Japanese-made stockings, in protest against that country's invasion of China. Then, too, in Manhattan, there was the burning question of the Spanish Civil War. Carl Rachlin could hardly wait to read each morning's issue of the *New York Times,* with its dispatches from Herbert Matthews, a brilliant American correspondent in Spain. That civil war was "a tremendous event" in the lives of young New York intellectuals, Rachlin said. And it was during the Spanish hostilities that he and his political friends first discovered Ernest Hemingway and John Dos Passos, "both of whom wrote brilliantly about the civil war."

Out in West Chester, Pennsylvania, Bayard Rustin was distant from the radical ferment among Manhattan's young intellectuals. Though Philadelphia, with its echoes of that ferment, was nearby,

Rustin's exposure to the reporting and discussion of major world events was chiefly through provincial papers, such as the *Daily Local News,* in his hometown. Rachlin considered him naive when, during one of their talks on the civil war in Spain, Bayard argued for nonviolent resistance by the loyalists, while he, Rachlin, believed in an outright military confrontation with the fascists. What, Rachlin wondered, could passive resistance achieve against the overwhelming weaponry at General Franco's ruthless command? In such a case, wasn't nonviolent resistance the equivalent of surrender? He had raised one of the key issues in moral pacifism, to which Rustin had begun attaching himself.

But during their discussions in Auburn, Rachlin recognized that Rustin's position on the civil war—naive or impractical though it was—reflected his genuine belief in nonviolence and in the Gandhian philosophy of nonviolent *resistance.* Some years afterward, Rachlin would himself begin a conversion to nonviolence. At first he could embrace it only as a political tactic. "But I came to see," he said, "that people like Bayard Rustin were attached to Christian-Gandhian nonviolence not just as a tactic but as a total way of life. Especially after observing Martin Luther King, I became convinced that nonviolence, if subscribed to at all, must be held as a full moral belief. By the early 1960s, I myself was totally a Gandhian."

When, at the end of their 1937 summer in Auburn, the four peace volunteers prepared to disperse, Carl Rachlin and Robert Bilheimer—impressed by Rustin, probably the first young member of the black intelligentsia they had ever met—invited him, bound for West Chester, to make a detour through New York City, where their parents lived. It was a good idea but without wholly good results. Rustin's meeting with the Rachlin family was cordial. The one with Robert Bilheimer's father was much less so. It was all one of Rustin's early lessons in the liberal spirit of New York City.

"My father," Bilheimer said later, "was then the business manager of the YMCA in Manhattan, and I had written to him, asking if my friend and I could meet him for lunch. The appointed meeting place was the 'Y' branch on West Twenty-third Street. After I introduced Bayard in the lobby, my father said, 'Son, may I speak with you for a minute?' We walked a few paces away from Bayard, and my father, in considerable distress, asked why I had not told him my friend was a Negro. He said he could not have Bayard for lunch there at West Twenty-third Street. I replied that it had never occurred to me to tell him what Bayard's color was. My father excused himself, and in a few minutes he returned and escorted Bayard and me to a room where one table was set up in private. There the three of us had lunch. I was mortified. Bayard kept up a fine conversation, saying nothing about the situation. At the end, he thanked my father and took his leave of us. I knew him well enough to know that he must have been outraged. But he clearly understood my mortification, and he was willing to leave it at that."

For several weeks after Rustin returned home, he was bored and restless, with nothing challenging to do. Educated, but without a degree from either of the two colleges he had attended, he found himself at intellectual loose ends. He was nearly unemployable as well, being intellectually overqualified for the modest jobs generally available to young black males in West Chester. A number of them—"wiser" than he—had not even aspired to a college education. For a while after returning from Auburn, Rustin worked with a landscape artist, planting young trees on a large estate outside West Chester. Although Quaker philosophy encouraged humble and self-effacing work with the hands, Bayard decided after a week or two that the work of planting trees was not for *his* hands; nor was self-effacement one of the qualities that appealed to him. Since he no longer gave serious thought to a career in music or teaching, only one option seemed to remain—social activism, which had always lurked among his ambitions and which he had given a try during his summer in Auburn.

He therefore began riding the trains into Philadelphia to investigate the possibilities for political action. In the city, he saw nothing more attractive than the activities of the communist movement, whose soapbox orators were making an aggressive pitch for black member-ship. There was then no racial issue in America so controversial as the Scottsboro case, and the communist organizing machinery exploited it fully. The case had begun in 1931 and, with its series of convictions and appeals, was to drag on throughout the decade.

The communists were in fact among the first to organize and finance the legal defense of the nine black youths who had been charged with raping two white women on a freight train passing through Scottsboro, Alabama. In the southern social climate of the time, their plea of innocence was futile. The Scottsboro boys, Irving Howe and Lewis Coser later wrote, were "utterly bewildered Negroes who had been caught up, almost arbitrarily, in the injustice against their people that was part of the very fabric of the South. As the communists soon proclaimed, the Scottsboro boys were simply victims. . . . Both of the women were shown to be of dubious virtue, and one of them, Ruby Bates, recanted damaging testimony and became a speaker at Scottsboro defense rallies." The Scottsboro issue became an interna-tional cause. And it may (or may not) have been the crucial influence upon Bayard Rustin's migration to New York City, where he would spend the remaining fifty years of his life.

Returning from one of his journeys into Philadelphia, Rustin announced to his family that he had had his fill of life in West Chester. "He came down the stairs one day," his aunt Anna recalled, "carrying a great big suitcase. He said he was leaving. I tried to stop him but I couldn't. I ran after him, up East Union Street, and when I caught up with him I talked him into coming back home, so that we could all rea-son soberly over the matter. My mother, Julia, was crying when I brought him back into the house. He was the apple of her eye, and she couldn't stand the thought of his leaving. But we should have known that Bayard would never leave without saying goodbye to his grand-mother. I opened the suitcase as soon as he set it down, only to find that there was nothing in it. He had played one of his antics, but it was also a way of showing us how serious he was about getting out of West Chester."

Rustin left West Chester soon after, in the winter of 1937. Later, he would claim that his aunt Bessie (who had moved to New York in 1930) invited him to join her in Manhattan, where she would help him to resume his college education. Alternately, he would say, "I first encountered communists at a public meeting on the Scottsboro Case, where a man approached me and asked if I was interested in passing out literature in the black neighborhoods of Philadelphia. Later . . . the communists sent me to the College of the City of New York." There was probably some truth in both versions, despite his leaning to narrative embroidery.

In Manhattan, Rustin first shared an apartment with his aunt Bessie, a teacher in the public school system, and her husband, Pierre LeBon, a Haitian émigré who was a chef in a midtown hotel. The LeBons lived on Saint Nicholas Avenue, near 155th Street, in the section of Harlem that was still called Sugar Hill—for the successful and wealthy members of the black bourgeoisie who began occupying the area in the early 1920s. The name, coined from a mixture of envy and mockery, had been conferred by Harlem's sardonic working class, who knew that the rents up there were so steep that only Negroes with lots of money ("sugar") could afford them. But by the late 1930s and early 1940s, Sugar Hill was no longer a preserve of the black middle class. Poorer folks, from lower down in central Harlem, had been moving up into its splendid apartment buildings—erected and first occupied by rich white Protestants, Catholics, and Jews. In the late thirties, almost all those houses retained their elegant facades; but indoors, a number of them had begun showing signs of social and economic decline.

In Harlem, Rustin made his first friendships among a group of youngsters who gathered regularly at the intersection of 151st Street and Convent Avenue. According to one of them—Howard Wallace, who became a community officer in the New York Police Department—"there were five or six of us who hung out together, all in our late teens. One day, Bayard suddenly showed up. We wondered where the hell he came from. He spoke in this crisp British accent. We had never heard any American talking like that. After a while, we began calling him 'English.' He was a stickler for the proper pronunciation of words. We couldn't open our mouths without him trying to correct us. He caused a lot of argument. But he was a friendly guy, and he fit in easily. Hardly anyone could resist his gift of gab. Not long after Bayard arrived in the city, he and I shared a part-time job as ushers at the New Utrecht Theater, over in Brooklyn. Next door, there was an ice cream parlor, a gathering place for Jews and Italians in the community. Many afternoons when I arrived at the theater to relieve Bayard, he would be holding forth with all the Jewish intellectuals, discussing politics and other issues of the day. They loved him. He held them spellbound."

The Harlem Rustin saw when he moved there in the late 1930s was not quite the vivacious black cultural mecca it had been during the roaring twenties. The Great Depression had inflicted deep spiritual and physical wounds. But Harlem managed to retain a good deal of its old social élan; and Rustin, from his bland small-town background, found it to be "a vital and dynamic community." Its dwindling high society still threw grand parties, to which they invited only guests of their own style and status. There lingered in the atmosphere an afterglow of the Harlem Renaissance—that explosion in literature and art and intellectual assertiveness. The major churches and their powerful preachers still presided over middle-class cultural standards, while scores of little storefront chapels ministered to the religious needs of the poor. It was still the era of big bands and swing music and crowded dance halls, like the Rockland Palace and the Savoy Ballroom.

Rustin would recall aspects of that time and its places: "Each Thursday night—which was then known as 'maids night out'—all the smart dudes dressed up and all the girls, who worked for rich white folks downtown, came in and lined the walls of the Savoy. The lindy hop, from the 1920s, was still a popular dance craze. The young men, who must have been practicing at home all week, threw the girls over their heads, under their legs, around their waists. It was unbelievable. The big bands of Duke Ellington, Chick Webb, Benny Goodman, and

Jimmy Lunceford all played at the Savoy. You could hear them a block away. People started dancing as soon as they got off the trains at Lenox Avenue and 135th Street.

"On Sunday mornings after church, there was a fashion parade up and down Seventh Avenue—men wearing spats and tilted hats, and walking elegantly with canes. And competing with all that elegance were the street jitterbugs—young dudes wearing spectacular broad-brimmed hats and wide-shouldered zoot suits, with chains looping down from their waists to the tips of their alligator shoes.

"On Saturday and Sunday evenings, especially in the summertime, young college-trained men from the South would hang out around the YWCA at 137th Street, near Seventh Avenue. That was where the working-class girls from the South were staying. And some of those girls would also hang out around the YMCA at 135th Street, between Seventh and Lenox avenues. They were all scrubbed and well dressed, half of them pretending they weren't really from the South. 'Where you from?' 'I's from Chicago, honey.' They were ashamed to say they came from the South.

"A few blacks like myself got occasional jobs from the WPA [Works Progress Administration], paying $42.50 a week. That doesn't sound like much, but during the Depression you could live fairly well on it. Along 125th Street, you could get a hot dog and a big mug of beer for a nickel. So even when you were down to your last ten cents you could buy your lunch. Besides, the bars gave out free cheese, free salami, free pickles, and free crackers."

In the spring of 1938, Rustin registered as an evening student at the City College of New York, on Convent Avenue in west Harlem, not far from his aunt Bessie's apartment on Sugar Hill. He was admitted first as a nonmatriculated student, auditing courses that appealed to him. Not until September 1940 did he become a limited matriculant, receiving sixteen credits for courses he had audited in English, history, Latin, French, algebra, political science, music, and general science. In his first semester as a matriculant, Rustin seldom sat for examinations, so that he received a final grade only in economics. It seems he was more interested in reading the assigned texts than in qualifying for a degree, and he took exams only in the subjects that interested him most. Furthermore, his political agenda on campus competed with his academic work; and the CCNY faculty may not have been surprised when he dropped out, in June of 1941.

At an early point in his enrollment at CCNY, Rustin supported himself by working as a substitute teacher at Benjamin Franklin High School. Later, he was the part-time director of a WPA-sponsored youth center in Harlem, where (according to one of his students there) "he taught some kind of modern dance—not really ballet but quite graceful." On occasions, Rustin supplemented his income by attending the Apollo Theater, on West 125th Street, and volunteering as a last-minute replacement for any vocalist who failed to appear.

In September 1939, the Harlem choral director Leonard DePaur, who was auditioning singers for the all-black Broadway musical *John Henry,* starring Paul Robeson, invited Rustin to join the production's chorus. DePaur had heard him sing a program of spirituals at Mother Zion AME Church in Harlem. Rustin jumped at the offer, for it not only would guarantee him a weekly income but give him an opportunity to meet Paul Robeson—who was nearly as legendary as John Henry himself.

After a four-week trial run in Boston and Philadelphia, *John Henry* opened at Broadway's Forty-fourth Street Theater on January 10, 1940. But the mixed reviews—their plaudits reserved mostly for Robeson's singing—were ominous. "The play never rises to the stature of its hero," the *Herald Tribune* complained. The *Post* found it "nice to listen to" only "when Mr. Robeson and the chorus" were "giving it their all." The *Times*'s Brooks Atkinson called it "an uneven show with music that is also of uneven quality," serving "chiefly to renew acquaintance with a man of magnificence." The show, fatally wounded by such notices, closed within a fortnight. But Rustin had enjoyed meeting Robeson, his senior by fourteen years. "I was absolutely taken with him," Bayard later told Robeson's biographer Martin Duberman. "He was so large, so full of life, and so totally respectful of everybody. Almost anyone could knock on his door, go in, sit and talk with him, although he was the superstar."

During the *John Henry* run, Rustin met the guitarist and blues singer Josh White, who had played the main supporting role. Not long after the show closed, White organized a vocal quintet called the Carolinians, whose other members were Bill White (Josh's brother), Carrington Lewis, Sam Gary, and Bayard Rustin. In June, the Carolinians recorded *Chain Gang,* their first album. But its explicit blues and work songs fell so harshly upon many American ears that Columbia Records almost regretted releasing it. Josh White was considered a communist sympathizer, owing partly to the company he kept and partly to the political reputation of nightclubs in which he and the Carolinians often appeared.

One such club was Café Society Downtown—at Sheridan Square in Greenwich Village—which the impresario Barney Josephson had been operating since December 1938. Perhaps the first integrated nightclub in a white Manhattan neighborhood, Café Society Downtown came to be called the wrong place for the right people. Josephson's inclusive racial policy was probably meant as a rebuke to the once elite white-owned Cotton Club, in the heart of Harlem, where blacks had been admitted only as waiters and entertainers. "I wanted a club," he later told Whitney Balliett of *The New Yorker,* "where blacks and whites worked together behind the footlights and sat together out front." His revolutionary policy of open accommodations attracted a large number of left-wing intellectuals—as well as government agents, who marked Café Society Downtown as a place run and frequented by communists. Josh White and Josephson's brother Leon would later be subpoenaed to testify before the House Un-American Activities Committee. "Though Bayard and his young friends, including me, went to Café Society Downtown," Charles Bloomstein remembered, "our favorite club was the Village Vanguard, which was also integrated. The Vanguard was more left-wing and less expensive than Café Society."

Politically, Rustin would not have been out of place in either of those establishments. He was a left-winger himself, a member and organizer of the Young Communist League at City College. Rustin contributed a portion of his earnings to the YCL and did only enough academic work to preserve the misleading appearance that he was studying for a degree. Politics and not scholarship was his true mission on the CCNY campus—an apparent confirmation of his earlier statement that communists in Philadelphia had recruited him for service in New York. According to Mark Naison, a historian of the communist movement in the black inner city, "From the early '30s on, the Party made a practice of sending talented black organizers all over the country into Harlem, convinced that the Party's progress in that community would be crucial to its overall success." George Chaney, a party organizer, added, in his autobiography: "The democratic revolution had come to Harlem. In the churches a new combination of religion and politics emerged. . . . The Party, too, had its place on the Avenue . . . though its slogan of Negro and white unity evoked mixed reactions and incredulity. . . . The people were accustomed to their separateness, to the mores of the ghetto, and received the whites who shared the Communist platform with suspicion—believing that somehow the thunder against Jim Crow was inspired by ulterior motives."

But whatever Rustin's status as a young communist organizer, he gained it chiefly among the white students at CCNY, a hotbed of radical activism in the thirties and forties. The basement of the school's cafeteria building was subdivided into alcoves, in which various student groupings engaged one another in fierce ideological combat. Meyer Liben, a CCNY graduate, wrote in retrospect:

> In the alcoves it was dark, Dostoevskian dark, corresponding, no doubt, to the soul's needs at the time.
>
> The discussions down there . . . often turned into arguments . . . and these of a sometimes violent nature. When that happened a crowd gathered around the contestants, the way kids do, waiting for a fight to explode. . . . The political discussions ranged from the sectarian to the loftiest, most utopian

matters, from issues of the day to questions of the "withering away of the state." . . . The political spectrum at the college, as compared to that of the population at large, was somewhat eccentric. There was no doubt a Republican somewhere among the students. There were, of course, Democrats, but their position was not considered a political one—to be a Democrat meant that you wished to become a lawyer, teacher, civil servant, and were protecting your future.

The radicals ranged from right-wing Socialists . . . to splinters from the Trotskyist left wing. In between was a bewildering variety—Austro-Marxists, orthodox Communists, Socialist centrists, and Socialist left-wingers. . . . We also had in our midst philosophical anarchists, supporters of the IWW, and all kinds of sympathizers, fellow-travelers, and indeterminists.

Rustin shared an alcove with the Young Communist League, many of whose members had enrolled at CCNY partly to elude the problem of joblessness during the Depression and partly to avail themselves of the free tuition for which the college was known. But despite their un-American ideology, they were viewed as young idealists. "As the Depression deepened," Irving Howe and Lewis Coser wrote, "the idea of Communism began to strike fire in the minds of an important section of American youth. Those who joined or were influenced by the Young Communist League were never to comprise more than a small minority of their generation—but a minority that, because of its devotion and energy, left its imprint upon many others. No matter how hostile one may be toward the politics of these young Communists, honesty requires the admission that some of them were among the best of their generation, among the most intelligent, selfless, and idealistic."

Because of his pigmentation, Rustin was the most striking and conspicuous occupant of the young communists' alcove at CCNY. Milton Kramer, an undergraduate at the college, "was visiting the basement one evening, when I saw this black man in the communist alcove.

I asked myself, 'Well, who have the communists snared this time? Who is this Negro they have fronting for them?' We didn't say 'black' in those days. 'Negro' was the term almost everyone used." Morton Calvert, another student, was struck as much by Rustin's intellect as by his color: "I shared a good deal of alcove conversation with Bayard. He was a distinguished, distinctive member of the evening-student body."

Since, as Rustin admitted, he was at CCNY as a phony student, his real purpose being to organize and agitate on behalf of the Young Communist League, much of his reading was confined to radical literature: writings by Lenin and Bakunin; *The Communist Manifesto,* by Marx and Engels; *The Coming Struggle for Power,* by John Strachey. At CCNY, as in Philadelphia, he joined protest rallies in support of the Scottsboro "boys." He also claimed to have played a leading role in the communist takeover of CCNY's student senate, its campus newspaper, and, later, the American Student Union—a nursery for some of the left-wing intellectuals who entered American public life during and immediately after World War II.

But Rustin did not sever his ties with the nonpolitical, nonintellectual friends he had made in Harlem. "I used to follow Bayard when he visited a communist cell at 146th Street near Saint Nicholas Avenue," Howard Wallace remembered. "The cell was right next door to a place we called Kirby's Pool Room. When you were broke and had nothing, that was a good place to go. The people there were friendly. Whatever they had to eat and drink they shared with you. Bayard was like a big sport. When we went into Williamson's Restaurant, on 150th Street, he would treat everybody.

"Occasionally, he invited me to hear the young revolutionaries in their meetings at City College. I saw Josh White at some of those meetings. I also saw the singer Lillian Roth, who later wrote the book *I'll Cry Tomorrow.* Although I wasn't a revolutionary myself, I didn't mind listening to all the stuff the City College radicals discussed. But I was always embarrassed when I attended their meetings, for they always ended by taking up a collection, and I never had anything to give."

Milton Kramer, a pacifist who later befriended Rustin on campus, found him to be an unconventional sort of communist—aristocratic in manner, refined in sensibility. "Bayard knew the best soups and pâtés," Kramer said. "He turned me on to the best cheeses and wines. He was a good liver, with fine tastes—a Quaker who wasn't as Spartan-like as his brethren. I noticed, too, that he always wanted to be in the sun. He had something about being in the sun. We were walking through Harlem one day when he suddenly crossed to the other side of the street. Catching up with him, I asked why he had crossed over. 'The sun is shining on this side,' he said. It impressed me that he loved the sunny side of the street. Ever since then, I've always gone out of my way to walk in the sun."

What had chiefly attracted Rustin to the communist movement was its progressive stance on issues of racial injustice. Having found in the New Deal no program for civil rights—unless it was the sympathetic roving ambassadorship of Eleanor Roosevelt—he concluded that "if blacks were to get anywhere," they would have to ally themselves with a movement more radical than the Democratic Party. Nor did he believe such a movement could emerge within the Socialist Party, despite the humanitarian leadership of Norman Thomas. He was later to change his mind, but he felt then that "the Norman Thomas social-ists took the view that while civil rights were important you couldn't help blacks by concentrating on civil rights. It was their position that only when you changed the economy into a socialist economy would blacks automatically get their civil rights. Well, I was impatient. I didn't want to wait."

He therefore fell into the seductive arms of the communists, the only predominantly white national movement that had committed itself to a civil rights program for blacks. "The communists were pas-sionately involved and I was passionately involved," he said. "So they were ready-made for me."

Rustin was ecstatic early in 1941 when the Young Communist League assigned him to organize and lead a campaign against segrega-tion in the armed services. But in June 1941, when the Nazis invaded the Soviet Union, he was called in by the communist leadership and ordered to disband his campaign against racial segregation in the military—since such a campaign was no longer in the best interests of Moscow. Hitler's invasion, he was told, now required a Soviet-American solidarity against Germany; and to continue the fight for desegregation in the armed forces would be disruptive to the American military machinery and hurt the prospects for an effective alliance with the Soviet Union.

As Wilson Record later explained in his definitive study, *The Negro and the Communist Party:*

> No longer was President Roosevelt a warmonger, leading the country toward a blood bath to preserve the interests of Wall Street; he was now cast in the heroic role of leading the American forces against the Axis drive for world conquest. The war was no longer one whose outcome would further enslave the darker races. . . .
>
> Whereas during the preceding period the rights of American Negroes could best be secured by "getting out and staying out of the imperialist war," these same rights could be guaranteed now only by all-out support of the military effort. The attack on the USSR was an attack on all racial minorities.

But for Rustin a light had failed. He now saw, he said, that "the communists' primary concern was not with the black masses but with the global objectives of the Soviet Union," objectives that "were bound to conflict with the necessities of the racial struggle." Disillusioned, Rustin broke with the communist movement, and he was to remain one of its sterner critics for the rest of his life. He also dropped out of City College and went off to establish new alliances, with organizations that shared his commitment to civil rights progress and radical religious pacifism.

Chapter 4

In Fellowship

The day in June 1941 that Rustin quit the Young Communist League, he walked from the heights of Sugar Hill down to the "valley" of central Harlem and renewed a slight acquaintance he had had with A. Philip Randolph—the labor and civil rights leader who was to be one of Rustin's more important influences. Then twenty-nine, to Randolph's fifty-two, Rustin was somewhat like a prodigal son, going home to his roots after squandering a portion of his early idealism in an alien ideological lifestyle. He had made Randolph's acquaintance some months in the past, when he visited the latter's office on West 125th Street. That was the headquarters of the Brotherhood of Sleeping Car Porters, which the staunchly anticommunist Randolph had founded in 1925 and had been leading ever since—despite the heavy fire he drew from communists hostile to his social democratic leadership of oppressed black workers.

In that first meeting with Rustin, Randolph had been personally cordial but politically reserved. For he learned early in the conversation that his charming and articulate visitor was an ally of the communist movement—an unpleasant discovery that Randolph did not remark upon till near the end of their interview.

It isn't now clear why Rustin had wanted to see Randolph, whose anticommunist stance was widely known. As a trade union leader and a member of Norman Thomas's American Socialist Party, Randolph was one of the nation's prominent social democrats; and communists did not usually wish to share the same room, breathe the same air, with the likes of Randolph and Thomas. Indeed, American communists regarded Randolph as one of their worst enemies in the black community, a leader whose gradualist and ameliorative measures frustrated the communist program for revolutionary political and social change in the black precincts of the nation. The communists had tried to wreck Randolph's presidency not only of the Brotherhood of Sleeping Car Porters but also of the National Negro Congress, to which he was elected in 1936, at an inaugural conference in Chicago. And Randolph had come to despise communists—particularly what he called their policy of "rule or ruin"—nearly as much as they despised him.

But whatever had motivated Rustin to seek his first audience with Randolph, he was immensely impressed by the elegance of manner and spirit with which Randolph received him. "This man of great dignity and inner beauty," he later said, "stood up, walked from behind his desk, met me in the middle of the room, shook hands, and offered me a seat." Rustin was all the more impressed with the Randolph persona because "I was then nothing, a nobody." But he correctly discerned that while Randolph's style "was an innate part of his personality," it was also an effective social tactic, a kind of "moral judo that threw opponents off balance."

In their first encounter, Randolph admired Rustin's keen intelligence and his desire—even as a communist—to energize the efforts on behalf of black progress. They had much else in common, though they did not both know it then. Randolph had himself been an evening student at the City College of New York, in the years just before World War I. He had also been a campus radical, albeit in the democratic socialist movement of Eugene Debs. And he, too, had dropped out of CCNY, without qualifying for a degree. There were other resemblances, beyond skin color. Rustin's maternal grandfather was a deacon in the

African Methodist Episcopal Church in West Chester, Pennsylvania; Randolph's father had been the pastor of an AME chapel in Jacksonville, Florida. Both men shared a vanity in acquired speech, puzzling to their fellow African Americans and to more than a few white Americans as well. Randolph spoke in a grave cadence, which he probably thought of as the cadence of the great abolitionist preachers and speakers of the mid and late nineteenth century—particularly those in New England, though there was also an old southern gravitas in the style of his delivery. Rustin, more of a modern Anglophile, favored the crisp accent and diction of the British upper class.

One thing Rustin and Randolph certainly didn't share, when they first met, was a common political ideology. Though Randolph had seen that in the early moments of their conversation, he had kept a silence about it. Born in 1889, raised with courtly southern manners, he almost always maintained a Victorian-Edwardian reticence in exchanges that were fraught with embarrassment—up to the point where he recognized that candor was no longer avoidable. So it was virtually at the end of his first talk with Rustin that Randolph sprang the remark "I am sorry to know that you are associated with the communists. I think you are going to discover that they are not really interested in civil rights. They are interested in utilizing civil rights for their own purposes." Whether or not Rustin contemplated a reply, Randolph stood and extended a hand, indicating that their time had expired.

But his parting prophecy was correct; for it was a sudden shift in Soviet policy on the race question that compelled Rustin to resign from the Young Communist League. Indeed, when the disillusioned and contrite Rustin returned in June of 1941, for his second visit with Randolph, it was to volunteer his services to a mass civil rights march on Washington that the veteran black leader was mobilizing. Randolph readily assigned Rustin to the youth arm of the march organization—a project designed to protest against the exclusion of black workers from the nation's defense industry, which was busily producing armaments to aid the Allied cause in Europe.

•   •   •

But as energetically as Rustin threw himself into action, he was a late-comer to the March on Washington project. Preparations had begun in January 1941; and when he came on board, only about a week remained before the date, July 1, Randolph had set for the event. As if delivering an ultimatum, Randolph had thrown that deadline at President Franklin D. Roosevelt. In letters to the President, and in at least one personal confrontation at the White House, Randolph had told Roosevelt—who feared the potentially violent outcome of a black mass demonstration in Washington—that he would cancel the march only if the President issued an executive order banning racial discrimination in all munitions factories. Roosevelt had stiffened against the effrontery of such an ultimatum. But upon further reflection—especially after his wife, Eleanor, described to him the militant preparations for the march she had seen in New York—he relented. In late June, he issued Executive Order 8802, declaring that "there shall be no discrimination in the employment of workers in defense industries or government because of race, creed, color, or national origin." Honoring the promise of his ultimatum, Randolph then called off the proposed march.

This decision triggered an explosive dissent among his youth orga-nizers, including Bayard Rustin. Their political passion allowed for nothing like the honor Randolph had displayed toward Roosevelt. They wanted a march, no matter what; for they had been excited by the prospect of a confrontation with the federal government in the nation's capital. They felt, moreover, that beyond the provisions of Executive Order 8802, Randolph should have pressed for immediate desegrega-tion of the armed forces—a campaign Rustin had been leading before losing his faith in the Young Communist League. The radical youth organizers not only denounced Randolph's cancellation of the march—a decision praised throughout the country as an important victory for civil rights—but also conspired to keep their activities alive until Randolph rescheduled the march on which they had set their hearts.

But the conspiracy failed, after Randolph issued a public statement reprimanding the young renegades. Its strictures were outlined under these headings: "(1) The Main Objectives of the March had been Won.

(2) To Rally the Masses, Objectives Should be Kept Simple. (3) The Youth Were too Enamored of the Romantic Flavor of Demonstration. (4) Organizers in the Youth Division Were Dilettantes. (5) Some Members of the Youth Division were Communist Dupes. The historian Herbert Garfinkel later called Randolph's statement an instructive "lecture on the nature and strategy of mass movements."

Did Randolph mean to include Bayard Rustin among the youth organizers he described as communist dupes? It would not be surprising if he did. After all, Rustin had only recently withdrawn from the communist movement; and conceivably, he would not so soon have rid himself entirely of its influence. Although they were to resume their collaboration a few years later, Rustin broke with Randolph in the late summer of 1941—mostly because he felt a deep remorse over his part in the insubordinate rebellion that had been so embarrassing to Randolph's leadership. But in retrospect, Rustin would always regard the canceled march of 1941—with its threat of a massive nonviolent protest in Washington—as "the symbolic inauguration of the modern civil rights movement."

From Randolph's black March on Washington crusade, Rustin shifted over to the predominantly white pacifist movement. Specifically, he began working for the Fellowship of Reconciliation—the American branch of an international organization of Christian pacifists—which was then led by A. J. Muste, one of Randolph's many associates in the white liberal community.

Born shortly after the outbreak of World War I, the Fellowship of Reconciliation (FOR) had been conceived in the very first spasm of those hostilities. More than a hundred Protestants, from various parts of Europe, were meeting at Lake Constance, in Germany, when the guns of August 1914 brought their convention to a premature conclusion. As the conferees dispersed hastily to their different homelands, two of them—Henry Hodgkin, a British Quaker, and Friedrich Siegmund-Schultze, a Lutheran pastor in Germany—pledged, between themselves, to continue sowing "the seeds of peace and love, no matter what the future might bring." The two were to meet again only four months later, at Trinity College, Cambridge, where another gathering of Protestants founded the Fellowship of Reconciliation. "One must choose between the sword and the cross," wrote Britain's Muriel Lester, who was to become one of the FOR's indefatigable emissaries throughout the world. "Thus," she added, "the Fellowship . . . was formed, providing us with anchorage as well as with a chart for all adventuring." Richard Roberts, a Presbyterian minister who attended the meeting at Trinity College, further explained the FOR's mission: "Through all the years, peace had been chiefly conceived as the absence of war. . . . For us, peace was something to be waged, as war was waged."

On a visit to the United States in November 1915, Henry Hodgkin addressed a conference of Protestants in Garden City, Long Island, at the end of which the American branch of the FOR was inaugurated. Its earliest members included Tracy Mygatt, Frances Witherspoon, and their associate Jessie Wallace Hughan, a Barnard graduate with a Ph.D. in political science. They became progressive activists in what was then a fragmented and largely civic-minded American peace movement. Hughan recalled that it was the Reverend John Haynes Holmes, "a hot pacifist" (at the Community Church in Manhattan), who invited her circle of friends to the meeting in Garden City; and that "after we heard the ringing message of Henry Hodgkin we gradually realized that here was the uncompromising peace group for whose existence we had been longing." Still, Jessie Hughan, a spirited pacifist from an upper-middle-class family in Brooklyn, wasn't too fond of the term "reconciliation." It "sounded too mild" to her. So it isn't surprising that some years later, in 1923, she helped to launch the War Resisters League—as a secular, more muscular, complement to the Fellowship of Reconciliation.

Other early members of the American FOR included such wartime and postwar intellectuals as Norman Thomas, then a young Presbyterian minister in East Harlem; Evan Thomas, Norman's brother, who served an excruciating imprisonment at Fort Leavenworth for his conscientious objection to military service; Reinhold Niebuhr, a rising theologian in New York City; Paul Jones, a socialist-leaning

Episcopal bishop from Utah; Howard Thurman, the leading African American religious thinker at that time (a professor of religion at Howard University); Harry Emerson Fosdick, the pastor of the Riverside Church in Manhattan; John Nevin Sayre, a clergyman in Suffern, New York; Rufus Jones and Henry Cadbury, Quaker intellectuals and founders of the American Friends Service Committee; Roger Baldwin and Scott Nearing, radical civil libertarians; Oswald Garrison Villard, an editor of *The Nation,* grandson of the abolitionist writer and orator William Lloyd Garrison; and A. J. Muste, a young clergyman of the Dutch Reformed Church, who had been a classmate of Norman Thomas's at Union Theological Seminary in New York.

Muste was to become the most renowned leader of the FOR in America, a future that seemed most unlikely at one stage in his career. In 1915, he abandoned his Dutch Reformed ministry in upper Manhattan in favor of a Congregational pulpit in Newtonville, Massachusetts. There he began a radical priesthood against the war in Europe, but when his pacifist sermons offended a number of communicants whose sons were risking their lives in the world conflict, he was relieved of his appointment. Converted later to left-wing politics, Muste joined the Trotskyist faction of the American labor movement, where he became a radical trade unionist and a leader in the debates surrounding Marxist-Leninist thought. Returning from a meeting with Trotsky in Switzerland, Muste paused in Paris; and there, while visiting Saint Sulpice Church, he underwent another conversion—back to Christian pacifism. This earned him the ridicule of former associates in the left-wing movement. Sidney Hook, the philosopher and Marxist scholar, later wrote mockingly of Muste's circular intellectual journey, "When he became a revolutionary Marxist he publicly abandoned his pacifism. . . . He could not have been very well versed in either one or the other, despite his religious training, for when he finally vomited up his hastily swallowed Marxism, he returned to his early beliefs with the passion of someone newly converted." Reflecting upon criticism of that sort, Muste was to say, in a piece of his own writing: "I surmise that not a few of my associates of that period claim that I never ceased being a pacifist at heart and therefore never was a true-blue Marxist-Leninist—and there is something to that. At any rate, I never abandoned certain ethical attitudes which had been and are now part of my pacifism."

In August 1940, after he had resumed his pacifist ministry, Muste was elected to lead the Fellowship of Reconciliation in America. And his successful candidacy reflected the outcome of a philosophical debate that had erupted in the FOR during the 1930s—whether the organization should be pragmatic or absolute in its pacifism, limited or total in its commitment to nonviolence.

The latter point of view—absolute pacifism, total nonviolence—had prevailed, and it facilitated Muste's elevation to the FOR leadership. But it also caused the resignation of tough-minded religious intellectuals, Reinhold Niebuhr among them. Explaining "Why I Leave the FOR," in an article for *The Christian Century,* Niebuhr wrote in 1934: "The Fellowship controversy has revealed that there are radical Christians who can no longer express themselves in pacifist terms. I think we have to leave the Fellowship of Reconciliation with as good a grace as possible. . . . We must find more solid ground for the combination of radicalism and Christianity than the creed of pacifism." By "radical Christians," Niebuhr probably meant "Christian radicals"; for in the context of that debate, it was the "radical Christians" who urged an absolute commitment to pacifism and nonviolence.

At all events, those in the FOR who shared Niebuhr's position felt that pacifists were not morally bound to be nonviolent in all circumstances, certainly not when immoral forces threatened to destroy not only democratic freedom but also the civilized values upon which that freedom depended. Hence, they argued, it was politically unrealistic, even irresponsible, for the Fellowship to assert a policy of total pacifism—especially at a time when the barbarities of Hitlerism were already foreshadowed in Europe. Could total nonviolence deter the Nazis?

But radical pacifists like A. J. Muste were not so interested in such a question. To them, nonviolence was as sacred a human value as any in the world, requiring an unconditional commitment to the peaceful res-

olution of conflict. Nonviolence was not for them a tactical or pragmatic option but a total way of life. Those who were influenced by the
teaching and preaching of A. J. Muste stood ready to be broken for their
ideals and convictions. Not surprisingly, Muste was the only pacifist
leader to whom they applied the term "saintly."

Describing the FOR's stance during World War I, Muriel Lester
wrote: "We could not conceive of God as a nationalist; we knew that,
strange as it might appear, the Germans were as dear and precious in
His sight as the Allies." Muste sounded a similar note when, early in
World War II, he declared: "If I can't love Hitler I can't love at all." To
the average listener, such a statement might have marked him as a
lunatic. After all, most sane clergymen in the United States despised
Hitler. A leader of the Unitarian Church said, in 1941: "The Unitarians
have always admired the Samaritan who bound up the wounds of the
stranger set upon by robbers, but today they work to rid the Jericho
road of thieves."

When Muste spoke of loving Hitler, he was addressing an understanding audience of Quakers, religionists who subscribed to the ideal
of radical human brotherhood, who believed, as he did, in hating the sin
and not the sinner. One non-Quaker in that audience was the political
journalist Milton Mayer. Astonished by the remark about loving Hitler,
Mayer decided to confront Muste at the end of the meeting. However,
he later lost his nerve. "Some seventeenth sense told me I was out of my
class," Mayer wrote. It occurred to him as well that Muste had been
"saying something to himself," that his "voice picked it up and ampli-
fied it," that it "came from the very center of the man." Still, Mayer
added, "I thanked God (à la Swinburne) that I was not a Christian. . . .
It was hard enough to be a Jew, even in America, and desperately hard
in Germany; but anything was better than having to be a Christian and
love your enemies."

As old men gave money to Muste, Mayer said, so did "young men,
in and out of the ministry, and across the country, gravitate to him in
their search for the good, the true, and the beautiful." Bayard Rustin
was among the young people Muste attracted to the Fellowship of

Reconciliation. "I learned more about nonviolence from him than in all my subsequent reading," Bayard told Nat Hentoff, Muste's biographer. "I carried over his lessons to my later work with Martin Luther King."

Soon after passage of the Conscription Act, late in 1940, Rustin had applied for classification as a conscientious objector. "Bayard was among the first in our group to be called," his Harlem friend Howard Wallace remembered. "He appeared before a draft board near City College, and when he began explaining his opposition to war, half the people on the board couldn't understand what he was saying. With his Oxford English, he seemed to be speaking above their heads. Anyway, he talked them into accepting his claim, and when the hearing ended, a member of the board referred him to A. J. Muste. That's how he came to work for the Fellowship of Reconciliation, the first job that gained him recognition in this country."

Actually, Rustin had met Muste a few months earlier, at a conference of the American Friends Service Committee that summer, in Syracuse. John Swomley, who was then Muste's deputy at the FOR, recalled that the two men were introduced by Norman Whitney, a prominent Quaker living in upstate New York—with whom Rustin later formed a close friendship. "I was deeply impressed [with Muste]," Bayard told Nat Hentoff. "He wasn't at all the fuzzy liberal pacifist type I'd expected. He didn't try to proselytize me, although he did explain several principles of nonviolent direct action. At the end of our talk, he said simply that if I examined all the possible positions I could take, and measured them against my background and experience, I'd come to the right decision." Rustin was also to find, when he began working with the FOR, that Muste was "realistic"; that what friends and critics called his "saintliness" was "combined with unusual political shrewdness"; that he knew and admitted "enough about the existence of evil not to share the easy optimism of the average pacifist."

Muste was himself impressed by his first meeting with Rustin; and before they parted in Syracuse, he invited Bayard to attend the FOR's twenty-fifth annual conference in September, at Lake Chautauqua, New

York. According to William Hefner, a delegate at that conference, Muste "presented Rustin to us as one who, in his lifetime, would probably have a national influence in helping to solve the racial discrimination problem in the United States." Rustin was then still an evening student at City College, where he would soon begin organizing the communist-sponsored campaign against racial segregation in the armed services.

Months later, not long after he withdrew from A. Philip Randolph's March on Washington movement, Rustin joined a team of peace volunteers to Puerto Rico, sponsored by the American Friends Service Committee. He was the only black member of the eleven-man team—indeed, he was to be one of the few blacks in the American pacifist movement—but he had lobbied aggressively for his inclusion. "Bayard felt strongly that not only white students should be on the delegation to Puerto Rico," said Curt Regan, who had organized the mission on behalf of the AFSC. Rustin wasn't unaccustomed to being a conspicuous black in a predominantly white setting—as he had been in the Quaker community of his native West Chester; in the peace delegation to Auburn during the summer of 1937; in the Young Communist League at CCNY. He was what his friends and political colleagues called racially self-liberated: never uncomfortable with, and always challenged by, his minority status in white groupings. William Sutherland, one of the rare black comrades in the pacifist movement, was to say, "Bayard thrived on being a special voice among whites. They accorded him a recognition that blacks did not. Many blacks would try to cut him down to size, but he was idolized in white circles. His gifts and abilities were more readily acknowledged by white radicals and pacifists than by blacks on the whole."

In Puerto Rico, Rustin carried out an important assignment A. J. Muste had given him: to investigate the problems facing conscientious objectors there. On his return to New York, Rustin presented a cogent analysis of those problems; and Muste wrote, in mid-August 1941, to thank him for his "very detailed and comprehensive report." It was a sign not only that Muste was growing in his admiration for Rustin's abilities but also that Bayard was being auditioned for a job on the national staff of the Fellowship of Reconciliation.

Reviewing the Fellowship's twenty-sixth annual conference, in September 1941, Muste called it "the most significant and historic" so far. It was surely the largest yet. And Muste's self-congratulatory tone was understandable, for that gathering marked the first anniversary of his FOR leadership. The Lakeside, Ohio, meeting was also significant for being the occasion on which Muste announced three key staff appointments to his new administration: James Farmer as race relations secretary; George Houser as youth secretary; Bayard Rustin as secretary for student and general affairs. Those positions were to be revised and rotated in later years. But Farmer and Houser and Rustin—joined subsequently by the Reverend Glenn Smiley—were probably the finest staff appointments Muste ever made. Farmer and Rustin were black; Houser and Smiley were white. And, in a sense, they were Muste's gifts to the future movement for racial and social reform in America.

Like Houser and Smiley, Farmer had been trained in the Protestant ministry. The son of a Methodist clergyman in Texas, he had studied at Howard University's School of Religion. And in 1942, some months after becoming the Fellowship's race relations secretary, he founded the Congress of Racial Equality (CORE), which—along with Randolph's March on Washington movement—pioneered the nonviolent mass struggle against segregated public institutions in the United States. George Houser, also the son of a Methodist minister, was a graduate of Union Theological Seminary. "I was a product of the 1930s," he said later. "The Social Gospel, putting the Christian ethic into practice on the social scene, was the credo that moved me. I was a pacifist as well as a supporter of organized labor and all efforts to challenge racial discrimination and segregation. I joined the Young People's Socialist League, affiliated with Norman Thomas's Socialist Party. And as a seminarian I supported A. Philip Randolph's Brotherhood of Sleeping Car Porters."

In November 1940, Houser and a number of seminarians at Union Theological were among the first young Americans arrested for resisting the recently legislated military draft. They were tried and sentenced to a year and a day at the penitentiary in Danbury, Connecticut. Upon his release—with time off for good behavior—Houser continued his studies at the Theological Seminary in Chicago. There he later helped James Farmer to organize CORE, of which Bayard Rustin was the first field secretary. And in the early 1950s, Houser and Rustin were to be among the cofounders of the American Committee on Africa, the first interracial organization in the United States to support the struggle against colonialism and apartheid in that continent.

By 1942, most leading activists in the Fellowship of Reconciliation were also disciples of Mahatma Gandhi. Beyond A. J. Muste himself, they included Rustin, Houser, Farmer, Glenn Smiley, and the Reverend J. Holmes Smith. Almost all of them had been drawn to Gandhian philosophy and methodology by their reading of such influential texts as Thoreau's essay on civil disobedience; Gandhi's autobiography; *My Gandhi,* by John Haynes Holmes; *The Power of Nonviolence,* by Richard Gregg; *The Conquest of Violence,* by Bartolemeo de Ligt; and *War Without Violence,* by Krishnalal Shridharani.

The latter was probably the most influential. Written by a former associate of Gandhi—later a doctoral student at Columbia University—it was adopted by FOR activists as a blueprint for nonviolent mass resistance. Muste called it "the most important explication" of Gandhian principles that had yet appeared. Bayard Rustin said later, "Shridharani's book became our gospel, our bible." James Farmer consulted it while planning CORE's earliest activities in nonviolent direct action. Glenn Smiley (who, with Rustin, was to be a Gandhian counselor to Dr. Martin Luther King during the epochal Montgomery bus boycott of 1955–56) regarded the publication of Shridharani's work as "the most significant event in the history of the American FOR." Smiley recalled: "A small number of people in New York City, including A. J. Muste, A. Philip Randolph, and John Haynes Holmes, met to discuss the book and its possible application to the racial conditions in the United

States." It was "a tiny pebble" thrown into a pond, he added, but its "resulting ripples and waves were to have an extraordinary influence upon the future of civil rights activism in America."

J. Holmes Smith, a former Methodist missionary, was not—like some of his colleagues in the FOR—a newcomer to Gandhian thought and method. He had lived in India until the late 1930s, when the British authorities, ruling him persona non grata, expelled him for working too closely with Gandhi's independence movement. In at least one sense, Smith may have welcomed the expulsion. As an American clergyman, he would no longer have to devise an answer to Indians who asked him this embarrassing question: "Why do you come out here to tell us about Christianity when in your own country they lynch colored people?"

But it was after reading Shridharani's book that Smith, under FOR auspices, set up a Gandhian ashram on Fifth Avenue, near 125th Street. The Harlem ashram became a retreat for a variety of peace radicals, most of them belonging to the Fellowship of Reconciliation. The black civil rights attorney Conrad Lynn would remember it as "the gathering place of absolute pacifists," many of whom "had refused to register for conscription."

In its location, appearance, and accommodations, the ashram was a resort that only genuinely selfless Gandhians could love. It stood opposite a saloon called the Bucket of Blood—scarcely a suitable neighbor to a house of pacifism and nonviolence. When John P. Roche, a student at Hofstra University and a member of the Socialist Party, visited the ashram for an interview with Bayard Rustin, he left with this "vivid memory": the place was so "filthy," the food so "awful," that he failed to see "how anyone could think this sort of commune was really the way to live." James Farmer, who lived there briefly in 1943, was repelled by its "dark and dingy" walls; its "old, cheap, and tasteless furniture." He considered its "unpalatable" food "an inducement to fasting."

But the Harlem ashram had been designed for meditation, not for the provision of physical comforts. It was meant to be a center for the study of nonviolent strategies and tactics, for the development of spiritual discipline, for the cultivation of an ascetic Gandhian sensibility. Within its dingy walls, creative political meetings examined the principles of *Satyagraha* and considered how they might be applied to pacifist and other social struggles in the United States. Those discussions led to the founding of at least two organizations, both ad hoc satellites of the FOR. One, led by J. Holmes Smith, was the committee for Non-Violent Direct Action (NVDA), reflecting A. J. Muste's and the Fellowship's commitment to both antiwar activism and the black struggle for civil rights. The other organization, headed for a while by Bayard Rustin, was the Free India Committee—a reciprocal gesture to Gandhi, whose philosophy, while inspiring the struggle for India's self-determination, had helped to energize the movement for nonviolent mass resistance in America. Beyond Rustin, other leading lights of the Free India Committee included such peace, labor, and civil rights activists as Muste, John Swomley, A. Philip Randolph, John Nevin Sayre, Sidney Hertzberg, Hazel Whitman, Pauli Murray, Ernest Lefever, William Hefner, William Sutherland, and James Farmer. In 1943, leaders and members of the Committee staged frequent demonstrations at the British consulate in New York and at the embassy in Washington—where, on almost every occasion, they were arrested for disturbing the peace.

For most of the 1940s, the Fellowship of Reconciliation occupied national headquarters in a small three-story building at 2929 Broadway, next door to Columbia University. The accommodations were shared by A. J. Muste and his executive assistant, Doris Grotewohl; the Reverend John Nevin Sayre, who had been designated Muste's coleader of the American FOR; John Swomley, the chief deputy leader, and his administrative secretary, Catharine Raymond; Ernest Bromley, a field representative; Marion Bromley, a general office secretary; Bayard Rustin and his secretarial assistant, Martha Higashida (Martha Huset, after she married); Alfred Hassler, editor of *Fellowship,* the FOR's monthly magazine; and Hassler's assistant editor, Constance Muste, a daughter of A. J. Muste. In 1943, office space was made for James Farmer and George Houser, whom the FOR called back from Chicago to a reassignment at national headquarters.

Reflecting the FOR's poor financial position, its office furnishings on upper Broadway were, Marion Bromley later reported, "maybe just a notch up from the shabby." The chief reward to workers at the Fellowship's headquarters was the spiritual satisfaction they gained from serving the pacifist cause in which they deeply believed. When Bayard Rustin joined the staff in September 1941, his base salary (and that of other field representatives) was fifteen dollars a week—raised a year later to $18.75. In November 1941, the FOR had reason to remind its employees that they worked under a vow of virtual poverty—though all of them, well enough educated, could easily have found more lucrative employment elsewhere. Rustin certainly could, probably somewhere in the progressive sector of organized labor. At its national committee meeting, late in 1941, the FOR acknowledged that its staff payments were "obviously minimum . . . by many standards of subsistent wages." Therefore, the committee said, employees should be genuinely committed to "the Fellowship way of life," should be willing to undergo "whatever sacrifices it may require."

In June 1948, Constance Muste announced in the *Fellowship* a munificent improvement in salaries: "Take-home pay for office workers and unmarried executives . . . is now [an annual] $1750, approximately $2000 before taxes. Take-home pay for married executives reaches the top of about $4000." Bayard Rustin was unappeased, complaining bitterly that he deserved to be paid as well as married executives, including A. J. Muste. It was one of the few occasions on which he had said anything critical about his revered mentor in the pacifist movement. But beyond gripes over paychecks, Marion Bromley remembered that "the FOR staff was truly a family," presided over by the fatherly A. J.

Rustin was the liveliest and most engaging member of that family. "Bayard was certainly the star of the FOR field staff," according to Marion Bromley. "He was a special favorite of A. J. Muste. Like A. J., he had had some earlier experience on the political left. He was devoted to A. J., looked up to A. J. as his guru. He could be a slippery customer when it came to keeping a dinner engagement, unless it was an engagement with Muste and his wife, Anne. A. J. was such a wise and self-confident leader that Bayard knew he couldn't pull any of his shenanigans with Muste. Bayard respected A. J. for that, and A. J. loved and respected him in return. One of Bayard's female admirers, who wrote to him regularly at the office, always addressed him as 'Pet.' And in a way, he was a pet of the whole FOR community."

There were other reasons as well for Rustin's popularity at 2929 Broadway. Ernest Bromley (Marion's husband) was impressed with Bayard's "advanced knowledge and judgment"; his impish humor; his gift for brilliant conversation; his compelling style in political argument—as when he would "wave a long extended forefinger, while crisp paragraphs, in an Oxford accent, poured from his mouth." Ernest Bromley also recalled this occasion in the early 1940s: "Bayard and I were walking along Broadway one day, when he spotted a cheese shop. He darted in, because he loved all sorts of cheeses. When I joined him in the shop, the proprietor—who had apparently said something uncomplimentary to Bayard—was standing there stunned and speechless. A long forefinger gestured scoldingly at him, and a clearly enunciated Oxford accent poured down upon him. Never before, I could imagine, had this shopkeeper been so addressed. Bayard left the shop in an amiable mood, bearing a packet of his favorite cheese." Catharine Raymond, of the secretarial staff, once invited Rustin out to lunch on Broadway. "In the street," she recalled, "we met a woman who couldn't conceal her disapproval of a black man and a white woman walking together. Bayard bowed to her very cordially, greeted her as if she were an old friend, and inquired about her family—all of this before the woman could recover her poise."

Catharine Raymond was also struck by Rustin's artful maneuvers at contentious staff meetings: "It amused me to watch how he got his way with some controversial project he was proposing. He would start by outlining his plan in a completely neutral manner. Then he would explain the reasons he thought his plan might not work. By this time, he would have aroused enough feeling in enough people to guarantee a lively discussion. And as it usually turned out, most of the original opponents of his project would end up voting for it. I never was sure that any of them understood just how skillfully Bayard had manipulated them into a support of his position."

In those staff meetings, "Rusty," as almost all his friends and coworkers called him, enjoyed the steady support of A. J. Muste. A close father-son relationship had developed between them—so much so that in the FOR they came to be called Muste-and-Rusty. William Sutherland, one of Rustin's few black associates in the FOR, would remember: "When Bayard and A. J. took positions at our strategy sessions, the rest of us looked at one another and rolled our eyes to heaven, in acknowledgment of the Muste-Rusty axis. They didn't have to plan their common positions ahead of time. They operated naturally together." And when Glenn Smiley came in from his base in California to attend meetings at national headquarters, he couldn't help noticing that Rustin and Muste "meshed quite well politically."

Like most members of the staff, John Swomley, Muste's deputy, recognized that Rustin "was a very talented person with a fine mind," that he "could think rapidly and well," that he was "very imaginative, creative, and affable." Nor was Swomley unaware that "Muste looked upon Bayard as his own son." But Swomley, who supervised all the field representatives, was not, like Muste, so indulgent toward Rustin. Neither was he, like Catharine Raymond, amused by Bayard's manipulative tactics at staff meetings. Swomley often saw Rustin as "imperious and unwilling to tolerate opposition—though he would back off and yield graciously when necessary." Swomley could not recall later ("my memory may be faulty") that he ever had "any serious difficulties" with Rustin. But "there were times when I had to deal with problems involving him; for while he was generally respected by his colleagues, some felt that he was a prima donna, who wanted to have things his own way; and unless Muste or I or a staff consensus opposed him, he usually got what he wanted."

Swomley's balanced recollections do not quite conceal the fact that there was a subterranean tension in his relationship with Rustin. He was Rustin's immediate supervisor; and it was in Rustin's "imperious" character to bridle against any supervision that didn't come from the highest level of leadership—such as A. J. Muste's. Consequently, Swomley cannot have helped resenting, even subtly, the favorite-son status Rustin enjoyed with Muste, a status that undermined Swomley's immediate authority over Bayard. Rustin felt, secretly, that Swomley was less than fond of him, a feeling he shared with friends outside the Fellowship. One of them, Milton Kramer—the young pacifist Rustin had met at City College—was to say, "Bayard told me about things that were going on at the FOR, and I gathered that he wasn't so comfortable with John Swomley, nor Swomley with him." It was also James Farmer's impression that "Swomley was less than warm in his attitude toward Bayard."

Swomley may have been much more comfortable with Farmer. They were old acquaintances. As theological students (Swomley at Boston University, Farmer at Howard), they had been colleagues in the National Council of Methodist Youth—where Farmer had impressed everyone, Swomley recalled, as "a persuasive and powerful speaker." It was on Swomley's recommendation that Muste had hired Farmer to be the Fellowship's race relations field secretary.

Therein lay the source of another problem. Whether or not Rustin felt that he was the more qualified for the position to which Farmer was appointed, the relationship between the two was never to be cordial, though never hostile either. It was to be one of keen rivalry. That may have been what Farmer had in mind when he said later (referring to the Fellowship's professional staff) that "the infighting was fierce." George Houser, who worked harmoniously with all factions, could see that "Bayard and Jim Farmer weren't buddies," though they "had a strong respect for each other's abilities." Farmer himself explained many years later, "To be perfectly candid, we were rivals. Think of an organization that was largely white, with two rather talented black staff members of national standing. Inevitably, they would bump heads, and persons would sometimes be pitting one of them against the other. I think Bayard understood what was happening, but still the situation kept us from being warm friends."

Rustin's political relationships in the early 1940s were not confined to the FOR. He made and maintained acquaintances within the Socialist

Party and also within the War Resisters League—the secular and more radical wing of the pacifist movement. One of the young socialists he befriended was John P. Roche. During an early stage of his political and intellectual quest, Roche had imagined himself a religious pacifist and considered joining the Fellowship of Reconciliation. But after a discussion with John Nevin Sayre, he decided that pacifism was not his path, that he could not in conscience oppose the use of arms in all circumstances. Hence he resigned himself to membership in the Socialist Party, which was not absolute in its opposition to war. "That's when I met Rustin," he recalled. "And I often saw him when he attended the Socialist Party's Youth Committee Against War. At first I thought Bayard was West Indian. His affectation of speech led me to believe he came from a British background. I later learned otherwise. As a young man, he was a strange character, blending spectacular rhetoric with the qualities of a sybarite. When I saw and heard him, I thought of Alexander Hamilton and Oscar Wilde combined."

Some evenings, after he left the FOR office on upper Broadway, Rustin rode the IRT subway down to Greenwich Village. At clubs like Max Gordon's Village Vanguard, he listened to jazz, the blues, and contemporary political songs. According to his friend Charles Bloomstein, who accompanied him on occasion, "Bayard particularly liked a song that Richard Dyer Bennett sang there: 'So give three cheers for the white and blue—there's no need to cheer for the red.' Bayard liked that song because he had recently broken with the young communists. We hung out at other places in the Village as well. At a bar named Julius's, on Waverly Place near West Tenth Street, we drank lots of beer at fifteen cents a glass. Bayard later developed a taste for good Scotch and vodka, but in those days cheap beer was all he could afford. We called that bar 'Dirty Julius's,' because it had thick cobwebs hanging from the ceiling. There was also a restaurant named Julius's, at Waverly Place and Seventh Avenue. We called that one 'Clean Julius's,' partly because we couldn't afford to eat there."

It was on one of his early visits to Greenwich Village that Rustin first met Bloomstein, an antiwar activist, who would become his life-long political colleague and confidant. With eleven other radical pacifists, Bloomstein—a member of the War Resisters League—shared a brownstone on Waverly Place near Bank Street. Rustin often visited the cooperative for dinner, mostly at the invitation of a young white man—the son of a prominent business executive—with whom he was then in love. The man later became a Catholic priest and disappeared into the upper echelons of his church.

"Whenever Bayard came to our communal house in the Village," Bloomstein recalled, "after-dinner talk ran well past midnight. But they were fascinating discussions. As young peace activists, we were full of piss and vinegar. We believed that our pacifism was going to save the world. We recognized no ideological reason for war. Warfare was just something that had to be resisted. And when our discussions weren't about pacifism, they were about Shakespeare, Freud, and the great novelists. Bayard was an enthusiastic and self-assured leader of our talks—vigorous in his presentations, charismatic in his style of argument. As a young man, he had great powers of expression, exceptional clarity of thought, intense emotional projection, and a wonderful command of language. It was clear, even then, that he was going places, that he would become an impressive person on the national scene."

Part II

Chapter 5

On the Road

Rustin's position as the Fellowship's field secretary for youth and general affairs was in perfect accord with his love of travel and his gifts for communication. A major requirement of his job, he replied to a young correspondent in the 1940s, was the ability to make a persuasive case for pacifism, "to present an unpopular point of view without contention." It was partly an impossible requirement. His powers of persuasion were beyond doubt, but not even the saintly Gandhi, one of his exemplars, could have presented unpopular views without contention. Still, as his pacifist colleague William Sutherland said, the Fellowship was lucky to have a missionary of Rustin's ability propagating its values and convictions: he not only "delighted in ideas and tactics" but was also "one of the few activists who combined the talents for singing and public speaking."

A. J. Muste charged all FOR field secretaries to "spread the message" of pacifism and "stimulate the organization of local groups and cells." Rustin could not have been more obedient to Muste's command. Beginning late in 1941, he crisscrossed the United States, organizing new pacifist groups for the Fellowship of Reconciliation; lecturing on college and high-school campuses; addressing civic and religious audiences; teaching workshops in the Gandhian technique of nonviolent direct action; visiting Civilian Public Service work camps, where one variety of conscientious objectors were interned during World War II; interceding on behalf of Japanese American families who were forcibly relocated from the West Coast after the bombing of Pearl Harbor. In September 1942, Rustin reported to the FOR's national office, in New York, that in the previous eight months he had traveled ten thousand miles through twenty states, performing his tasks as an organizer and a spokesman for the pacifist movement.

Although he wasn't the FOR's race relations field secretary, he did have A. J. Muste's permission to involve himself in issues of racial discrimination—for Muste was no less concerned with the cause of black civil rights than with that of war resistance. While stamping his leadership upon the FOR, Muste had expanded its traditional role—to include not only pacifist agitation but also a commitment to the struggle for black progress in America. This, some critical observers say, was simply in line with a strategy generally adopted by radical organizations: broadening their mandates by recruiting a diversity of adherents. But it is to be doubted that Muste was employing such a strategy. His genuine belief in pacifism went hand in hand with a strong commitment to the struggle for African American progress and dignity.

Energized by that belief and commitment, Rustin, on his national speaking tours, came to be recognized as probably the most militant civil rights advocate in the United States. His provocative addresses to one gathering or another included topics like "Racial Exploitation in America"; "A Minority in Our Democracy"; "Race, Religion, and Nationalism"; "Can Nonviolent Non-Cooperation Win Freedom for the American Negro?" It was in such speeches that he failed to meet one of the main requirements of his job: to present an unpopular viewpoint without contention, without alienating some of those he sought to persuade.

In June 1943, after he addressed an audience at the Bethel Baptist Church, the Dayton, Ohio, *Journal* reported with alarm: "While he emphasized that he was not in sympathy with Germany, the speaker said Hitler has been more honest than President Roosevelt and Prime

Minister Churchill. For instance, he explained that Hitler does not pretend friendship with the Jews on the one hand and punish them on the other. . . . He said that Churchill does not intend to bring racial equality, but rather intends to retain the status quo. He stated that much is said about equality in this country, yet the government, even in the armed forces, is one of the worst offenders."

When, four months later, he delivered a similar address ("Racial Aspects of the War") at Westminister House in Eugene, Oregon, the city's *Daily Herald* considered it too inflammatory to print. According to Orval Etter, the FOR man in Eugene, Rustin raised this question in his speech: "Why fight and die abroad to squelch the doctrine of Aryan supremacy while at home we are victimized by white racism?" Barbara Younger, a *Herald* reporter, submitted an enthusiastic account of Rustin's address, but it was just as enthusiastically killed by her editor. In Etter's words "The editor believed that Bayard had advocated that American blacks stop participating in the nation's armed forces. I learned that soon after Bayard's Westminister House talk the FBI was called in to investigate his Eugene visit."

Whether or not Rustin had urged black nonparticipation in the war, it would have been consistent with his pacifist beliefs; and he had certainly heard enough on his national tours to give him the impression that large numbers of blacks were reluctant to serve in the armed forces. One of his earlier reports to FOR headquarters (in September 1942) had stated: "I have heard many say they might as well die right here fighting for their rights as die abroad for other people's. It is common to hear outright joy expressed at a Japanese military victory. For thousands of Negroes look upon successes of any colored people anywhere as *their* successes. . . . No situation in America has created so much interest among Negroes as the Gandhian proposals for India's freedom. In the face of this tension and conflict, our responsibility is to put the technique of nonviolent direct action into the hands of the black masses."

One black mass leader who had already adopted a version of Gandhi's nonviolent technique was A. Philip Randolph. His canceled March on

Washington was modeled upon the Gandhian tactic of nonviolent mass pressure, influenced greatly by the exegesis of Gandhian methodology in Shridharani's *War Without Violence.*

After calling off his planned June 1941 demonstration in the nation's capital, Randolph, from his base in Harlem—and with the economic support of the humble Brotherhood of Sleeping Car Porters—went on to organize a March on Washington Movement throughout the United States. And he dangled that movement—with its constant threat of a massive march—as a Damoclean sword over the various heads of national government in Washington. A great American visionary, Randolph was not so good at nuts-and-bolts organizing, for which he relied upon members of his retinue.

In any case, the longer he hesitated to unsheathe his Damoclean sword, the more it seemed that he was merely bluffing. Perhaps he simply couldn't find the right moment or the right set of circumstances in which to act. But meanwhile, the troops he had mobilized were becoming restless. "When," they asked, "is Randolph going to let us march? What is a march movement that doesn't march?" Pauli Murray, a young civil rights militant—who later became one of the first female Yale-educated priests in the Protestant Episcopal Church—wrote to Randolph in the early fall of 1942: "Somewhere between the mass meetings of last summer and today, the March on Washington Movement has lost ground rather than gained it. . . . I get the impression from reading the press that you are a leader without a movement." Murray's criticism bore a certain resemblance to that of Bayard Rustin and other youth leaders when Randolph canceled the 1941 march.

Discovering, now, the restiveness of his militant following, Randolph took a mollifying step. He announced that at the next conference of the March on Washington organization—scheduled for the summer of 1943, in Chicago—he would inaugurate a nationwide campaign for civil disobedience. Though not the march on the nation's capital that his disciples fervently wanted, it was an initiative to which they could give their pent-up energies. In the promised civil disobedience campaign, Randolph said, he would urge blacks to resist all laws that violated their basic rights as citizens.

It was now the turn of conservative elements in African American society to register *their* protest. Startled by Randolph's nationwide project, they denounced it as a recipe for race warfare. "A. Philip Randolph," said the black-owned *Pittsburgh Courier,* "is guilty of the most dangerous demagoguery on record. The 'March on Washington' plan was bad enough; but alongside a call for civil disobedience, it seems sane."

Randolph's announcement of the civil disobedience campaign was something Bayard Rustin had long been wanting to hear, and it was a project the Fellowship of Reconciliation was eager to support. In January 1943, A. J. Muste wrote to congratulate Randolph on "the vision, intelligence, and courage represented by this step." If carried out in "the true spirit of nonviolence," he added, "this action of yours may well prove to be as epoch-making as Gandhi's own inauguration of a similar movement in South Africa in 1906." The FOR, Muste said, would "be glad to render any help possible in the achievement of your goal." And after hearing Randolph restate his plan at a meeting in Ohio, Rustin wrote to Muste in New York: "[Randolph] spoke in a way that convinced me that he's really concerned to develop an understanding of nonviolence by the American Negro. . . . I feel much better about the whole situation now."

Accepting Muste's offer of assistance, Randolph asked that Rustin and James Farmer be assigned temporarily to the March on Washington Movement—chiefly to help organize the Chicago conference at which the civil disobedience campaign would be launched.

Rustin's enthusiasm for Gandhian nonviolent resistance was growing. The method required not only an absolute lack of fear, he felt, but also the rigid self-discipline that prevented emotionalism from displacing cool and creative thinking. James Farmer, himself a Gandhian, must surely have shared those sentiments. He was not, however, as keen about Randolph's planned campaign as Rustin and Muste were. Though Farmer was second to none in his personal regard for Randolph, his skepticism about the campaign may have been rooted partly in jealousy. He had recently founded the Congress of Racial Equality—pledged to the principle of nonviolent direct action—and he appears to have hoped that *his* organization would be the first effective arm of the Gandhian movement in America. "Muste and Rustin had been elated," Farmer wrote more than forty years later. "I had my misgivings. Someone suggested that I was simply piqued that it was going to be [the March on Washington Movement] and not CORE [leading the civil disobedience campaign]. . . . I thought MOW could not do it, and if it tried there would be shootouts in the South and bloody massacres. I feared a fiasco that would set back a nonviolent movement in the United States for decades." Farmer's credentials as a race radical were beyond question, yet his objections were remarkably similar to those raised in the conservative African American community.

More than two thousand adherents and friends of the March on Washington Movement turned up in Chicago for Randolph's big conference, June 30–July 4, 1943; and delegates from fourteen states pledged their overwhelming support of Randolph's call for a nonviolent campaign against all forms of racial discrimination in public accommodations. Rustin and Farmer (despite his reservations) addressed the conference on the Gandhian technique of mass resistance. And Rustin closed the meeting, singing from his repertoire of Negro spirituals: "It's me, O Lord, standing in the need of prayer." J. Holmes Smith, a member of the FOR delegation, reported later to Muste, "There was something about the conference all the way through that was spiritually impressive."

But the much-discussed national campaign—in whose conception Smith saw "the Divine Hand at work"—never got off the mark. It was crippled at the outset by an eruption of race rioting in Detroit and later in Harlem. In fact, Randolph's critics were quick to blame his proposed campaign for fueling the outbreak of racial disorder. Nor did the March on Washington Movement long survive, fading away in the late 1940s. "The great wartime upsurge of Negro mass action had run its course," wrote the historian Herbert Garfinkel. The vacuum created by the death of Randolph's movement was to be filled by a number of its Gandhian progeny—the first being James Farmer's Congress of Racial Equality, followed by the emergence, in the late 1950s, of nonviolent street protests, led by Martin Luther King. A. J. Muste's Fellowship of Reconciliation played an important role in those developments: Farmer's founding of CORE had been sponsored and subsidized by the FOR; Bayard Rustin was CORE's first field organizer, while he and Farmer were on the Fellowship's payroll; Rustin and the FOR's Glenn Smiley were to be Dr. King's chief Gandhian counselors during the 1955–56 Montgomery bus boycott, which propelled him into national leadership.

On his national speaking tours for the Fellowship, Rustin encountered much the same forms of discrimination and segregation that were the daily lot of the black masses. He was refused service and accommodation at restaurants and hotels; ordered to ride in the back of buses and segregated compartments of trains. To such indignities he responded with what his white colleague George Houser called "a stimulating one-man crusade, challenging Jim Crow nonviolently." Rustin's usual procedure was the one he recommended in his "Lesson Plan on Nonviolent Action," which he wrote for distribution by the Fellowship:

> An effective technique to be used by Negroes in the South, where education for nonviolent direct action has been absent, is the "Why?" method. Here the victim of discrimination proceeds as though equality existed. Upon being told to move into a Jim Crow [railroad] car, for example, he simply asks, "Why?" Although finally he may be forced to accept the consequences of his position—such as being arrested or being moved to a segregated area—he has raised a vital issue.

Rustin raised such an issue in Indianapolis, when the proprietor of a luncheonette refused to serve him a hamburger. He asked, "Why?" It wasn't the practice of restaurants in Indianapolis to serve Negroes, she told him. He asked, "Why?" Whites would not enter a restaurant in which blacks were seated, she said. "Have you ever served Negroes?" he inquired. "No," was the predictable reply. "Then why do you believe that doing so would offend your white customers?" Sparing the proprietor an answer, Rustin proposed that she join him in an experiment: He would sit by the front door with a hamburger on his plate; he would not begin eating it for ten or fifteen minutes; if, during that time, his presence deterred whites from entering, then he would gladly leave the premises. Fifteen minutes later, several whites had walked into the luncheonette, blind to Rustin and his uneaten meal. The proprietor then replaced his cold hamburger with a freshly cooked one and asked, "What will you have to drink?" It was a small but significant victory, a vindication of his belief that reconciliation could be achieved through thoughtful and nonviolent assertion.

But the technique wasn't always so successful. Not long after the confrontation in Indianapolis, he had a most excruciating one in Knoxville, Tennessee. Ordered to move to the back of a bus, he asked, "Why?" And, dissatisfied with the reason, he refused to move. The bus operator summoned the police: Rustin was brutally beaten and then thrown in jail.

According to Wilfred Gamble, the principal in the 1940s of Lincoln Normal School in Marion, Alabama—where Coretta Scott studied before she met and married Martin Luther King, Jr.—Rustin was always alone on his travels. Lincoln sometimes arranged accommodation for Rustin, protecting him from nasty confrontations with white-owned hotels and guesthouses. "Bayard was always determined to test the segregation laws of the South," Gamble later recalled. "He would deliberately sit in the front of a bus; and when the driver told him to move further back he would always say, politely, 'Thank you, but I like this seat fine.' Almost always, he would be met at the next police station and ordered to get off the bus. At times, he was badly beaten by the police. During World War II, I asked him whether he would register for sugar rationing, an emergency wartime measure. 'No, thank you,' he said. 'I'll just do without sugar for the duration.' That was one of the simple ways in which he protested against the war. He was that consistent in his pacifist beliefs, and he made a profound impression upon our students and our teaching staff."

His message of nonviolent resistance was particularly influential among college students, some of whom would remember his example for decades. Wallace Nelson, a black undergraduate at Ohio Wesleyan University, was converted to pacifism—he became a conscientious objector—only after Rustin made an appearance on campus. "I was interested in nonviolence," Nelson said some forty-five years later, "but I didn't quite know how one should behave in certain situations. I was always yelling and getting dragged out of public places when I protested against racial discrimination. It was Bayard Rustin who explained and demonstrated to me the demeanor you should adopt: never raise your voice; never make a ruckus; simply insist on your dignity and your rights as a human being. I later mastered that technique in all trying circumstances. In the early 1940s, scores of young people, black and white, were similarly influenced by him." Carolyn Lindquist, one of Nelson's white classmates, would "never forget that man and his nonviolent approach to solving problems." With his "passionate conviction" and his "quiet work behind the scenes," she recalled, "he was one of the unsung heroes of my time." Gay Morenus Hammerman was always to remember one of Rustin's visits to the University of North Carolina at Chapel Hill: "Someone told me that the man coming from the Fellowship of Reconciliation was a wonderful speaker. I would have gone to the meeting anyway, for I wanted to hear a real pacifist. Pacifists were rare in our area at that time, when we had seen that pacifism left democracy and decency helpless before vicious aggression. But there was no compromise in Rustin's message. He preached the importance of pacifism and nonviolence under all circumstances. I was very impressed with his message. It has remained my standard for pacifism ever since." A former student at the Oakwood School—a Quaker institution in upstate New York—recalled "a marvelous speech" Rustin made there about the nonviolent resolution of conflict. "He concluded by singing beautifully to us a program of black spirituals and Elizabethan songs. His voice had an extraordinary range, unaffected by his apparent love for alcohol and cigarettes."

Despite his charismatic appeal as speaker and singer, Rustin experienced a number of personal embarrassments among whites from whom he had expected better—whites who were not yet ready to associate cultural and intellectual excellence with people of his color. On his first national tour for the Fellowship of Reconciliation, late in 1941, he appeared at a church in Ohio to fulfill a speaking engagement. Arriving early, he sat alone at the back of the auditorium. John Mecartney—then a young Methodist clergyman, with whom Rustin was later to work in the pacifist movement—recalled: "When the meeting began, the guest speaker seemed not to be there. Finally, someone said, 'Why don't we ask the Negro janitor sitting back there if he has seen the speaker in any part of the building?' We approached the man and asked him that question. 'I am Bayard Rustin,' he said. We had never known many black people, and never dreamed that Bayard Rustin would be black. Well, we learned a lot that night. Not only did Bayard give us a brilliant presentation of peace issues but he also raised our consciousness in matters of race relations. We would never be the same again."

Denny Wilcher, a young white pacifist living in Washington, D.C., was "entranced and intrigued" when he first heard Rustin speak, at a conference in the Midwest. The blacks he was used to seeing and hearing were mostly from the Deep South, and "Rustin was totally different, in culture and language." Some time later, when Rustin visited Washington to deliver an address, Wilcher asked his parents "if Bayard could spend a night with us—for there were no hotels in which blacks could stay." His father, a Methodist minister, consented immediately. "But my mother, an old sort from Virginia, said to me, 'Son, you can bring him here to stay, but I shall have to leave and spend the night at your sister's apartment. I couldn't spend a night in the same house with a black person.' Of course, Bayard wasn't exactly a person of black stereotype—not with his education and wonderful speech. But my mother didn't know all of that, and she probably wouldn't have cared. She was so conditioned by her upbringing in her part of Virginia that she couldn't emotionally accept the idea of a black person staying at her house. I was deeply embarrassed. But whatever Bayard may have felt when I reported back to him, he revealed no sign of embarrassment. He relieved me of my own—so great were his self-esteem and his understanding of American race relations."

John Nevin Sayre, the FOR's coleader, wrote to A. J. Muste in the early 1940s, praising one of Rustin's performances on the West Coast: "Bayard is doing a grand job." Not all supporters of the FOR held him in such grand esteem as he made his way through the towns and cities of America. To some, his combination of self-confidence and sparkling verbal display seemed troublingly like arrogance—though they were probably just expressions of his entertaining personality. Nor was everyone comfortable with his occasional lapses into narrative embellishment—yet another mark of his diverting character.

Margaret McCulloch, a board member of the FOR, then living in Nashville, wrote to Muste in July 1942:

> *Bayard Rustin has been here, and I liked him—a brainy zealous youngster on fire to right the wrongs of his people. But, frankly, {he is} very far as yet from a universal Christian base. Race freedom is his first passion; Christianity and humility are second. . . . He is still very immature in social action—intensely theoretical, without adequate insight into the inner workings of human motivations. He is a fine youngster, and I think we should hold on to him and give him a chance to grow within the Fellowship. . . . But at present he is just a promising young thoroughbred colt. {Rustin was then thirty years old.} He has yet to be broken and become bridle-wise. Until he matures, I'm sure he shouldn't be sent into areas of race tension, as he is likely in his zeal and naivete to do far more harm than good. . . . Can't you use Bayard for a while in Northern white groups, already fairly receptive and liberal—and then find him some tough local assignment in which he would have to stick through thick and thin, meeting the actual consequences of all his own actions, and learning the tough stubbornness of the defects of his own people as well as of whites? I believe such an experience would make a man of him, and he might then be a fine travelling secretary. Not now.*

It was probably the most unfavorable evaluation of Rustin that Muste had ever received. And he found it hard to accept, partly because he disagreed with most of its judgments, partly because of his own high intellectual regard for Rustin, partly because Bayard was like a son to him. Yes, he replied to McCulloch, Rustin ought to be given the sort of tough assignment she suggested. Then he came to his apostle's defense: "On the whole, my impression is that he is nearer to what you call a universal Christian base than you think. True, he is young and a little too inclined to want to cover ground. . . . On the other hand, he has demonstrated a very sweet, generous, courageous, and devoted spirit in many situations. I think all of us here at the national office feel that he probably has an unusually significant future before him and that he is ready for greater responsibilities."

Begging to differ, McCulloch submitted a new set of charges against Rustin: the "inaccuracy" in his reporting of events; his "lingering adolescence"; his "self-dramatizing quality"; his want of a "fuller Christian maturity." In reply, Muste respectfully but firmly stood his ground: "I think your criticism of Bayard's presentations of his experience is probably correct," he said. Nevertheless, "I have great faith in him. And I pray fervently that he may grow in grace." To Bernard Junker, another of Rustin's critics, Muste wrote: "I do think that in many ways he comes nearer to working out imaginative techniques for dealing with the racial situation than anyone else we have."

"Anyone else" would have included James Farmer. Rustin first met Farmer in the spring of 1942, at an FOR conference in Ohio. From Farmer's standpoint, there was some tension in the encounter, for it took place on what he had reason to regard as his own turf. The FOR's secretary for race relations was based in Chicago, his mandate "to carry on interpretive work" among blacks and whites in the Middle West, "to do his share of organizing and promoting the work of the Fellowship." Farmer's position was generally considered to be more important than Rustin's. But at twenty-two, he was Bayard's junior by eight years, a fact that, together with the closeness of the Muste-Rustin axis, might have shaken his feeling of security. In his travels for the Fellowship, Rustin often acted, with Muste's approval, as though *he* were the race relations secretary. It all contributed, in any case, to a subtle rivalry that would always mark the Farmer-Rustin relationship in the FOR—two talented blacks "knocking heads," as Farmer was to put it. "Bayard impressed me as being very bright, very articulate, very outspoken, and as a very excellent singer," he said later, recalling their first meeting. "I was struck by his wonderful rendition of Negro spirituals, his entertaining skills, his ability to move an audience. He was enormously popular with the young people. But I didn't get to know him at that conference. I got to know him a little while after, when the Congress of Racial Equality was founded."

In February 1942, Farmer—strongly influenced by Shridharani—wrote a memorandum to A. J. Muste (subsequently revised), proposing the formation of an interracial Gandhian organization, under the umbrella of the FOR. Unlike the Fellowship, it should not be an anti-war grouping. "Peace," Farmer explained some years later, "was number one with him [Muste], whereas for me the priority was racial equality." Thus, his proposed organization would be engaging in nonviolent direct action—protests and sit-ins against racial segregation and discrimination. Coming from the Fellowship's race relations secretary, it wasn't so wild an idea; and Farmer's revised and refined blueprint brought into being the Congress of Racial Equality.

At a meeting in Chicago a few months later, Muste gave his reluctant blessing to Farmer's brainchild. His reluctance was understandable. He and the Fellowship had been asked to fund the launching of CORE—to continue paying the salaries of Farmer and some of his fellow organizers—while in all other respects the infant Congress insisted on establishing and maintaining an identity independent of the FOR. Muste feared, moreover, the weakening of FOR's leadership, as well as demands upon the political and financial support of its membership. He would have been happier if Farmer had consented to make CORE a formal arm of the Fellowship.

"Jim, you can't hide your pacifism," Muste told Farmer during the meeting at which the matter of CORE was debated and settled. Farmer replied that he wasn't trying to hide his pacifism, that he wanted CORE "to be a mass movement," that "the masses of blacks will not become pacifists." Muste added, "By the way, Bayard agrees completely with me." Farmer wasn't surprised. He had already heard that "Rusty" shared Muste's positions on almost all issues. "Rustin," he recalled, "sat impassively as I walked up front to make my presentation" for the founding of CORE. Bernice Fisher, one of his aides in the new organization, later said to him, "What a pity you and Bayard have to be on opposite sides of this. What a team you'd make."

But Rustin was as much a civil rights activist as a pacifist, and he did not refuse Farmer's invitation to serve as the first field organizer of CORE. On his national speaking tours for the Fellowship, he spent a portion of his time, albeit the lesser portion, drumming up membership for the new group. Although Rustin wasn't as deeply involved in CORE affairs as Farmer was, his double role exemplified the problem Muste had feared: that CORE's reliance upon the resources of the Fellowship would be a drain upon its leadership and membership.

Farmer's passion for building CORE into a national movement became harder and harder for Muste to bear. Farmer, he complained at one point, was now doing little or no organizing work for the Fellowship, a complaint also made by J. Holmes Smith.

Along with Rustin and Farmer, Smith was a member of the FOR delegation to the 1943 conference in Chicago at which A. Philip Randolph announced his civil disobedience campaign. He wrote later to Muste: "Rusty and I compared notes, and found ourselves in full agreement. . . . We wanted to confer with Jim, also, but he disappeared before the last two days of the conference. . . . We are not gossiping about it, but we do feel the need for a very frank conciliatory conference about his attitude." On the same issue, Muste also heard from John Swomley, his chief executive assistant: "Bayard is very angry at Jim Farmer. He says that at the crucial [Randolph conference in Chicago] Jim was [often] on the other side of town, planning CORE activities."

All of this contributed to the gradual unraveling of Farmer's ties to the FOR—especially since not even Swomley, his earliest champion in the organization, was now eager to defend him. "I am convinced that we must effect some reorganization if we are to hold Bayard's loyalty and if we are to count on him for the future," Swomley wrote to Muste in the summer of 1943. "I am also convinced we must do something about Jim. . . . Make Bayard the race relations secretary . . . unless [Jim] should consent to making CORE an official project of the FOR. . . . Otherwise, I suppose we must either dismiss him or use him to the fullest in FOR work, until he resigns." Making CORE an official project of the FOR was not an idea Farmer was ever likely to consider. Still, the Fellowship was on the horns of a dilemma. It was as reluctant to lose Farmer as it was eager to keep Rustin. "Pacifist Negroes of *their* ability are hard to find," Swomley said, in one of his notes to Muste. That was true—although it ought to have been clear to Swomley by then that antiwar activism had ceased to be a priority with Farmer.

He resigned from the Fellowship in the spring of 1945. "Muste called me into his office and told me that I was still not organizing, not signing up members for the FOR," he recalled in his autobiography. "I was not asked to resign, but it was clear that Muste wanted me to do so. So I obliged him." Farmer was now free to devote himself wholly to the building of CORE.

Bayard Rustin and George Houser were then appointed cosecretaries for race relations—a position Farmer had suspected Rustin was angling for. Rustin was then in prison as a conscientious objector, and did not assume his share of the appointment until after his release, in 1946.

Rustin's mixed feelings about James Farmer included a great admiration for Farmer's talent as a public speaker—a remarkable tribute from one who was himself among the more impressive political orators in America. Rustin would recall later in his life: "I don't think anybody could make a better speech, could use a platform more creatively. Jim was, I think, the best platform man, after Martin Luther King. When it came to organizational detail, Jim was easily bored. And when it came to new ideas, I would say that George Houser and I had many more than he did. But when it came to presenting ideas to the public, Jim could outdo us, ten to one, anytime."

Chapter 6

Conscience and Consequence

Late in 1940, when Bayard Rustin appeared before his draft board in Harlem, he applied for, and was granted, classification as a conscientious objector—based chiefly on his membership in the Religious Society of Friends, one of the historic peace churches. Under the Draft Act of that year, those whom the Selective Service recognized as genuine conscientious objectors were given three options: enlisting as noncombatants in the armed forces; performing tasks of national importance in civilian work camps; or—if they refused those choices—accepting incarceration in federal penitentiaries. Since genuine conscientious objection was recognized mostly on religious grounds—where a draftee's denominational teaching abjured violence in all its forms—many young men who sought exemption from military service, for reasons of social or political conscience, did not qualify and were automatically subject to imprisonment for violating the conscription act.

On November 13, 1943, soon after Rustin returned to New York from a speaking tour of the West Coast, he was ordered by his draft board to report for a physical examination—a statutory requirement of conscientious objectors who were about to be assigned for work in Civilian Public Service camps. Rustin refused to appear, having changed his mind since 1940: he no longer wanted a privilege granted chiefly to religious conscientious objectors. He had come to feel that if all conscientious objectors—the religious and the nonreligious—were not treated equally he would rather risk the extreme penalty of federal imprisonment. His adoption of that position reflected the intervening moral influence of radical pacifist leaders like Evan Thomas and the Reverend John Haynes Holmes, a staunch antiwar preacher at the Community Church in Manhattan.

Evan Thomas—who then held a dual membership in the religious Fellowship of Reconciliation and in the secular, more militant War Resisters League—took the view that since civilian work camps were created by the government, they aided and abetted the government's system of conscription. In his judgment, they were to be resisted much as the draft should be. Thomas, who underwent an excruciating imprisonment for conscientious objection during World War I, wrote to A. J. Muste (whose FOR cooperated with the government's running of Civilian Public Service camps): "I condemn it [the CPS system] with my whole being. It not only fails to respect the consciences of others but it establishes a precedent which is exceedingly dangerous to all civil liberties." Largely over that issue, Thomas later resigned from the Fellowship of Reconciliation, while maintaining his membership in the War Resisters League.

John Haynes Holmes had reemphasized *his* position in an article for the Fellowship's monthly magazine:

> It is a pity that the conscription act confines conscientious objection . . . to religious grounds. For there is, or may be, conscientious objection which is not religious at all, but economic, political, or humanitarian in its motivation. To the religious objector there comes something like shame that he enjoys at the hands of the government a recognition and protection which are denied to certain other men; and gladly he would extend the law, like the borders of Isaiah's tent, to include all who are like-minded with him on this fundamental issue.

Swayed by these arguments, Bayard Rustin chose imprisonment over the protections to which he was entitled as a religious conscientious objector. Rustin's chief pacifist mentor, A. J. Muste, might have advised him differently; but Muste must have known the moral imperatives to which his strong-willed proselyte was susceptible.

To the draft board that summoned him for a physical examination Rustin replied:

> *I cannot voluntarily submit to an order stemming from the selective service act. War is wrong. Conscription is a concomitant of modern war. . . . Conscription for war is inconsistent with freedom of conscience, which is not merely the right to believe but to act on the degree of truth that one receives, to follow a vocation which is God-inspired and God-directed. . . . Though joyfully following the will of God, I regret that I must break the law of the State. I am prepared for whatever may follow.*

What followed may have been worse than Rustin had prepared himself for. He probably thought that he would been sentenced to a year and a day in jail—as George Houser had been. He was mistaken. And the much higher price he paid reflected his public agitation against the war. At a protest meeting—held at New York City's Labor Temple, in Greenwich Village—federal agents saw and heard him urging young men to come forward and burn their draft cards. John Mecartney, the young Ohio clergyman, was entitled to an automatic deferment from the draft; but he decided to forfeit that privilege after hearing Rustin's address to a church gathering. "I didn't think my automatic exemption was fair," Mecartney said later, "for no other professional or occupational groups were exempt only on the basis of their work. I wanted to make a personal witness. I thought sitting out the war in a theological college would be too safe. Rustin's eloquent case was for breaking with the whole system of war, as an act of civil disobedience—and I adopted that approach myself. So Bayard helped me to go to jail in the early 1940s."

• • •

On January 12, 1944, two months after his defiant reply to the draft board, Rustin was arrested by a United States marshal in New York. At his trial, on February 17, he was found guilty of violating the Selective Service Act and sentenced to three years in a federal prison. Eleven days later, after being allowed to put his personal affairs in order, he surrendered at Federal Detention Headquarters, on the West Side of Manhattan, from which he was later dispatched to the penitentiary in Ashland, Kentucky.

"The place [the FOR's national office] is somber—and quiet!—now that you are gone," Doris Grotewhol, Muste's secretary, wrote to Rustin at the detention center. Alfred Hassler, the editor of *Fellowship,* could scarcely imagine the charming and gregarious Rustin locked up "in a house of sorrow, and loneliness, and fear." "It is hard to think of you in prison," Muste said in a letter. John Nevin Sayre wrote to Rustin's Quaker grandmother, Julia, expressing his esteem for what "must be a rare woman" and assuring her that Bayard was highly regarded in the pacifist community. "The ordeal of prison which he must go through will be a hard one," Sayre added. "Like all suffering, the effect is to make a man better or worse. In Bayard's case, I believe it will be better, but the severity of temptation is such that I think we must continuously pray for him." The "severity of temptation" may have been a politely phrased reference to Rustin's homosexuality, which was then an open secret to all at the FOR's national office.

Julia Rustin replied: "Bayard's birthday is March 17, St. Patrick's Day. In a letter to me he asked that at 7 p.m. [on that day] I read the 56th Psalm, and he would be reading it at the same time." One of the thirteen verses of that psalm states: "In God I will praise his word, in God I have put my trust; I will not fear what flesh can do unto me." Whatever she understood by the "severity of temptation," the doting grandmother continued: "Oh! I do realize the temptation which can and will come to him in prison. But I also know that the Heavenly Father has promised to keep all those who are placed in his charge. . . . So, Mr. Sayre, while I am concerned and anxious about Bayard, I have no real fear, as I live in the promises of God. And I love the 91st Psalm—'He that dwelleth in the secret place of the most High shall abide under the shadow of the Almighty.'"

The Fellowship of Reconciliation was to retain Rustin on its payroll throughout his imprisonment; and he was to ask that his salary be sent to his aging grandparents.

He was only one of the many radical pacifists in the FOR and the War Resisters League whose conscientious objection landed them in penitentiaries and civilian labor camps across the country. Well known in the antiwar circles of the time, they included Charles Bloomstein, Bronson Clark, Robert Currier, David Dellinger, Ralph DiGia, Joseph Felmet, Roy Finch, Larry Gara, Alfred Hassler, William Hefner, George Houser, Bernard Junker, John Mecartney, Wallace Nelson, James Peck, Igal Roodenko, William Sutherland. Those and others were high on A. J. Muste's pacifist roll of honor—"the young men to whom I felt most akin," he would recall.

Rustin arrived at Ashland on March 9, 1944. After surrendering all personal possessions (except his Bible), he was fingerprinted; assigned a prison identity number (2705); issued a regulation uniform; and then placed in temporary quarantine. During that period, he—as all new inmates did—underwent a battery of psychological tests and familiarized himself with the penitentiary's rules of conduct.

Released from quarantine, he renewed acquaintance with a number of the conscientious objectors who had preceded him to Ashland. They welcomed him as both a nationally known peace activist and a potential leader of their campaigns against racially segregated accommodations in the prison community. He immediately joined those campaigns—particularly hunger strikes against segregated seating in the dining hall—for which he was often thrown into solitary confinement.

"Both morally and practically," he wrote to the prison warden, "segregation is to me a basic injustice. Since I believe it to be so, I must attempt to remove it. There are three ways in which one can deal with an injustice. (a) One can accept it without protest. (b) One can seek to avoid it. (c) One can resist the injustice nonviolently. To accept it is to perpetuate it. To avoid it is impossible. To resist by intelligent means, and with an attitude of mutual responsibility and respect, is much the better choice."

Rustin's comrades had dragged him into prison activism somewhat earlier than he had wanted. When he arrived at Ashland, he hadn't yet decided what social or political role he would play among the inmates—though, as he well knew, Muste expected all imprisoned peace activists to demonstrate against unacceptable conditions at the penitentiaries. Rustin had written to Peggy Deuel, at the FOR office in San Francisco: "I go to prison with high hopes of making some contribution, rather than with the idea of setting up protests. It may be, of course, that it will be necessary, ultimately, to do some protesting; but that is not upper in my thinking." What may then have been upper in his thinking was revealed some time after his first confrontations with the prison authorities.

Despite those confrontations, Rustin had come to form a cordial relationship with his principal jailer, Warden E. G. Hagerman. He was surprised to discover that Hagerman held a Ph.D. degree and was related to the Brethren, which, like the Religious Society of Friends, was one of the historic peace churches in America. He also felt that Hagerman, for all his stern enforcement of prison discipline, was "a good fellow." So did A. J. Muste. After visiting Rustin and others at Ashland, Muste reported to an executive council meeting of the FOR: "I am convinced . . . that Dr. Hagerman . . . is an exceptionally intelligent official."

Rustin applied to the warden for appointment to the prison's education department—to help "effect attitudes for the better." He wanted to conduct courses in reading, grammar, English composition, dramatics and vocal training, and music for beginners. He also suggested a course in American history, with emphasis on the contributions racial minorities had made to the nation's cultural life. Hagerman was willing to grant all but the last request. He didn't think that Rustin, with his radical politics, would be the appropriate teacher of a course in

American history—surely not at a penitentiary where the majority of inmates were southern whites. But Rustin's students responded well to his tutelage in other subjects. "Being taught by a Negro," he wrote to a friend in Manhattan, "is for them a revolutionary situation." He particularly enjoyed teaching music (he formed a choir) and dramatics. From friends and acquaintances he requested printed collections of Negro spirituals and sixteenth-century religious compositions by Palestrina, Orlando di Lasso, and Michael Praetorius. "The fellows here," he informed one of those colleagues, "lean toward the most weak and sentimental hymns with the most sickly melodies. We are trying to change tastes gradually, and so we have a Bach chorale and several spirituals with great beauty and simplicity." In dramatics, he staged what a number of his fellow inmates called a memorable performance of O'Neill's *The Emperor Jones.*

For a period, Rustin spent many of his evenings teaching himself to play the lute an old friend in New York sent him. With help from Robert Currier, a violinist on his cell block, he was soon able to play a decent version of Bach's Chaconne for unaccompanied violin. He felt that certain qualities of that work—what he described as its "dancing mood" and "brittle tones"—were more beautifully expressed by the lute than by the violin. Not all of his neighbors on the cell block could endure his nightly practice sessions. "He drove us nuts," Larry Gara recalled. "We had to lay down the law that he could practice only so many hours in the evenings." But William Hefner would have a somewhat different recollection: "It was the guards Bayard drove crazy. Most of us loved listening to the Elizabethan songs he sang while teaching himself to play the instrument." Rustin reveled in his lute playing, partly because it was one of the few prison experiences over which he had sole authority. "When you're dealing with people all the time and nothing is ever settled," he said some years later, "it's a great pleasure to strike a C chord and know that it's a C chord."

After racial segregation in living and dining accommodations, the prison regulation Rustin detested most was the censorship of correspondence, periodicals, and books. Bronson Clark wrote from Ashland to a pacifist publication in the East: "He [Rustin] has trouble getting letters out. Few of them are returned to him . . . so one would assume they are piling up in Washington." This suggested the censor's disapproval of opinions Rustin was expressing in his letters, so it is surprising that opinions like the following managed to get through to one of his correspondents in New York:

> *I should have known that such letters {perhaps the ones piling up in Washington} would pass with difficulty. But I prefer to lose my privilege of writing—have material held up or sent to the FBI— before I should pusillanimously or expediently write material . . . so harmless as to please the limited minds that are selected to pass on it. . . .*
>
> *When I came here I was misguided enough to sign censorship papers, in effect giving away my birthright. . . . This I now see is a mistake, and am pledged to correct it. . . . I've decided to write what I most feel and believe.*

On the subject of reading material sent to him, and censored, at Ashland, he went on:

> *If I were to continue to consult officers here as to books I may or may not read, I should not merely seem to recognize their right to control my reading . . . but also I should forfeit my right under the Constitution to read any desired material for intellectual and spiritual growth. . . . I have decided not to request permission to receive printed matter. . . . The responsibility for censorship (usurpation of the inmate's rights) rests upon the bureaucrats. . . . I shall not help them to rule me. . . .*
>
> *Be aware that tyranny is no harsh term for the deeds practiced here. While we are held behind a wall (which appears a fence) and behind bars (which seem mere windows), we are held slaves to a state which "grinds the faces of the unfortunate in the dust. . . ." One is*

held by men who refer to their "sense of duty" and "the law," but they
themselves cannot see that, more accurately, they are obstructing
justice. They stand between the inmate and his basic rights; they
reduce rights to privileges; and to a sickly whine of {their}
helplessness to be just.

When a censor later confiscated Rustin's copy of *Equality* (a monthly newsletter edited by James Farmer of CORE), he "kicked up a fuss," Bronson Clark remembered. "Bayard stated," Clark said, "that he would have hundreds of his friends and dozens of organizations send him stuff by the pound," thereby exposing "the rather stupid" policy of censorship. The censoring authorities relented. Rustin was handed his next copy of *Equality,* which he accepted, he told the powers, "not as a privilege you are granting me but as a right."

He reported no further infringements of his right to read the magazines and books that were mailed to him. He regularly received *The Christian Century, Life, The Nation, Newsweek, The New Leader, The New Yorker, The Progressive, Time,* and *Politics*—a journal of radical opinion, edited by Dwight Macdonald. Friends now freely sent him books like Lillian Smith's *Strange Fruit;* Richard Wright's *Black Boy;* Antoine de Saint Exupéry's *The Little Prince;* Erich Fromm's *Escape from Freedom;* P. A. Sorokin's *The Crisis of Our Age;* Henry S. Canby's *Whitman, An American;* H. P. Howard's *America's Role in Asia;* and William James's *The Varieties of Religious Experience.*

In March 1945, Rustin replied to his young white friend Davis Platt—a college student in Manhattan—who had written to ask his opinion of George Santayana:

I came to respect Santayana not only for his prodigious mind and
his contributions to thinking but also because he seems to defy being
stamped or pigeon-holed. He writes superbly, with a poetic feeling
that is simultaneously lyric and intense.
Santayana was one of the small but gifted group of American-
born literati who found America a poor soil for writing. {Rustin

seems to have forgotten that Santayana, though he was raised in New England and later taught philosophy and literature at Harvard, was born in Spain.} Others in that group were Logan Pearsall Smith . . . and Gertrude Stein. . . . Though removed from our soil they had a great influence upon American thought and upon our literary forms. Smith {a Pennsylvania Quaker, who migrated to Britain and became a prominent figure in the literature and culture of Bloomsbury} certainly influenced the essay here and abroad, and Stein's influence is still more to be felt, I believe. . . .

I have always admired Santayana. . . . Some months ago Life *did a most unfortunate article on him, accusing him of existing in an ivory tower. In the fervor of war and war activity, they {at* Life*} apparently have lost sight of the "great action in non-action." Surely they failed to see that the effect of his thought . . . is more basic than war work, and unquestionably more permanent.*

Rustin's most faithful reporter on cultural happenings in the world outside, especially in New York, was Doris Grotewohl. A native of Burlington, Iowa, and a graduate of Berea College, Grotewohl cherished Rustin much as Muste did. It was she who sent him most of the magazines and books he read at Ashland, and even bought him strings for his lute. She kept him informed of what was happening at their old musical haunts in Greenwich Village—at Café Society Downtown and the Village Vanguard, and at a late-night place called Nick's, where she heard the jazz trumpeter Muggsy Spanier and the singer John Raitt, the Broadway star who sometimes entertained pacifist gatherings in New York. One summer evening while she sat awaiting the start of a concert at Lewisohn Stadium, she wrote to tell him:

Beecham is conducting. The program looks pretty good—
Overture to Prince Igor; Scheherazade; *some Tchaikowsky;*
Rachmaninoff's Second Piano Concerto. *These concerts always excite me—the realization that night after night thousands turn out to get an evening of good music. . . . And, too, it's a colorful sight. Women*

*seem to have gone in for yellow and gold tones. . . . Lots of bright
green and splashes of reds in hats, dresses, and coats. . . . The
orchestra is coming on stage now, and though it's 8:20 and still
light, the electric lights are beginning to come on.*

She was the main source of news about his grandparents. When
she told him of their desire to visit him, he discouraged the idea. He
felt they were too old to undertake the long journey to Kentucky;
moreover, he didn't want Julia to see him behind bars. Grotewohl had
met the elder Rustins in June 1944, when she visited their home in
West Chester. "I was amazed to find that your grandfather is going to
be 80 on August 14," she wrote. Although Janifer Rustin was in fail-
ing health, Grotewohl found him charming: he said to her, "I'll soon
be 80, and Julia is 71, but we're still courting." They were a "precious"
couple, she wrote, adding: "I can now understand the source of your
insight into people and [your] faith in something greater than any one
of us."

In August 1944, she wrote to tell Rustin of "your grandfather's fear
that he wouldn't live to see you again." Seven months later, when the
old man's condition worsened, the FOR sent Bayard one hundred dollars, enabling him (escorted by a prison guard) to return home for a
visit. A few weeks later, he received word that Janifer had died. Not
permitted to attend the funeral, he wrote to a friend: "God knows ever
more than I do the love that was in his every act. None of us can remember a single unkindness in him. His compassion took me from the dark-
ness and cruelness of a fatherless world. He wept for me. He guided me
by word and example. He sacrificed and slaved to educate me. But most
of all he loved me as his own."

In Rustin's segregated cell block at Ashland, a locked gate barred
blacks, on the ground floor, from visiting whites, on the floor above.
Most blacks were quite satisfied with the arrangement: mainly from the
South, they had no history of mixing with whites. But as Rustin and his
white pacifist comrades were chiefly northerners, the locked gate lim-

ited the interracial socializing to which they were accustomed. Refusing, as usual, to accept segregation voluntarily, Rustin challenged the policy against interracial visiting. And after lodging a number of protests with the authorities, he was allowed to fraternize with his fellow conscientious objectors on the upper floor—but only on Sunday afternoons, when they usually listened to a radio concert by the New York Philharmonic.

There were to be consequences that Rustin may not have anticipated. The nonpacifists on the upper floor included a Kentuckian named Huddleston, who at the end of one concert warned the black visitor never to return. Rustin reappeared the following Sunday afternoon—with results that Bronson Clark described in a letter to his wife:

> *Huddleston went to the utility room and got a stick, the size, in diameter and length, of a mop handle, and came back to hit Bayard over the head. The boys did not know what was going on till Huddleston hit Bayard a mighty blow. . . . They jumped and got between Huddleston and Bayard, and started taking the club from Huddleston. But Bayard asked them to stop, which they did. Huddleston continued to beat him with the club. . . . The club splintered and broke, but was still large enough to use, {when} Huddleston stopped. . . . It was a perfect example of what Richard Gregg described in his* The Power of Non-Violence. *Huddleston was completely defeated and unnerved by the display of nonviolence, and began shaking all over, and sat down.*

Rustin described the incident to Doris Grotewohl: "As you know, there are many inmates here who are conditioned to believe that persons of my 'expression' (to quote Father Divine) should 'stay in their place.'" But, he said, his pacifist response to Huddleston's attack "served as an example to all" of the effectiveness of nonviolent resistance: overwhelming an attacker without fighting on his terms. Warding off Huddleston's blows, Rustin had sustained a fracture to his left wrist, and for a while, his usually neat handwriting deteriorated into an ungainly scrawl. "Perhaps this will force you to join a majority for a change, and become a right-handed man," Grotewohl chided him. But he had scored a victory, of whatever dimension. Dr. Hagerman assured him that there would be no further restriction upon interracial visiting, on Sunday or any other day.

In August 1945, when Rustin instigated another of the several failed attempts at desegregating the dining hall, he was put in solitary confinement. Not long after his release, he and his pacifist coconspirators were handcuffed and bundled off to Lewisburg, Pennsylvania. "Lewisburg," Larry Gara recalled, "was a rough and dangerous place, filled with some of the worst criminals in America. Before we got there, it had been a hotbed of conscientious objector resistance, where pacifists like David Dellinger and William Sutherland had helped to lead long and bitter work strikes against censorship and racial segregation. So when we arrived at Lewisburg, the warden [William Hiatt] was well experienced in handling agitators like us."

Hiatt immediately sequestered the troublemakers from Ashland. "We didn't see much of Lewisburg," Gara said. "We didn't see the general prison population. They kept us away from everybody else and kept everybody else away from us. They gave us a big dormitory for ourselves. In the library we could read whatever we wanted; and we could dine with whomever we pleased. We were isolated within our own world, a prison within a prison." Confirming Gara's version, Rustin remembered: "They simply washed their hands of us. They said, 'Give them what they want. Keep them to themselves. We don't want them infecting others with their liberal ideas.'" Hiatt's policy rendered them politically impotent, for, Rustin said, "it was difficult to operate in a situation where you were cut off from the other prisoners." It was in those circumstances that Rustin completed his incarceration, in June 1946, having served twenty-eight of the thirty-six months to which he was sentenced.

He later reminisced at length about aspects of his penitentiary experience: "By some prison officials we [conscientious objectors] were considered the worst scum on earth, because we had refused to fight for our country, and because we were college educated. We used to say that the difference between us and other prisoners was the difference between fasting and starving. We were there by virtue of a commitment we had made to a moral position; and that gave us a psychological attitude the average prisoner did not have. He felt either that he had done something wrong, and that he should be punished for it, or that he had done nothing wrong, and society was brutalizing him. We had neither the guilt nor the feeling of being brutalized. We had the feeling of being morally important; and that made us respond to prison conditions without fear, with considerable sensitivity to human rights. We thought we were making a contribution to society, in the same way that Gandhi, who was our hero, had said to a British judge: 'It is your moral duty to put me in jail.' That was our feeling. It was by going to jail that we called the people's attention to the horrors of war.

"Still, what is oppressive about prison is that one is unable to be a human being. He is unable to make a single decision about anything he thinks important. A bell rings, and you are permitted to take a shower. A bell rings, and you can go and eat. A bell rings, and you must leave the dining room. A bell rings, and you can go to the library. A bell rings, and you must leave the library. A bell rings, and you have no lights at night. A bell rings, and you get up in the morning. A bell rings, and you must leave your cell. A bell rings, and you can go for physical exercise. A bell rings, and you can see the warden. A bell rings, and if you are in the middle of a sentence you must stop talking to the warden. These books you may read, those books you may not read. All of that robs people of their inner capacity to be human beings. And almost all the violence in prison springs from that."

Rustin was released from Lewisburg on June 11. A month earlier, he had written to an official of the prison system, seeking "to discover the amount of money I shall receive." He itemized what his minimal financial need would be in the first week of his readjustment to civilian life. "When I told the warden that I would need $45 or $50 to see me through, he suggested that I turn to charitable organizations or to borrowing." Actually, there was a statutory provision for the amount of money prisoners should receive upon their release. Perhaps Rustin's case was an exception, but his occasional tendency to narrative inflation should probably be taken into account here. (Some forty years later, he told a group of high-school students at his alma mater, "When we came out of federal penitentiary, they gave us one suit, one change of underwear, one change of socks, and ten dollars.")

Twenty-eight months of imprisonment had reduced Rustin's size and weight. The suits he once wore—some still at his aunt Bessie's apartment—were now too roomy for him. "Bayard came out of penitentiary with a very small waist," his old Harlem friend Howard Wallace recalled. "When he saw what we were wearing, he wanted to know where he could buy such suits, cheaply. We took him over to a Jewish store in Brooklyn, a place that stocked the latest styles at low prices. He bought a couple of suits there, at twenty-five dollars each. Though they were inexpensive, they were of a very high quality. Today each would run you about four hundred dollars."

It must have been in one of those suits that Rustin appeared at 2929 Broadway on a Monday morning in June 1946 to undertake his new position as race relations secretary (together with George Houser) for the Fellowship of Reconciliation. Where A. J. Muste was concerned, that wasn't a moment too soon. He had missed Rustin's work for the Fellowship. Three months before Bayard's release from Lewisburg, Muste had written to remind him: "There are tremendous and pressing demands for the kind of service you are in a position to render."

Chapter 7

Journey of Reconciliation

Within a fortnight, Rustin was on the road again, as a radical activist and lecturer for the Fellowship of Reconciliation. Since there was no immediate need now for antiwar agitation, he urged his audiences to adopt the Gandhian methodology of nonviolent civil rights struggle. And as he had done in the past, he functioned as a one-man civil disobedience movement in his travels across the United States. He occupied "white only" railroad compartments; sat in at "white only" hotels; and refused to budge unless he was forcibly ejected.

On the evening of January 18, 1947, he arrived in Saint Paul, Minnesota, to fulfill a speaking engagement. A reservation had been made for him at the Hamline Hotel. But when Rustin checked in, a desk clerk took one look at him and said that there was no booking in his name. Not unused to receptions of that kind, Rustin calmly informed the young woman that one of his hosts in Saint Paul—Professor Russell Compton of Hamline University—had made the reservation. Compton had indeed done so, but he hadn't thought it necessary to inform the hotel that Rustin was black. The desk clerk walked into an inner office, for a consultation with her superiors. She reemerged to say that there *was* a reservation for Bayard Rustin, but that it was now, at 8:00 P.M., too late for the hotel to honor it.

Rustin telephoned his plight to the Reverend Clarence Nelson, a leader of the local NAACP. Nelson called Professor Compton, who said that Rustin's reservation had been made for 9:00 P.M. When this was relayed to Rustin, he saw it as the usual runaround; and he told the hotel management that he and his luggage would be occupying the lobby all through the night. News of the standoff spread, and prominent residents of Saint Paul, black and white, left their homes to join Rustin's sit-in at the Hamline Hotel. Early in the morning hours, the management relented, offering Rustin one of its best rooms. But he refused it, accepting, instead, the hospitality of a white family.

"I am surprised the university did not tell me that the visitor would be a Negro," the hotel's manager said later. "To tell the truth, this is the first time we have ever bumped into this kind of situation, and we were at a loss." Rustin's technique, the *St. Paul Recorder* commented, "consists in the nonviolent direct action approach. 'Sitting it out,' 'holding your ground,' appealing to the 'moral heart' of the individual, and seeking to win him to your position on the basis of conscience are some of the tactical tools of Mr. Rustin's philosophy."

"I got into a series of conferences all over the country, from California to Maine, Florida to Oregon," Rustin recalled. "These were interracial institutes and workshops, to which we invited lecturers like Eleanor Roosevelt, Margaret Mead, and Otto Klineberg of Columbia University. We were urging blacks and whites to understand the Gandhian techniques of nonviolent resistance. We were getting whites to face their responsibility for an alliance with the blacks who were in political motion. In some of these interracial institutes and workshops, blacks and whites would divide up into teams—challenging segregation in restaurants, theaters, and other places of public accommodation. Very often we would invite mayors, congressmen, and city council members to hear our case against segregation and discrimination. Then we would have an interracial dinner in some segregated town. That was what we [CORE and the FOR] did in those days."

While conducting a workshop in interracial cooperation, Rustin organized a sit-in by civil rights activists at a YMCA cafeteria in the nation's capital. Washington was still one of the most segregated towns in America, and Rustin and his colleagues had been told that the cafeteria would serve them only if they took their meals in the kitchen. A. C. Thompson, a member of CORE, who joined the sit-in, was to recall:

"Wanting to drive us from the cafeteria, the management poured huge amounts of ammonia into the air-conditioning system, and the fumes damn near asphyxiated the lot of us. What would we do now? Some quick thinking was required. It was here that I first observed Bayard Rustin's tactical resourcefulness. Bayard found a telephone and made an emergency call to the fire department. He told them that the cafeteria's kitchen was on fire, that diners were dropping like flies from smoke inhalation. When the firemen arrived, they recognized what the true problem was. They scolded the management in the harshest terms and ordered them to clean up their act. That saved our demonstration, we continued our sit-in, and the cafeteria was later desegregated. But it was Bayard's quick-witted response that rescued our campaign. It was an example of why he stood in the 1940s as a model for intelligent thinking about the struggle for civil rights."

On July 6, 1944, not long after Rustin entered the Ashland penitentiary, Irene Morgan, a twenty-eight-year-old black woman, boarded a Greyhound bus in Gloucester County, Virginia. Weak from recent surgery, she took the first unoccupied seat she saw—which happened to be in the section of the bus legally reserved for whites. At a stop in Saluda, the driver ordered her to move to the back. She refused to do so, and the police were called and placed her under arrest.

At her trial, Morgan was convicted on two counts: resisting arrest and violating the Virginia law against integrated seating on vehicles of interstate transport. She paid a fine of ten dollars on the first count, but—on the advice of the NAACP, which aimed to test her case in the higher courts—she appealed the latter decision. In 1946, after the Virginia Supreme Court upheld the conviction, the NAACP took

Morgan's case to the United States Supreme Court, where it was argued by Thurgood Marshall. By a vote of seven to one, the court concurred with Marshall that the Virginia code was not only unduly burdensome but also unconstitutional, a violation of statutes governing interstate commerce.

Despite that victory, the invalid Virginia law, and similar laws elsewhere in the South, continued to be enforced. Bus companies simply ignored the Supreme Court ruling, and local blacks flinched from asserting their right to integrated seating. Only an organized movement from the North could risk blazing so dangerous a trail.

Late in 1946, Bayard Rustin and George Houser, the FOR cosecretaries for race relations, began planning an interracial invasion of the South, aimed at enforcing compliance with the Supreme Court's decision in *Morgan* v. *Virginia*. This would take the form of bus rides through the region, an enterprise Rustin and Houser described as a Journey of Reconciliation. "The Journey was not meant to be just another testing of existing laws," the Reverend Homer Jack, one of its participants, later explained. "It was primarily to ascertain whether an unpopular court decision could be enforced by using the spirit of aggressive goodwill or, more accurately, nonviolent direct action."

The NAACP, then led by Walter White, volunteered the service of its southern attorneys, for a number of the bus protesters were bound to be arrested. "The NAACP was absolutely necessary to our adventures in the South," Rustin said. "Without the promise of support by the NAACP's legal team throughout the region, we didn't dare go in. Anything could happen to us if we didn't have NAACP lawyers coming to our assistance along the way."

But neither White nor the traditionally nonconfrontational NAACP thought highly of the effort in direct action, however nonviolent its leaders were. Addressing an audience in New Orleans on November 22, 1946, Thurgood Marshall warned that a "disobedience movement on the part of Negroes and their white allies, if employed in the South, would result in wholesale slaughter with no good achieved." He went on to criticize "well-meaning radical groups in New York," which seemed to believe that nonviolent tactics used in India could be successfully applied against segregation in the United States. Marshall's topic in New Orleans was "The Next Twenty Years Toward Freedom for the Negro in America." He clearly did not foresee or imagine the rise of a civil rights mass movement in the late 1950s, whose effectiveness, particularly in the South, owed a good deal to the Gandhian style of its leadership and conduct.

By "well-meaning radical groups in New York," Marshall could only have been referring to the Fellowship of Reconciliation and the Journey into the South that Rustin and Houser were organizing. After reading Marshall's remarks in the *New York Times,* Rustin replied with an article in the *Louisiana Weekly:*

> I am sure that Marshall is either ill-informed on the principles and techniques of nonviolence or ignorant of the processes of social change.
>
> Unjust social laws and patterns do not change because supreme courts deliver just decisions. One needs merely to observe the continued practice of jim crow in interstate travel, six months after the Supreme Court's decision, to see the necessity of resistance. Social progress comes from struggle; all freedom demands a price.
>
> At times freedom will demand that its followers go into situations where even death is to be faced. . . .
>
> Resistance on the buses would, for example, mean humiliation, mistreatment by police, arrest, and some physical violence inflicted on the participants.
>
> But if anyone at this date in history believes that the "white problem," which is one of privilege, can be settled without some violence, he is mistaken and fails to realize the ends to which men can be driven to hold on to what they consider their privileges.
>
> This is why Negroes and whites who participate in direct action must pledge themselves to nonviolence in word and

deed. For in this way alone can the inevitable violence [they encounter] be reduced to a minimum.

The Journey of Reconciliation, planned at the FOR's national office in New York, was to be a two-week pilgrimage (April 9–23, 1947) through Virginia, North Carolina, Tennessee, and Kentucky. Its inter-racial team—eight blacks and eight whites—comprised Rustin and Houser, the leaders; Nathan Wright, a religious social worker; Conrad Lynn, a civil rights attorney; Wallace Nelson, recently released from a three-year imprisonment for conscientious objection; Andrew Johnson, a law student; Eugene Stanley, a student in agronomy; Dennis Banks, a jazz musician; William Worthy, an activist in A. Philip Randolph's March on Washington Movement; Louis Adams, a Methodist minister; James Peck, a radical journalist; Ernest Bromley, a clergyman attached to the FOR; Joseph Felmet and Igal Roodenko, former conscientious objectors; Worth Randle, a biologist; and Homer Jack, a Unitarian minister, an original member of CORE, and a leader of the Chicago Council Against Racial and Religious Discrimination.

Late in March, all sixteen met in Washington for a two-day orientation session. The nonpacifists lacked training in the principles of nonviolent direct action; and nearly all needed to be drilled in the proper techniques of challenging segregation in the South. Rustin and Houser therefore drafted these instructions:

> *If you are Negro, sit in a front seat. If you are white, sit in a rear seat.*
>
> *If the driver asks you to move, tell him calmly and courteously: "As an interstate passenger I have a right to sit anywhere in this bus. This is the law as laid down by the United States Supreme Court."*
>
> *If the driver summons the police and repeats his order in their presence, tell him exactly what you said when he first asked you to move.*
>
> *If the police ask you to "come along," without putting you under arrest, tell them you will not go until you are put under arrest.*
>
> *If the police put you under arrest, go with them peacefully. At*

*the police station, phone the nearest headquarters of the NAACP, or
one of their lawyers. They will assist you.*

*If you happen to be arrested the delay in your journey will only
be a few hours.*

The Journey set out from Washington on the morning of April 9,
with interracial groups of two or three occupying the front and back
seats of Greyhound and Trailways buses. And for the next fortnight or
so, they proceeded through Richmond, Petersburg, Bristol, Roanoke,
Amherst, Charlottesville, Lynchburg, Raleigh, Durham, Chapel Hill,
Greensboro, Winston-Salem, Asheville, Weaversville, Louisville,
Nashville, and Knoxville. According to Wallace Nelson, "We had
meetings every night, as we went from one town to another. Rustin was
the most colorful figure among us. He sang on the buses, and he was
usually our main speaker at local meetings, where we explained the
meaning and importance of the Supreme Court's decision. Bayard
impressed everyone with his high-class British accent. People in the
South weren't used to hearing Negroes like him."

There were to be the inevitable arrests, though fewer than the freedom riders had feared. On April 11, Conrad Lynn was arrested in
Petersburg. "People on the bus were being inconvenienced," he recalled,
"but only a few complained. They seemed to sense that a much larger
issue was at stake. Unfortunately, a considerable crowd of local citizens
had gathered outside the bus, and they were threatening to beat me up,
and worse. Black people in the crowd looked apprehensive. The bus station porter, a diminutive, roly-poly black man of uncertain age, placed
his foot on the lower step of the bus and looked at the crowd. 'Let's take
the nigger off!' he said. 'We don't want him down here!'" Lynn found
that students at the all-black Virginia Union University were much in
accord with that feeling. Many of them, he said, "were unwilling to
admit that they had suffered discrimination in public transportation";
they "pretended that racial oppression did not exist for them."

Bayard Rustin, Andrew Johnson, and James Peck were later
arrested in Durham, another stronghold of the black bourgeoisie, whose

members seemed satisfied enough with the segregated order of things. "Whenever they emerge from their prosperous homes, they ride in cars," Peck reported. "These people . . . opposed our Journey, as many prosperous Negroes oppose action which threatens their privileged status. They tried to get the local NAACP to call off the meeting which it had planned for us in a church." Peck and Dennis Banks were arrested in Asheville and charged with breaking the local Jim Crow law. At a court hearing the next day, they were astonished to discover that neither judge nor prosecutor had ever heard of the Supreme Court's decision in *Morgan* v. *Virginia.*

The most frightening threat of violence occurred when Rustin, Peck, Johnson, Roodenko, and Felmet arrived in Chapel Hill. Holding tickets for a bus to Greensboro later that afternoon, the five spent the morning hours as guests of the Reverend Charles Jones, a white clergyman, and his wife. The pastor of the Chapel Hill Presbyterian Church was an old acquaintance of Rustin's and had once served on the national council of the Fellowship of Reconciliation. After lunch with the Joneses, Rustin and his colleagues left to begin their journey to Greensboro. But they had hardly settled into their bus seats when Rustin, Roodenko, Johnson, and Felmet were dragged out and arrested for violating North Carolina's law against racially integrated seating in public conveyances. Somehow James Peck (who, with Roodenko, was one of the two white New Yorkers) escaped the attention of the police, and while his comrades were being heard for bail, the sullen southern mood took a decidedly menacing turn. As Peck recalled:

> White cab drivers were hanging around the bus station, with nothing to do. They saw our Trailways bus delayed, and learned the reason why. Here was something over which they could work out their frustration and boredom. Two ringleaders started haranguing the other drivers. About ten of them started milling around the parked bus. When I got off to put up bail for the two Negroes and two whites in our group who had been arrested, five of the drivers surrounded me. "Coming down

here to stir up the niggers," snarled a big one with steel-cold grey eyes. With that, he slugged me on the side of the head. I stepped back, looked at him, and asked, "What's the matter?". . . My failure to retaliate with violence had taken him by surprise.

Another of the milling drivers exclaimed, "They'll never get a bus out of here tonight."

An alarmed bystander who heard the statement—a member of Chapel Hill Presbyterian Church—rushed to phone his minister. The Reverend Mr. Jones drove up some minutes later, made an accurate survey of the situation, and offered to take the besieged freedom riders on to their next stop, in Greensboro. But early in the journey, Jones's rearview mirror reflected a number of taxicabs trailing his automobile. Who could tell—who couldn't imagine?—what might transpire on one of the lonely back roads of North Carolina? Making a swift detour, Jones sped the imperiled five back to his home, getting them through his front door a moment before the angry pursuers arrived.

Emerging from their cabs with sticks and stones, the drivers advanced menacingly upon the clergyman's colonial-style residence— when a leader of the mob gave a restraining signal. His followers began to withdraw, though they had by no means abandoned their violent designs. A flood of terrifying phone calls began, one of which warned the minister and his wife, "Get the niggers out of town by nightfall, or we'll burn your house down." The group of "niggers" included three whites, but in the circumstances, and in that place, they had been tainted by their association with a minority of black "blood."

It was now time for the Reverend Mr. Jones to make some urgent phone calls of his own. Reaching a number of students at the nearby University of North Carolina, he implored them to organize a fleet of automobiles to spirit Rustin's delegation out of town. He next called the police, who, predictably, were deaf to his appeal for a protective convoy. Only after he threatened to bring a civil action against the police department, should any violence befall his guests, did a patrol car arrive. Its sole occupant was "the nicest man on the police force," Jones's wife, Dorcas, recalled. He and the fleet of student-owned vehicles escorted the freedom riders across the Chapel Hill County line, from which they made their way safely to Greensboro.

But the crisis their presence had stirred was not over. "We spent that Sunday evening with friends," Dorcas Jones remembered. "Late that evening, my husband, Charles, sent his preaching assistant to our house to see if things were all right. Someone, believing him to be Charles, threw a brick at him. We had young children, and we feared for them. The police chief said he couldn't protect us, so I took the children and stayed with friends in the mountains for about a week. Charles remained in Chapel Hill and helped to plan a town meeting. There he presented the facts of the case, and got things straightened out with the cabdrivers."

Without Jones's intervention, Rustin recalled, "we would have been in serious trouble, indeed." He later wrote to a friend in Minnesota:

> *When we went into the buses of the South, we knew that there would be some violent reactions brought to the surface. . . . We also had to accept violence unto ourselves. But unless we were naive, we also knew that the lynch mob at Chapel Hill, which was frustrated from getting us, might very well wreak its vengeance upon other Negroes in the community. And the fact is that they responded with violence not only to Negro members of the community but {also} to white ones. . . . You cannot take a stance for truth and justice without automatically involving other people, and causing some suffering.*

To Gay Morenus Hammerman, who was a coed at the University of North Carolina, Chapel Hill seemed, in some ways, too tender a setting for the sort of violence Rustin and his traveling party barely escaped. "Chapel Hill," she would remember, "was as idyllic as its name. The whole place, campus and town, smelled of arboretum flowers in the spring, and their petals blew across your face as you walked to class along the dirt paths Thomas Wolfe loved." Nor had the community been wholly hostile to liberal causes. Defying a sector of racist feeling, Dr. Frank Graham, a progressive leader of the university, had presented the black soprano Dorothy Maynor at a song recital before an interracial audience—an unusual event in the South of that day. And Charles Jones had permitted his church to be used for a meeting of the Congress of Industrial Organizations, known for its racially integrated unions.

Elsewhere in North Carolina, the Journey of Reconciliation sparked considerable debate over local conventions and attitudes. The *Greensboro Daily News* editorialized:

> If interracial collaborators are determined to test the Jim Crow regulations in intra-state traffic, there is nothing to do about it save let them go ahead. . . .
>
> Of course, there is the natural resentment that men of both races should come from other states and use buses at Chapel Hill and Durham for carrying out their experiment. . . .
>
> Anyhow, let's not help grow a fresh crop of martyrs. The seating arrangements are part of our state traffic regulations; but if they run counter to federal law all of us know which will prevail.
>
> Above all, it is to be hoped that none of our own residents who invite this sort of seemingly unnecessary embroilment upon us will be permitted to use it for purposes of personal exploitation.

A reader responded:

> One gathers from your editorial that North Carolina is being made a martyr in the cause of justice as interpreted in our democratic ideology. How could such be the case unless the citizens of our great state were in opposition to the basic democratic ideals of our nation? If the legality of inter-state travel . . .

is being questioned—in light of the decision of our highest tribunal in the case of Irene Morgan v. the Commonwealth of Virginia—does this state stand in the role of martyr, unless we are committed to ideals contrary to those of a democratic society?

The consensus in North Carolina may or may not have been reflected in the decision of Judge Henry Whitfield. On May 20, 1947, the Chapel Hill judge found Rustin and his comrades guilty of violating the state's Jim Crow bus statute. Rustin and Andrew Johnson were assessed court costs and sentenced to thirty days on a chain gang. Igal Roodenko and Joseph Felmet, both white, were socked with ninety days. That was sixty days beyond the statutory limit, and Whitfield justified it on grounds that white liberals were even more objectionable than the blacks whose cause they espoused. Rustin recalled, "He said to me, 'Well, I know you're a poor misled nigra from the North. Therefore, I'm going to give you thirty days.' Then, very angrily, he said, 'Now Mr. Rodenky'—purposely mispronouncing Roodenko's name—'I presume you're Jewish, Mr. Rodenky.' Igal said, 'Yes, I'm Jewish.' The judge said, 'Well, it's about time you Jews from New York learned that you can't come down here bringing your nigras with you to upset the customs of the South. Just to teach you a lesson, I gave your black boy thirty days, and I now give you ninety.' Later on, I said jokingly to Igal, 'See, there are certain advantages to being black.'" There is no record of what Judge Whitfield said to Joseph Felmet, but it could not have been much kinder than what he told Roodenko. Felmet was a native of Asheville, North Carolina, and Whitfield may well have considered him a traitor to the racial customs of his region.

The convictions were appealed. In March 1948, Judge Chester Morris, a superior court justice in Hillsboro, imposed a uniform thirty-day sentence on all four defendants. That ruling was appealed as well, for Rustin wanted their case to be heard by the U.S. Supreme Court. But it did not get beyond North Carolina's Supreme Court—which upheld the convictions in January 1949 and ordered the appellants to surrender for service in a local chain gang. Rustin was not surprised when their NAACP attorneys dropped the case and advised against petitioning the highest court of the land. "Roy Wilkins," he recalled, "had told me some time earlier that we would probably have to go to jail. Wilkins said, 'The black lawyer who had the ticket stubs, proving that you were interstate passengers, now claims he has lost the stubs— although we believe he was paid to destroy them.'"

Rustin had been out of the country since November 1948, visiting parts of Europe and India as a spokesman for the American Friends Service Committee and the Fellowship of Reconciliation. When he returned, in February, and heard that his imprisonment was now a fait accompli, he told an interviewer: "Our conviction, unfortunately, is one more demonstration to the colored majority of the world of the failure of American democracy. America cannot maintain its leadership in the struggle for world democracy as long as the conditions exist which caused our arrest and conviction."

Much earlier, in the spring of 1947, when the Journey of Reconciliation returned from the South, its participants had been ecstatic, proud of their heroic challenge to the system of segregated public transportation. "Bayard was radiantly elated by the mostly positive results of our action," recalled Worth Randle, a white member of the sixteen-man team. Liberal organizations in the North were elated as well. In February 1948, Bayard Rustin and George Houser were among the recipients of the Thomas Jefferson Award for the Advancement of Democracy, presented by the Council Against Intolerance in America.

The Journey of Reconciliation achieved no dramatic breakthroughs. Blacks did not suddenly begin flocking to the front seats of interstate conveyances, and it would be some time before the bus companies began enforcing the Supreme Court decision in *Morgan* v. *Virginia.* The Journey's achievement was mostly psychological or symbolic, signifying the possibility of future nonviolent mass action in the South. That was essentially the view held by Rustin and Houser.

Accepting the Jefferson Award on April 11, 1948—at a dinner in the Waldorf-Astoria—Rustin declared that the Journey of Reconciliation had been undertaken "not only to devise techniques for eliminating Jim Crow in travel but also as a training ground for similar peaceful projects against discrimination in employment and in the armed services." He added, "No single injustice more bitterly stands out in the hearts and minds of colored people the world over than the continuation of discrimination and segregation in our military forces."

By then he had already begun a struggle against the latter injustice: he had joined the Committee Against Jim Crow in Military Service and Training, organized by A. Philip Randolph in November 1947. But the outcome of that collaboration with Randolph (they disagreed over whether or not the campaign had achieved its objective) would cause another temporary rift in their historic alliance.

The Committee Against Jim Crow was formed not long after the Truman administration proposed the enactment of Universal Military Training, a conscription program in which no provisions were made for the elimination of racial segregation in the military. The new proposal was particularly alarming to two constituencies. One was Randolph's Gandhian wing of the black movement (with its abhorrence of racial segregation in all forms); the other was the racial wing of the pacifist movement (with its principled resistance to military conscription). As it happened, Bayard Rustin belonged to both constituencies; the leaders (Randolph and Muste) had worked closely in the past; and they now pooled their specific political concerns into a common fight against Universal Military Training.

According to John Swomley, then an officer in Muste's FOR, it was he, Swomley, who first alerted Randolph to the racial implications of the proposed UMT. Swomley had been working temporarily in Washington, monitoring provisions for the new conscription act, when he "became convinced that it was possible to defeat UMT and at the same time desegregate the armed forces." On returning to New York, he consulted with Randolph, Rustin, and William Worthy, of CORE; and in those talks, Swomley said, "we agreed to form a national Committee Against Jim Crow in Military Service."

Led by Randolph, the committee attracted national attention. It did not succeed, however, in blocking passage of the UMT legislation or in persuading President Truman to abolish racial segregation in the military. The prospects for success were not improved by an explosive exchange Randolph had with Senator Wayne Morse, of the Armed Services Committee.

Testifying before the committee in March 1948, Randolph declared that he would counsel young black men to refuse induction in the segregated armed forces. That sparked his exchange with the senator from Oregon, who was not unfriendly to the cause of civil rights.

SENATOR MORSE: Let me assume that a country proceeds to attack the United States [making] it perfectly clear that our choice is only the choice of war. Would you take the position then that unless the government granted the demands which are set out in your testimony . . . you would recommend a course of civil disobedience to our government?

RANDOLPH: . . . if the government does not change its policy . . . in the interests of the very democracy it is fighting for, I would advocate that Negroes take no part in the army.

MORSE: I understand . . . you would still recommend a program of civil disobedience.

RANDOLPH: Because I believe that that is in the interest of the soul of the country.

MORSE: Do you have any doubt then that this government . . . would necessarily follow a legal course of . . . applying the legal doctrine of treason to that conduct?

RANDOLPH: I believe that is the price we have to pay for the democracy we want. . . . I would be willing to face that doctrine on the theory and on the grounds that we are serving a higher law than the law which applies the act of treason to us when we are attempting to win democracy. . . . We would participate in no overt acts against our government. Ours would be one of non-participation in the military forces of the country. We would be willing to absorb the violence, to absorb the terrorism, to face the music, and take whatever comes.

None of that won Randolph support on Capitol Hill or in the White House. By early June, as the UMT bill made its inexorable way through Congress, Randolph received no assurance that the proposed legislation would outlaw segregation in the military. Hence, with Bayard Rustin as his most militant aide, he was now ready to proceed with the civil disobedience campaign he had threatened to lead during his testimony before the Armed Services Committee.

"The draft bill," *Newsweek* reported on June 7, "has run head-on into a sore and angry issue in American life: race segregation. Back of the whole issue loomed something new: the threat of a mass refusal of Negroes to submit to a draft under present conditions. . . . It raised the specter of a major crisis in American life." Randolph could not be ignored as insignificant, *Newsweek* added, "because he is one of the more respected Negro leaders in the country." Nor could he be dismissed as a communist agitator, for, as a democratic socialist, he had spent much of his career opposing communists. He *was* ignored, however: Congress passed the new conscription act on June 19, with no clause against Jim Crow in the armed services. Incensed, Randolph wrote to President Truman on June 21, "Sincerity demands that you veto an act that is pregnant with indecency." Near the end of June, when he had received no response from Truman, he launched the League for Nonviolent Civil Disobedience—an offshoot of the Committee Against Jim Crow in Military Service. The League would not be dissolved, Randolph announced, unless and until Truman issued an executive order banning racial segregation in the armed forces.

Marking its alliance with the pacifist movement, the League's principal activists included Bayard Rustin, James Peck, and George Houser, all of whom had played heroic roles in the interracial Journey of Reconciliation.

As field director of the League for Nonviolent Civil Disobedience, Rustin was Randolph's chief of staff. He advised Randolph on strategy and tactics; wrote almost all the League's correspondence and public statements; organized support groups across the country; collected pledges of noncooperation from young blacks eligible for the draft; and planned public meetings at which Randolph would speak, especially in Harlem.

When Randolph addressed one of those Harlem meetings in July, voices from the audience—massed in front of the Theresa Hotel—asked him directly: What do you want us to do? "My answer is this," he replied. "You should not register under this draft act." That was an invitation to arrest, for Randolph knew that his advice was in violation of the new law—a violation punishable by a fine of ten thousand dollars and/or five years in jail.

"On that fateful afternoon," James Farmer wrote later, "expectant crowds swarmed through the streets . . . to hear [Randolph's] thunder and to see if the government's lightning rod would strike. Federal agents and plainclothesmen were easily identifiable by their set jaws and icy eyes. . . . Randolph had deliberately violated the Selective Service and Training Act. . . . Most reporters waited . . . to see if handcuffs would be put on the premier leader of black Americans at the time. Wisely, the feds and the local police made no attempt to arrest him."

Most blacks felt that the government did not wish to make a martyr of Randolph only a few months before the November elections. Indeed, Truman's fear of alienating the black vote in 1948 may have accounted in part for the concession he made soon after Randolph's defiant speech in Harlem. On July 26, the President issued Executive Order 9981, declaring that "there shall be equality of treatment and opportunity for all persons in the armed services, without regard to race, color, religion, or national origin"; and that "this policy shall be put into effect as rapidly as possible."

While Randolph was welcoming this as a victory for his campaign, Bayard Rustin, his chief intellectual operative behind the scenes, was not. Distrusting the language of the executive order, Rustin felt it did not commit itself explicitly against "segregation" in the military.

Truman's wording, he later told readers of *Fellowship,* was designed "to split the movement and make Negroes believe that they had won a victory while in fact nothing had been gained."

Thus, Rustin and his fellow pacifists in the anti–Jim Crow campaign balked when Randolph ordered them to dismantle the League for Nonviolent Civil Disobedience. Well, he told them, they should arrange a press conference at which *he* would announce the League's dissolution. Combining insubordination with duplicity, they arranged Randolph's press conference for an afternoon in August and a press conference of their own at midmorning of the same day—intending to upstage their leader.

At *their* meeting with the press, they denounced Truman's executive order, assailed Randolph's readiness to accept it, and declared themselves "morally bound to continue the civil disobedience campaign until the object for which the League was organized is accomplished." That object, in their view, was a categorical statement that "desegregation" of the military was now a matter of national policy. Randolph's press conference, at four in the afternoon, was a feeble anticlimax, attracting a mere handful of reporters.

The subsequent rift between Rustin and Randolph—their last— would not be healed for more than two years. Rustin recalled, decades later: "It was nearly three years before I dared to see Mr. Randolph again, after the terrible thing I had done to him. When I walked into his office, he stood and came towards the door to meet me. I was so nervous I was shaking, waiting for his wrath to descend upon me. He shook my hand and said, 'Bayard, where have you been? You know I've needed you.' From then until the day he died he never once said a word about what I had done to him.

"But I and my colleagues were young and radical in the 1940s. We were crazy. And my experience with Randolph prepared me for an understanding of Stokely Carmichael, H. Rap Brown, and the other militants who came along in the 1960s."

Looking back more than forty years later, Houser reflected: "We in the nonviolent movement of the 1940s certainly thought that we were initiating something of importance in American life. Of course, we weren't able to put it in perspective then. But we were filled with vim and vigor, and we hoped that a mass movement could develop, even if we did not think that we were going to produce it. In retrospect, I would say we were precursors. The things we did in the '40s were the same things that ushered in the civil rights revolution. Our Journey of Reconciliation preceded the Freedom Rides of 1961 by fourteen years. There is definitely something to the phrase 'an idea whose time has come.' Conditions were not quite ready for the full-blown movement when we were undertaking our initial actions. But I think we helped to lay the foundation for what followed, and I feel proud of that."

Chapter 8

"Rustiji"

In December 1946, while planning the Journey of Reconciliation, Rustin wrote to Charles S. Johnson, the president of Fisk University: "As you know, I have been interested for some years in the nonviolent revolution which Gandhi and Nehru have been leading in India." Could Johnson assist him in obtaining a foundation grant for a one-year visit to the subcontinent? Johnson suggested an approach to the Julius Rosenwald Fund, and Rustin applied to the organization, stating his desire "to study the psychology underlying nonviolent resistance with Gandhi at his ashram." His application failed, however, despite glowing recommendations by A. Philip Randolph, A. J. Muste, and Rayford Logan, a professor of history at Howard University. His dream did not come true until late in 1948, when the American Friends Service Committee selected him as its delegate to an international pacifist conference. Even so, his dream was only partly realized; for when he arrived in India, Gandhi, whom he passionately wanted to meet, had passed from the scene, having been assassinated in January.

Rustin sailed to London on October 1, 1948, hoping to spend a two-week vacation there before proceeding to India. But his fortnight in London, the first of many visits he was to make to that city, would be anything but relaxed. He found himself flooded with invitations to address pacifist gatherings in the British capital—even in parts of France and Germany—on the subject of race relations in the United States.

Returning to London from one of his speaking engagements on the Continent, he learned that the international pacifist meeting in India had been canceled. He was making plans to fly back to New York—the Fellowship of Reconciliation insisted on his immediate return—when Muriel Lester intervened. An international ambassador for the Fellowship, the Englishwoman had been invited to India by Devadas Gandhi (the Mahatma's son); and she wrote to the FOR in New York, requesting that Rustin be allowed to accompany her. Lester, who had been a friend and confidante of the slain Indian leader, regarded Rustin as a bright young star of the pacifist movement—and he admired her "inner authority" and her "great prophetic voice."

On their arrival in India, both were greeted warmly by Devadas Gandhi. "Muriel and I have been taken care of beautifully," Rustin wrote to John Nevin Sayre. Gandhi introduced Rustin to the Governor General C. Ragalopalachari, who invited him for a stay at Government House in New Delhi. On December 17, when he made a guest appearance at the All-India Congress Party convention, in Jaipur, he met and conferred with Prime Minister Jawaharlal Nehru and Deputy Prime Minister Sardar Patel.

In and beyond New Delhi, Rustin also formed acquaintances with young Gandhian intellectuals, one of whom, Devi Prasad, recalled many years later, "He met us and gave us some idea of what was going on in the world of nonviolence in the United States. He sang spirituals that won everybody's heart. The Martin Luther King phenomenon had not yet started, but we got a very profound impression that Bayard was doing Gandhi's work in North America."

Not everyone who heard him on his Indian rounds was so impressed. The American consul general in Bombay informed the State Department that Rustin was speaking "in an inflammatory manner regarding racial conditions in the United States"; that his remarks were "being highlighted and given an anti-American slant in the Indian press"; that, altogether, he was fostering an "unfortunate impression." Yet one private American report made a somewhat different emphasis. A correspondent for the *Chicago Tribune* wrote to his paper that Bayard Rustin was "receiving a warm welcome" for his speeches on "racial intolerance in America."

Traveling through India, Rustin did not view his surroundings as with the lens of a tourist camera but identified himself with forms of the national culture. In small towns and villages, he adopted the Indian manner of greeting—pressing his palms together, fingertips pointing outward, and bowing gracefully from the waist. "Nothing makes the Indians quite as happy as greeting them Indian style," he wrote to the Reverend George L. Paine, a pacifist minister in New England. "To touch a woman in public," he said, "is considered the highest vulgarity." Thus, shaking hands was "counter to a good deal of Indian culture"—although many "liberated women" in the Gandhian movement were "perfectly willing to shake hands." During much of his time on the subcontinent, Rustin discarded his Western attire in favor of Gandhian calico and sandals. He developed a taste for Indian cuisine. When dining in rural areas, he joyfully squatted on the floor, as his hosts did; and in some of those areas he retired at nights in Indian "sleeping rolls." This adjustment to aspects of Indian culture was not just an act of social diplomacy. It reflected the pleasure he took in adapting himself to local customs wherever he traveled.

Near the end of Rustin's scheduled four weeks in India, Muriel Lester wrote to Sayre and Muste, requesting that Bayard be permitted to remain awhile longer. She felt that his effectiveness in India was "three times as much as [that of] a white pacifist"; it was "a perfect example of God's providence," having him over there. "He's getting far more notice than if he were one of a crowd," she said. "His quiet ways, his commanding stature (he really looks like a military man of valor in his Indian-style homespun), his irresistible friendliness, and his savoir faire endear him to all. . . . He's getting into the very centre of power here, and perhaps no one else could work so effectively with Nehru against militarism—but for February and March [1949], or for just February, he's utterly necessary for the colleges of this country." Confirming Lester's judgment, a member of the Gandhian movement in South India also wrote to Sayre: "I cannot say too strongly what a tremendous contribution it [an extension of Rustin's stay] would be.... He can do a job here that no white westerner can do at the moment.... We need a man like him in the colleges just now." It seems ironic that rising Indian thinkers should have been so captivated by the pacifist example and tutelage of a black American, who had come to their country seeking a deeper understanding of one of their own philosophers.

John Nevin Sayre favored Lester's appeal for an extension of Rustin's visit. A. J. Muste did not, almost demanding Bayard's immediate return. Unlike others, Muste failed to see what significant contribution Rustin could make to the politics and Gandhian programs of India. Moreover, he said, the Fellowship of Reconciliation had an urgent need for Rustin's work in America. Elaborating, he wrote to Lester:

> *Bayard's qualities are such that he will practically never be in any country without the demand developing that he stay longer.... We might easily slip into a situation where ... he was a roving ambassador of the {International} FOR rather than a member of the {American} FOR staff.... I am disposed to think that Bayard ought not to take on this roving ambassador role at this stage.... He needs to develop his own spirit at certain points, before undertaking that kind of mission.*
>
> *More fundamental than this is a consideration that in the long run a person's effectiveness outside his own country depends upon whether he has first made a major contribution at home. Unless a person has proved over a considerable period of time in a situation where he has to assume continuous responsibility ... his work elsewhere is bound to be shallow. Furthermore, until he has rooted*

himself in one situation and developed a "following" there, he
represents himself rather than being the representative of a
movement. . . . It is like the official in a national labor federation
who has no standing in his own union. . . .

Now, of course, Bayard has already gone a considerable distance
with respect to all this; but I am strongly of the opinion that he ought
to dig into the American situation, at least for several years, before
coming to be regarded as a person who can be called out of that
situation for extended periods of time.

That was a surprisingly stern and rigorous evaluation by an admiring mentor. But much of it was influenced by Muste's fear of losing his talented protégé—particularly to the International FOR, based in London, a city with which Rustin had begun to fall in love. Bowing to Muste's wishes, Bayard sailed from Bombay at the end of January 1949; arrived in London on February 18; and flew back to New York a few days later.

He had found in India that many inheritors of the Gandhian legacy were being less than faithful to it. Reporting to the FOR national committee in May, he said that while Gandhi's movement remained "nonviolent in means," it had become "essentially violent in its end"—especially in fostering, as it did, the growth of nationalism. Even Gandhi's "strict followers" in the Indian government, he said, favored "a budget of which 50% is for war," thus encouraging the development of a militarist feeling in their society. Nevertheless, Rustin added, the situation in India was not without a hopeful side: "There are the Gandhi youth groups which do stand for his principles, and others which are convinced of the valid use of nonviolence."

On his return from India, Rustin's star in the Fellowship of Reconciliation, and in the pacifist movement as a whole, glowed brighter than ever before. "He came back from India so full of enthusiasm," the FOR's Catharine Raymond recalled, "that some of us teased him by nicknaming him Rustiji." John Swomley's supervisory authority over Rustin began to decline. "My feeling," Swomley told A. J.

Muste, "is that he should arrange his own schedule . . . as to the area in which to work."

But before choosing his preferred area of work, Rustin surrendered to a court order in Hillsboro, North Carolina. It was time to begin serving the thirty-day sentence the state had imposed on him two years earlier for his role in the Journey of Reconciliation. He was assigned to a prison camp in Roxboro, where he did his time (later reduced to twenty-two days) working on a chain gang. He was to recall some of the more brutal of those hours:

"We had chains on us when we left the prison and went out to work on the roads. We were chained to one another while we used picks and shovels. It was a very harrowing and ugly experience. People were hanged on the bars [of jail cells] by their wrists, their feet dangling above the ground. This was a terrible thing, because it could cause your testicles to swell. People were put into a hole—just a hole in the ground—for two or three days if they misbehaved. No toilet, nothing. Every morning they gave you a pail of water, so that you had enough to drink. But no water for washing. On one occasion when the guards insisted that I entertain them by dancing, I refused. They took out pistols and shot at the ground around my feet, trying to make me dance. Of course, I wouldn't do it."

In August 1949, the *New York Post* serialized a five-part article by Rustin, titled "Twenty-Two Days on a Chain Gang," which stirred wide public comment. John Nevin Sayre described it as "a creative response to a rough situation" and "the most thrilling piece of FOR literature" he had read in some time. Joseph Felmet, who had also worked on the Roboro chain gang, called the *Post* series a "spellbinding exposé" of the "inhumane" experiences he himself had shared. Most important, Lee M. Brooks, a professor of sociology at the University of North Carolina, wrote to inform Rustin that his multipart article had sparked the beginning of prison reform in that state. The director of prisons and other civic officials in Raleigh were determined, Brooks said, "that the present convict system must be discarded. We want you to feel that your experience and cooperation have been all to the good for the future benefit of correctional trends in North Carolina." The Journey of Reconciliation, undertaken to reform the system of segregated bus transportation in the South, may be said to have achieved reform in a quite unintended direction.

For some three years after his release from the chain gang, Rustin's activities consisted mainly in helping to lead Gandhian-style campaigns against America's development of nuclear weapons and its programs of war preparedness. In those pacifist initiatives, he was one of the principal members of an ad hoc group called the Peacemakers, cosponsored by the FOR, the War Resisters League, the Catholic Worker Movement, and the Women's International League for Peace and Freedom. Rustin was a particularly zealous advocate of unilateral disarmament. Speaking at Lancaster, Pennsylvania, on an evening in March 1950, he urged the laying down of all arms "so that we are completely without a military."

A month earlier, he had written to Muste, proposing demonstrations at the gate of Los Alamos "or some such place, to obstruct the coming in of [nuclear] materials." A tactic of that sort would surely not be an unusual form of pacifist activism. But Rustin went a step further, suggesting the renouncing of citizenship as a "very sound" stratagem of protest and as a method of resisting "with our whole beings." Most of his colleagues in the Peacemakers instantly dismissed that suggestion as a "crackpot" idea, one the American people would rightly regard as pro-communist. Even Muste, who was almost always in accord with Rustin's thinking on strategy, was obliged to acknowledge that on this occasion his resourceful protégé had been carried overboard.

One idea that all the Peacemakers endorsed was Rustin's proposal of a week-long Fast for Peace, designed to end with a rally in the nation's capital on Palm Sunday of 1950. "The important thing is not the number of persons who give up eating for a week," Rustin announced in a press release, "but the number who give up war from now on" and dedicate themselves to "saying NO to the government in a way that might once have been treason but now is common sense."

The Fast for Peace, held on schedule, had no noticeable effect upon military policy, in America or elsewhere. But the small group of pacifists would probably have been surprised if their protest against eating had ended as a successful protest against war. They were much more accustomed to the heroism of moral and personal witnessing than to the achievement of practical victories.

Exploiting the guilt that many Americans felt over the dropping of atomic bombs upon Japan, the Peacemakers campaigned not only against the building of nuclear weapons but also against America's involvement in the Korean War, which broke out in June 1950. It was at a street demonstration in Manhattan, marking the first anniversary of the Korean conflict, that Rustin met a young intellectual activist he came to admire greatly. That was Michael Harrington—a democratic socialist in the prophetic tradition of Eugene Debs and Norman Thomas—with whom Rustin was to establish a close political alliance until the early 1970s, when they broke over American policy in Vietnam.

Harrington, a twenty-three-year-old writer when he attended the Peacemakers' street demonstration in June 1951, had been sent there to represent the Catholic Worker Movement, led by Dorothy Day. Participants in the rally, Harrington remembered, gathered beforehand in Central Park, and "there I met Bayard Rustin, an intense Negro with more than a touch of a British accent, who asked coolly if we were going to get arrested. I was still a well-mannered youth from St. Louis, and I listened with frightened fascination while my new friends argued the pros and cons of defying the police if we were ordered to move on. I was enormously relieved when it was decided that revolutionary strategy that day did not require a confrontation with the forces of order."

But there was to be confrontation of another sort when the Peacemakers and their adherents had marched to the venue of their rally in Times Square. Harrington was the opening speaker, followed by Sidney Aberman, a leader of the War Resisters League; and their militant antiwar addresses stirred an ominous restlessness within a section of the audience. Particularly inflamed was a bystander who misread a

"Catholic Worker" banner as "Daily Worker." Denouncing the rally as a communist plot, he attacked a number of the Peacemakers, tore up their picket signs, and began advancing menacingly upon the stepladder podium, from which it was David Dellinger's misfortune to be speaking.

Bravely, if not so wisely, Dellinger descended from the platform and confronted what he saw as "this raving maniac." "Go ahead and hit me," he shouted, invoking a version of Gandhian response to violent attack. The "maniac" obliged, knocking him cold and continuing to pound him as he lay senseless on the ground. "I lost all memory of what I thought I was doing," Dellinger said later. Gradually regaining his senses, he struggled to his feet and wobbled back to the platform to resume his remarks. "I'm glad you hit me," he began, at which point Bayard Rustin intervened. "Dave," he hollered, "you're groggy, you don't know what you're saying. Get the hell off the ladder." Seizing a broken picket sign, he handed it to the enraged man and offered himself to be beaten with it. The "maniac" did not oblige, having expended enough of his violence. Rustin then climbed the stepladder and delivered what one of his colleagues called "a most moving speech." Dellinger's assailant then came forward, apologized, and withdrew from the gathering, although Rustin implored him to stay.

Once more, a pacifist demonstration failed to achieve its declared purpose—in this case, to alter the conduct of the Korean War. But by influencing the remorseful retreat of Dellinger's attacker, it successfully exemplified a form of Gandhian witnessing. Exponents of this Gandhian method sometimes paid an excruciating physical price, and their willingness to do so passed beyond all ordinary understanding. Only they could explicate the philosophy to which they so readily sacrificed their bodies.

One of them, George Houser, explained: "This means that a person trying to practice nonviolence will refuse to retaliate violently. He merely absorbs the physical punishment. This sounds crazy to the average person, who has been taught to protect himself by retaliating when attacked, even if he does take a beating in the process. Why, then, is non-retaliation essential to the nonviolent approach? . . . From the negative standpoint, if nonviolence is forsaken by the minority group . . . it means that the police can be called to arrest them. . . . From the positive point of view, non-retaliatory action may make possible the winning of the support of the public, of the police, and of the opposition."

Chapter 9

A Passage to Africa

Until the early 1950s, American pacifists took no interest in African affairs, and it was somewhat by accident—after one of their failed adventures in Europe—that they began doing so. In autumn of 1951, four members of the Peacemakers (David Dellinger, Ralph DiGia, Arthur Emery, and William Sutherland) flew to Paris, on the first leg of a planned mission to the Soviet Union. In Paris, they mounted bicycles, intending to pedal the rest of their journey to Moscow, distributing antiwar leaflets along the way. "But we never got there," Sutherland, the black participant in the enterprise, later recalled. "We got no farther than the Russian army headquarters in Austria, where they compelled us to abandon our mission." While his comrades returned straightaway to New York, Sutherland made a detour through London.

From a few African students he met in Paris, he had learned about the growing intensity of anticolonial struggles in their different countries; and he surmised, correctly, that larger pools of English-speaking Africans—students and other nationalists-in-exile—were to be found in the British capital. He wished to gain from them a deeper and broader understanding of the modern winds—especially those of political self-determination—that had begun blowing through areas of their continent.

During Sutherland's inquiries in London, he was invited by a community of Quakers in Birmingham to address them on the subject of his aborted journey to the Soviet Union. At that meeting, he shared the platform with Jacob Mahlapo, a South African intellectual, whom the Birmingham Friends had asked to speak on current developments in the struggle against apartheid. Mahlapo would have been well versed in such matters, for he edited *The African World,* a monthly journal published in London. After his own speech, Sutherland learned from Mahlapo's that the African National Congress planned to inaugurate, in the summer of 1952, a massive nonviolent campaign against the apartheid laws of South Africa.

Back in New York, Sutherland excitedly told Bayard Rustin and George Houser what he had heard from Mahlapo and urged them to commit the FOR strongly behind the ANC's civil disobedience campaign. But the cosecretaries for race relations and the FOR didn't at first share Sutherland's imported passion. Their primary obligations, they felt, were to antiwar causes in the world at large and to civil rights activism in the United States. "I double-crossed them, however," Sutherland said. "I assembled packages of literature, mailed them to South Africa, and alerted ANC leaders to the existence in America of the Fellowship of Reconciliation and the Congress of Racial Equality. In no time, the South African activists were writing to Rustin and Houser, appealing for help."

George Houser was to confirm much of this more than forty years later, in his political autobiography, *No One Can Stop the Rain:*

> My introduction to the African liberation struggle began with the "Campaign to Defy Unjust Laws," sponsored by the African National Congress. . . . The year was 1952. Word about plans for a forthcoming massive nonviolent Defiance Campaign . . . to resist the apartheid laws came to me from my friend and co-worker Bill Sutherland [through] a South African

editor whom he had met in London. Sutherland and I were
both pacifists, and had worked together on numerous projects
to combat segregation in the United States by nonviolent
methods. His opinions meant a lot to me.

Nevertheless, my first reaction to Sutherland's enthusiastic
reports, urging us to active support, was hesitant. A lot was
going on right here at home. I felt overwhelmed by existing
commitments, and was not eager to take on new ones.
Sutherland's persistence had its effect, however. Somewhat
protestingly at first, I began to reach out for more information;
and together he and I, along with Bayard Rustin, began to plan
a program.

That program, sponsored by the FOR race relations department,
was launched by a group called Americans for South African Resistance,
the first organized effort in the United States on behalf of any African
freedom movement. Its founding agenda was limited to fund-raising.
But in 1953, after the government of Prime Minister Daniel Malan had
crushed the ANC's civil disobedience campaign, Americans for South
African Resistance broadened its program to include political action.

In September of that year, it restructured itself and, as the
American Committee on Africa, extended its interest to anticolonial
struggles in West Africa—particularly Ghana (then called the Gold
Coast) and Nigeria. George Houser became the first executive secretary
of the American Committee on Africa. And by 1955, the issues had so
engaged him that he resigned his position with the FOR to work as a
full-time leader of the Committee—which later extended its concerns
across the black continent, all the way to East Africa. Julius Nyerere,
the first leader of self-governing Tanzania (formerly Tanganyika),
would later recall: "The Committee [on Africa] had no money to give
us nationalist leaders, but that was not what we wanted. What it gave
us was a knowledge that we were not alone in the world . . . that our
demand for independence had sympathy and support in a very powerful
country."

• • •

Not long after William Sutherland returned from London, he and Houser and Bayard Rustin began vying for the distinction of being the first to visit the African continent. Sutherland got there in 1953 and was never again to live in the United States: he married a West African writer, raised a family in Ghana, and later settled in Tanzania, where he worked closely with Julius Nyerere. Houser went to the continent in 1954, the first of his many visits there. But Rustin, intensely competitive, had beaten his two colleagues in the race to Africa, having arrived there late in 1952. Sutherland was to say, with a self-mocking chuckle, "It was I who brought home from London the news that ignited Bayard's interest in Africa, and the next thing I knew, he had gotten himself a trip and gone to Africa ahead of me."

Rustin's trip, cosponsored by the Fellowship of Reconciliation and the American Friends Service Committee, was designed to link the American pacifist movement with leaders of the West African independence struggle—especially Ghana's Kwame Nkrumah and Nigeria's Nnamdi Azikiwe, both of whom had once studied at Lincoln University, in Pennsylvania.

En route to his discovery of West Africa, Rustin paused in Britain to attend an international meeting of Quakers: the third World Conference of Friends, held at Oxford University in July–August 1952. There he made an even stronger impression upon British pacifists than he had in 1948, when, on his way to India, he addressed components of the peace movement in London.

"Bayard, Norman Whitney, and I worked closely together," Stephen Cary, an AFSC delegate to the Oxford meeting, recalled. "The conference was tightly controlled by the English Quakers, and in the end, all three of us were terribly frustrated. There was no chance for the free winds of spirit to blow, and that was reflected in the final statement the conference drew up. It was a six-page single-spaced tome, heavy as lead.

"We therefore decided to write a statement of our own and present it to the conference as a livelier, more readable, addition to its official release. We agreed that it should be no longer than three paragraphs and, as Bayard suggested, that the language should sing. We sat up one evening till three in the morning and struggled to draft the document we felt was needed. Bayard wrote much of it, and Norman Whitney, who was a professor of English at Syracuse University, did the polishing. We produced a brief and marvelous statement."

Its final paragraph urged,

> Let us join together throughout the world to grow more food, to heal and prevent disease, to conserve and develop the resources of the good earth to the glory of God and the comfort of man's distress. These are among the tasks to which, in humility for our share of the world's shame, and in faith to the power of love, we call our own society and all men and nations everywhere.

The Rustin-Whitney-Cary statement was barred from the minutes of the Oxford conference. Perhaps it was deemed too strong. But the thoughts that motivated it had been aired earlier by Rustin on the convention floor. Godric Bader, a British delegate to the meeting, would never forget what he heard. "I first met Bayard there," he said later. "And I was thrilled when he spoke at the closing session, getting the official conference statement changed to something that had some life and purpose. I remember Bayard saying, in singing tones, 'Christianity is a revolutionary faith.' The 'world revolutionary' was typical of his whole approach to life."

On August 29, Rustin flew on to Accra, Ghana, where he was to have audiences with Kwame Nkrumah, the prime minister in a limited form of self-government. Nkrumah, then forty-three, headed the Convention People's Party, formed to guide his country's struggle for complete freedom from British colonial rule. Rustin found him to be a charismatic national figure, revered by his people as a sort of political witch doctor.

No one in Ghana, Rustin said later, was "held in such respect, love, fear, and awe." Nkrumah's "crowded day," he reported,

Usually begins at 4 a.m. Before he can wash and pray, the people have come to his gate to consult with him. One morning I met him at 7 for breakfast. Already he had received many people and done what he could to help them with their various problems. Still more people lined the verandah and waited at the gate to be admitted. He was suffering from a cold that morning and had had only four hours of sleep, but he didn't look tired, and he showed no irritation. One man, who was quite ill with malaria, insisted on seeing Nkrumah. He was sure no doctor could cure him. Nkrumah took one look at him, smiled, helped him into a car, and had him driven to the hospital. The man went away smiling: Kwame Nkrumah had laid hands on him.

It might have been adoration of that sort which encouraged Nkrumah to build a cult of personality around himself. By 1952, he was no longer the "poor struggling student" Peter Abrahams, the black South African novelist, had met in London during the late 1940s. Now visiting the prime minister in Accra, Abrahams was astonished by the personal transformation: "Tribal myths had grown up around him. He could make himself invisible at will. He could go without food and sleep and drink longer than ordinary mortals. He was, in fact, the reincarnation of some of the most powerful ancestral spirits. He allowed his feet to be bathed in blood."

Yet Bayard Rustin was impressed with Nkrumah's "calm and quiet deliberation." Despite the "stories of his miraculous powers," he could be "a sound, down-to-earth political realist." Above all—because of the political reasons for his visit to West Africa—Rustin was glad to hear from Nkrumah that the struggle for Ghana's independence would be influenced by Gandhian principles. Still, Rustin harbored some skepticism. He wrote back to Norman Whitney in Syracuse, saying that "nonviolence here is one of expediency" and under it lay "hate, fear, and potential violence."

Looking around Accra, Rustin was surprised by resemblances he saw to certain black lifestyles in Manhattan. "My experience here has been staggering," he told Whitney. "In this dirty, poor, ambitious city, I find much that I find in Harlem. We [African Americans] left here in 1619, yet the people here sing, walk, laugh, cry, dance, and strive in a way that is like 125th Street and Lenox Avenue. I seem to know and to understand them as I do nowhere else but in Harlem."

In Nigeria, where he arrived on September 13, Rustin toured the "bush" regions, observing forms of indigenous art and tribal governance. He encountered "sculpture in wood and stone that made the realistic classical works of Greece and Rome seem cold and photographic"; and he observed "a system of decentralized democracy" whose "degree of individual freedom is like nothing the West has yet devised." The latter may have sounded surprising to those of Rustin's correspondents in America who knew him to be a keen student and passionate advocate of Western democratic procedures and institutions. He may have seen in practice what an Ibo historian had written:

> The communities live under a government of elders, who fix the laws and customs. Every family group has the right of selecting its eldest man, provided he is married, to be its council representative. If the eldest man is an idiot or has a mental deficiency, the immediate successor is selected in his stead. . . . At the head of the council is a president or chief whose decision in cultural matters, laws, and customs as handed down from the ancestors, is final. There are no written laws or customs, but the men are full of memory and follow the trends of their fathers very carefully. The opinion of elders is not neglected in matters affecting the general well-being of the community. Privilege of suggestion (franchise) is given to every young man, once he is married.

But Rustin spent most of his Nigerian visit in Lagos, the capital, where he held talks with Nnamdi Azikiwe, leader of the independence movement. "Zik," as his people called him, was an affluent

Janifer Rustin and Julia Davis Rustin, Bayard's grandparents. (Courtesy Bayard Rustin Estate)

Bessie Rustin LeBon, one of Bayard's "sister"-aunts, at whose home he lived when he first arrived in New York City. (Courtesy Bayard Rustin Estate)

Bayard Rustin (fourth from left, front row), with West Chester High School track team, 1932. (Courtesy Henderson High School, West Chester, Pa.)

Rustin (far right) with Wilberforce
University's vocal ensemble.
(Courtesy Bayard Rustin Estate)

Rustin listening to Dr. Evan Thomas at a
retreat held by the War Resisters League,
Bound Brook, New Jersey, in the summer
of 1942. (Photo Sidney Moritz)

A. J. Muste during the 1940s.
(Courtesy Fellowship of
Reconciliation)

Catherine Raymond, Rustin, and
George Houser, near the FOR
national office on upper Broadway,
Manhattan, in the late 1940s.
(Courtesy George Houser)

Rustin, an unidentified member of CORE, James Farmer, and George Houser at a meeting in Chicago, 1943. (Courtesy George Houser)

Rustin and George Houser sit-in at a restaurant in Toledo, Ohio, during the early 1940s. (Courtesy George Houser)

A contingent of the Journey of Reconciliation just before boarding buses in the nation's capital, 1947. Left to right: Worth Randle, Wallace Nelson, Ernest Bromley, James Peck, Igal Roodenko, Bayard Rustin, James Felmet, George Houser, Andrew Johnson. (Courtesy Swarthmore College Peace Collection)

Rustin conversing with Prime Minister Nehru at a session of the All India Congress Party, 1948. (Courtesy Fellowship of Reconciliation)

Rustin with Muriel Lester in India, 1948. (Courtesy Fellowship of Reconciliation)

Leafletting at an antiwar demonstration in Philadelphia,
circa 1950. (Photo Gamble Brothers)

Rustin conferring with Kwame Nkrumah in Accra,
Ghana, 1952. (Courtesy Fellowship of Reconciliation)

Accompanied at the
harpsichord by Margaret
Davison during an in-
formal recital of classical
and religious songs in
the early 1950s.
(Photo Zeller)

Meeting with Nnamdi Azikiwi, the Nigerian independence leader, while visiting Lagos in 1952. (Courtesy Bayard Rustin Estate)

Rustin marches with Dr. Martin Luther King, Jr., during the Montgomery bus boycott, 1956. (Courtesy Bayard Rustin Estate)

Rustin circa 1965.

An interlude with Malcolm X during a debate at Howard University in October 1961. Student Council president and debate moderator Michael R. Winston is at right. (Photo Moorland-Spingarn Research Center, Howard University Archives)

businessman, with extensive holdings in real estate, farming, banking, and publishing. And his political popularity in West Africa was rivaled only by Nkrumah's. "A few miles outside Lagos," Rustin later wrote of his first meeting with Azikiwe, "there stands a large four-story residence surrounded by well-trimmed lawns and palm trees. On the second floor of this house there is a collection of books, said to be the finest personal library on the west coast of Africa. I was ushered into that spacious library to meet Nnamdi Azikiwe. . . . The telephone rang every few minutes. The calls came from simple people and from men of great power; for the room in which I sat is the nerve center of the Nigerian independence movement." That movement was represented by the National Council of Nigeria and the Cameroons; and on another of Rustin's visits, Azikiwe presented him with a copy of the NCNC's constitution, upon which the constitution of a self-governing Nigeria would be modeled. The document, Rustin noticed, drew strongly from the principles of liberty enshrined in the Constitution of the United States. "I have never met two men more alike than 'Zik' and Nehru," Rustin was to say. "Each is fiery and sensitive. Each has a world view. Each has the love of his people. Each is willing to expend his all for the people. And each respects the ideals of Gandhi."

Soon after returning to New York, in October 1952, Rustin prepared a series of articles for the Baltimore *Afro-American,* a weekly paper that liked to accredit him as a press correspondent. The pieces were not published, but Rustin wrote in one of them:

> The admiration of the West African for the Negro American is astounding. I talked with men and women in every economic and political group, and found many of them measuring their progress by the Afro-American. Dr. Azikiwe put it this way: "In Africa the Negro American is our standard of measurement." A scientist is not "excellent" or "brilliant;" he is a "budding George Washington Carver." A singer of promise is "a Paul Robeson." In part this respect springs from

the fact that the men who have voiced the people's desire for freedom are men who were educated in America. . . .

The education of these men differed greatly from that of the average [African] student in British universities. In America they came face to face with Mr. Jim Crow, and they saw him countered by men skilled in struggling for freedom and justice. Men like Walter White, A. Philip Randolph, and W. E. B. Du Bois inspired and encouraged the college boys, who, now mature men, will set Africa free. They returned home with both the vision and the skill equal to that task.

In Rustin's cordial talks with Azikiwe, the Nigerian leader had asked him to consider returning for a six-month assignment with the national independence movement, helping to train young activists in the techniques of nonviolent resistance. But the Fellowship of Reconciliation was not wholly in favor of the idea. John Nevin Sayre felt that Rustin and the FOR "ought to concentrate on promoting pacifism in the United States, particularly in the South." But taking a different view, a pro-Muste faction in the Fellowship argued that "some special attention to Africa is warranted as part of the FOR's responsibility"; that "there is a real tie-in between our work among Negroes and inter-racial work" in Africa; that Rustin was uniquely qualified to undertake that work in Nigeria. The latter viewpoint prevailed, and the FOR approved Rustin's return to Nigeria, scheduled for June 1953.

There was one condition, however. Because the FOR treasury, always meager, was unable to underwrite Rustin's six-month sojourn, it would be necessary for him to make a speaking tour of the United States, raising the funds for his African mission. In April, Rustin received an offer from Azikiwe that would have made all further fundraising unnecessary. Writing to remind Rustin of "the proposition we discussed while you were here," Azikiwe promised him an important position with *The Pilot,* one in a number of newspapers the wealthy Nigerian owned. "Zik" promised also "to pay your transportation from the United States and back, at the expiration of your term of service," and ended by applauding Rustin's willingness "to spend some time and talent in Africa to aid in its progress."

But it was all too late. By April, an occurrence in California had forced Rustin to cancel his plans for a return to Nigeria; had shattered his twelve-year alliance with the Fellowship of Reconciliation; and had brought his political career to the brink of ruin.

Part III

Chapter 10

Fallen Angel

On January 21, 1953, Rustin arrived in Pasadena, California, on a leg of the speaking tour he had undertaken to raise funds for his planned return to Nigeria; and that evening, under the auspices of the American Association of University Women, he addressed a gathering at the Pasadena Athletic Club.

At the end of his speech, members of the audience milled around him, offering their congratulations on his articulate and informative account of political developments in West Africa. As the congratulatory circle gradually thinned and dispersed, two young men, who had been looking on from a distance, approached him, added their words of praise, and invited him to join them at a party nearby. Perhaps they had heard something about his personal history; perhaps—as Rustin may even have thought—they were simply being friendly to a stranger. In any case, theirs was an invitation Rustin would have been wise to refuse. The next morning's issue of the *Los Angeles Times* reported that "Bayard Rustin, a 40-year-old nationally known Negro lecturer," was arrested on "a morals charge," when the police—investigating a parked car near the Green Hotel (where Rustin was registered)—discovered him in sexual acts with two young men. That afternoon, he was arraigned before Judge Burton Noble; and after pleading guilty, he was sentenced to sixty days in a county jail.

Although Rustin may indeed have been entrapped, as he said later, it was not then a believable claim—for he had employed it on more than one occasion in the past. Recalling the California event many years afterward, David McReynolds, of the War Resisters League, had this to say: "Bayard told me that he was sure he had been framed in Pasadena. But I discounted it, partly because I thought he hated to admit that he was stupid enough to be caught. I once said to Bayard that among the qualities I admired in him was that he was the only person I'd ever met who knew that roughly half of everything he said at certain times was a lie. He laughed, in his roguish manner." If there was a scintilla of truth in Rustin's claim that he had been entrapped in Pasadena, then why were his two male companions arrested and sentenced to sixty days in jail?

A. J. Muste was devastated by the news from California. He deeply loved Rustin's political imagination; he had long known of Rustin's sexual preference; and he had always advised Bayard to indulge that preference only in his purely informal hours—not while he was undertaking an official mission for the Fellowship of Reconciliation. Muste felt that Rustin's conduct in Pasadena had not only strained, severely, their father-son relationship but also damaged, fatally, his political usefulness to the FOR. Phoning Rustin on the West Coast, Muste informed him that he was no longer acceptable as a representative of the Fellowship; if he didn't resign his position as a field secretary, he would be fired.

Soon after, Glenn Smiley, the FOR's representative in California, visited Rustin at the Roncho Honor prison farm. "Bayard was in tears," Smiley recalled. "He was most repentant over the homosexual incident, because of the grief it had brought A. J. Muste. He told me, 'I have talked with A.J., and have, of course, resigned my position with the FOR.' I questioned this decision, but he hastened to add that the decision was irrevocable."

Like Muste, Rustin's colleagues on the FOR staff had never been unaware of his sexual orientation. He hadn't ever concealed it from them, and it hadn't diminished their esteem for him—except, as Smiley said, "when it involved the police." His openness about his gay lifestyle sprang from a feeling that he was entitled to be whatever he was, even at a time in America when homosexuality was prosecuted as a crime. But Muste had reached the end of his patience with Rustin, viewing Bayard's conduct in California as a sign that he was insufficiently sensitive to the cause and public image of the Fellowship.

Rustin later explained that he had been confronting and acknowledging his homosexuality ever since his boyhood. When he first became aware of it, he recalled, he discussed it with his grandmother. "I never said, 'You know, I'm gay.' I told her I enjoyed being with guys when I joined the parties for dating. And she said, 'Is that what you really enjoy?' I said, 'Yes, I think I do.' Her reply was, 'Then I suppose that's what you need to do.' It wasn't an encouragement, but it was a recognition. So I never felt it necessary to do a great deal of pretending. And I never had feelings of guilt."

His high-school classmate Charles Porter never observed signs of Bayard's homosexuality. "I never heard the word 'gay' or 'homo' when I was young," he recalled. "Such people were called 'funny,' and we could never socialize with them, for we were raised in a strict society. Up to about the age of ten, boys and girls had separate parties. Beyond that age, they were encouraged to mix and play games, under supervision. I never saw any reason to be suspicious of Bayard. From my observation, he was just another guy in our friendship circle. My parents would have forbidden us to play together if they had suspected anything questionable about Bayard's sexual behavior."

Rustin's accounts of the early acceptance of his homosexuality differed in various tellings. His pacifist comrade William Sutherland recalled, "Bayard told me that he didn't take it easily when he discovered his homosexuality. He said he went into the woods and beat his legs with sticks, because he was so different. And then, in defiance, he went out and became a great football player and track athlete in his high school. He was going to show 'em." Rustin said on another occasion that he didn't consciously begin cultivating homosexual relationships until 1932, when, at the age of twenty, he entered Wilberforce University: "It was in college that I came to understand that I had a real physical attraction to a young man. He was from California, and in the holidays he used to come with me to my home. I had a bedroom of my own, with twin beds in it. He slept in his bed and I slept in mine. We didn't have a physical relationship, but there was a very intense friendly relationship."

His grandmother Julia—always indulging him to a fault—may have looked leniently at that relationship. But his grandfather was very near scandalized. An upstanding Victorian-Edwardian gentleman—and a pillar of the local African Methodist Episcopal church—Janifer could not easily abide a relationship of that sort under his roof. He protested vehemently to Julia, whose Quaker tolerance in such matters he did not share. But she pleaded successfully for his understanding. "So I never went through the trauma about coming out of the closet," Bayard said later. "And I have always sympathized with those people who, for one reason or another, go through the great trauma I never experienced." But traumas there would be. They were to figure among the reasons he terminated his studies at Wilberforce and, later, at Cheyney State Teachers College.

When Rustin moved to Harlem in 1937, at the age of twenty-five, he soon found himself drawn to an elite society of homosexuals, most of them residing in the well-to-do neighborhood called Sugar Hill. "In the black aristocracy," he remembered, "there was a great number of gay people," and the Harlem community "accepted them as decent and respectable, as long as they made no public display of their gayness." He visited the homes of church organists and choirmasters, ostensibly to probe their expertise in music. "But they could tell what my sexual orientation was, for gay people have a certain telegraph system among themselves." Prominent among the homes he visited was that of Hall

Johnson, leader of the famous Hall Johnson Choir, which had appeared in a number of successful Broadway productions, notably Marc Connelly's *The Green Pastures.* "Johnson's apartment," he recalled, "wasn't necessarily a hangout for gays. It was a hangout for musicians and people in the arts. But if you happened to be gay or lesbian, then you were there too."

In the Harlem of the late 1930s, Rustin also met Alain Locke, the sophisticated aesthete, critic, and academic intellectual, who had been among the major promoters and explicators of the black literary renaissance that flowered between the 1920s and early 1930s. Educated at Harvard and the University of Berlin—as was W. E. B. Du Bois, himself a major influence in the renaissance—Locke taught at Howard University but spent a good deal of his time in Harlem. "I got to know Locke very well," Rustin said in a reminiscence. "He was gay, and he held open house for the literati and for younger writers like Langston Hughes and Richard Wright. I suspect he was more a model for me than anyone else then was. He never felt it necessary to discuss his gayness. He universalized his affection. He carried himself in such a way that the most people could say about him was that they suspected him to be gay." Langston Hughes was "not gay," Rustin remembered. "He was just totally without sex."

Although Rustin did have heterosexual relationships, they were not frequent or intense enough to define him as bisexual. Most women he met or worked with were strongly attracted to him, partly because of his charm and intellect, partly because of his physical appeal. "Bayard was the best lay I ever had," one of them was to say. The civil rights attorney Carl Rachlin recalled a gathering of pacifist students at Cheyney State, in the late spring of 1937, where Rustin "danced with all the women, and they all loved dancing with him." A psychotherapist whom Rustin had reason to consult in the spring of 1953 said later, "Bayard was charming with women, and they loved him. His homosexuality made female admirers angry. They didn't want a charming and good-looking man like him to ignore them. They wanted the flattery of his attention." Gay Morenus first saw Rustin when he came as a speaker to the University of North Carolina in 1947: "Physically, sexually, he was the most compelling man I have ever seen, before or after. He was tall, broad-shouldered, broad-chested, bronze, with sculptured features, strongly marked cheekbones, and very lively speaking eyes. He was thoroughly Negro, and at the same time the uncategorized, unclassifiable essence of manhood." Milton Kramer, one of Rustin's old pacifist friends, recalled, "When I was having sexual problems with my girlfriend, Bayard gave me the wisest advice. I can't imagine how he came to know so much about women. But he did. And he steered me in the right direction with that girl."

Rustin's own sexual affairs were not always so orderly. Kramer added, "He was a very sensual person, an active liver, and his homosexuality was very much a part of who he was. At a point in the early 1940s, he and a boy named Richard were very intense lovers. Richard was a very delicate and sensitive white lad, who came from a wealthy family in Connecticut. His father was an executive in one of the big steel companies. But Richard's affair with Bayard became very stormy, and I think I know why it did. Bayard fooled around a lot. He wasn't a monogamous person. He responded to life wherever it was."

Davis Platt, another of Rustin's young lovers in the 1940s, made a similar discovery, one that ended their relationship. When they first met, Platt had recently been accepted by Harvard and Yale and Columbia. He couldn't quickly decide which of those institutions he wanted to attend. But the decision was made for him when he learned that Bayard Rustin worked at the FOR office, just across from the Columbia campus. He enrolled at Columbia and took an apartment nearby. Platt admired Rustin's elegant speech, his sense of humor, his devotion to nonviolence and pacifism, his fondness for Elizabethan music, his excellent singing of Negro spirituals. "He had broad musical tastes and an absolutely glorious tenor voice," Platt said. They regularly attended concerts in classical and popular music, "and I gave him his first lute after he was sent to prison as a conscientious objector." On visits to his relatives in Paoli, Pennsylvania, Platt drove over to West Chester, not far away, with gifts and flowers for Rustin's grandparents.

"Bayard was a mentor to me in many ways," Platt would remember. "He was surely more experienced in sex than I was. He had even slept with women, far more successfully than I had up to that time. He had no shame at all about being gay, and that was very strengthening to me. Being gay was a terrible secret I had to keep from anybody I knew and respected. But Bayard felt he had a right to be who and what he was. The time came, however, when I had to ask Bayard to leave my apartment. He was sleeping around, and I just didn't feel I could deal with that. There is no question he was promiscuous. He was attractive to an awful lot of people, black and white."

Few activists in the New York pacifist movement were uncomfortable with the bold flaunting of his sexuality. One of them, Rascha Hughes, recalled, "During the late 1940s, a married couple in our movement weren't getting along so well. Bayard saw that opening and couldn't resist exploiting it. In a short time, the marriage was completely destroyed. The husband, a lovely man who played the viola, said to me after he got involved with Bayard, 'You know, I've never been so happy.' He was like a child who had suddenly discovered something new about himself. But Bayard wasn't discovering anything new about himself. He was like a predator."

Before A. J. Muste relieved Rustin of his position with the FOR, he had long been patient with reports of Bayard's sexual conduct. James Farmer recalled that mothers in different parts of the country wrote to Muste, "complaining that Bayard had led their sons astray." According to John Swomley, "Other episodes were reported to us," after which " A. J. and I had a discussion with Bayard wherein we indicated that if there was another occasion involving substantial publicity, we would have serious doubts about his remaining on the staff."

But James Farmer spoke up on Rustin's behalf, despite their ambivalent and competitive relationship. He told Muste and Swomley that Bayard was entitled to his sexual preference, whether or not he worked for the Fellowship. Muste didn't agree entirely. While conceding that Rustin's private life was his own, he argued that the FOR was

itself entitled to censure his conduct when it drew embarrassing publicity to the work he did for the Fellowship. It was imperative, Muste
emphasized, that Rustin restrain his sexual behavior whenever or wherever he appeared as a representative of the FOR. Surely that wasn't an
unreasonable demand. "Muste was one of the wisest persons I ever
knew," Milton Kramer said. "He had a deep understanding of moral
and political problems. Valuing Bayard's political abilities and also loving him like a son, Muste feared losing Bayard's services but also
wanted to see him grow as a whole human being. He was ready to do
what was right for the Fellowship and what was right for Bayard. After
they had a talk about the problem of sexual behavior, Bayard promised
Muste that he would control himself in the future." But the power of
impulse or the force of habit defeated the best intentions of his pledge,
for the problem did not disappear.

In the summer of 1944, while serving his imprisonment as a conscientious objector, Rustin was placed in solitary confinement on a
charge of sexual misconduct. He claimed that he had been set up by
guards who wished to curtail his militant political activities in jail.
There may have been some truth to his claim. But entrapped or not, he
appears to have been guilty as charged. Unhappy with the report that
came to him in New York, Muste visited Ashland for a talk with
Rustin. But he wasn't satisfied with the explanation he heard, and on
his return to New York he wrote to Bayard:

*During the . . . conversation I had with you at Ashland . . .
you spent a couple of hours detailing "evidence" that the charges
against you were a frame-up, for which there was absolutely no
basis. . . . Yet a couple of hours later you admitted guilt as to
certain charges.*

*Now it seems to me that the first thing you have to do as a
sensible human being, not to say a pacifist, is to try to understand
how the administrators involved must think of you. You have been
guilty of gross misconduct, specially reprehensible in a person making
the claims to leadership and—in a sense—moral superiority. . . .*

Furthermore, you had deceived everybody, including your own comrades and most devoted friends.

In characteristic remembrance of his personal and political admiration for Rustin, Muste added: "It is not easy to write about these things and be sure that one's true and full meaning is conveyed—and that my love for you and hope in you shines through."

More than a week after hearing from Muste, Rustin wrote to Davis Platt: "I sense that I have betrayed you and the things for which we stand. I offer no defense. I accept your and A. J.'s alternative as the only one. There is one and only one choice for me, for I must do the work that fits my hands. . . . It is not going to be easy to overcome the causes or results of this situation, but I am pledged to pull through." Pulling through was to be more difficult than Rustin feared it would be. He wrote to Platt a few months later: "I have not seen completely to the bottom of the problems of my life. . . . The single-sex life here is no arena in which to make a clear judgment." Not until the 1970s, during the last twelve years or so of his life—when he settled permanently with Walter Naegle—did he make a firm decision about controlling his gay lifestyle. In 1952, when he wrote to a student at the Putney School, in Vermont, he may have been thinking not only about the tests of political commitment but also about a difficult side of his personal history. "To hold a philosophy of nonviolence in a time of crisis," he said, "depends to a large extent on an inner discipline, and one may think he has it when he has not. It is very easy for us to make, in a calm intellectual atmosphere, a judgment as to how we would behave, only to discover that in a time of emotional crisis we have not enough emotional strength to carry through. And, in a sense, all of us face this problem."

Now, in January 1953, with his arrest and imprisonment in California, had come the most publicized, embarrassing, and destructive episode in his sexual history. Perhaps its saddest aspect was that it finally exhausted A. J. Muste's paternal faith in Rustin. John Swomley wrote to him: "I must tell you what a real blow this has been to A. J. I don't think I have seen him looking so haggard and upset before. . . . You must know that he has to a very real degree looked upon you as an adopted son." Swomley added: "All of us deeply love you . . . and want to assure you of our abiding concern and care." Reflecting the high regard of most peace activists, David McReynolds, of the War Resisters League, also wrote to Rustin in his West Coast jail: "I'm with you all the way. My confidence in you is unshaken. No paragon is unsoiled. . . . I do not come bringing this letter as an act of Christian charity toward a fallen brother, for I'm not that kind of Christian, and besides, brother, I'm fallen myself."

But Rustin was particularly moved by the letter from Swomley, for they hadn't always worked smoothly together. As Muste's chief assistant, Swomley was empowered to supervise all the FOR field secretaries; and Bayard Rustin often balked at taking orders from anyone but A. J. Muste. But now, from prison, Rustin replied lengthily and conciliatingly to John Swomley. In what was probably the humblest letter of his life, he wrote:

> *In some ways, your letter meant more to me than many of the others I received—for it reveals that more sensitive side of you that you should reveal more often. . . . Thank you for your hope and faith. . . . I was sorry to have to resign from the FOR, because in the last years I had begun to feel that the gulf . . . between us was just about bridged. You may not realize it . . . but I was really trying to work more in the spirit of team work. In the past, this has not been easy for me; for I have been very self-centered and filled with pride.*
>
> *But I know that, in God's way of turning ugliness and personal defeat to triumph, I have gone deeper in the past six weeks than ever before, and I feel that I have at last seen the real problem. It has been pride—self.*
>
> *In most of the dramatic ways, the so-called big ways, I was prepared to give all. I would, I believe, have died rather than join the army. But in the small and really primary ways, I was as selfish as a child. I am sure that in a way I must have known this. Now I*

feel *it, and know that pride must be overcome.*

No matter where I work in the future, where I live and with whom I am, I have pledged before God that I will live more nonviolently in the small ways that support the big ones, if they are to be real.

While sex is a very real problem, and while it has colored my personality, I now see that it has never been my basic problem.

I know now that for me sex must be sublimated, if I am to live with myself and in this world longer. For it would be better to be dead than to do worse than those I have denounced from the platform as murderers. Violence is not so bad as violence and hypocrisy. . . .

So no matter where I am in the future, John, I shall always feel a certain closeness to you—a closeness that has grown from strife reconciled. When you pray, think of me. For in the new life, I shall need more prayer and love than before. I trust you will not dismiss this letter as coming from the Bayard you have known, for God's mercy has permitted something new to be added. . . .

Special affection to A. J. who does not realize that his love has kept me from going lower than I have, and whose everlasting faith has accompanied me through hell.

It was reminiscent of Oscar Wilde, who, in a time of his crisis, had remarked that there's no higher moment than when a man kneels and confesses the sins of his life.

When Rustin returned to New York from California, in March, one of his first meetings was with A. J. Muste. By then Muste may or may not have seen the moving confessional Bayard had written to John Swomley; in any case, it didn't matter. Muste was no more forgiving now than he had been in January, when he demanded Rustin's resignation—an adamancy that, to some, seemed at odds with the name and spirit of the religious-pacifist organisation Muste led. John Muste, A. J.'s son, was to recall that 1953 meeting with Rustin:

"My father had reluctantly told the family about Bayard's trouble on the West Coast. So it was not a surprise when he came home early one afternoon and told me and my mother that Bayard would be coming to see him, and that while we could say hello to Bayard if we wished, their conversation would be private.

"Bayard was one of my mother's favorites among A. J.'s group of colleagues. On one occasion, when she was ill, Bayard and Bill Sutherland transported a harpsichord to our fifth-floor apartment; and Bayard sang and played an impromptu concert for her. Because of her fondness for Bayard, my mother had been genuinely shocked at the apparently incontrovertible evidence of his sexual preference, and she had trouble deciding whether to say anything to him. But she did, when Bayard came to our home that March; and I also spoke with him very briefly, before he and A. J. retreated to a separate room.

"Later that evening, over dinner, my father told us about their talk. It was clear, he said, that Bayard could no longer represent the FOR with youth groups. But he had advised Bayard to seek treatment for his 'problem.' At that time, the 'enlightened' view was that homosexuality was a curable condition, susceptible to psychotherapy. Bayard agreed to look for treatment."

During their talk, Muste had held out one last hope to Rustin. Could he, finally and conscientiously, promise that there would be no future episode like the one that had landed him in trouble on the West Coast? Rustin replied that being human—and the future being so unpredictable—he could not, in honesty, make so firm a promise. He had made such a promise in the past and had been unable to keep it. Little was left to be said on the matter. His tenure with the Fellowship of Reconciliation was over.

His brilliant future in the organization was aborted as well. "Rustin had been thought of as Muste's successor," his former comrade Larry Gara said. "But of course, all of that was smashed by his arrest in California." David McReynolds felt, "His sexual life was something he had to follow, it was part of his nature. However, he did a lot of existential acting out, all of which put the Fellowship at risk. But his was a great loss to the FOR. Not only was he the Fellowship's most popular lecturer; he was also a genius at tactical matters. His fine sense of tactical reality was something A. J. Muste did not have. He had a gift for involving ordinary people in political action. For instance, it was Bayard who first gave me a true understanding of nonviolence. He brought to the Gandhian principle a dialectic which said that one ought to absorb suffering in order to resolve conflict; that conflict was inevitable; that the role of pacifists was to confront it creatively. Bayard was being groomed by the Fellowship to become an America Gandhi. The position was cut out for him. Unfortunately, it was all destroyed by the incident in California."

Catharine Raymond, who worked at the Fellowship's national office, added, "Bayard's abilities were apparently boundless, although we did wish he had more self-discipline. In other words, he was an angel, but we wanted him to be an archangel."

Chapter 11

Beginning Again

Not long after leaving the Fellowship, Rustin complained that A. J. Muste and the FOR had cut him off, penniless. This was not true in one sense, though it may have been true in another. While he was still in prison, the Fellowship's executive committee had met and resolved to do "all we can to help Bayard in the various ways that may be required." And records of the organization did show that from January to May 1953, he received checks totaling $830.20. The FOR, John Smiley said, "was always living on the financial edge, all of us lived on subsistence pay." Yet "it would have been completely out of character for A. J., who had looked upon Bayard as a son, to have sent him penniless into the streets." The main point of Rustin's complaint may therefore have been that after twelve years of service to the Fellowship, he was deserving of substantial severance pay.

He had other reasons as well to find Muste wanting in generosity. When, at the end of March 1953, Rustin began consulting Dr. A., a young psychoanalyst on Park Avenue, Muste wrote to the therapist:

> *As I understand it, the sum of $15 per session has been*
> *mentioned. I suppose there is virtually no way of answering the*

*question, how long the analysis will take. However, if there is any
approximate figure that you can give . . . it would obviously help us
in determining for how long a period we {at the FOR} may need to
undertake some financial obligation.*

*Secondly . . . I thought it might be appropriate for me to
mention . . . that the salary which Bayard has been paid as a staff
member of the FOR is a pretty modest one. When taxes are deducted,
it amounted to about $2800 a year. Out of this, he has paid for
several years, and will continue to pay for several years more,
approximately $500 annually to repay a loan . . . which one of our
members made to him in order that he might be able to buy a small
home for his grandmother in West Chester. . . .*

*As you know, he is now no longer on the staff of the FOR. . . .
He should be able to get work, though it may not prove too easy to get
satisfactory employment, and the chances of his being able to make a
substantial salary are certainly very slight. . . .*

*I want to make it very clear . . . that we are well aware of the
fact that the $15 sum is by no means a high one from a professional
point of view {there were to be two sessions a week}; and that it will
make no difference in our determination to do whatever is necessary to
enable Bayard to meet his obligations, if he is not in a financial
position to meet them promptly himself.*

But Rustin's psychiatric sessions were scarcely under way when
Muste wrote again to Dr. A., virtually withdrawing his original offer.
Surprised and annoyed, the doctor replied, "The tone of your letter suggests simply that you have changed your mind. Couching that change
of mind in terms like 'we are strongly of the opinion that you would
consider it very bad for us to provide' [financial assistance] creates a situation of basic dishonesty. . . . The necessity for him [Rustin] to borrow
cannot be changed. . . . Bayard cannot have a high esteem of your relia-
bility or honesty in the future."

The annoyance Dr. A. then felt was still in his voice thirty-five
years later, when he explained: "Coming back to New York, after his

traumatic experience in California, Bayard was without a job, and he was ashamed about the jail sentence he had served. It wasn't a noble sentence. It wasn't like going to jail as a conscientious objector, as he had done in World War II, or as prominent pacifists like Roger Baldwin and Evan Thomas had done in World War I. Bayard was a very depressed person when I began treating him, and I hoped he could rely heavily on Muste's moral support.

"Through all of Rustin's misery, I appreciated who he was and came to admire him; for I myself came from parents with a background in progressive politics. Then there developed the rotten business of Muste offering to pay for Rustin's treatment and later deciding that he wouldn't. It was as if he and certain officers in the FOR had said, 'Well, Bayard can get a job helping to move furniture.' I think they were saying, in effect, 'He's male and he's black. So why can't he go out and shine shoes?' That's the way it sounded to me. And in fact, Bayard did have to go out and do a few menial jobs, in order to stay alive. But he did some jobs that were artistic as well. He began repairing other people's harpsichords and musical instruments. Still, there came a time when he ran out of money, and I had to pull strings to keep him in therapy. Because I was also an attending psychiatrist at Roosevelt Hospital, I transferred him to Roosevelt, where he could become a clinic patient. So he continued his treatment with me, without having to pay. And I eventually got him over his depression.

"At the beginning, his warm feeling for A. J. Muste was a centerpiece of the therapeutic sessions we had. He wanted very much to present Muste as a kind and fatherly man. But as we continued working together, I got him to recognize that if such a person was a friend and father, then who needs enemies? I helped him to recognize that Muste wasn't quite the saint that he, Rustin, wanted to see—that in the end, Muste didn't really give a damn about him. Bayard and I were both uneasy about dredging up those deep feelings. And when I saw him a while later, he told me that although he had come to acknowledge those feelings, he was still uncomfortable with them. I let him know that it was okay for him to feel uncomfortable."

Rustin eventually got over his uncomfortable feelings. And Dr. A. was correct in predicting that Bayard would come to lose his sense of Muste's paternal solicitude for him. In his predicament, during the early months of 1953, Rustin was to gain from socialist and secular peace leaders the faithful moral support that Muste and the religious Fellowship of Reconciliation had withheld from him. It caused him to wonder about the Christian values of the organization he had served— the values of forgiveness and reconciliation. He was never to forget that Muste abandoned him in the worst crisis of his personal life. They were to work together again, within other peace organizations, but always under the brooding cloud of Rustin's memory. William Sutherland recalled in the 1980s, "Bayard and I were in Zimbabwe, observing the elections. We had breakfast together one morning. He cried when he remembered how Muste had abandoned him in 1953. He said he went hungry. He said he would never again allow himself to be in such a situation." "Bayard was not ashamed of his homosexuality," Tom Kahn, his close friend and intellectual aide, would recall, "but was quite outfront about it. He had a strong ego, so that he was willing to put himself out on the line. A part of him said, 'I'm also a child of God. I also have a soul and a personality made in the image of God.' That side of him could not accept Muste's condemnation. Therefore, while he later forgave Muste's action against him, he always remembered it. Something would occur to remind him of Muste's abandonment, and he would speak out with considerable bitterness."

For some time before his arrest in California, Rustin had broken up with Davis Platt. He had taken a small apartment at 217 Mott Street, in downtown Manhattan, neighboring "Little Italy." The building at 217 housed a veritable commune of artists, radical pacifists, former conscientious objectors, activists in the black and white civil rights movement (mainly the Congress of Racial Equality). Rustin's neighbors and friends included Margaret Davison, an amateur pianist and harpsichordist; her husband, Robert, a doctoral student at New York University; Robert Currier, a violinist with the New York Philharmonic;

Currier's wife, Ruth, a dancer with the José Limon company; Rascha Hughes, a Japanese American activist in the Fellowship of Reconciliation; James Robinson, an officer of CORE and a professor of English; his wife, Helen, an aspiring mezzo-soprano; Ralph DiGia and Igal Roodenko, pacifist radicals in the War Resisters League; Sally Sullivan, a student at the New School for Social Research; and her husband, Tom, who worked for the Liberal Party in New York. They were a close-knit group, of which Rustin may have been the only black member.

William Sutherland, who lived over on the Lower East Side, often came to visit his pacifist friends. "It was a time," he recalled, "when Bayard, especially before his trouble on the West Coast, was at his most lively and joyful; when he was always singing and playing the lute; when his youthful talents and ambitions found their most creative expression." Margaret and Robert Davison, probably Rustin's closet friends in the Mott Street group, often invited him to dinner. Whenever they visited their country home on Long Island, they allowed him the freedom of their apartment, with its well-stocked refrigerator and wine cabinet; and on their return they almost always found that Rustin had cooked a meal for them and left it on the stove. At her harpsichord, Margaret enjoyed accompanying Bayard's singing of spirituals, madrigals, and operatic arias. For decades after, she was to treasure an antique music stand Rustin gave her in the early 1950s.

During the months of joblessness that followed his expulsion from the FOR, Rustin engaged in one of his main hobbies—collecting discarded antique furniture and musical instruments. Some of these he repaired and kept for his own use; others he sold to help support himself. He once came upon an old piano on a side street of New Orleans; had it renovated by a firm in Boston; and later sold it to a wealthy collector for three thousand dollars. "Bayard's apartment had the look of a museum," Ralph DiGia said. "He picked up a lot of his antiques off sidewalks in Greenwich Village, particularly where old Italian families were throwing out their fine pieces of European furniture. Such families, now wanting a more American look to their apartments, were going in heavily for modern furnishings. But Bayard, with a good eye for art and antiques—and their future value—grabbed up much of the old stuff. Many years later, he ended up with one of the best private collections of antiques in New York."

DiGia had known Rustin since the mid-1940s, when they were jailed as conscientious objectors. But it was chiefly after Rustin moved to 217 Mott Street that DiGia came to recognize him as "a great guy," with a fine mind and impressive political skills. Those skills and abilities had first caught DiGia's attention—the attention as well of his colleagues in the War Resisters League—when Rustin and George Houser led the 1947 Journey of Reconciliation to the South. They were to be further impressed by Rustin's collaboration with A. Philip Randolph in the 1947–48 campaign against Jim Crow in the military.

Ralph DiGia and the War Resisters League had also been looking admiringly and enviously at Rustin's effective work for the Fellowship of Reconciliation: his eloquent national lectures; his recruiting of an idealistic young membership; his antiwar activism; his missions to India and West Africa. The War Resisters League had no staff person of Rustin's versatility: black, pacifist, socialist, anticolonialist, interracial in values, nonviolent in convictions. "Bayard made me feel that being white in no way compromised my relationship with a radical pacifist struggle on behalf of blacks," Sally Sullivan recalled. "He never made me feel that I was white; only that I was very important to the social movement. He had an extraordinary way of pulling people into political action." The WRL had long wanted such a man in the leadership of its organization.

While working for the Fellowship, Rustin, along with A. J. Muste, had sat on the national council of the secular War Resisters League; and when he lost his position with the FOR, he had offered to withdraw from the WRL's advisory council. But a majority in that body refused to accept his resignation, for they now saw the chance they had long been awaiting: to recruit him into the activist leadership of the League. "Bayard was then in urgent need of money," Igal Roodenko said later. "He had applied for a job packing boxes and was told he was overqualified. We responded to his plight with a predatory organizational greed. We said, 'We can get him now,' for we had always begrudged his outstanding work for the Fellowship."

At a meeting in the Greenwich Village apartment of Jessie Wallace Hughan, cofounder of the WRL, Rustin's supporters on the national council drafted a statement of their intention to work with him "in our common cause of war resistance." And in the summer of 1953, Rustin was appointed executive secretary—chief program officer—of the War Resisters League. According to Roy Finch, a leader of the executive committee, "Bayard was the most valuable man in the whole pacifist movement. We were lucky to have him working for us. He had style, something that was sadly lacking in the rather grubby world of the peace movement. Helping to get him into the WRL was one of the things in my life I was most proud of, and it was one of the best things that happened to the War Resisters League." Some years later, a deep ideological rift was to develop between David Dellinger and Rustin. But in the 1950s, Dellinger, who supported Bayard's appointment, considered him to be "the most creative nonviolent activist" of their generation, "truly inventive, courageous, and brilliant."

Those were views that A. J. Muste had once shared. Perhaps he still did, despite his disillusionment with Rustin's conduct of his personal life. At all events, Muste abruptly ended his association with the WRL, loath to maintain an alliance with any group that would elevate Rustin to a position of leadership. It was one of the unlovelier episodes in Muste's estrangement from Rustin. Ralph DiGia called it "one of the saddest things in Bayard's life."

Abraham Kaufman, a former leader of the War Resisters League, was surprised—yet also not so surprised—by the harshness of Muste's turn against Rustin. "I greatly admired A. J. in many ways," Kaufman said later, "and I never knew him to act vindictively. But I formed the impression that he was convinced that Bayard could not control his sexual needs and stay out of trouble. Furthermore, the Fellowship of Reconciliation, to which 'respectability' meant a great deal, could not afford the publicity of another event [like Rustin's arrest in California]. This area of conduct mattered less to the WRL. The [secular] WRL, younger than the religious FOR, had a history of greater flexibility and was readier to risk its public image. I saw Bayard as a trustworthy comrade and friend. I did not think of his homosexual preference. Hiring him gave the WRL an excellent organizer and thinker."

Muste later reconsidered his decision. After retiring from his leadership of the FOR, late in 1953, he resumed his association with the WRL; and this entailed a renewal of his collaboration with Rustin—though with none of the mutual personal warmth that marked their earlier relationship. "Muste was one of those rare people who continued to grow as he got older," David McReynolds said. "He had started out as a very devout minister of religion, and he had gone through a later period of Marxist-Leninist conviction. Yet he had remained a total puritan. He had some growing up to do, which he did. Despite his Marxist-Leninist phase, he had never been a bohemian, had never been open-minded about sexual orientation."

At any rate, it was the War Resisters League that rescued Rustin from what had looked like political oblivion. He was to be the WRL's executive secretary for twelve years, and during that period he reenergized the organization, as it had resuscitated him. In strengthening its pacifist programs, he allied it more closely than it had been to the international crusade against nuclear weapons; bolstered its relationship with the civil rights movement in America; and associated it with freedom struggles on the African continent. A roving troubleshooter, he revisited Africa and established ties with the movements of Kenneth Kaunda in Zambia and Julius Nyerere in Tanzania. David McReynolds remembered, "When one social problem or another came to his attention, he would always say to me, 'Why don't we take this on?' And he would help me to think through strategy—how to involve those who, like myself, were not very brave; how to organize levels of action. So he left a stamp on me as well." But McReynolds, who later became the WRL's executive secretary, was careful to add, "Of course, you can't separate A. J. Muste from the work Bayard did for the War Resisters

League. For instance, the links to Africa were forged jointly by Rustin and Muste."

Rustin had also been deeply hurt by the coolness of the American Friends Service Committee after his arrest. The AFSC, for which he had done excellent work, now seemed more than reluctant to acknowledge him, even after his rehabilitation in the War Resisters League.

In the spring of 1954, the AFSC assigned Stephen Cary, a staff officer, to convene a working group of intellectuals. They were to discuss and shape a pacifist stance toward the nuclear arms race and the threat of a Soviet-American confrontation. Cary selected the most thoughtful group of pacifist intellectuals he could imagine. Only Bayard Rustin was not endorsed. "People at the AFSC urged me to write Bayard off the list," Cary reported later. "They were embarrassed by his homosexuality, which became public knowledge after the matter in California. But I resisted. I told them I didn't give a damn what Bayard was. I had known him in the past. We had attended Quaker conferences in England, where Bayard was the most brilliant of the American delegates. I wasn't going to write him off my list. I wasn't going to put him on the shelf. To me, Bayard was a marvelous human being. He stood out for the great clarity of his thought and speech, his astonishing grasp of issues, the depth of his intellectual analyses of political problems."

That summer, Cary's group assembled at Haverford College for a week-long conference, at the end of which they produced a seventy-page document, later published as *Speak Truth to Power*. The historian Lawrence Wittner called it "the most sophisticated and widely read of the Quaker policy analyses." In *The Progressive* magazine, where it first appeared, Robert Pickus, one of its coauthors, explained,

> *Speak Truth to Power* marks the first attempt . . . to present a distinctively pacifist analysis. It presents a reasoned case for the unqualified rejection of reliance on military power; not in the future, after world law and agreements on universal disarmament are achieved, but *now*. It was written in the belief that

pacifist insights and . . . the actions which spring from them constitute the essential moral and political acts of our time.

When, in 1955, the document appeared in *The Progressive,* it sparked one of the livelier political debates of that era, notably among public intellectuals like Robert M. Hutchens, Lewis Mumford, Gordon Allport, Erich Fromm, Norbert Weiner, Hans J. Morgenthau, George Kennan, Dwight Macdonald, Karl Menninger, Reinhold Niebuhr, and Norman Thomas. Their differing statements appeared in *The Progressive* that year.

But what most engaged Stephen Cary was that none of the intellectuals he recruited to his working group made a more creative contribution to the drafting of *Speak Truth to Power* than Bayard Rustin did; and that was a vindication of his refusal to heed the objections the American Friends Service Committee had made to Rustin's inclusion in the group. Cary recalled, a few decades later:

"It was a great week that we all had at Haverford. We were talking about the relevance of pacifism in the modern world, trying to break new ground. And there developed in our gathering two sharply different viewpoints about how we might deal with the Soviet Union. On the one hand, Robert Pickus took the position that we *had* to see the Soviet Union as a dangerous power, the focus of evil. On the other hand, Milton Mayer argued that the devil is in all of us, that the devil is a traveling man, here one day, there the next. Mayer was saying that we would be wrong to regard the Soviet Union as the only embodiment of political evil in the world. It was a titanic clash, because Pickus and Mayer were brilliant advocates. They would argue back and forth about Plato and Aristotle and about every important philosopher since the beginning of time. Theirs was a marvelous exercise in intellectual pedantry, and guys like me simply couldn't keep up with them.

"There were only two members of our group who could stay with the brilliance of Pickus and Mayer. One was A. J. Muste. The other was Bayard Rustin. But Bayard was the key person. Not only could he argue with Pickus and Mayer on their own terms; he could also quote

Aristotle and John Locke as easily as they did. So he became the great reconciler among us. When Pickus and Mayer were floating up into intellectual space, Rustin brought them back to the ground and supplied them with the ideas they needed to compose their differences. A. J. Muste could have played such a role, but it was Bayard who did, day after day, sometimes until two or three in the morning. Without him, *Speak Truth to Power* could never have been written. That was one of the richest weeks of my career."

When the discussion appeared as a booklet, Rustin was not listed among the coauthors. "Bayard reminded us of his arrest on the West Coast," Cary said, "and urged that his name not be included among the writers of the document. He said, 'It will be a valuable publication, and my name on it right now will be hurtful to circulation.' I said, 'Bayard, you know this thing couldn't have been written without you.' But I couldn't persuade him to change his mind. Before he left Haverford, he sang two beautiful spirituals to us: 'Nobody Knows the Trouble I've Seen' and 'There Is a Balm in Gilead.' The effect was overwhelming. And then he said, 'Gentlemen, I'm at peace. It's been a wonderful week. Just leave my name off.' Especially after that week, I was never able to assign a moral dimension to people's sexuality. Bayard gave me a sense, a meaning, of diversity and community that I have always treasured."

In 1954, Rustin renewed his acquaintance with a young man he had met some years earlier at a Quaker academy in upstate New York. Frank (as we shall call him) was then reading for a graduate degree in English at Columbia, where he would soon be appointed an assistant dean. "Bayard had still not fully recovered from his depression of 1953," Frank recalled. "He seemed very down and vulnerable, and we fell in love. There was then a lot of casual love in the homosexual lifestyle, promiscuity and all, with no emotional depth. But Bayard recognized that I was a high-quality type, and our relationship became quite steady and deep." On an early visit to Rustin's apartment on Mott Street, Frank was generally disappointed by what he saw. Beyond the impressive pieces of antique furniture Rustin had been collecting, the apartment looked to him like "a rat hole." "I felt strongly moved to find a decent place for both of us to live in."

With the help of Robert Gilmore—one of Rustin's Quaker friends in Manhattan—Frank found such a place on West 107th Street, between Broadway and Amsterdam Avenue. They "colonized" the building, Rustin liked to say, referring to the fact that he was the only black tenant; they were probably the only gay couple as well. Rustin was not, of course, the legal tenant. If he, with his sparkling British accent, had telephoned to express an interest in taking the apartment, he would have been invited to come on up and look it over; but when he appeared, in all his blackness, he would have been told that the place had just been let to someone else. The legal tenant *was* Frank; and not surprisingly, the building superintendent soon began objecting vehemently to Rustin's presence in the apartment. Frank argued resolutely, however, that nothing in his lease barred him from having a roommate of his choice. "The superintendent didn't know that all the exquisite and valuable old furniture in the apartment belonged to Bayard," he said later. "He thought it all belonged to me. So he relented. He thought I was rich and therefore a tenant well worth keeping."

Describing aspects of their life on the Upper West Side, Frank added, "Bayard's aesthetics were of a very high level. He had exquisite taste. Had he been rich, there would have been nothing vulgar or flamboyant or ostentatious about his home. It would have been in superb taste. He had a wide-ranging interest in antiques and a specific interest in old musical instruments. In our apartment there was a fine seventeenth-century harpsichord, which he had restored and which he played occasionally. But he almost never practiced. He just sat down and played beautifully, getting along on his tremendous natural talent. He was good at cooking, and we usually ate off pewter plates. He knew every detail of aristocratic dress and clothing, aristocratic speech, aristocratic manners. He knew the whole mystique of an aristocratic dinner party.

"Our relationship ended in 1958, when I walked out on Bayard and got married. I had met a woman at Columbia; and as we got closer, I came to recognize that I wanted her to be the mother of my children. The rejection was emotionally devastating to Bayard. I don't think he quickly recovered after I broke the news to him."

Living at the intersection of Broadway and 106th Street, near the apartment Rustin shared with his companion, was a wealthy attorney and political intellectual named Stanley Levison. Bayard and his friend were often invited over for social evenings at Levison's apartment. Rustin and Levison had apparently known each other for some time; both were to become close advisers to Dr. Martin Luther King, Jr.

In its later campaign to discredit King and the black civil rights movement, the FBI alleged that Stanley Levison had an affiliation with the communist movement. Perhaps Bayard had first met Levison in the late 1930s, when Rustin was a member of the Young Communist League at City College. If so, Rustin had no memory of such a meeting. Furthermore, he stated after the FBI allegation, he saw nothing in Stanley Levison's work with Dr. King to suggest that Stanley was in the service of the communist cause. If you don't waddle like a duck, Rustin said, then you're not a duck. His earlier life among communists would have qualified him to recognize whether Levison waddled like a left-winger in Dr. King's movement—unless, out of a sense of honor, he was suppressing what he recognized. But Rachelle Horowitz, who began working with Rustin in the late 1950s and became one of his key aides in the civil rights struggle, would always continue to believe that Levison, whom she observed closely, had links with the communist movement.

"Bayard and I were frequent guests in Levison's apartment," Rustin's roommate on West 107th Street recalled. "We were always being invited there. Bayard seems to have met Stanley some time in the past, but under what circumstances I cannot be sure. Bayard knew an endless number of people. At times he told me about their backgrounds, at other times he didn't. However, I couldn't help forming the impression, however fugitive, that he and Levison were old acquaintances.

"But all that aside, during my relationship with Bayard I formed the much stronger impression that he was a most unusual political being: deeply committed to the triumvirate of democratic social reform, nonviolence, and racial justice. His message was that you couldn't have one without the other two. In whatever movement he worked, he saw one or another of that triumvirate as an element of his total commitment to a social method. And that was part of why I admired him so greatly."

Part IV

Chapter 12

Mission to Montgomery

On December 1, 1955, the police in Montgomery, Alabama, arrested Rosa Parks, a highly respected member of the black community, for her refusal to move to the back of a bus. Four days later, the Montgomery Improvement Association, which may have selected Parks for the heroic role she played, launched its historic boycott of all the city's buses. Leaders of the MIA—notably E. D. Nixon, a veteran organizer in the Brotherhood of Sleeping Car Porters—could not have realized that they were inaugurating a decade of black mass protest in America. Nor could they have guessed that they were embarking upon a long struggle, that what they had planned as a one- or two-day boycott would drag on for more than a year, despite the intervention of the Reverend Dr. Martin Luther King, Jr.

The energy that sustained the boycott through to its triumphant ending was King's adoption (unsurely and imperfectly at first) of nonviolent direct action. This entailed the spirit and techniques of Gandhian resistance that had been pioneered in the United States (during the early and mid 1940s) by organizations like the Fellowship of Reconciliation and the Congress of Racial Equality, as well as by peace and civil rights activists like A. J. Muste, A. Philip Randolph, George

Houser, James Farmer, and Bayard Rustin. When, late in December, Farmer learned of the principled and tenacious struggle in Montgomery, which Dr. King had emerged to lead, he meditated to himself: "The nonviolent movement in America is airborne. Why am I not more exuberant? Is it because it is not I who leads it? Is there a green-eyed monster peering through my eyes? I had labored a decade and a half in the vineyards of nonviolence. Now, out of nowhere, someone comes and harvests the grapes and drinks the wine." That someone was, of course, Dr. King.

King, then aged twenty-six, was an improbable leader of the mass movement in Montgomery. Recently graduated from Boston University's School of Religion, he was a surprisingly accomplished and inspiring preacher at Montgomery's Dexter Avenue Baptist Church, his first ministerial appointment. However, he had no experience in public leadership and no aspirations of that kind. But he had been chosen. As Bayard Rustin said later, a divine hand had been laid on him.

Among those who recognized the divine hand—those who had heard King's powerful sermons at the Dexter Avenue church—was E. D. Nixon. At an early stage of the bus boycott, Nixon and others approached the young minister and invited him to assume leadership of their movement. King wasn't strongly drawn to the idea. He didn't see that as what his religious calling was about. But they bullied him, going so far as to say that if he didn't accept their invitation he would be seen as a coward. He was the only black preacher in Montgomery to whom they could turn, the only one whose pulpit did not seem to be compromised by sub rosa understandings with the white power structure. King gave in and agreed to lead the bus boycott movement. The white Montgomery opposition then turned on him. On January 26, 1956, he was arrested and later convicted for driving his automobile at thirty-five miles an hour in a twenty-five-mile-per-hour zone. On January 30, his house was bombed. And on February 1, a bomb was tossed into the residence of E. D. Nixon.

All of this presented King and the boycott movement with a severe moral test. Should they absorb all that violence, in order to accomplish their objective, or should they retaliate in kind? King, who had read Gandhi at Boston University, understood some of the spiritual restraints that were necessary. But he also knew that while most of his followers in Montgomery were Christian in their values, they had little or no experience in absorbing violence without retaliation, had never been called upon to adopt the Gandhian principle of resistance. Even he was not yet fully committed to the demands of Gandhian methodology.

In February 1956, Bayard Rustin, at the War Resisters League, received a telegram from Lillian Smith—the white liberal southern novelist, author of the nationally acclaimed *Strange Fruit*—urging him to go to Montgomery as an adviser to Dr. King. She also wrote to King, telling him that Rustin was one of the few outsiders from the North she would trust to work with the emerging black movement in the South. A former board member of the Fellowship of Reconciliation, Smith, having met Rustin in the 1940s and been impressed with his knowledge of Gandhian technique, felt that he would be useful to both King and the politically inexperienced Montgomery Improvement Association. "Lillian Smith had once traveled with me around the country," Rustin recalled, "observing interracial institutes that I conducted in different cities. And she therefore considered me a kind of minor authority on nonviolence. So it was she who brought me to King."

Despite King's academic exposure to Gandhi's philosophy, what he and the Montgomery movement still lacked, and what Rustin could provide, was practical experience in the self-discipline that Gandhian activism required: resolute resistance without resort to violence. And what Lillian Smith feared was that the local movement might succumb to violent provocation, thus jeopardizing its goodwill or eroding its moral authority. For instance, after the bombing of his house, King had applied for permission to carry a handgun in his automobile; and there was a firearm at home for the defense of himself and his family. He may or may not have realized that Gandhian precept frowned upon even the owning of weapons. "I had merely an intellectual understanding and appreciation of the position," he said later, "with no firm determination to organize it."

Not all of Rustin's political associates in New York shared Lillian Smith's belief in his usefulness to the struggle in Montgomery. At a meeting in A. Philip Randolph's office, the majority disapproved of Rustin's going to the South. They feared that aspects of his personal and radical history might be harmful to the effort King was leading. But a minority of two prevailed: Randolph and Muste strongly endorsed Rustin's mission. Randolph had heard from E. D. Nixon that Rustin's services would be more than welcome; besides, he and Muste shared Rustin's view that the Montgomery boycott could be the springboard for a black mass movement all across the South. The War Resisters League instantly released Rustin to work for an indefinite period in Alabama, for, as David McReynolds said later, "Bayard was too talented and many-faceted to be confined."

Dr. King was out of town when Rustin arrived in Montgomery, and he reported instead to the Reverend Ralph Abernathy, whom E. D. Nixon had told to expect the visitor from New York. There was indeed much useful work for him to do, Abernathy assured Rustin, receiving him cordially. He could write instructive position papers for the MIA and drill young demonstrators in the techniques of Gandhian struggle— not nonresistance, as some critics misunderstood it to be, but direct and vigorous nonviolent action.

Rustin, not ready to devote himself fully to such a program until he introduced himself to Dr. King, looked around Montgomery and conferred with Nixon. "They can bomb us out and they can kill us," Nixon told him, "but we are not going to give in." Strolling beyond his hotel late one evening, Rustin saw the all-night shifts of armed black men— illuminated by strings of lightbulbs—who had been organized to guard the homes of Abernathy and King. His nighttime walk was unwise, an attendant at the hotel told him when he returned. There was an air of warfare in Montgomery, he was advised, and elements hostile to the bus boycott would probably attempt to mark and kill him as an agitator brought in from New York. Moreover, he should at all times keep the window drapes in his hotel room drawn tightly.

Soon after Dr. King returned to the city, Rustin visited the home of the protest leader; he was surprised by his gracious reception. Coretta Scott King, who met him at the front door, recognized him instantly as a former lecturer for the Fellowship of Reconciliation; she remembered his speaking at her high school in Marion, Alabama, during the early 1940s. Waving aside the letter of introduction he was handing her—from Ruth Neuendorfer, a former teacher at Lincoln High School in Marion—she said, "I know you, Mr. Rustin," and invited him in. Mrs. King later recalled their conversation, while awaiting her husband's return from an engagement in town: "Bayard told me how strongly he felt about our work and the possibility of its developing into a nonviolent movement all over the country. He also spoke of his admiration for my husband. When Martin came home, though they had never met before, they had a wonderful talk [in which] Bayard offered to help in any way he could."

Rustin, almost forty-four, was Dr. King's senior by some seventeen years. He explained his controversial history: his sexual life; his radical past in the left-wing movement; his imprisonment as a conscientious objector during the war; his work with A. Philip Randolph and A. J. Muste; his continuing pacifism and civil rights activism; and, as a disciple of Gandhi, his total commitment to nonviolent action. King, Rustin said later, was impressed by any political alliance with Randolph and Muste, both of whose careers he admired greatly. Silent about certain other aspects of his visitor's life and background, King told Rustin that the Montgomery movement would welcome all the help it could get.

On February 26, a Sunday evening, Rustin made another call at Dr. King's home. Accompanied by the black journalist William Worthy, he wanted to congratulate King on a sermon he had delivered that day at the Dexter Avenue church. White southerners, King had said, "should not be hated," for "the most prejudiced mind in Montgomery, in

America," could become "a mind of goodwill." A successful bus boycott, he'd added, would be a victory "not for Montgomery Negroes alone" but also for justice, fair play, and democracy in the nation as a whole.

But upon entering King's residence, Rustin was alarmed by the sight of a gun resting on an armchair in the living room. That item was out of place in the home of a Gandhian leader, and he told King so, when they sat and talked in the kitchen. "If in the heat and flow of battle a leader's house is bombed and he shoots back," Rustin remembered saying to his host, "then that is an encouragement to his followers to pick up guns. If, on the other hand, he has no guns around him, and his followers know it, then they will rise to the nonviolent occasion." Not long after that discussion, the Kings decided to rid their household of firearms.

"It seemed to me," Rustin later told an interviewer, "that King had read about Gandhi, and that his reading had tilled the ground, created a readiness for his gradual deepening in the philosophy of nonviolence. But he was still working out of the framework of Christian love. It was hard to argue with Martin if the argument was merely about the strategies and tactics of nonviolent action. His attachment to nonviolence reflected his belief that only the blood of Jesus could clarify the world. That was good, because it took Martin through some difficult straits. Yet he would also raise questions about the problem of adhering wholly to Christian nonviolence. I believe he soon came to see what I had recognized while working with Gandhi's movement in India—that you ought not to separate the secular from the religious. So King's Christian-based nonviolence began drawing increasingly upon the practical strategies and tactics Gandhism had adopted."

King himself was to confirm much of that analysis in an article he contributed to *The Christian Century* in the spring of 1960. "Christ furnished the spirit while Gandhi furnished the method," he wrote, describing his role in the Montgomery bus protest. "The experience in Montgomery did more to clarify my thinking on the question of nonviolence than all the books I had read."

During and after the bus boycott, King and Rustin formed one of the more creative alliances in the civil rights movement. "He became very close to us," Coretta King recalled, "and was tremendously helpful to my husband."

In his work with the Montgomery Improvement Association, Rustin not only advised on proper Gandhian procedures but also wrote correspondence and publicity material; composed songs for the regular mass meetings; organized car pools and other alternatives to bus transportation. "At one point, King was about to give up," he remembered. "We were having a meeting, when he said, 'I can't go on. These people can't walk anymore. Where are we going to get cars?' When the meeting adjourned I got on the telephone and called A. Philip Randolph in New York. 'Mr. Randolph, there's a need for automobiles,' I said. 'Do you think we can get enough middle-class blacks to give up their automobiles?' Randolph laughed and said he didn't think so. 'But I'll tell you what to do,' he said. 'Go up to Birmingham, where the steelworkers are making enough money to afford two cars. Ask them to donate their second car.' So we did. And that helped to save the boycott."

Rustin also raised funds from sympathetic organizations in the North. "If the job of nonviolent education is [to be] done, even inadequately," he wrote to the War Resisters League, "it must be done by money from pacifist sources. We must not fail in this unique situation. This is an effort to avoid war—race war—but war nonetheless." From a wealthy Quaker in Manhattan he obtained a loan of five thousand dollars for the MIA. He may also have shared in the decision to discard the term "bus boycott" (implying an illegal restraint of commerce) in favor of "bus protest." "Boycott," he wrote a friend in New York, was too narrow a term, suggesting "a desire to hurt economically." It was the white community's failure to negotiate, he said, that "created what we never intended—economic loss."

But as he had been warned after his arrival, his presence in the city was not wholly welcome, even by elements within the MIA. Certain of its members were troubled by what they learned about areas of his personal and political history—possibly from hostile sources in the police. He wrote to a colleague at the War Resisters League:

I have been followed by police cars, and never go out after dark alone. There are two white girls down from the North as reporters who have been stopping me in public for information. Today I had to ask them not to speak to me except by phone. I have a lot of inside dope, and they all want it, but I can't take a chance. On two occasions when these girls came to me, two police officers came and stood over us with the most menacing expressions. When I called one of the girls to ask her not to contact me publicly, she told me to be careful, {that} every move I made was being watched; that I should be prepared to leave town by car at a moment's notice; that the rumor was being spread by a reporter on The Advertiser, *the local paper, that I was a communist NAACP organizer; and that the Rev. Abernathy, {allegedly} trained in Moscow, and I were planning a violent uprising. So I must be prepared if necessary to leave here.*

That would indeed become necessary. Already cool toward Rustin—and further unnerved by the hostile surveillance he was attracting to the MIA—a number of his detractors in the organization felt that the time had come for him to leave town, a feeling they communicated to A. Philip Randolph. At a hastily called meeting in his office, on West 125th Street, Randolph addressed more than a dozen representatives of pacifist, civil rights, and trade union organizations. In view of the complaints he had received, Randolph asked the gathering, should Rustin be recalled from Montgomery? The consensus was that he should be; and, concurring, Randolph telegraphed Rustin, informing him of the decision. But Bayard did not return immediately to New York. Instead, he withdrew from Montgomery to an outpost in Birmingham, where he continued, secretly, to communicate with Dr. King.

John Swomley, who succeeded A. J. Muste in the leadership of the Fellowship of Reconciliation, had arranged a Gandhian replacement even before Rustin's forced departure from Montgomery. Swomley had never favored Rustin's mission to the South, and he now seized the opportunity to provide King with what he considered a more appropriate adviser—Glenn Smiley, the FOR's ablest exponent of Gandhian methodology. Feeling no animosity toward Smiley, Rustin welcomed him to Montgomery and introduced him to Dr. King.

John Swomley had instructed Smiley to avoid any contact with Rustin, but that wasn't the kind of instruction Smiley was disposed to heed. He and Rustin had been friends and comrades since the early 1940s, when they began working as field secretaries for the Fellowship. Born in Texas, Smiley was a Methodist clergyman in Redlands, California, and he had occasionally invited Rustin to preach the social gospel at his church. Smiley regarded Rustin as "a cherished friend" and "an orator of great ability." He was to write some time later: "My principal inspirations have come from Jesus and Mahatma Gandhi, and my American guru has been Bayard Rustin. . . . It was he who taught me the philosophy and essential tactics of nonviolence, even as we shared the heat of the civil rights battles of the 1940s." For all those reasons, Smiley, to Swomley's great displeasure, made no attempt at avoiding Rustin. Nor could Swomley have been happy with a report he received from Smiley after Rustin had left Montgomery to establish secret communication lines with Dr. King and the boycott movement. It was "unfortunate" that Rustin had been forced to leave, Smiley said, for "Bayard has had a good influence on King" and was "in on all the strategy."

Glenn Smiley, now the only experienced Gandhian theoretician in Montgomery, soon became one of Dr. King's most valuable advisers and trusted confidants. He was to find, as Rustin had, that King was not yet a thoroughly confirmed Gandhian and that certain activists in the Montgomery Improvement Association were still bearing arms. He and King agreed, he said later, that "I would teach him everything I knew about nonviolence, since, by his own admission, he had only been casually acquainted with Gandhi and his methods." Still, Smiley had been deeply moved by his first conversation with King. "I've just had one of the most glorious yet tragic interviews I have ever had," he wrote to Muriel Lester of the international FOR. "I believe God has called

Martin Luther King to lead a great movement. But why does God lay such a burden on one so young, so inexperienced, so good?" King could become "a Negro Gandhi," Smiley added, "or he can be made into an unfortunate demagogue, destined to swing from a lynch mob's tree."

Unduly modest or not, Smiley considered himself a poor substitute for Rustin in Montgomery; but, he told John Swomley, the bus boycott movement was "potentially the most exciting thing I have ever touched." He was to serve King impressively up to the victorious conclusion of the boycott, in December 1956. A number of King's associates felt that Smiley may have played a more valuable role than Rustin did—although that judgment was probably influenced by a personal animus toward Rustin, who, despite his brilliance, and because of his closeness to King, was disliked by many who contended for the leader's attention. According to David Garrow, King's biographer, the Reverend Robert Graetz believed that while Smiley and Rustin contributed to King's adoption of nonviolence, "most of the credit for giving form and substance to this principle must go to Glenn Smiley." Graetz and others resented Rustin's assertiveness and King's reliance upon his advice. Harris Wofford was to recall, in a memoir: "Even the shrewd and intelligent help of Bayard Rustin verged on a kind of manipulation I disliked. Steeped in Gandhian lore, with extraordinary personal experience in nonviolent action, Rustin seemed ever present with advice, and sometimes acted as if King were a precious puppet whose symbolic actions were planned by a Gandhian high command."

Early in March 1956, Rustin slipped out of Birmingham for a covert visit to Montgomery, but his return to the city was soon discovered. He awoke a morning or two later to find his photograph prominently displayed in *The Advertiser.* "Who is this man?" the caption inquired. "He is wanted for inciting a riot." Moreover, said an accompanying news item, he was misrepresenting himself as a correspondent for *Le Figaro* and the *Manchester Guardian. Le Figaro* had denied any connection with the "impostor," the report added. Rustin was required to beat a hasty retreat from Montgomery. "I'll never forget," he recalled, "that Dr. King whisked me out of town in a car, with a car behind, to Birmingham."

If Rustin had indeed misrepresented himself as a writer for the publications in question, he was not wholly a journalistic impostor. Ever since 1952, when he made his first visit to West Africa, he had been an accredited correspondent for the Baltimore *Afro-American*. Besides, he was writing an account of the bus boycott for *Liberation* magazine, of which he was a coeditor; and the magazine did publish his "Montgomery Diary" in its issue of April 1956. Concerning *Le Figaro* and the *Manchester Guardian*, Rustin wrote to Dr. King from Birmingham: "For the record, at no time did I say that I was a correspondent for either of those papers. I did say that I was writing articles which were to be submitted to them, and this is now in the process of being done."

Rustin returned to New York on March 8, having found his stay in Birmingham to be nearly as untenable as the one in Montgomery. Among those who regretted his departure from the South was Homer Jack, a white civil rights activist and clergyman from Evanston, Illinois, who, on a visit to Montgomery, had observed Rustin's work with King and the boycott movement. Not only was Rustin "especially effective in counseling with the leaders of the protest," Jack wrote in a report to pacifist comrades in the North, but "his contribution to interpreting the Gandhian approach to the leadership cannot be overestimated."

In his own report to the War Resisters League, from which he had been on leave, Rustin stated: "The leadership in general is exploring the principles and tactics of nonviolence. All . . . are clear that they will have no part in starting violence. There is, however, considerable confusion on the question as to whether violence is justified in retaliation to violence directed against the Negro community. At present, there is no careful, nonviolent preparation for any such extreme situation. The Rev. Martin Luther King . . . is developing a decidedly Gandhi-like view, and recognizes that there is a tremendous educational job to be done within the Negro community. He is eagerly learning all he can about nonviolence, and evidence indicates that he is emerging as a regional symbol of nonviolent resistance in the deep South."

In New York—mostly at WRL headquarters (5 Beekman Street) and the editorial offices of *Liberation* (110 Christopher Street)—Rustin continued his efforts on behalf of Dr. King and the struggle in Montgomery. He drafted an article, revised and edited by King, titled "Our Struggle." The first piece of political journalism that carried King's byline, it was aimed at galvanizing support in the North and appeared in the April 1956 issue of *Liberation.* Not long after, Rustin and the War Resisters League played a leading role in organizing the Committee for Nonviolent Integration, designed to aid the cause of King's work. Its prominent cosponsors included James Farmer, the Reverend Harry Emerson Fosdick, the Reverend Donald Harrington, Murray Kempton, A. J. Muste, A. Philip Randolph, and the Reverend Gardner C. Taylor. At one meeting of the Committee, King, on a short visit to New York, emphasized the need for bicycles and station wagons, to help lessen the cost of car pools in Montgomery.

To guide his New York activities on behalf of the bus boycott, Rustin, in his communications with King, asked constantly for reports on the state of the movement. King wrote him a lengthy account:

Though finances were "holding up well," out-of-town contributions had fallen off "tremendously" during the previous three months; the MIA still needed all the funds it could get, for "we are spending at present approximately five thousand dollars weekly," mostly for "the transportation system and the running of the office." The people's enthusiasm had not waned; they were "determined never to return to Jim Crow buses"; the mass meetings were "still jammed and packed"; and those who had wanted to use guns in the beginning were "gradually coming to see the futility of such an approach." Reactionary forces were still attempting "to block our transportation system"; insurance policies "have been cancelled on more than half of our station wagons," and "we have confronted insuperable difficulty" in getting them reinsured. On the more hopeful side, "At present, we are awaiting a decision of the Supreme Court. As you know, the Federal District Court, in a decision back in May, declared segregation unconstitutional in public transportation. In order to delay the situation, the city and state appealed the decision to the United States Supreme Court. The court will reconvene in October. Our lawyers feel that the Supreme Court will render its decision before Christmas or by January."

In New York, Rustin helped to organize another pro-Montgomery grouping, called In Friendship. One of its cofounders was Stanley Levison, Rustin's Upper West Side neighbor, who was later to be among the counselors upon whose political judgment King most strongly depended. The third cofounder of In Friendship was a strong-willed feminist, formerly of the NAACP, named Ella Baker—who, unlike Rustin and Levison, was never to gain a trusted seat at King's right hand. Baker did not defer reverentially to the tradition of male leadership, feeling that women were just as qualified for positions on the front line of the black struggle.

In Friendship established headquarters on East Fifty-seventh Street, in office space donated by Levison, who also provided the original funds for the group's operation. Rustin's staff at In Friendship consisted chiefly of Rachelle Horowitz and Tom Kahn, socialist undergraduates at Brooklyn College, who had been referred to him by Michael Harrington. For years to come, Horowitz and Kahn were to be Rustin's ablest intellectual assistants in the civil rights movement. "Mike Harrington had known Bayard from earlier days," Horowitz remembered, "and after one of Mike's speeches to the Young Socialist League at Brooklyn College, he told Tom Kahn and me that we could do a very good thing by going up to an office in the East Fifties, where Bayard was building support for the Montgomery bus boycott. We went up and volunteered. We stuffed envelopes, worked on leaflets, and helped coordinate big fund-raising events Rustin and In Friendship were organizing. It was our first experience in the civil rights movement."

One of those fund-raising events, in May, was a rally at Madison Square Garden, which netted approximately twenty thousand dollars for the Montgomery Improvement Association. On December 5—the

first anniversary of the bus boycott—In Friendship staged an even
larger fund-raising affair, a concert at the Manhattan Center called
"Salute to Montgomery," which featured performers like Tallulah
Bankhead, Harry Belafonte, and Duke Ellington. Coretta Scott King
(who had studied at the New England Conservatory of Music), was to
remember singing a program of classical music and then telling "the
story of Montgomery in words and song." Perhaps from no other city in
the North did the Montgomery struggle receive the solid moral and
financial support that Rustin and In Friendship mobilized in New
York.

A vindicating decision by the United States Supreme Court brought
the bus boycott to a triumphant end on December 21, 1956, three hundred eighty-one days after it began. Early that morning, Dr. King and
his resident Gandhian tutor, Glenn Smiley, were the first to board a
desegregated bus in Montgomery. In a chat with King the previous
evening, Smiley had said, "Tomorrow I want to be paid. . . . I have been
working here for the whole year . . . and now I think it is time to collect
my salary." "I will pay you anything within my power," King replied.
"Name your price." He was surprised and amused by Smiley's modest
demand: "I want to be the first to ride by you on an integrated bus." So
it was, King later reported, that "I rode the first integrated bus in
Montgomery with a white minister, and a native Southerner, as my
seat-mate."

Bayard Rustin was not present at the celebration, though King had
invited him to fly down from New York. He would content himself
with reflections upon principles he considered indispensable to the success of the yearlong struggle in Montgomery. The victorious bus boycott, he said a while later, was "a post-Gandhian contribution" to the
theory and practice of nonviolence. "Not one of the Negro leaders in
Montgomery was a pacifist when the struggle began."

Chapter 13

Advising the Prince

"As an aide to Dr. King," Rustin wrote some years after the bus boycott that began King's rise to the pinnacle of black leadership, "I felt . . . that a victory at Montgomery would have no permanent meaning in the racial struggle unless it led to the achievement of dozens of similar victories in the South. In practical terms, this meant that the movement needed a sustaining mechanism that could translate what we had learned during the bus boycott into a broad strategy for protest in the South." That sustaining mechanism was to be the Southern Christian Leadership Conference, which Rustin conceived and charted, in collaboration with Ella Baker and Stanley Levison.

To Baker, the SCLC was a needed counterbalance in the civil rights field—dominated by the old and prestigious NAACP—while Levison viewed it as the dawn of black protest activism on a national scale. Soon after the victory in Montgomery, Rustin discussed with Dr. King the possibility of establishing the mechanism for a southern mass movement, with King as its leader, its hierarchy composed predominantly of black clergymen throughout the region. King was not immediately enthusiastic. He didn't see how an all-southern protest movement could be organized. "I can show you how to do it," Rustin said, and

King gave him the green light to draw up the plans.

With important contributions from Baker and Levison, Rustin drafted seven Working Papers and presented them to King. A preamble to the seven-point blueprint emphasized certain of the objectives and conditions required for a mass movement: "economic survival"; a bold expression of "just grievance" and "group pride"; a belief in the principles of "direct action" and "community sharing"; "a unified leadership"; "community spirit through community sacrifice"—all "based on the most stable institution in Negro culture, the church."

After studying Rustin's seven documents, King called a two-day conference (January 10–11, 1957) at Atlanta's Ebenezer Baptist Church, of which his father was pastor. There he discussed the SCLC project with more than sixty ministers, drawn from twenty-nine towns and cities across the South. Mostly superstars of the black pulpit, they included Ralph Abernathy (Montgomery), Fred Shuttlesworth (Birmingham), Joseph E. Lowery (Mobile), Ted Jemison (Baton Rouge), A. L. Davis (New Orleans), Sam Williams (Atlanta), and C. K. Steele (Tallahassee). Rustin flew down to Atlanta, wanting to monitor the discussion of his plan. He was not disappointed. Influenced strongly by King, the gathering endorsed the proposal for a Southern Christian Leadership Conference. King, Rustin recalled, "spoke movingly on the power of nonviolence," at "one of the most important meetings that have taken place in the United States." A few weeks later—at a meeting in New Orleans on February 14—King was elected leader of the newly formed SCLC, the organization in which he rose to national prominence. It was Bayard Rustin, the SCLC historian Adam Fairclough later wrote, who "helped to place King at the head of a new organization of black Southerners."

Because the SCLC was largely his brainchild, Rustin seemed eminently qualified to be its first executive director. But his candidacy was opposed by a number of the ministers who had objected to his work with King during the Montgomery bus boycott. He might not, however, have accepted the position if it had been offered him. He enjoyed the wide range of his commitments within the civil rights, socialist, and pacifist movements. He owed a particular obligation to the War Resisters League, which had stood by him at a critical point in his career and which readily granted him leaves of absence to work with the black movement. Besides, he saw himself as an intellectual enabler—a strategist and tactician—not, as he would say, a dry-as-dust administrator.

After Rustin, the next logical candidate for the directorship of the nascent SCLC would have been Ella Baker, one of the best grassroots organizers in America. Baker was indeed appointed acting executive secretary of the SCLC. But when, after nearly two years, her "acting" appointment was not upgraded, she came to the conclusion that the SCLC did not want a woman—surely not one as outspoken as she was— to be its permanent executive director. Quitting her position in 1960, Baker went on to help organize and build the Student Nonviolent Coordinating Committee.

"I had known," she said later, "that there would never be any role for me in a leadership capacity [at the SCLC]. First, I'm a woman; I'm not a minister. And, second, I'm a person who feels I have to maintain some degree of personal integrity, and [be guided] by my own barometer of what is important and what is not. I knew that my penchant for speaking honestly about what I considered [desirable] directions would not be tolerated. The combination of being a woman and an older woman presented problems. I was old enough to be the mother of the leadership. The basic attitude of men, especially ministers, as to what [should be] the role of a woman in their church setup [was] that of taking orders, not providing leadership. This would never have lent itself to my being a leader.

"I even heard something to the effect that I hated Martin [Dr. King]. But I think this stems from the fact that I did not have the kind of awe for the charismatic role that he had gained, or was playing. Martin wasn't basically the kind of person—certainly at the stage when I knew him the closest—[to] engage in dialogue that questioned the almost exclusive rightness of his position. And because I had no such awe, I would raise questions that I considered fundamental. I think I

accepted the fact that he was there in the role of having been pronounced a great leader, as a result of the Montgomery situation. But
I've never been able to feel that this symbolic value [displaces] the need
for knowledgeable leadership. I've never felt it necessary for any one
person to embody all that's needed in the leadership of a group or people. This comes back to my old cliché about a leadership-centered
group [SCLC] as against a group-centered leadership [SNCC]. The
group came first in my mind. The most important thing was to develop
people to the point where they don't need the strong savior-type
leader."

She stuck so faithfully to her principles that Bayard Rustin told
Taylor Branch, one of Dr. King's biographers, "Ella Baker was very
tough on Martin. I literally saw her drive him to tears. He couldn't
endure much criticism. He loved to be surrounded by people who said
'yes.'"

On February 14, 1957, the day Dr. King was elected leader of the
SCLC, he telegraphed President Eisenhower, urging him to visit the
South and address the issues of racial segregation and discrimination.
"In the absence of some early and effective remedial action," the tele-
gram said, "we shall have no moral choice but to lead a Pilgrimage of
Prayer to Washington. If you, our President, cannot come South to
relieve our harassed people, we shall have to lead our people to you."
Eisenhower—usually silent on racial issues until they boiled into a cri-
sis—did not reply.

A month later, when King and A. Philip Randolph met in Ghana,
which was celebrating its independence, they discussed the idea of an
SCLC-sponsored Prayer Pilgrimage to Washington. Randolph, who
was not unaware of King's plan—Bayard Rustin had already told him
about it—promised his full support. And on returning to the United
States, Randolph further enlisted the backing of Roy Wilkins, the
NAACP leader.

At that time, as Ella Baker put it, King and Randolph and Wilkins
were "the triumvirate leadership" of black America, "Randolph being

the link that could bridge" philosophical and organizational differences. There were indeed such differences. Mass action in the streets was not high on the NAACP's agenda: court litigation and congressional lobbying were its priorities. And after the victorious bus boycott in Montgomery, Wilkins—head of the largest and most important civil rights organization in America—was not among those celebrating King's sudden arrival into national celebrity. He also feared that King's newly established SCLC might draw membership and money away from the old NAACP chapters in the South. Consequently, Wilkins might not have agreed to support the planned Prayer Pilgrimage had not the conciliating Randolph urged him to do so.

The Prayer Pilgrimage was organized chiefly by Bayard Rustin, on NAACP premises at 20 West 40th Street in Manhattan; and to the satisfaction of all concerned, it was billed as a joint venture of the SCLC and the NAACP. Rustin's deputy organizer was the not-yet-disillusioned Ella Baker; and they were assisted by an interracial group of student volunteers—particularly Rustin's white Brooklyn College protégés, Rachelle Horowitz and Tom Kahn.

But what became the popular signature of civil rights activism in the 1960s—mass protest in the streets—was still frowned upon in the late 1950s, even by elements in the North. When Horowitz invited Rustin to discuss the Prayer Pilgrimage with a group of young socialists at Brooklyn College, its president, Harry Gideonse, objected to his appearance on the campus. "Dr. Gideonse," she recalled, "was an authoritarian figure, and he feared that Rustin would disrupt the campus by coming there to espouse the theory and practice of mass protest. McCarthyism was still very strong. But insisting on our right to invite whomever we wished, we turned for help to John Hope Franklin, chairman of the history department. He was the first black to hold such a position at a predominantly white college, and Gideonse was proud to have appointed him. Franklin shrank, at first, from involving himself with our dispute. He seemed a very bourgeois and responsible gentleman. He told us he didn't believe in the kind of activism Rustin promoted, that he disliked mass movements and protests in the streets.

But when we begged him to do something, he interceded with Gideonse, and Bayard was allowed to come and speak."

Gideonse and Franklin may also have been troubled by allegations of Rustin's recent association with communists. In February 1957, not long before the Prayer Pilgrimage, a dissident faction within the American Communist Party invited A. J. Muste—along with a number of ex-communist and noncommunist progressives—to observe the party's national convention in New York City. The "impartial observers," as they were called, included Bayard Rustin; Dorothy Day, of the Catholic Worker movement; Lyle Tatum, of the American Friends Service Committee; Roy Finch, of the War Resisters League and *Liberation* magazine; George Willoughby, of the Committee for Conscientious Objectors; Alfred Hassler, of the Fellowship of Reconciliation; and the writers Milton Mayer and Sidney Lens. They may have considered themselves impartial observers, but J. Edgar Hoover and the FBI did not: If you were attending a conference of communists, then you were a communist—unless you were there under the auspices of the FBI.

The invitation to Muste and his delegation had come from John Gates, editor of the party's newspaper *The Daily Worker* and a leader of its reformist faction. Recent events abroad—particularly Moscow's brutal crushing of the Hungarian uprising in 1956—had shaken American communist solidarity with party headquarters in the Soviet Union. John Gates's faction wanted the party in the United States to end its subservience to directives from Moscow. He wished, in effect, to fashion a form of communism that would be responsive chiefly to American conditions; to reconstruct it as an institution for radical social education; to bring it, where possible, into a cooperative relationship with progressive noncommunist forces in the United States. It was mainly for the latter reason that Gates had invited Muste to observe proceedings at the 1957 convention. But the FBI, whose agents monitored the meeting, saw Muste and his group as fellow travelers of the Communist Party, not as informal and impartial guests. In support of that view,

Hoover informed the Senate Internal Security Subcommittee that Muste had a long history of fronting for communist causes. That hadn't been true since the late 1930s, when Muste abandoned his Marxist-Leninist convictions and returned to his ministry as a Christian pacifist.

But as a civil libertarian, Muste had not lost his tolerance for political views with which he disagreed. He was among the signers of a petition to President Eisenhower recommending amnesty for communists jailed under the Smith Act. In 1950, when Paul Robeson was barred from appearing on the major concert stages of America—on grounds that he was an apologist for the Soviet Union—Muste had urged the Fellowship of Reconciliation to present Robeson at a public song recital in New York City. The concert did not take place, however, elements within the FOR and other liberal constituencies having discouraged the idea: Freda Kirchway, editor of *The Nation,* felt that while the concert was a right thing to do, it might be politically counterproductive; Robeson's allies on the left might misconstrue and exploit the artistic and humanitarian purpose of the event. Norman Thomas, leader of the Socialist Party, told Muste that the pro-Robeson gesture would be "confusing to the general public," and he would not consider associating himself with an occasion designed to aid anyone with Stalinist leanings.

After attending the 1957 Communist Party convention, Muste became one of the leading organizers of a group called the American Forum for Socialist Discussion, which was accommodating to members of John Gates's dissenting faction. The American Forum was a collective of left and liberal intellectuals, committed, Muste explained, to the "study and serious untrammeled discussion among all elements that think of themselves as related to historic socialist and labor traditions . . . however deep and bitter their differences may have been." At Muste's request, Bayard Rustin agreed to serve on the Forum's forty-member national committee.

He may have regretted that decision when, in the ensuing controversy over Muste's alliance with left-wingers, the FBI classified the American Forum as a front for communist subversion. "The communists don't belong in jail," Norman Thomas said, "but they also don't belong in any party with which I want to be connected." Roger Baldwin, of the American Civil Liberties Union, saw the Forum as the latest example of Muste's "romantic nonsense." Romantic nonsense or political tolerance, this was how Muste later explained it to his biographer Nat Hentoff: "I've always tried to keep communication open between radicals and nonradicals. . . . You always assume there is some element of truth in the position of the other person, and you respect your opponent for hanging on to an idea as long as he believes it to be true. On the other hand, you must . . . make him realize what you consider to be the larger truth. . . . You keep the lines of communication open, and you act on your own ideas."

Rustin's involvement with the politics of the American Forum reflected the degree to which he shared Muste's intellectual analysis. As a member of the democratic socialist movement, he abhorred communism—or had come to do so after his dalliance with it in the late 1930s—but did not believe disillusioned communists should be barred from redemption within the fold of the democratic left. Tom Kahn, his close personal friend and fellow socialist, recalled the issues that led to Rustin's association with Muste's initiative in the American Forum.

"After the Hungarian Revolution of 1956," Kahn said, "the American Communist Party split up. And there began a great debate in the democratic socialist community over whether there should be a realignment of political forces on the left. A. J. Muste emerged as the chief spokesman and architect of the idea that if a new socialist movement was created it could include dissident communists. And out of that idea the American Forum was born. Max Shachtman [a former Trotskyist] was dead set against the idea. He felt that the best way to recruit decent elements from the Communist Party was to keep the party isolated. He and Muste had a dramatic confrontation over that issue; and Rustin sided with Muste, for he wasn't then as close to Shachtman as he later became. Bayard and Muste were pacifists. Shachtman was not.

"But as the politics of the American Forum got out of hand, Rustin began gravitating toward Shachtman's point of view. He realized that

you couldn't really build a mainstream democratic left in this country
with communists in it. Bayard also recognized that if he was to work
effectively with the emerging civil rights movement, it would make no
sense for him to support Muste's strategy. From that point on, Rustin's
relationship with Shachtman became quite strong. I once arranged a
private meeting so that all three—Muste, Shachtman, and Bayard—
could sit down and confront the issue. Muste and Shachtman, the two
warhorses from the 1920s, had a go at each other that I shall never forget. It reflected very sharply divergent views of how socialists could be
effective within the civil rights movement. Shachtman carried the day
in that argument. And I think that where national civil rights activism
was concerned, it ended all serious collaboration between Bayard and
Muste."

Rustin resigned from the American Forum. He did not, he wrote to
Muste, "question the sincere desire of those who remain in it [so as] to
keep the marketplace of ideas free." He was resigning, he said, "to
refrain from compromising, in the eyes of a confused public, those with
whom I am currently associated in other very important endeavors." He
was referring to his association with Dr. Martin Luther King, A. Philip
Randolph, and Roy Wilkins; the cause of the Southern Christian
Leadership Conference; and the Prayer Pilgrimage to Washington,
aimed at petitioning President Eisenhower and the federal government
for a speedy implementation of the 1954 school desegregation order.

The Pilgrimage massed at the Lincoln Memorial on the afternoon of
May 17, 1957, the third anniversary of the Supreme Court's order.
There were about thirty thousand participants, drawn from labor, student, religious, and civil rights organizations. Though the turnout was
smaller than Rustin and his team of organizers had hoped to see, it was
still the largest interracial civil rights demonstration yet held in the
nation's capital. Attending celebrities included Sidney Poitier, Jackie
Robinson, Harry Belafonte, Mahalia Jackson, Ruby Dee, Sammy Davis,
Jr., and the novelist John Oliver Killens. Paul Robeson was there as
well, but, his biographer Martin Duberman reported later, Robeson

"was ignored"; the organizers "asked Robeson antagonists Roy Wilkins and Adam Clayton Powell Jr. to speak, but not Robeson." Such programs were not improvised as they went along, however. Speakers were selected in advance. So if Robeson was ignored, it wasn't while he stood expectantly in the audience but in the earlier process of selection. And in omitting him from their prepared list of speakers, organizers were following specific instructions—especially from the staunchly anti-communist Randolph—to allow no sign of left-wing participation in the event. For sections of the federal officialdom were already branding the civil rights movement as a creature of communist subversion.

At the Lincoln Memorial, Michael Harrington recalled, "The program was, like every civil rights demonstration I have ever attended, too long. Every faction [of the movement] had to be given the right to make a speech." Randolph spoke; Wilkins spoke; as did a large number of activists and celebrities. But the highlight of the afternoon was the speech by Dr. King, his first to a major protest gathering outside the South.

There had been an interesting conceptual or stylistic debate over the address King was to deliver. Dissatisfied with what he had seen of the first draft, Bayard Rustin suggested certain changes in emphasis and language: "a clear statement on nonviolence"; an analysis of the racial struggle, voting rights, and a cooperative relationship with organized labor; "the need to expand the struggle on all fronts." "The question of where you move next [after the successful boycott in Montgomery]," Rustin said, "is more important than any other question Negroes face today." King accepted items of Rustin's advice but balked at making a small change in the dramatic language he planned for his oration: he wanted the phrase "Give us the ballot" to resound throughout the closing passages of his speech. Feeling that militant blacks didn't want the federal government to *give* them anything, Rustin urged this stronger declaration: "We demand the ballot." No, King said, that wouldn't convey the rhythm and music of his natural delivery. When Rustin insisted on his point, the young preacher, then only twenty-eight, issued this gentle reminder: he needed no advice from Rustin in the art of engaging and inspiring an audience. The argument was over. This, then, was King's peroration at the Prayer Pilgrimage to Washington:

> Our most urgent request to the President of the United States and every member of Congress is to give us the right to vote. *Give us the ballot,* and we will no longer have to worry the federal government about our basic rights. *Give us the ballot,* and we will no longer plead with the federal government for the passage of an anti-lynching law. . . . *Give us the ballot,* and we will transform the salient misdeeds of bloodthirsty mobs into the abiding good deeds of orderly citizens. *Give us the ballot,* and we will fill our legislative halls with men of goodwill, send to the sacred halls of Congress men who will not sign a Southern manifesto. . . . *Give us the ballot,* and we will place judges on the benches of the South who will do justly and love mercy. . . . *Give us the ballot,* and we will quickly and nonviolently, without rancor or bitterness, implement the Supreme Court's decision of May 17, 1954.

More electrifying on the platform than it probably reads, King's was a brilliant performance. Michael Harrington, himself a masterful political speaker, had heard what he called "an orator in the black Baptist mode, the last survivor of a great American rhetorical tradition." King, he said, had engaged his listeners "on a level deeper than speech," had summoned up "a vision of a new birth of justice in America" so dramatically that "grown and grizzled men had tears streaming down their faces." Bayard Rustin had to confess: "I learned from the occasion that Martin had a gift for saying things in a poetic way, that he had a greater understanding of the psychology of blacks than I did." Dan Wakefield reported in *The Nation* that "the crowd was on its feet to this man who has become their symbol." King's address, wrote James Hicks, editor of New York's *Amsterdam News,* marked his emergence as "the number one leader of sixteen million Negroes in the

United States." It was an emergence for which Rustin—as organizer of the Washington event and principal architect of the Southern Christian Leadership Conference—could take more than a small measure of credit.

James Hicks was not so discerning when he went on to make the absurd charge that Randolph and Wilkins had dragged their feet toward the Prayer Pilgrimage, "with the direct hope that the march would fail and that the threat of King's leadership would die aborning." In fact, without the full support of Randolph and Wilkins, Rustin could not have organized the Pilgrimage as successfully as he did. Wilkins wrote to C. B. Powell, publisher of the *Amsterdam News:* "Including mailings and telegrams, as well as the larger items, the NAACP put $9,000 into supporting the Pilgrimage. We submit that no one sinks $9,000 into a project that he hopes will fail. No one spends $9,000 and then 'drags' his feet."

During one of the furloughs the War Resisters League often granted him to work with the developing black protest movement, Rustin became Dr. King's and the SCLC's special assistant in New York. He performed the required duties from an office at the Harlem Labor Center, on West 125th Street, where he functioned together with Stanley Levison and the Reverend Thomas Kilgore, a board member of the SCLC. "But Bayard was the mastermind," Kilgore remembered.

By then Levison—whom Rustin had introduced to King after the Montgomery bus boycott—had begun emerging as one of the key political and intellectual aides to the SCLC leader. So much so that a degree of sibling rivalry was to develop between Levison and Rustin over whose counsel had the stronger influence upon King's thinking. But at an early stage of that rivalry, Rustin was still closer to King's ear than Levison was. Much more than Levison did, he maintained a wide network of relationships—liaisons useful to King's rise in national importance—with northern liberals, socialists, pacifists, trade unionists, and a variety of religious leaders.

For King's guest appearance at an anniversary dinner of the

Fellowship of Reconciliation, Rustin urged the SCLC leader to pay special tribute to the early civil rights efforts of former FOR stalwarts like A. J. Muste and John Nevin Sayre. "Much of the new movement among Negroes in the South today," he wrote to King, "would not be possible without the many long years of work that these men have carried on." For King's speech to a convention of the Negro American Labor Council (led by A. Philip Randolph), Rustin advised: "The emphasis should be on the Negro-Labor alliance. It [the NALC] should know that you understand labor and its history—that you are a 'Labor Minister.'" Most of the funds Rustin raised for the SCLC were contributed by Jewish organizations and sectors of the trade union movement.

With Levison, Rustin helped in revising early drafts of King's first book, *Stride Toward Freedom,* partly an account of the Montgomery bus boycott and the role King played in its leadership. "King wrote his books completely by himself," Rustin said later. "But when he was terribly busy, moving from place to place, he would ask me or Levison to give him notes. He would accept some of these, and he would reject others. We always prepared our notes in triple space, so that he could write between the lines. And he almost always did. When there were things that required a particularly careful formulation, he would say, 'I want you to give me a first draft on what you think.' But the bulk of what he wrote he did by himself." Early in February 1958, King mailed Rustin an unfinished chapter of *Stride Toward Freedom,* requesting "any additional suggestions you would like . . . concerning things that would be added as well as deleted." A month later, King sent Rustin another chapter, asking him to "go over it and give your reaction." When King's English publishers requested the names of people in Britain and the Commonwealth for the promotion of his book, he turned the matter over to Rustin, who had traveled in Europe, Africa, and India. "I do not know such persons," King wrote to him, "but I am sure you do. Please send the names and addresses of these persons to me."

When *Stride Toward Freedom* appeared, in September 1958, Rustin was not mentioned in the acknowledgments. This caused an acquaintance to write to him, inquiring why. "In regard to King's book and my name being left out," he replied, "that was my decision, and a very sound one, I believe. Reactionaries in the South have distributed several pieces of literature accusing King of being a communist, and linking me, as a 'communist agitator,' with him. I did not feel that he should bear this kind of burden. A New York lawyer [Stanley Levison] who has put thousands of dollars into the King movement, and who helped on the book a great deal, also asked that his name not be listed. For your information, the first draft of King's book listed the tremendous help which I had given him and the movement. I mention this only because I would not want you to think that Martin is the kind of person who would take my name out because of fear. I want you to know that I insisted he do so."

Three days after the publication of his book, King was autographing copies in a Harlem department store, when he was stabbed, nearly fatally, by a deranged woman. His three-month convalescence kept him from attending another of the mass demonstrations in Washington that Bayard Rustin organized—the Youth March for Integrated Schools, in October 1958.

Delivering the keynote address at the Lincoln Memorial, a spiritual mecca of the civil rights movement, A. Philip Randolph explained the "central and dominant purposes" of the march: to dramatize "the God-given right of every child, regardless of race or color, religion or national origin or ancestry, to receive an education in the public schools, free from the insult of segregation and discrimination"; and to help "awaken, inform, arouse and mobilize people to the realization of the patriotic duty of every American citizen to support the Supreme Court decision for the desegregation and integration of public schools as the law of the land." Randolph then aimed his remarks at those in the federal government, principally J. Edgar Hoover, who had denounced the march as a communist-inspired promotion. "The leadership," he said, "completely rejects and unequivocally condemns communists and communism and their support, organizationally and financially. We realize that democracy and freedom, which communists openly denounce as bourgeois prejudices, are the only framework within which the Negro and other minorities, including the labor movement, can achieve their rights."

Six months later, in April 1959, Rustin organized a second Youth March for Integrated Schools, at which the triumvirate of black leadership—King, Randolph, and Wilkins—dominated the proceedings. But most others in the usual procession of orators, especially those without name recognition, were overshadowed by the charismatic Harry Belafonte. One of them, Curtis B. Gans, was most unfortunate in Rustin's late reshuffling of the lineup. "As my time to speak approached," he said later, "Bayard was worried that the program wasn't sufficiently interesting to the audience, and he decided to reorder the program. In my stead, he put Belafonte on, and with Harry came a crowd of 17,000 screaming females, charging the platform. I've never had a tougher act to follow." Later that afternoon, Belafonte was the center of a different kind of attention, when—leading a delegation of marchers to deliver a statement to President Eisenhower—he was barred at the gate of the White House. It was once more a sign of the President's general indifference to issues arising from racial segregation and discrimination.

Like the Prayer Pilgrimage of 1957, the Youth Marches of '58 and '59 signified the gathering momentum of the civil rights protest movement: the gradual awakening of a consciousness that had been stirred by the 1955–56 Montgomery bus boycott. As the chief organizer of those demonstrations, Bayard Rustin was, indisputably, a major force behind the momentum they generated. And the student volunteers who aided his organizing efforts—notably Rachelle Horowitz, Norman Hill, Maya Angelou, Tom Kahn, Robert Moses, Eleanor Holmes Norton—were among the many young people he attracted to the cause of civil rights activism. Like Rustin, a number of them were socialists, who viewed the growing black protest movement as one of the most hopeful political developments in the United States—"a revolution in the making," as Horowitz said.

"Our country," she added, "had become intimidated by McCarthyism. An apolitical climate had pervaded the college campuses. Now, suddenly, here was a movement for social justice—sparked by Martin Luther King and the Montgomery bus boycott—waking us up. If you considered yourself a radical, then supporting that movement was the thing to do. You simply had to be there."

Chapter 14

Radical Jet-Setter

In the late 1950s, while helping King and Randolph to nurture the new protest movement, Rustin occasionally undertook missions abroad on behalf of the pacifist community. He felt as strong an attachment to pacifism as to civil rights activism; but as executive director of the War Resisters League—which loaned his services to King and Randolph—he enjoyed an official status in the pacifist movement that he did not in the civil rights struggle. Rustin rejoiced in his pacifist missions abroad not only because of his devotion to their objectives but also because of his passion for globe-trotting. "Bayard," the WRL's Igal Roodenko said, "was always flying off for meetings and engagements with top nonviolent groups in Europe, India, and Africa. He was a leading member of the radical jet set."

On August 2, 1955 (even before he first met Dr. King in Montgomery), Rustin flew to London for a two-week vacation, preceding a conference in the Netherlands of the Third Camp, an organization of international pacifist intellectuals that advocated nonalignment with the major cold-war power blocs. After the meeting in Holland, he shortened his visits to Sweden and Norway, in order to return for a court trial in New York, scheduled for September 14. A few months earlier, he was among twenty-nine pacifists who had been arrested in down-town Manhattan for refusing to cooperate with a civil defense air raid drill, ordered by the federal government. Appearing before Judge Hyman Bushel, Rustin and his codefendants—including A. J. Muste and Dorothy Day—justified their action on grounds of civil disobedi-ence: they were bound by conscience to resist all preparations for nuclear warfare. Judge Bushel found them all guilty of violating an emergency federal statute; but lenient in his punishment—probably because of a respect he had formed for Muste—he admonished and dis-charged them with suspended sentences.

On June 19, 1957, not long after organizing the Prayer Pilgrimage to Washington, Rustin wrote to Dr. King: "Because of an international conference which I must attend in connection with my [pacifist] work, I am leaving for Europe today." That was to be a world conference of the War Resisters League, from which he returned to New York at the end of July.

On April 3, 1958, after embarking upon a pacifist journey through Europe, scheduled to end with an antiwar rally in Red Square, Rustin stopped off in London. He had been invited there to address the next day's historic peace march from Trafalgar Square to the village of Aldermaston, in Berkshire. That demonstration, planned as a protest against Britain's development of nuclear weaponry, was the first in an annual series. The Aldermaston Marches were to invigorate British pacifism, which had been dormant since World War I. And credit for that reawakening belonged jointly to the radical Direct Action Committee (DAC), with which Rustin had an American alliance, and the somewhat less militant Campaign for Nuclear Disarmament (CND). The early 1950s, said Michael Foot, of the British Labor Party, had not been "an estimable or adventurous period in Conservative Britain." Now, with the sudden emergence of the Aldermaston March movement, "the horror of nuclear weapons" had provoked an "adequate response" to the fear of total destruction.

The movement's inaugural demonstration (lasting from Good Friday to Easter Monday, 1958) assembled at Trafalgar Square, before setting out on a fifty-mile walk to Aldermaston, the village where Britain's nuclear research facilities were situated. The gathering of more than ten thousand at Trafalgar Square included Bertrand Russell and Philip Toynbee; Canon L. J. Collins, of Saint Paul's Cathedral; Aneurin Bevan, Tom Driberg, Fenner Brockway, and Michael Foot, of the British Labor Party; the Reverend Michael Scott, a fighter against apartheid and colonialism in Africa; the writers Doris Lessing, John Osborne, and Kenneth Tynan; the Reverend Martin Niemoller, a German theologian in exile; Peggy Duff, one of the more militant peace activists in Britain (she titled her autobiography *Left, Left, Left*); Hugh Brock, editor of the influential *Peace News;* and April Carter and Michael Randle, young radical pacifists in the Direct Action Committee.

Bayard Rustin was the only American on the program at Trafalgar Square, and in his speech (following those by Russell, Toynbee, Bevan, and Foot) he told the assembly: "There must be unilateral [disarmament] action by a single nation, come what may. There must be no strings attached. We must be prepared to absorb the danger. We must use our bodies in direct action, noncooperation, whatever is required to bring our government to its senses. In the United States, the black people of Montgomery said, 'We will not cooperate with discrimination.' And the action of those people achieved tremendous results. They are now riding the buses with dignity, because they were prepared to make a sacrifice of walking for their rights."

Michael Foot, among the elite of British political orators, was to remember that afternoon's speechmaking chiefly for "the limpid beauty" of Bertrand Russell's sentences. But the DAC's Michael Randle said later, "Bayard Rustin delivered what many regarded as the most powerful speech of that Good Friday afternoon, linking the struggle against weapons of mass destruction with the struggle of blacks for their basic rights in America."

Randle, who had heard Rustin speak at a number of pacifist gatherings, was not surprised by the performance at Trafalgar Square. From their first meeting, in the spring of 1952—at a Quaker conference in

Oxford—he had found Rustin to be "an immensely powerful, impressive, and somewhat intimidating" figure. "I don't think," he said, "I had ever met anyone who could order his thoughts so effectively: telling you in the heat of a debate that there were x number of factors to consider and then laying them out—one, two, three—without seeming to pause for reflection. He would sometimes put his points with all the vehemence and authority at his command, but end up with a merry chuckle or a loud laugh. He would be laughing at his own astuteness in making his points, or laughing in a teasing way at his adversary."

Not long after the march from Trafalgar Square, which Rustin accompanied all the way to Aldermaston, four members of the Committee for Non-Violent Action (CNVA) arrived in London from New York. Marvin Gewirtz, Lola Stone, Lawrence Scott, and Morton Ryweck had come to join Rustin on the next leg of their peace journey across Europe to Moscow. Rebuffed in their attempts to hold talks with Prime Minister Harold Macmillan and Foreign Secretary Selwyn Lloyd, they flew on to Paris, where they were cordially received by a number of French deputies. This was Rustin's second visit to Paris, and he was exhilarated. "Bayard was a lively person," Gewirtz recalled. "He could not be weighed down even by so grave a problem as the threat of nuclear destruction, which we were going to protest in Moscow. He exulted in the beauties of Paris. One lovely day, as we strolled down the Champs Élysées, I saw him jump and click his heels, expressing his sparkling sense of life."

Moving on from Paris, through brief stops in a number of other European cities, Rustin and the CNVA delegation arrived in Helsinki on May 1. While awaiting visas to enter the Soviet Union, they toured the city, which Rustin found architecturally appealing. "Bayard loved walking down the major avenues," Gewirtz said. "But someone of his color was a rare sight in those northern streets. During one of his walks, he encountered a group of four- and five-year-old children. They had never seen a black person in their lives, and they ran to hide behind their parents. But Bayard was amused, and his reaction was wonderful.

Laughing heartily, he walked up to the children and began playing with them."

Rustin and his peace team, unable to obtain entry visas to the USSR, were not to reach their destination. After the Soviet Embassy had stalled them in Helsinki for several days, they abandoned their mission to Red Square and headed back to the United States.

En route, Rustin stopped off again in London, the European city he was to visit most often in his life. He was as enchanted by its cultural style and atmosphere as he was by the speech of its educated classes, whose accents he had begun cultivating during his boyhood. London was also where he maintained the largest number of his intellectual relationships overseas—with such liberals and radical pacifists as Michael Randle, April Carter, Michael Scott, Muriel Lester, Peggy Duff, Hugh Brock, Percy Bartlett, Tony Smythe, Godric Bader, and Adam Roberts. When visiting the city, he usually lodged at the Friends International Centre, near Gordon Square in Bloomsbury. He liked not only its Quaker accommodations but also its adjacency to London University, the British Museum, the offices of *Peace News,* Housman's pacifist bookshop, and Dillon's university bookshop.

London's artifacts also fired his imagination. He spent a good deal of his time browsing through the antique shops and flea markets of Brighton Road and Portobello Road, evaluating and acquiring quaint clocks and walking sticks, rare music boxes and fob watches. He occasionally ventured into Britain's northern counties. On one excursion, Godric Bader, his guide, was astonished to observe his knowledge of and enthusiasm for the dripstone sculpture of ancient Britain—life-size heads and busts ornamenting the walls of medieval churches and monasteries. Drip stone, a kind of onyx marble, which some early sculptors used as raw material, took its name and origin from stalagmites and stalactites. "One sunny afternoon," Bader recalled, "I had the incredible experience of watching as Bayard, hacking away with a stonemason's saw, removed a dripstone bust from the ruins of a deconsecrated plague church in Northamptonshire. The English plague of the Middle Ages had wiped out a third or more of our population. Villagers' and other houses were destroyed, but the churches remained. And the walls of this church in Northamptonshire still stood, alone in the fields. Here was this tall, lithe, strong Negro, silhouetted against the sky, cutting away at one of the dripstone figures attached to the ancient church. It looked, for all the world, that the infidels had arrived to remove early Christianity. Bayard was appalled at our apparent indifference to the stonework of past ages."

But, Tony Smythe remembered, "Bayard's evident fascination with Englishness was centered in London, not the countryside. He heightened his British accent especially when he was in the city. He liked to think he was submerging himself in the local culture." Adam Roberts, impressed by Rustin's "beautiful rendering of English," felt that "Bayard wanted to prove that he wasn't copying the American white man, that he was better than the American white man." April Carter found him to be "charming and extremely intelligent in all things political," though she couldn't help noticing that, like certain elements he admired in the British upper class, he could also be "rather high-handed, personally arrogant."

It was Michael Randle who was most insightful regarding Rustin's Anglophilia: "I think Bayard was attracted to the measured style and quiet self-assurance of a certain type and class of the English person. He met mainly the people from high-middle-class backgrounds, many of them educated in our elite public-school system but, at the same time, people with liberal or radical political views. He liked what he saw of the British penchant for understatement and the strand of liberalism in its political culture. And yet a part of him was also attracted, I think, by the assertiveness he observed among the English ruling elite, the sense that it was their role in life to give orders and have others carry them out. At his grandest and most authoritative—and he could be both—he assumed the persona of an English aristocrat. He could be abrasive when he assumed his lordly manner. He didn't gladly suffer fools or 'foolishness'—a term he liked to use. His accent then became distinctly upper-class English, the tone that brooked no contradiction. He had the style to carry it, and he used it to good effect. But I don't think he was ever blind to the shortcomings of British society, particularly its racism."

At times, Rustin assumed his lordly persona as a form of seriocomic put-on. Returning to London from a visit to Africa in 1962, he wished to consult with Randle, who was probably his closest pacifist comrade in the city. Randle was in jail, however, serving a six-month sentence for leading a peace demonstration outside the U.S. Air Force base at Wethersfield, in Essex. Undeterred, Rustin traveled to Essex and bluffed his way into the prison. "It was something that should never have happened," Randle said. "Visits were strictly rationed to one a month. Not even my wife, Anne, ever succeeded in getting an extra visit. But Bayard phoned the prison and, putting on his best British accent, said how vital it was for him to see his 'deah friend' Michael before returning to the United States for his important work with the Reverend Dr. Martin Luther King. The liberal governor of the prison was won over instantly and gave his permission for a special visit. Bayard loved dressing up for a role. Wearing a long black coat that ran down to his ankles, he swept up to the jail in a taxi and strode into the visiting room, holding himself very erect. Officers and inmates alike were so impressed that, by evening time, word was all over the prison that I had been visited by an Ethiopian prince." To Eileen Brock, whose husband, Hugh, edited *Peace News,* "it was an example of Bayard's ability to get his way and his enjoyment of being exotic."

In the summer of 1959, when France announced plans to test its first nuclear device in the Sahara, the news was alarming to the international peace movement as well as to a number of countries in West Africa, particularly Ghana. The Ghanaian government and people feared that nuclear fallout would devastate their cocoa industry, a vital source of national revenue. They felt, moreover, that nuclear testing on African soil was a new form of European colonialism. So they were heartened when the British and American peace movements collaborated in organizing protest demonstrations at the nuclear site. The chief sponsors of the pacifist Sahara Project, as it was called, were activists in Britain's

Direct Action Committee (DAC), supported by similar activists in America's Committee for Non-Violent Action (CNVA), of which Bayard Rustin and A. J. Muste were prominent members.

At first George Willoughby, a leader of the CNVA, opposed involvement with the Sahara Project, feeling that the CNVA might be seen endorsing the Algerian struggle for independence from French colonial rule. "I don't see," he wrote to Rustin, "how the Sahara Project can operate" without being sucked into crosscurrents of the French-Algerian conflict. A peace protest, Willoughby said, could not afford to become enmeshed with "the international intrigue that is part of the North African struggle."

Rustin and Muste did not share Willoughby's reservations; they were committed, unconditionally, to pacifist witnessing. So was William Sutherland, who was then living in Accra, working as a special assistant to Ghana's minister of finance, K. A. Gbedemah. Willoughby relented only when Sutherland told him that West Africa had an urgent need for the CNVA's support, that the region was relying heavily upon American participation in the Sahara Project.

Toward the end of 1959, a DAC-CNVA aggregation assembled in Accra to plan their two-thousand-mile journey from Ghana northward to the French nuclear installations. Although the idea had originated with the DAC, Michael Randle had reason to fear that Rustin, with his penchant for giving orders, would seek to dominate preparations for the Sahara Project. He was correct: Rustin did take over. But, Randle recognized, consolingly, coordination of the enterprise could not have been in more capable hands. "Bayard was a brilliant organizer," he said, "with an amazingly quick understanding of the tasks needed to carry out a particular project. He had confidence in his own authority, his ability to take hold of a situation and exercise leadership by delegating tasks. In many ways, he was fascinated by power, and he derived an immense satisfaction from using it to good effect. He displayed himself to be a formidable politician, with a keen sense of where power lay in a given situation and what political options were realistically open. He and William Sutherland did a crucial job of steering the Sahara Project through the minefield of Ghanaian politics, enlisting the wholehearted support of Nkrumah and the Ghanaian government."

The Sahara protest team set out from Accra on the morning of December 6, 1959, its original eight-member force augmented to nineteen—partly because of Rustin's insistence that Africans be included. Traveling by Land-Rovers and a four-ton truck, they plotted a journey through rural Ghana, the Upper Volta, Niger, the French Sudan, up to the Algerian border. It was their plan, upon arriving at the border, to encamp in the shadow of the French nuclear site and, if they failed to disrupt plans for the explosion, to risk being destroyed by it.

Their scheme failed, however, even before they reached the Algerian border. They had barely crossed into the Upper Volta when a division of French troops blocked their passage. Two further attempts were similarly repelled. In the face of overwhelming military odds, the Sahara Project collapsed on January 17, 1960, and the frustrated participants began their long retreat to Accra. Bayard Rustin had withdrawn some time earlier. Under pressure from A. Philip Randolph, who needed him to resume his organizing activities for the civil rights movement, he had returned to New York.

Because Randolph had not objected to his role in the Sahara Project, Rustin was surprised when, late in 1959, he began hearing from Stanley Levison and Tom Kahn that Randolph was displeased by his absence from the struggle at home. Randolph "was shocked by your departure," Kahn wrote, adding that Rustin should have known it wasn't in Randolph's manner to discourage "your leaving, feeling it improper to exert pressure on you." Randolph now began exerting pressure, however. He wanted Rustin back in the States to organize a project he and King and Wilkins planned for the summer of 1960: demonstrations at the Democratic and Republican national conventions, demanding progressive civil rights planks in the parties' platforms.

Rustin therefore found himself in the middle of a tug-of-war between the two political causes to which he was equally committed, pacifism and black protest activism. One movement was virtually demanding his return home, while the other was insisting that he remain with the antinuclear project in Africa. He wished they would resolve the contest between themselves, thus relieving him of a most unpleasant decision—choosing one above the other. "What is happening here is very important," he wrote to Randolph, "but, as you know, as I have said again and again, I am an American and must not get cut off from the struggle at home. I sincerely need your advice." No such advice was forthcoming. Instead, Ralph DiGia, of the War Resisters League, wrote to him:

> *I imagine you are pretty essential to the {Sahara} project and that the Africans . . . would feel very let down . . . for you to pull out. . . . Randolph and {Levison} state that you are essential {over here}, that the civil rights movement is the greatest thing for peace {and} the worldwide struggle for equality. They want you back. Meanwhile we {in the pacifist movement} want you to stay. From the pacifist viewpoint, this Sahara Project has much more potential than the civil rights stuff. Which will turn out to be more important I don't know, {but} from the WRL viewpoint the Sahara Project should take precedence. . . . You personally stand to lose some prestige, no matter what you decide. . . . If you were arrested and deported back here by January 1, everybody would be happy.*

As DiGia said, Rustin was indeed "in a tough spot," a predicament confirmed when Tom Kahn again wrote to him: "We are categorically convinced that you should return by the first [of January]. While we understand the problems you face, coming back to a disgruntled band of pacifists, the situation is such that they cannot have the final say in the matter." If the pacifists' "inflexible position" made a collective decision impossible, then "Randolph's firmness on your role" in the civil rights movement would also "preclude compromise. I don't believe he has ever before taken so strong a stand on you, and we should be heartened by this." Rustin arrived back in New York on January 5, 1960.

Pressure for his return had come from another source as well. At a board meeting of the Southern Christian Leadership Conference in the late fall, Dr. King had proposed, and a majority had agreed, that Rustin be invited to become the SCLC's associate director and an administrative assistant to its leader. King recognized that the SCLC, after two years of existence, had yet to develop an effective grassroots program, particularly in the area of voter education. He felt also that Rustin's administrative assistance would allow him, King, to devote more time and energy to building the SCLC into the formidable mass organization Bayard himself had envisioned. "One of the reasons you are so valuable is because of your acquaintance with so many people," Stanley Levison wrote to him in Ghana. "He [King] is now more vividly conscious of the public relations problems involved in [his move from Montgomery to Atlanta], and is dependent on your guidance and imagination. He is eager to have you start as early as the first part of December."

Rustin was not eager to accept a position that would require him to move from New York to Atlanta. And he had other reservations. He felt that he would not be welcome by certain of his old critics in the SCLC hierarchy; that they would undermine the effectiveness of his work for the organization by reviving talk about his sexuality. But Tom Kahn, as much a personal companion as a gifted intellectual aide, urged him to accept the position in the South. "People are going to make trouble for you from now until you've got both feet in the grave," Kahn wrote to him. "Hasn't a vicious cycle been created whereby you have calculatedly avoided real public prominence in order not to expose yourself and others to attack? Invulnerability comes only with total anonymity. That you cannot have. It seems to me that we must always expect sniping, and from friends."

Kahn was also motivated by his strong interest in a socialist-labor-civil rights alliance. And he believed that with Rustin, a socialist, helping to lead the emerging black movement in the South, the struggles for social and racial progress would be united. In the end, Rustin declined the SCLC offer. He preferred to continue playing his marginal but vital role with all civil rights leaders and organizations, and to preserve his official relationship with the pacifist movement, based in New York.

Chapter 15

Exile from the Kingdom

Not long after his return from Africa, early in 1960, Rustin began work on the project A. Philip Randolph had called him home to organize: demonstrations at that summer's national party conventions. But first Randolph had had to heal the rift that developed between himself and the War Resisters League, over the issue of Rustin's role in the Sahara Project. Writing to Edward Gottlieb, chairman of the WRL, Randolph requested that Rustin's leave of absence be extended, owing to the importance of his contribution to the black struggle. Gottlieb granted the request, but fearing that Rustin might be gradually stolen from the pacifist movement, he was careful to emphasize, in his reply to Randolph: "We do not wish Bayard Rustin's relationship with our staff to be severed. We are accordingly retaining him in his present capacity [executive secretary] but detaching him for service with you and Martin Luther King."

Rustin had scarcely begun organizing the conventions project when a more urgent demand for his services intervened. In February, the state of Alabama indicted Dr. King on charges of perjury and tax evasion. Randolph, stunned by the news—as were almost all pro–civil rights constituencies in the country—wrote immediately to King, assuring him of "my absolute faith in your integrity." Already, Randolph added, "preparations are being made to give you concrete, organized, and systemic support."

That concrete organized effort took the shape of an ad hoc group called the Committee to Defend Martin Luther King. The committee, whose formation Randolph announced on March 3, established headquarters at the Harlem Labor Center, with the objective of raising $200,000 to help defray the costs of King's legal defense. Randolph, one of the committee's two cochairmen—the other was the Reverend Gardner C. Taylor, of Brooklyn's Concord Baptist Church—appointed Bayard Rustin its executive director, assisted chiefly by Stanley Levison, as an important fund-raiser for King's SCLC. To underscore its prestige, the committee then mobilized an interracial cosponsorship, comprising prominent actors, musicians, trade unionists, writers, clergymen, political and civic leaders.

Much of the targeted $200,000 was to come from concerts, promoted with the help of Harry Belafonte and Sidney Poitier; from fund appeals to labor, liberal, Jewish, and other religious institutions; and from full- or half-page newspaper advertisements.

One of those ads, in the March 29 issue of the *New York Times,* netted thousands of dollars. But it got the *Times* in serious trouble, a protracted and costly libel litigation—whose outcome would uphold and affirm vital principles of American press freedom. The text of that controversial advertisement—written partly by the playwright Lorraine Hansberry and approved by Bayard Rustin, who had commissioned it—contained these statements:

> Small wonder that the Southern violators of the Constitution fear this new, nonviolent brand of freedom fighter. . . . Small wonder that they are determined to destroy the one man who, more than any other, symbolizes the new spirit now sweeping the South—the Rev. Dr. Martin Luther King. . . .
>
> Again and again, the Southern violators have answered Dr. King's peaceful protests with intimidation and violence. They

have bombed his home, almost killing his wife and child. They have assaulted his person. They have arrested him. . . . And now they have charged him with "perjury"—a felony under which they could imprison him for ten years. Obviously, their real purpose is to remove him physically as the leader to whom the students and millions of others look for guidance and support and thereby to intimidate all leaders who may rise in the South.

Offended by the term "Southern violators of the Constitution," L. B. Sullivan, a city commissioner in Montgomery, sued the *Times* for libel, claiming damages in the amount of $500,000. Four other Alabama state officials followed suit, asking a total of three million dollars in compensation. Those complaints aimed not only to punish the *Times* financially but also to inhibit its reporting of civil rights affairs in the South.

From unexpected quarters, Bayard Rustin also came in for a fusillade of criticism. Mentioned in one of the libel suits were a number of black clergymen, officers of the Southern Christian Leadership Conference, whose names had appeared as cosigners of the offending advertisement; and they now denounced Rustin for using their names without permission. Understandably, he hadn't thought it necessary to seek permission, for they were all cosponsors of the Committee to Defend Martin Luther King. The ministers were implacable, nevertheless, and demanded that Rustin be fired from his position as director of the committee. "The attack upon Bayard," one of his volunteer assistants recalled, "came from the usual quarters in the SCLC—people who were jealous of his relationship with King and had strong political disagreements with him. They used any excuse to undermine his role in the movement." Such people did not include L. D. Reddick, an early historian of the SCLC and a close associate of its now beleaguered leader. In a letter to A. Philip Randolph, deploring "the vicious attack that has been made upon Bayard," Reddick emphasized that "it would be a great mistake to let him resign under this kind of pressure." But

Randolph seldom yielded to pressure of that sort. He quelled the uprising against his handpicked director of the King defense committee, and
Rustin went on with his work.

The *New York Times* was to make a dogged fight for its case, through
the unfriendly southern judiciary and all the way to the Supreme Court
of the United States. Not until March 1964—after the flowering of the
King-led protest movement—was the main issue in *Times* v. *Sullivan*
resolved. In a majority opinion, written by Justice William Brennan,
the Court ruled that freedom of the press included the right to publish
statements without malicious intention, absent knowledge that such
statements were inaccurate. Further, Brennan wrote, "We hold today
that the Constitution delimits a State's power to award damages for
libel actions brought by public officials against critics of their official
conduct." In his book *Make No Law,* a study of *Times* v. *Sullivan,*
Anthony Lewis called the Brennan decision "a landmark of freedom"
that "transformed American libel law." It could therefore be said that,
through the *New York Times,* the black protest movement had, unintentionally, contributed to a transforming landmark in the system of
American justice. And in that contribution Bayard Rustin, director of
the Committee to Defend Martin Luther King, had played a marginal
but important role.

Paul Barnes, a young black socialist in 1960, would remember his own
role in the last fund-raising affair Rustin organized for the King defense
committee: "Early in May, I went down to City Hall Park, where the
pacifists were protesting against civil defense drills in New York. I
wasn't a pacifist, but I was interested in the issue of nuclear disarmament. There were about five hundred people in the park, and when a
siren sounded, the police gave us until the count of ten to get out of the
park and take shelter in the nearest subway. But hardly anybody moved.
And at the count of ten the cops said, 'Okay, you're all under arrest.'
They grabbed about twenty people, threw them into paddy wagons,
and took off.

"At that point, I saw Bayard Rustin and David Dellinger, standing away in the background. I had never met them, but I knew who they were. I went up to them and said, 'I think we ought to go and get ourselves arrested.' Bayard looked at me, smiled roguishly, and replied, 'I don't believe in knocking at the jailhouse door.' Being a fresh kid, I then jumped on a park bench and made a rousing five-minute speech. Later, as I was leaving the park, Bayard stopped me and asked, 'Are you working?' I told him I wasn't. 'Come up to my office at five o'clock,' he said. I went up to his office in Harlem and he recruited me on the spot, to help publicize a big fund-raising concert for Dr. King at the 369th Regiment Armory. He put me on a sound truck and sent me off, distributing leaflets and making speeches.

"The concert [on the night of May 17, 1960] was a tremendous event. Harry Belafonte, Sidney Poitier, Sarah Vaughan, Ossie Davis, and Ruby Dee were there. The big armory was filled to capacity. And after all those people had paid good money to get in, Bayard still had some of us roaming the aisles, passing hats and cans. We collected about ten thousand dollars in bills and coins. There was a Jewish lawyer named Stanley Levison, who was Bayard's friend and Dr. King's money man. At the end of the concert, Levison selected two of us to carry the ten thousand dollars from the armory [on 142nd Street] to the office of King's defense committee [on 125th Street]. I carried one of the two heavy boxes of money, and I thought my shoulder would break under its weight. Moreover, can you imagine carrying all that cash through the streets of Harlem late at night? I was glad none of the street gangs guessed what we had in those boxes. What a hit they would have made!

"Working with Bayard Rustin was one of the most interesting experiences of my life. He was the fastest man thinking on his feet I've ever seen. No one could stop him with a question. He was in total control. He was good at fund-raising and even better at consciousness-raising. Everyone who worked with him loved him."

Altogether, the King defense committee raised approximately $85,000, well short of the $200,000 it had set as a target, but sufficient to cover a major portion of King's legal expenses. Arraigned in

Montgomery on May 25, he was acquitted three days later by an all-white jury—causing him, his biographer David Garrow wrote, to express his surprise at "the white Southerner's ability to do justice." But he may simply have been lucky in the particular individuals who constituted his jury.

At a press conference in Harlem on June 9, Randolph and King announced that Bayard Rustin had resumed his organizing of the civil rights demonstrations planned for the national political conventions that summer: the Democrats' at Los Angeles, beginning on July 11; the Republicans' at Chicago, on July 25. Rustin's memorandum to Dr. King suggested a set of demands to be made at the party conventions: Both parties should "repudiate" all segregationists; declare racial discrimination to be "unconstitutional"; endorse the southern sit-ins as "having the same validity as labor strikes"; support the reduction of congressional representation in districts that denied blacks the right to vote; uphold the Supreme Court's 1954 school desegregation decision as "morally right and the law of the land"; condemn colonialism and racism "in all [their] forms, East and West."

But, for reasons that were not clear, the Reverend Adam Clayton Powell, Jr., who represented Harlem in Congress, opposed black protest action at the Democrats' gathering. Addressing a meeting in Buffalo on June 25, Powell denounced the planned demonstration, declaring that Randolph was a captive of sinister interests and that King had fallen under the radical influence of Bayard Rustin. Powell's opposition, many observers believed, was motivated by two fears: that a civil rights picketing of the Los Angeles convention would harm the presidential candidacy of John F. Kennedy, whom he greatly admired; and that by alienating white southern congressmen, it would jeopardize his own candidacy for the chairmanship of an important committee in the House of Representatives.

Early in July, Dr. King, while visiting Brazil, received a startling message from a source close to Powell: Unless King fired Rustin and canceled the proposed demonstration, Powell would announce publicly that King and Rustin were involved in a sexual relationship. King immediately sent word to Randolph. Though Powell's charge was utterly without substance, he said, it was potentially damaging; therefore it might be wise to cancel the demonstration. Randolph advised King to stand fast against Powell's apparent blackmail for he could think of no charge more absurd than the one the Harlem congressman threatened to make. Nothing like homosexuality could be linked with King, whose alleged wanderings from the marital arrangement were faithfully within the heterosexual bond. Even if King withdrew from the planned demonstration, Randolph stated, he himself had no intention of doing so. King was reassured by Randolph's firm stand.

But he was ominously silent on the issue of Rustin. And when he broke that silence, a few days later, it was to inform Rustin, through an intermediary, that it would be advisable for him to sever all connections not only with King but also with the Southern Christian Leadership Conference. It was a crushing blow to Rustin. He had expected a vote of confidence from the SCLC leader, to whom he had rendered noble service since 1956. But wishing to spare King and the civil rights leadership an embarrassing public squabble, he quietly resigned.

He explained to the *New York Courier,* a black weekly published in Harlem:

> I cannot permit a situation to endure in which my relationship to Dr. King and the Southern Christian Leadership Conference is used to confuse and becloud the basic issues confronting the Negro people today. I cannot permit a situation to endure in which the best elements of the Negro leadership are attacked as a result of my relationship to them. . . . Those who have worked with me during my twenty years in the movement know that I have never sought high position or special privilege, but have always made myself available to the call of the leadership. Twenty-two arrests in the North and South, including time on a North Carolina chain gang, in the course of fight-

ing Jim Crow, are the recorded measure of my dedication, not to political power but to the ideals of our struggle. Nonetheless, Congressman Powell has suggested that I am an obstacle to his giving full, enthusiastic support to Dr. King. I want now to remove that obstacle. I have resigned as Dr. King's special assistant, and severed relations with the Southern Christian Leadership Conference.

A number of King's admirers were shocked by his decision to fling Rustin as a sop to Powell. A. J. Muste saw it as a failure of nerve. In an article for *Harper's* magazine, James Baldwin wrote that King "lost much moral credit . . . in the eyes of the young, when he allowed Adam Clayton Powell to force the resignation of his extremely able organizer and lieutenant, Bayard Rustin. Rustin . . . has a long and honorable record as a fighter for Negro rights and is one of the most penetrating and able men around. The techniques used by Powell . . . were far from sweet; but King was faced with the choice of defending his organizer, who was also his friend, or agreeing with Powell; and he chose the latter course."

The SCLC office Rustin had been operating in Harlem was taken over by Jack O'Dell, a friend and colleague of Stanley Levison. According to Rachelle Horowitz, "Levison, Bayard's great friend, just abandoned him and placed in his stead an alleged functionary of the communist movement." Rustin's chief aides dispersed—after helping him to organize every pro-King and pro-SCLC effort in the North since 1956. Horowitz took a job with the Workers Defense League. Tom Kahn entered Howard University, to complete the undergraduate studies that had been interrupted by his work for the civil rights movement. Norman Hill later became a program officer for the Congress of Racial Equality. Occasional volunteers like Stokely Carmichael and Robert Moses were to become activists in the Student Nonviolent Coordinating Committee. Rustin resumed, full time, his position as executive secretary of the War Resisters League. For more than two years, he would be in virtual exile from the mainstream of civil rights activism—"pushed . . .

to the sidelines," wrote Michael Harrington, a white socialist partisan of the black movement.

Now back with the War Resisters League, Rustin resumed not only his official duties to the organization but his pacifist globe-trotting as well. On December 4, 1960, he flew to London, spent twelve days in his spiritual home abroad, then proceeded to Bombay for an international meeting of the WRL. There he renewed his acquaintance with Devi Prasad, an intellectual who was deeply influenced by the teachings of Gandhi and Tagore. During Rustin's visit to India in the late 1940s, Prasad had been surprised and impressed by the dedicated black Gandhian from the United States. Meeting him again, in 1960, Prasad was even more impressed by the strength of Rustin's commitment to the principles of Gandhian nonviolent direct action. "Bayard was easily the most effective speaker at our Bombay conference," he would recall. "No one there defined the challenge of nonviolence as inspiringly as he did. Bayard emphasized that conflict was inevitable in the world; that there is no life without conflict; that if conflict couldn't be eliminated, then it was the task of the more conscious among us to transform it into a creative force for moral reconciliation and political reconstruction."

Returning from Bombay, in early January, Rustin made another of his irresistible stops in London, where he joined the Committee of One Hundred—a recently formed pacifist grouping—at an antinuclear rally in Trafalgar Square. He flew back to New York on January 14, only to learn that his services would soon be required in another international enterprise.

A peace "walk" from San Francisco to Moscow had begun a month before his return to New York. Sixteen pacifists, sponsored by the Committee for Non-Violent Action, had set out from the West Coast on a leisurely march across the United States. They were to fly from New York to London and from London to Paris, where they were scheduled to resume, on foot, their antinuclear protest journey to Moscow. The pilgrimage was planned to arrive in London on June 1; and at that point, or before that point, the CNVA needed Rustin to organize the remaining logistics of the passage through Europe to the Soviet Union.

Rustin therefore went back to London on March 5. There he set up headquarters in Chancery Lane, with the able assistance of April Carter, a young Oxford-educated activist in Britain's Direct Action Committee, whom he had first met at the Aldermaston March in 1958. While Carter managed the headquarters in Chancery Lane, Rustin flew from one European city to another, negotiating accommodations and speaking appearances for the marchers from San Francisco. Carter was later to confess her "surprise at how far Bayard was willing to treat a woman of twenty-three as his equal." There was "an element of tact," she said, "but it was all genuine."

After its ten-month journey from San Francisco, the peace march arrived in Moscow on October 2, 1961. Because it was the longest and most arduous pacifist journey ever undertaken, it deserved to be crowned with a modicum of success. It wasn't. It failed to exert the slightest influence upon the conduct of Soviet nuclear policy. But A. J. Muste, its leading architect, found a token of consolation in a *New York Herald Tribune* editorial. Though that conservative paper, a voice of the American establishment, couldn't be called an admirer of radical pacifism, it stated: "It is a long time since any group of foreigners has been permitted to challenge that enforced conformity [the Soviet Union]. Inhabitants of Moscow have had their first taste of the kind of diversity that exists in the West. . . . Through this tiny chink in the Iron Curtain a few seminal ideas have penetrated. They may not affect the current crisis, but they may grow."

On the back burner of pacifist strategy since the mid-1940s was the idea for an international peace army, first proposed by the Gandhian mystic Vinoba Bhave. Though not entirely in the form Bhave had conceived, the idea was resurrected in January 1962. Meeting that month in Beirut, a group of international pacifists, including Bayard Rustin, founded an organization called the World Peace Brigade. With A. J. Muste as one of its three cochairmen—the others being Britain's Michael Scott and India's Jayaprakash Narayan—the World Peace

Brigade pledged itself to alliances with peoples and movements engaged in "nonviolent struggle for self-determination and social reconstruction." And in forming its alliances, the Brigade identified itself chiefly with the nonviolent struggle in colonized parts of central Africa.

In February, Rustin flew to Addis Ababa for a conference of the Pan-African Freedom Movements of East and Central Africa (PAFMECA), a coalition whose secretariat was based in Dar es Salaam, Tanzania. In the Ethiopian capital, he conferred with Tanzania's Julius Nyerere, a cofounder of PAFMECA, and Kenneth Kaunda, who headed the movement for self-determination in Zambia. Kaunda, leader of his country's United National Independence Party and a devotee of Gandhian methodology, invited Rustin and a detachment from the newly formed World Peace Brigade to support a general strike he would soon be calling in Zambia, demanding universal adult suffrage. That support, Kaunda suggested, should take the shape of an organized march into Zambia.

Rustin and a team from the Peace Brigade planned their operation in Dar es Salaam, where Nyrere's political party, the Tanzania African National Union, provided them with office space and living accommodations. In a spasm of excitement, Rustin wrote to A. J. Muste, in New York: "The project is built around us. We are the new factor that has struck the nerve. We are the emotional drive in a very weary and difficult situation, and we must not fail, no matter what." But through no fault of theirs, the project would fail.

In March, the masses they mobilized set out from Tanzania, attracting new forces along the way; five hundred miles later, they were to assemble at the Zambian border, awaiting word from Kenneth Kaunda. But the word they awaited—when to begin their invasion of the border—never came. When Kaunda did send word, it was to say that the British Colonial Office in London had promised early elections, leading to internal self-government; the general strike had therefore been canceled. Rustin and his troops dispersed, the main elements retreating to Dar es Salaam, where the World Peace Brigade had recruited them.

The British government later lodged a strong protest with Julius

Nyerere for allowing Tanzania to be used as the base for a march into Zambia. Bayard Rustin was scolded by the American State Department: the embassy in Dar es Salaam warned him against any further meddling with the internal affairs of African countries. But Kenneth Kaunda applauded "the generous support" of Nyerere and the Rustin-led group from the World Peace Brigade. He was "heartened," Kaunda said, by their contribution "to our long efforts at achieving freedom . . . through nonviolent resistance."

Rustin would remain in Dar es Salaam for several months. With his friend William Sutherland, who had moved from Ghana to join Julius Nyerere's government in East Africa, he helped to organize a Gandhian program for the Tanzania African National Union, Nyerere's power base for years to come.

On Rustin's return to the United States in October 1962—after visiting his jailed comrade Michael Randle in Britain—he found the civil rights movement in an advanced state of agitation: The Congress of Racial Equality was undertaking its perilous Freedom Rides into the Deep South; the Student Nonviolent Coordinating Committee was growing in size and militant energy; Dr. King and the Southern Christian Leadership Conference were leading defiant street demonstrations, demanding voting rights and the desegregation of public facilities. In all those developments Rustin had played a pioneering role. But now he could only stand on the sidelines, exiled from the mainstream of civil rights action.

Rustin's contribution to the rise of the protest movement consisted partly in the generation of student leaders, black and white, he attracted to the avant-garde of civil rights activism. Most of them young enough to be his children, they included Norman Hill, Rachelle Horowitz, Eleanor Holmes Norton, Tom Kahn, Joyce Ladner, John Lewis, Robert Moses, Stokely Carmichael, and other militant idealists in SNCC.

Soon after arriving home from Dar es Salaam, Rustin, in his office at the War Resisters League, reread a letter the WRL had received two years earlier. At that dispirited point in his career—August 1960, some weeks after he had been pushed out of his work with Dr. King and the SCLC—he must surely have been cheered by what the letter said. It came from Jane Stembridge, a former student at Union Theological Seminary, who had moved to Atlanta to help administer the first national office of SNCC—a poor and struggling operation, off in a nook of the SCLC headquarters. Stembridge's letter thanked the WRL for Rustin's "inestimable help to us"; for his "concrete, penetrating suggestions"; for his "constant example in the fight for freedom, honesty, and peace."

One of her colleagues at that early SNCC office was Robert Moses, a future leader of the organization, who had been among the student activists who helped Rustin coordinate the 1958–59 Youth Marches for Integrated Schools. According to Rustin, it was at *his* suggestion that Moses, a brilliant intellectual from Harlem, went South and volunteered his services to the infant SNCC. Moses, who later became SNCC's most inspiring spiritual leader, was to recall his first days in the Atlanta office—licking stamps, while discussing Paul Tillich and Reinhold Niebuhr with Jane Stembridge. In her decision to do volunteer work for SNCC, Stembridge had reached the conclusion that in the end, everything came "to human relationships," that "love alone is radical." Moses was to display the radicalism of love by serving poor and unread blacks in some of the more backward and dangerous regions of the Deep South.

Through Tom Kahn, Rustin exerted a strong influence upon a group of student radicals at Howard University. Though one in a minority of white undergraduates on campus, Kahn became an ideological force in the university's Nonviolent Action Group, which included young SNCC militants like Courtland Cox, Ruth Howard, Bill Mahoney, Charles Cobb, Muriel Tillinghurst, Ed Brown, Joan Weaver-Smith, Michael Thelwell, and Stokely Carmichael. To their racial activism Tom Kahn added the democratic-socialist analysis he shared with Bayard Rustin, Michael Harrington, and Max Shachtman. In fact, it seemed to Michael Thelwell that Kahn had entered Howard mainly to cultivate black student activism from a democratic-left perspective.

"Tom," Thelwell recalled, "represented a socialist collaboration with the nonviolent black movement. Politically, he was far more sophisticated and experienced than any of us. Though shy and reticent, he taught us a great deal about politics and the techniques of radical action; and as we grew close to him, he introduced us to the polemical style of sectarian socialist discourse in New York City. It was all very fascinating and exotic to us.

"He also spoke glowingly of Bayard Rustin's political history and his Gandhian-pacifist-socialist approach to the black struggle. It is fair to say that after our first year at Howard, Rustin became our intellectual and political mentor. We adopted his view that the integration of American society required a radical coalition of social and interracial forces. We admired Bayard's intellectuality. He sometimes came to speak on campus, and he seemed far more creative, articulate, and analytical than others in the established civil rights leadership. He was an activist in direct action, a theoretician and a practitioner, a dramatic and romantic figure who had traveled throughout the world on behalf of peace and political freedom. We became Bayard Rustin people. He was a key influence at that early stage of our political development."

Late in 1962, the Howard group presented Rustin and Malcolm X in a public debate, a confrontation Rustin helped to engineer. The college administration had objected to Malcolm's speaking on campus without rebuttal by an opposing point of view. "I told Malcolm," Rustin recalled, "that I could arrange his appearance on the campus, but strictly on my terms. 'What are your terms?' he asked. I said, 'We'll have a debate. You'll present your views, and then I'll attack you as someone having no political, social, or economic program for dealing with the problems of blacks.' He said, 'I'll take you up on that.'"

The outcome was anything but what the predominantly pro-Rustin audience had confidently expected—particularly the student activists who were already impressed by Rustin's gift for logical analysis. Michael Thelwell was to retain this memory of the occasion:

"Bayard presented his position: the urgency of a nonviolent struggle against segregation and discrimination; the necessity for black inclusion in all the political, economic, and educational institutions of American life; the importance of organized mass pressure upon the federal government. Malcolm then took the floor, launched into his black nationalist message, and, astonishingly, turned the audience around. In an electrifying performance, he articulated many of the things that weren't being openly said by the black middle class; and he did so in such a biting and uncompromising style that he had the audience literally shouting. It was Malcolm's occasion. We felt that if he hadn't won the debate in analytical terms, he had certainly won the audience in visceral terms. Only when we cooled off the next day did we recognize that we had not been converted after all. The black nationalist position still wasn't a viable one. Malcolm had mesmerized us, but he hadn't shaken most of us out of our pro-Rustin position."

For a while longer—until he broke with the integrationist movement—Stokely Carmichael was among those who maintained the pro-Rustin position. "Bayard," he said later, "was one of the first I had direct contact with [of whom] I could really say, 'That's what I want to be.' He was like a superman, hooking socialism up with the black movement, organizing blacks." But not long after graduating from Howard, Carmichael began losing faith in Rustin's approach to the civil rights struggle, a transformation that led him gradually into a passionate embrace of Black Power.

"I think Bayard's influence upon the young SNCC activists at Howard University," Tom Kahn said in retrospect, "was more by the force and example of his political personality than by his ideas. Not all of them were taken with his perspective on the black struggle. What chiefly attracted them to Rustin was his being a type of black intellectual-activist they hadn't seen before—a radical and a cosmopolitan fighter for human rights. And because they were so fascinated by his example, they established a personal loyalty to him. That loyalty lasted for a while. But most of it began unraveling when he returned to the national civil rights leadership and organized the big march of 1963."

Chapter 16

The March on Washington

O ne winter afternoon in 1962, Rustin went up to Harlem from his office in downtown Manhattan, for a visit with his civil rights mentor A. Philip Randolph. They had been meeting regularly, though not frequently, since Adam Clayton Powell, Jr., helped to drive Rustin from his position as the key tactician and organizer for the developing protest movement. At their latest reunion, the men—Rustin then fifty and Randolph seventy-three—discussed two urgent issues of that time: the growing rate of black unemployment and the heroic street demonstrations Martin Luther King was leading in areas of the Deep South.

Randolph was moved to mention an idea he had broached at a recent gathering of the Negro American Labor Council, a trade union alliance he then led, in addition to his vice presidency in the AFL-CIO. The civil rights movement, Randolph said, couldn't more appropriately mark the centenary of Abraham Lincoln's Emancipation Proclamation than by organizing a massive Emancipation March on Washington, calling national attention to the unfulfilled social and economic promises of a hundred years. Would Bayard consider drafting the blueprint for such a march? Rustin could not have responded with more enthusiasm to the idea, which offered him an opportunity to regain the position from which he had been dislodged in the summer of 1960.

In January 1963, after conferring with Norman Hill and Tom Kahn, Rustin presented Randolph with an outline of the Emancipation March, entailing "the co-ordinated participation of all progressive sectors of the liberal, labor, religious, and Negro communities." The outline further proposed two consecutive days of nonviolent direct action, culminating in a great rally at the Lincoln Memorial, where "our concrete Emancipation Program" would be presented to the nation. Pleased by Rustin's plan, Randolph cleared it with the Negro American Labor Council, then began a campaign to win the collaboration of other major civil rights leaders.

His effort, after a successful beginning, was to become more difficult than he had imagined it would be. James Farmer and John Lewis—the leaders of CORE and SNCC, respectively—instantly agreed to participate, perhaps because they and their organizations shared Randolph's belief in Gandhian mass action. Dr. King and his SCLC shared that belief as well, yet King was not eager to join Randolph's project. Preoccupied with the SCLC's mass demonstrations in the South, he was also thinking of leading his own march to Washington, planned and executed from below the Mason-Dixon line. Randolph persisted; and with help from the Reverend Fred Shuttlesworth, prominent in the SCLC leadership, he eventually persuaded King to support the Washington project originating in New York. It was then, partly to accommodate King's major concern—civil rights rather than economic pressure—that Randolph renamed the proposed event a March on Washington for Jobs and Freedom. The accommodation was a mutual victory. It surely underscored Randolph's long-held conviction that black political advancement would be meaningless without accompanying economic gains.

There was a calculated motive behind Randolph's approach to King before seeking the participation of the NAACP's Roy Wilkins and the National Urban League's Whitney Young. As Bayard Rustin later explained it, Randolph always used King as a left leverage to the moderate centers of black leadership, feeling that the moderates would not wish to exclude themselves from a popular initiative in which the SCLC leader was involved. With King now aboard, Randolph expected no resistance from Wilkins and Young. He was mistaken. That his strategy was not so readily effective in 1963 was due, curiously, in part to the march's being the largest and most visible national undertaking in which the moderate leaders had ever been invited to share.

The National Urban League was traditionally a black social service agency, not a protest organization; and it feared jeopardizing its tax-exempt status by participating in the political enterprise Randolph had conceived. Still, hoping he might be able to influence his conservative board of directors, Whitney Young told Randolph that the NUL would consider joining the March on Washington if a number of conditions were met: The Urban League would have to be fully involved in planning the event; it would not want to be linked with a program of civil disobedience in the nation's capital; it would demand an equal say in the selection of a march director; and it would require an assurance that the demonstration would be interracial and nonviolent. Only one of those conditions was hard for Randolph to accept. How could the march abstain from Gandhian methodology when that was near the heart of its conception? Without employing techniques of civil disobedience, wouldn't the march be little more than a ceremonial display of grievance? But Randolph badly needed the Urban League's participation if his march was to represent the broadest coalition of civil rights forces in America.

He had a similar need for the NAACP's participation, but like Young, Roy Wilkins told Randolph that the NAACP would support the demonstration only if it canceled its plans for civil disobedience. The March on Washington could not be effectively staged without the support of the NAACP's treasury; its vast network of local groups across the United States; its prestige as the largest and oldest civil rights organization in America. Of such predicaments were compromises made. There would be no acts of civil disobedience at the March on Washington—no sit-ins on Capitol Hill or around the White House.

But while that decision placated the Urban League and the NAACP, it was deplored by students and young activists, including some who were prepared to assist Bayard Rustin's organizing of the Washington demonstration. A number of them would recover from their disappointment with Randolph's compromise—which they viewed as a cave-in to the moderate black establishment—but others never would. And it was to be the beginning of their disillusionment with Rustin, whom they accused of playing a role in Randolph's decision.

"For SNCC," recalled Mary King, "the march produced a canker that never healed." If the original plan hadn't been gutted, said Michael Thelwell, another SNCC activist, "then a crisis might have been forced" in Washington. Rachelle Horowitz, one of Rustin's planning assistants, was torn between two views of the compromise but resolved them on the side of pragmatism and the pressure to which Randolph and Rustin were forced to yield. "On the one hand," she said later, "I regarded the compromise as an incredible sellout. . . . Roy Wilkins and Whitney Young weren't going to join anything that would be embarrassing to John F. Kennedy, because they were very close to the President. I was in a funk for days. On the other hand, I came to recognize that the decision to scale down the militancy of the march was a sensible one. After all, we wanted the demonstration to be as broad-based as possible, reflecting a coalition of American conscience. We couldn't have achieved that objective if we had insisted on a program of radical confrontation with the government. We simply couldn't have it both ways."

But thanks to the Randolph compromise, the 1963 March on Washington was to be the first occasion on which all major civil rights leaders and organizations collaborated in a national undertaking. Their past relationships had been marked more by sectarian squabbling than by cooperation. James Farmer's CORE looked coldly at the NAACP's aversion to militant mass action in the streets. John Lewis's SNCC was almost always at odds with the moderate-to-conservative axis of Roy Wilkins and Whitney Young. James Forman, one in the cohort of

Lewis's leadership, was to recall that SNCC's relationship with the Urban League and the NAACP—"stormy" from the beginning—deteriorated into "irreconcilable differences." Wilkins took his own disdainful view not only of CORE and SNCC but also of Dr. King's SCLC, regarding them all as upstart organizations feeding off the prestige of the NAACP and the pioneering victories it had won through its long history of dogged and costly court litigation.

Bayard Rustin later reported this example of how the NAACP, founded in 1909, viewed the "upstart" protest organizations: "When Medgar Evers was murdered in Mississippi, all the black chieftains went down for his funeral, because one of our heroes had been martyred. As he entered the church, Dr. King was ushered to a place of honor on the platform. Displeased, Roy Wilkins walked over to King and said, 'This is an NAACP affair. We have not invited you here to come and take over.' King was so humiliated that he later said to me, 'How could Wilkins have done such a thing?' Martin didn't understand that the NAACP, which had put decades of service into the South, resented the fact that he, a young man, had now come along, at the right moment, to reap the credit. Wilkins was hurt that the world was so captivated by King's dramatic entrance into the black struggle, forgetting all the tedious work the NAACP had done to prepare the path."

Civil rights leaders of the 1960s, James Farmer was to say, weren't "joint chiefs of staff." They were "jockeying for position," for media attention, for foundation grants. And because King "was far away in the lead, envy of his visibility was inevitable." Only their common regard for A. Philip Randolph, elder statesman of the civil rights movement, could have united them in support of the March on Washington. Randolph, the journalist Murray Kempton wrote in 1963, "neither feels hostility" toward the younger black leaders "nor excites it in them."

The momentum gathering behind the proposed march was strengthened by events being televised from Birmingham in the spring of 1963, during the controversial street demonstrations Dr. King was leading in

Alabama. "Birmingham," Rustin remembered, "was one of television's finest hours. Evening after evening, television brought into the living rooms of America the violence, brutality, stupidity, and ugliness of [police commissioner] Eugene 'Bull' Connor's effort to maintain racial segregation." At the White House, President Kennedy was as appalled as were millions of other viewers. So much so that on the evening of June 11, he delivered his first major address to the nation on the subject of civil rights. "We face a moral crisis as a country and as a people," he said. "It cannot be met by repressive police action. It cannot be left to increased demonstrations in the streets. It cannot be quieted by token moves or talk. It is time to act. . . . Those who do nothing are inviting shame as well as violence. Those who act boldly are recognizing right as well as reality."

Kennedy was signifying his own readiness to act. "No President," his special assistant Theodore Sorensen recalled, "had ever before so forcefully recognized the moral injustice of racial segregation, and no President could ever therefore ignore his moral obligation to remove it." On June 19, Kennedy sent to Congress the most progressive civil rights message of his administration, hoping that while his proposed legislation made its way through the House and Senate there would be a cessation of hostilities in the streets. That did not occur. Nor did the civil rights leaders suspend their plans for a March on Washington, as Kennedy had also hoped they would.

On June 22, he invited the entire march leadership—the "Big Six" of Randolph, King, Wilkins, Lewis, Farmer, and Young—to a conference in the cabinet room of the White House. Those on the President's side of the table included his brother Robert, the attorney general; his vice president, Lyndon Johnson; and Arthur Schlesinger, Jr., a special assistant. Kennedy wanted the black leaders—"as gifted and impressive a group as one could find in the country," Schlesinger called them—to cancel the March on Washington, so as not to jeopardize passage of his civil rights bill. "We want success in Congress," he told them, "not just a big show at the Capitol. Some of these people [in Congress] are looking for an excuse to be against us. I don't want to give them a chance to say, 'Yes, I'm for the bill, but I'm damned if I'll vote for it at the point of a gun.' It seemed to me a great mistake to announce a March on Washington before the bill was even in committee. The only effect is to create an atmosphere of intimidation, and this may give some members of Congress an out."

Randolph, leader of the delegation, replied that while they understood the President's political problems, they had serious problems of their own. "The Negroes [particularly in the South] are already in the streets," he said. It was "very likely impossible to get them off"; and if they were bound to be in the streets, then it was "better that they be led by organizations dedicated to civil rights and disciplined by struggle rather than to leave them to other leaders, who care neither about civil rights nor about nonviolence." Restating and extending Randolph's theme, James Farmer said the leaders would be in an "untenable position" if they canceled the march "and then were defeated in the legislative battle"; frustration "would grow into violence, and would demand new leadership." Randolph and Farmer were probably thinking of Malcolm X's black nationalist contempt for "so-called" civil rights leaders and their movement for a racially integrated American society. Seeing how firmly his visitors held their ground, the President yielded a measure of his. "We're in this up to the neck," he told them. "We may all go down the drain as a result. . . . What is important is that we preserve confidence in the good faith of each other. I have my problems with the Congress; you have yours with your own groups. We will undoubtedly disagree from time to time on tactics. But the important thing is to keep in touch."

It was one of the best meetings Schlesinger could remember attending in his years at the White House, and when it ended he had a brief talk with Roy Wilkins—"the Negro leader whose intelligence and integrity the President particularly respected." Wilkins "whispered to me his sympathy for the President, in view of the pressures playing on him, the choices he had to make." The NAACP leader had a residual difficulty of his own, for he had not yet wholly resolved his tactical differences with others in the march leadership: Dr. King, unhappy with the concessions Randolph had made to Wilkins and Young in order to win their support of the march, still favored a program of civil disobedience at the coming Washington demonstration. As Wilkins put it, "Dr. King, who had no legislative experience, was thinking of applying . . . the tactics of Birmingham to the capital, a line of thought I considered disastrous." Hence, not long after the White House conference, Wilkins suggested another meeting of the march leaders, at which that and other remaining issues would be settled once and for all. It was scheduled to take place at New York's Roosevelt Hotel on July 2.

Dr. King could not have looked forward to that conference, fearing, conceivably, that it might spark yet another of his unpleasant clashes with the sardonic Wilkins. James Farmer, who had witnessed a number of those encounters in the past, was to write in his autobiography:

> At one meeting Wilkins leaned across the table and said to King, "One of these days, Martin, some bright reporter is going to take a good look at Montgomery and discover that despite all the hoopla, your boycott didn't desegregate a single city bus. It was the quiet NAACP-type legal action that did it.
>
> "We're fully aware of that, Roy," Martin replied with simple poise. . . .
>
> Roy appeared to ignore the reply and pressed the point.
>
> "In fact, Martin, if you have desegregated *anything* by your efforts, kindly enlighten me."
>
> Well," said Martin, "I guess about the only thing I've desegregated is a few human hearts."
>
> Roy conceded that one and nodded.

According to Rustin, who had also observed a number of such clashes, "Martin simply couldn't in-fight with Roy. Martin could stand up to the worst police brutalities in Birmingham, but he flinched from polemical exchanges with Wilkins."

At the July 2 meeting, King did not insist that the March on Washington adopt the confrontational tactics he employed in

Birmingham. The discussion dealt mainly with Bayard Rustin's role in the proposed demonstration.

Who, Wilkins asked Randolph, would be organizing and directing the march? Randolph had never doubted that it would be Rustin, architect of the original blueprint; he surely knew no one in the movement with Rustin's ability and experience at coordinating civil rights mass coalitions. When Randolph said as much, Wilkins was the only dissenter in the room. While he was well aware of Rustin's "organizational skill and brilliant mind," he did not consider Bayard the suitable director of a project so vital to the integrity and national prestige of the civil rights movement.

What, Randolph inquired, were the grounds of Wilkins's objection? First, Wilkins explained, there was the matter of Rustin's left-wing past: though he had long severed his ties to the communist movement, later becoming a democratic socialist, most Americans did not distinguish between communists and socialists. Second, Rustin had been imprisoned as a conscientious objector during World War II; and there again, few Americans knew or cared about the difference between draft resistance (conscientious objection) and draft dodging. Third, there was the problem of Rustin's sexual life. All three factors, Wilkins argued, could be used as ammunition against the March on Washington.

When Randolph solicited other opinions at the conference table, John Lewis gave his instant and unconditional endorsement of Rustin. "I felt," he said later, "that Bayard had the skill and capacity to pull the needed coalition of national forces together. He was our best organizer, with an all-inclusive view of American society." James Farmer concurred, despite his history of ambivalence toward Rustin. Lewis recalled what then transpired: "Dr King said he saw no reason why Bayard's past should bar him from directing the march. Well, that unleashed a tirade from Roy Wilkins. Roy ended up by saying, 'Martin, you're politically naive. And *you* need to dissociate yourself from some of the political people around you.' [That may have been a veiled reference to Stanley Levison, whom the FBI had linked with the communist movement.] It was a nasty scene. It took A. Philip Randolph to restore some peace and civility."

A compromise was reached. Wilkins and Whitney Young suggested that if Randolph named himself the official director of the march, then he could appoint whomever he wished to be his working deputy. "But I want you to know," Randolph emphasized, "that my choice will be Bayard." Retiring from the combat, Wilkins fired a parting shot. "Phil," he said to Randolph, "I'll have to go along with you on that. But I'm issuing a word of warning. We're going to hold you responsible for any embarrassment that might befall the March on Washington." Wilkins's objection was principled, not personal. Urbane and politically sagacious, he had always enjoyed an amicable working relationship with Rustin. Nor, despite Wilkins's fight against his appointment as march director, did Rustin lose his long-standing regard for the tough-minded leader of the NAACP. "Bayard had a high respect for those people in his political life who counterbalanced his tendencies toward the dramatic and the flamboyant," Tom Kahn said. "Roy Wilkins was such a person—coolly analytical, hardly ever carried away by emotion. He and Bayard had their differences, but their mutual respect remained intact. Later, when Rustin began organizing the march, he received more support from the NAACP than from any other civil rights institution."

Before the Big Six wound up their stormy meeting, they concluded two other items of business. They voted to add four white cochairmen to the march leadership: Matthew Ahmann, of the National Catholic Conference for Interracial Justice; the Reverend Eugene Carson Blake, of the National Council of Protestant Churches; Rabbi Joachim Prinz, of the American Jewish Congress; Walter Reuther, of the United Automobile Workers. And having enlarged their coalition into a Big Ten, they then scheduled the march for Wednesday, August 28.

As the chief organizer, Rustin had a mandate to mobilize at least 100,000 demonstrators in the nation's capital. They were to be drawn from around the United States and from a cross section of racial, political, and religious communities. They were to begin arriving in Washington early in the morning of August 28; were to be guaranteed all physical conveniences and every protection against outbreaks of disorder; and were to be on their way out of the city by dusk.

More than a few skeptics wondered whether a project of that dimension and complexity could be organized in the seven weeks from July 2 to August 28. "How," asked a writer for the *National Guardian,* "do you move [that] many people into a crowded, unfamiliar city—by rail, bus, plane, and private car—making certain that they arrive no earlier than 6 a.m. and no later than 10 a.m.? What do you do with them once they have arrived? How do you feed the hungry, refresh the thirsty, care for the sick, discipline the undisciplined? . . . How do you make certain that all these people get back on their buses at precisely 5.30 p.m., so that they leave the city by nightfall?" An official of Washington's police department was just as doubtful. "I simply don't see how they're going to make it," he said. "We spend nearly a year planning for the inaugural parade." If Rustin was daunted by the challenge, he bravely masked his fears. "I am a technician," he told an inquirer. "My job is to carry out policy as established by top leadership."

By mid-July he had a fully functioning headquarters at 170 West 130th Street, the Reverend Thomas Kilgore's Baptist church hall in Harlem. The offices were staffed by more than a hundred volunteers and paid workers, their wages and other office expenses met by donations and contributions from trade unions and the major civil rights organizations. Rustin's principal assistants included Tom Kahn and Rachelle Horowitz; Norman Hill, then a program officer for CORE; the trade unionist Cleveland Robinson, financial chairman of the march project; Joseph Overton, an officer in Randolph's Negro American Labor Council; Seymour Posner, a publicist loaned by the American Jewish Congress; Joyce Ladner and Courtland Cox, two of the activists in SNCC who were not totally disillusioned by the revised march program.

At march headquarters, Rustin maintained a steady communication with auxiliary offices at the NAACP, the Urban League, and an outpost in Washington, headed by the SCLC's Walter Fauntroy. When M. S. Handler, a reporter for the *New York Times,* visited the poorly furnished command post in Harlem, it seemed to him that Rustin and his industrious band were "bent on demonstrating that big things can be accomplished with a small outlay of money." Working sixteen-hour days, they wrote, printed, and mailed out thousands of news bulletins and instruction manuals; advised regional groups in the details of chartering buses, trains, and planes; coordinated the travel arrangements being made in scores of towns and cities across the United States. Rustin, chain-smoking Pall Mall cigarettes, presided over this beehive of activity, though he seemed almost always to be on the telephone— responding to the press, briefing cosponsors of the march, refining arrangements with federal authorities. It was "just like they were getting ready for D-Day in Normandy," one government official said, after surveying the preparations in Harlem.

In another military analogy, *Life* magazine commented: "Merely contemplating the possibilities for trouble and the logistics of the demonstration has given Washington officialdom its worst case of invasion jitters since the first battle of Bull Run." In a poll conducted by the *Wall Street Journal,* two-thirds of the respondents denounced the idea of a march on the nation's capital. "Tempers are bound to flare in the heat of the Washington summer," an alarmed clergyman wrote to the *Times,* "and there is danger that people will be injured and property destroyed."

An editorial in the *Herald Tribune* warned: "If Negro leaders persist in their announced plans to march 100,000-strong on the capital . . . they will be jeopardizing their cause. . . . The ugly part of this particular mass protest is its implication of uncontained violence if Congress doesn't deliver. This is the kind of threat that can make men of pride, which most Congressmen are, turn stubborn." Indeed, most congressmen—turning, or remaining, stubborn—declined invitations to join the marchers at the mass assembly planned for the Lincoln Memorial. William Jennings Bryan Dorn, a representative from South Carolina, replied to his invitation: "This attempt to force Congress to bow to demands is a dangerous precedent, and could some day lead to the overthrow of free government and destroy the liberties of our people."

No voice on Capitol Hill was more hostile than that of Senator Strom Thurmond. Aiming to torpedo the march by discrediting its chief organizer, Thurmond launched a blistering attack upon Bayard Rustin, calling him a communist, draft dodger, and homosexual. Circulated by the national media, Thurmond's attack confronted the civil rights leadership with much the kind of "embarrassment" Wilkins had feared when he opposed Rustin's appointment. Wilkins did not, however, hold Randolph responsible, as he had said he would. Nor did he heed the calls, mainly from moderate quarters of the black movement, for Rustin's dismissal or resignation.

To an irate member of the NAACP, Wilkins replied: "We have found in the past six weeks that he [Rustin] is a man of exceptional ability, who has delivered an extraordinary job on a project that should have required a full three months but is being completed in two. . . . It is the belief of all of us who have noted his work, regardless of our personal feelings, that . . . we could have done no better than the gentleman in question." Randolph's faith in his handpicked organizer remained unshaken as well. "Mr. Rustin," he said in a statement prepared for the press, "has more than satisfactorily conducted himself in the position with which he has been entrusted; and we have not the slightest intention of permitting his separation from that position." The march organization, he added, would not allow "corrupt" and "undemocratic elements to deprive our movement of so capable a leader." Especially after Randolph's defiant public endorsement, the storm blew over; and, heartened by the testimonials he received from the highest levels of civil rights leadership, Rustin resumed his preparations for the big march.

How—as the *National Guardian* had asked—do you discipline the undisciplined on a mass occasion such as the one being planned for August 28? In letters and telephone calls to Washington, Rustin arranged for the deployment of nearly two thousand policemen. And to supplement the local constabulary, he invited William Johnson, a black sergeant in the New York Police Department, to train and direct a large detachment of civilian marshals. Johnson's force of marshals were to act as peacekeepers, with no authority to make arrests; they were to encircle troublemakers and deliver them into the hands of the official police.

How do you feed the hungry and refresh the thirsty? Rustin and his crew instructed demonstrators to arrive in Washington with their own box lunches, preferably unspoilable cheese and peanut butter sandwiches, apples, cakes, soft drinks. The march organization would itself sell eighty thousand ham-and-cheese sandwiches as well as hot dogs and hamburgers. Water would be plentiful. The parade route, from the Washington Monument to the Lincoln Memorial, would be lined with bubbler spigots and 250-gallon water trucks.

How do you meet the demands of sanitation, illness, and exhaustion? There would be scores of mobile toilets and urinals. There would be clinics, ambulances, and first-aid stations, staffed by volunteer doctors and nurses. Parents were advised against bringing children under the age of fourteen. Bus captains were to equip their conveyances with aspirin, Band-Aids, salt tablets, spirits of ammonia, sunburn oils, and waterproof plastic bags (in case of carsickness). There would be lost-and-found booths for the reunion of friends and families. There would be thousands of army blankets for weary travelers who might arrive on the grounds of the Washington Monument before dawn.

The syndicated columnist Mary McGrory observed, with a touch of humor, that the March on Washington would be "the most elaborately nurse-maided demonstration of grievance ever held." What manner of thinking had produced this frenzy of careful preparations? "It was my theory," Rustin explained later, "that you avoided serious incidents and confrontations by imagining them in advance. It is by taking care of simple details that you reduce the possibility of disorder." Any demonstrator who still behaved disruptively would be "a traitor to our cause."

By August 24, Rachelle Horowitz, Rustin's transportation director, had recorded virtually every bus, train, and plane chartered for the journey to Washington. Her figures showed that there would be more than fifteen hundred buses, twenty-one special trains, and three airliners. There was no way of telling how many private automobiles there would be; but it was already clear that the size of the march would exceed the earliest and most optimistic estimate of its planners. "We were ecstatic," Horowitz said. "We had set out to organize a demonstration of 100,000, and we could now see that there would be at least twice that number. But Bayard cautioned us not to publicize our latest figures, so that if only 100,000 people did show up we could still claim a major victory."

On August 26, Rustin and leading members of his organizing team transferred march headquarters from Harlem to the Statler Hilton Hotel in Washington, there to supervise last-minute details. On August 27, they were joined at the hotel by eight of the march's ten cochairmen. Dr. King, one of the two absentees, was registered at the Willard Hotel. James Farmer, the other, was jailed in Plaquemine, Louisiana, where he had been arrested for leading a civil rights demonstration. A number of his colleagues in the North felt that Farmer had refused bail, had elected to stay in jail, so as to dramatize his heroic plight while other leaders were basking in the spotlight of the great March on Washington. Whatever his reason was, Farmer later regretted his absence from the capital.

The evening of August 27—while Rustin briefed the available cochairmen on the order of the next day's program—a surprising visitor appeared in the lobby of the Statler Hilton. It was Malcolm X, surrounded by a group of reporters, who eagerly took down his every word. What was *he* doing there, at the local headquarters of what he mockingly described as "the farce on Washington"? Why would the leading spokesman for black nationalism and separatism wish to be under the same roof with chieftains of the integrationist movement, men he often referred to as "so-called Negro leaders," "begging" for constitutional privileges that were theirs by right of citizenship? "Well," Malcolm replied to such an inquiry, "whatever black folks do, maybe I don't agree with it; but I'm going to be there, brother, because that's where I belong." That implausible answer was a nimble sidestepping of the real question; but he was skilled at elusiveness of that sort when the polemical occasion required it. Hearing that Malcolm X was holding court in the hotel lobby, Roy Wilkins replied, impatiently, to a reporter, "Look, we know Malcolm, and we're not surprised that he's out there. Whatever he says doesn't surprise or hurt us. We have business to take care of."

That business was, of course, to make final arrangements for the next day's demonstration. And this, in a statement the coleaders had issued earlier, was how they envisioned the march: "orderly but not subservient"; "proud but not arrogant"; "nonviolent but not timid"; "unified in purpose" but "not splintered into groups"; "outspoken but not raucous"; carried out with "the dignity befitting a demonstration on behalf of the human rights of twenty millions of people."

Early on the morning of August 28, a weekday, the streets of Washington seemed unusually serene and deserted. "The city was so empty," the writer Marya Mannes observed, "that it looked as if a plague had struck it, or as if ambush was being prepared for an enemy." The previous evening, thousands of white Washingtonians had abandoned the capital, taking temporary refuge in the suburban asylums of Maryland and Virginia. Thousands more, who hadn't decamped, elected to remain indoors on August 28, terrified of the advancing army called the March on Washington.

Few legislators wished to witness or welcome that invasion. According to Burke Marshall, of Robert Kennedy's Justice Department, "Washington politicians were scared to death of the march," fearing "totally and irrationally" that "people were going to march down Constitution Avenue throwing stones at them." Troops were on the alert across the Potomac. Roy Wilkins remembered that "the administration had the army preparing for the march as if it were World War II." Washington, he said, "seemed paralyzed with fear of black Americans." A few days earlier, Peregrine Worsthorne, of the London *Sunday Telegraph,* had cabled his paper: "There has been no protest of these dimensions in all American history, not even in the worst days of the

Depression. Not since the Civil War has so heavy and dark a shadow lain across the fair land of the free."

Bayard Rustin rose early on August 28, eager to see the first signs of the massive invasion he had spent two months organizing. He could imagine a fairly large number of demonstrators already gathering around the Washington Monument—from which, hours later, they were to begin their parade to the Lincoln Memorial. But at about six-thirty, when he and Rachelle Horowitz strolled over to the Monument grounds, they were shocked by what they saw. Hardly more than two hundred marchers had arrived, a poor augury of the 200,000 they secretly expected—or even of the 100,000 they had publicly announced. Had their estimates been wildly inflated? Would their project end in a humiliating failure?

Spotting Rustin on the Monument grounds, a few early birds from the press converged upon him. "Mr. Rustin," one of them said, "it is past six o'clock. You promised a march of more than a hundred thousand. Where are all the people?" Rustin fished a scrap of paper from an inner jacket pocket, studied it intently, and announced confidently, "Gentlemen, everything is going exactly according to plan." Horowitz, standing beside him, was astonished. As the transportation director, she knew that things weren't going according to plan. She could also recognize that nothing was written on the scrap of paper from which Rustin had read. "It was a masterpiece of bluffing and quick thinking," she said later. At the Willard Hotel, Coretta Scott King was "subdued and saddened" when she rose and switched the radio on. The morning news reported a sparse gathering at the Washington Monument, "a far cry from the 100,000 we had hoped for."

But even then—as police helicopters could see in the outskirts of the city—caravans of cars and buses were streaming toward Washington. By nine-thirty, about 40,000 demonstrators had arrived at the Monument. An hour later, that number had more than doubled. As it kept growing, the *New York Times* reported, a "great crush of humanity spilled over into Constitution Avenue, and edged westward in a great lava flow." When Coretta King eventually arrived at the

Monument grounds, her spirit "soared" at the "beautiful" sight: "that whole vast concourse [was] alive with 250,000 people," and almost "a fourth of that enormous crowd was white."

Before beginning its parade to the Lincoln Memorial, the crowd listened to freedom songs by Joan Baez, Odetta, Bob Dylan, Leon Bibb, Josh White, and the trio of Peter, Paul, and Mary. Between songs, arriving celebrities were announced—a long list that included Josephine Baker, Marlon Brando, James Baldwin, Paul Newman, Harry Belafonte, Sammy Davis, Jr., Ossie Davis, Ruby Dee, Diahann Carroll, Lena Horne, Burt Lancaster, Rita Moreno, Jackie Robinson, Sidney Poitier, and Charlton Heston. Before leading the Hollywood delegation to Washington, Heston had said, "We will march because we recognize the events of the summer of 1963 as among the most significant we have lived through; and we wish to be part of these events and these times, when promises made a century ago will finally be kept." His remarks, and many others on August 28, signified a moment of genuine interracial optimism never seen in America before or since.

The parade to the Lincoln Memorial began around midday, an unprecedented coalition of racial, religious, political, and professional groupings. A forest of picket signs proclaimed some of the major demands of the March on Washington: "Equal Rights, NOW." "Jobs for All, NOW." "Integrated Schools, NOW." "Voting Rights, NOW." "Freedom Rights, NOW." And as the marchers made their way along Constitution Avenue, hundreds of them linked arms and sang "We Shall Overcome" and "The Battle Hymn of the Republic." "Tens of thousands of these petitioning Negroes," said a writer for the *New York Herald Tribune,* "had never been to Washington before, and probably would never come again. Now here they were. And this was their Washington, their own Capitol, and that great marble monument was a memorial to the man who had emancipated them."

By 2:00 P.M. almost everyone in the procession had massed at the Lincoln Memorial—"the greatest assembly for a redress of grievances that this capital has ever seen," the *New York Times* reported. Not everyone agreed on the size of that assembly. From the platform, A. Philip Randolph, accepting the official police estimate, announced a congregation of 250,000. But Seymour Posner, the march's publicity director, distrusted all police estimates of black political gatherings, particularly this one. "I went crazy with that figure," he recalled. "I was standing next to Randolph, and I leaned over to him and said, 'Brother Randolph, I happen to know that there are at least 400,000 people here.' But Randolph was a man of principle. He said it would be improper to announce a figure larger than what the police gave him. I wasn't surprised when Rustin agreed with Randolph. Bayard was always protecting Randolph's integrity."

After preliminaries of singing and benediction, Randolph delivered the afternoon's keynote address. "Let the nation and the world know the meaning of our numbers," he declared with the resonance of a nineteenth-century abolitionist.

> We are not an organization or a group of organizations. We are not a mob. We are the advance guard of a massive moral revolution for jobs and freedom. The revolution reverberates throughout the land, touching every city, every town, every village where [blacks] are segregated, oppressed and exploited. But this civil rights demonstration is not confined to the Negro; nor is it confined to civil rights; for our white allies knew that they cannot be free while we are not. And we know that we have no future in which six million black and white people are unemployed, and millions more live in poverty. . . . Those who deplore our militancy, who exhort patience in the name of a false peace, are in fact supporting segregation and exploitation. They would have social peace at the expense of social and racial justice. They are more concerned with easing racial tensions than enforcing racial democracy.

Randolph was followed by a near interminable procession of speakers, cumulatively wearying to the thousands massed on one of the punishingly hot days of the Washington summer—though they applauded almost everyone and everything they heard. "Like their white political brethren," the *Times*'s James Reston wrote later, "the Negroes cannot run a political meeting without letting everybody talk." But the ordeal of standing and waiting could not have been more richly rewarded than when Randolph introduced the "moral leader of our nation" and the Reverend Dr. Martin Luther King, Jr., took the stage.

What James Reston didn't know was that not *everybody* was free to speak. The program at the Lincoln Memorial was not as smooth in conception and execution as it seemed to the tens of thousands who applauded it. There had been, and probably still was, a brooding feminist rebellion behind the scenes. Black female activists resented the predominance of male speakers; no woman had been invited to deliver one of the many major addresses. While the male civil rights leadership was fully represented at the microphone (Floyd McKissick substituted for the jailed Jim Farmer), the leader of the National Council of Negro Women, Dorothy Height, was conspicuously absent. Only Daisy Bates (who had led the struggle to desegregate Little Rock's Central High School in 1957) was allowed a brief ceremonial turn on the platform, to introduce five "Negro Women Fighters for Freedom."

Imperatively, those five included Rosa Parks, heroine of the 1955–56 Montgomery bus boycott. It was that event which not only produced the celebrated leadership of Martin Luther King, Jr., but also inaugurated the modern phase of black protest activism—a phase that had now reached its moral and popular zenith in the March on Washington. In fact, Anna Arnold Hedgeman, one of the newly disgruntled black women—she had been a passionate supporter of every mass initiative A. Philip Randolph had launched since 1941—now declared that the March on Washington would have been rightly called "Rosa Park's Day."

Perhaps the strongest voice of feminist complaint was Pauli Murray's. Then studying at the Yale School of Divinity, she was among the black civil rights activists who had admired Randolph since the early 1940s. Seethingly displeased with particular arrangements for the March on Washington, Pauli Murray wrote to Randolph a week before the event:

> *I have been increasingly perturbed over the blatant disparity between the major role which Negro women have played and are playing at the crucial grass-roots levels of our struggle and the minor role of leadership they have been assigned in the national policy-making decisions. . . . It is indefensible to call a national March on Washington and send out a Call which contains the name of not a single woman leader. Nor can this glaring omission be glossed over by inviting several Negro women to appear on the August 28 program.*
>
> *The time has come to say to you quite candidly, Mr. Randolph, that "tokenism" is as offensive when applied to women as when applied to Negroes, and that I have not devoted the greater part of my adult life to the implementation of human rights to {now} condone any policy which is not inclusive.*

Perhaps such a letter would have been more appropriately addressed to Bayard Rustin; for it was he who organized the program and procedures of the March on Washington. Rustin and Anna Arnold Hedgeman were not on the best of terms. She felt that he had emerged as too great an influence upon Randolph. For much the same reason—in addition to the clash of two large egos—Cleveland Robinson, financial chairman of the Washington march, did not hold Rustin in high esteem. They barely got along while coordinating the march. Whether or not Pauli Murray shared Anna Hedgman's feeling, her letter to Randolph echoed the earlier view of the feminist Ella Baker that black men did not want women to share the highest level of civil rights leadership.

But on August 28, 1963, yet another rebellion was seething behind the scenes. It had to do with the remarks that John Lewis, the twenty-five-year-old chairman of SNCC, had prepared for delivery at the Lincoln Memorial. Meant to describe the political idealism of student activists and the racial violence they were experiencing in the South, Lewis's text was unsparing in its attacks upon the Congress, the Kennedy administration, Republicans and Democrats alike. His prepared remarks went on to say: "The time will come when we will not confine our marching to Washington. We will march through the South, through the heart of Dixie, the way [General] Sherman did. We shall pursue our own 'scorched earth' policy, and burn Jim Crow to the ground, nonviolently. We shall crack the South into a thousand pieces and put them back together in the image of democracy."

Those radical metaphors were alarming to certain leaders of the Lincoln Memorial ceremony. Bishop Patrick O'Doyle, who was scheduled to deliver the opening invocation, threatened to withdraw from the proceedings unless Lewis modified the language of his prepared statement. "Lewis," Roy Wilkins said, "was denouncing the legislative process at a demonstration called in large part to back the [Kennedy] civil rights bill," and "that seemed like a double-cross." Lewis's supporters included the Reverend Fred Shuttlesworth. "I didn't think it was necessary for John Lewis's speech to be changed," he said later. "I didn't think we went up there to be little boys. We were suffering. People were going to jail. People were dying and would be dying." Predictably, James Forman—an exemplar of SNCC militancy, who had helped to draft Lewis's controversial text—considered it "a dynamite speech," one that "would puncture the tranquility of the march and the efforts of the Kennedy administration to make this look like a popular uprising in favor of his civil rights bill."

Unknown to the thousands gathering at the Memorial, an embarrassing disruption was averted when Randolph, in the cause of unity, persuaded Lewis to alter those passages in his address that Roy Wilkins and Bishop O'Doyle found particularly objectionable.

"So we had this hurried conference behind the Lincoln Memorial," Lewis later recalled, "and at one point in the negotiations Wilkins said that he had problems with the words 'masses' and 'revolution.' Bayard Rustin was pretty quiet, he wasn't saying much; but I don't think he liked what was going on. It was A. Philip Randolph who spoke up.

'There's nothing wrong with the word "masses,"' he said. 'And there's nothing wrong with the word "revolution." I use them myself. But we have come this far together, and let's try and stay together.' I couldn't be insensitive to Randolph's plea for unity. He was the highly respected elder statesman of the civil rights movement. And the March on Washington was his brainchild, something he had been dreaming about since 1941."

Still, with all its polite excisions and amendments, Lewis's was the most caustic and irreverent of the speeches delivered at the Lincoln Memorial.

Certain members of the Southern Christian Leadership Conference had censured Bayard Rustin for placing Dr. Martin Luther King, Jr., at the tail end of the day's program. They accused him of conspiring to weaken the impact of King's speech by delaying his appearance, until many in the assembly and the mass media had grown tired and drifted away. But it was precisely to prevent a sizable exodus from the gathering that Rustin had held back what he knew would be the afternoon's most arresting and anticipated speech. "Moreover," he explained, "almost all the other speakers had asked me to make sure they didn't follow King. They knew that King was the key figure at that time in civil rights history; and they realized that the minute King finished speaking the program would be over, that everybody would be heading home."

King's magnificent address ("I Have a Dream"), one of the more memorable in the annals of American oratory, needs no further recitation here. James Reston heard in it "an anguished echo from all the old American reformers: Roger Williams calling for religious liberty, old man [Norman] Thomas denouncing coercion, William Lloyd Garrison demanding emancipation, and Eugene V. Debs crying for economic equality." To Ned O'Gorman, a young Catholic layman, King "evoked the spirit of America as no one ever had in my generation." Listening to the radio in his Louisiana jail cell, James Farmer—who should or could have been in Washington—felt that King had risen beyond himself "by divine inspiration," that he had been "touched by a spirit which cannot be captured in our lifetime."

With King's buoyant message reverberating in their minds, the marchers began dispersing from the Lincoln Memorial at four-thirty, singing the anthem of their American aspirations, "We Shall Overcome." By six-thirty, they and almost all their conveyances had rolled out of the nation's capital, leaving much of Washington in nearly as deserted a state as it had been some twelve hours earlier. There had been none of the violence that residents and federal officials had feared. In fact, one of the worst criticisms of the March on Washington was that it had been too goodhearted a festival of protest—a festival in which SNCC's John Lewis was forced to revise his hard-hitting speech.

At a late-afternoon reception in the White House, President Kennedy congratulated the march leaders. The orderliness of their demonstration, he said, could only improve the prospects for his civil rights bill in Congress. Earlier in the day, when the nonviolent spirit of the march seemed beyond doubt, the President had issued this public statement: "One cannot help but be impressed with the deep fervor and the quiet dignity that characterize the thousands who have gathered in the nation's capital from across the country to demonstrate their faith and confidence in our democratic form of government." But with their history of unrequited faith in democratic government, it was probably hope and not confidence they were demonstrating.

What did it all mean, the March on Washington? Opinion was divided. The novelist Kay Boyle: "If one was an American, and believed in the equality of man, on the 28th of August, 1963, there was no other place to be." Malcolm X: "Who ever heard of angry revolutionists all harmonizing in 'We Shall Overcome' . . . while tripping and swaying along, arm-in-arm, with the very people they were supposed to be angrily revolting against?" James Baldwin: "The day was important in itself, and what we do with this day is more important." Syndicated columnist David Lawrence: "[It was] a day of public disgrace—a step backward in the evolution of the American system of government." The author and essayist Marya Mannes: "It was a wonderful and immensely important thing that happened here. And the only pity of it was that the people who fled it, the people who deplored it, the people who resented it, missed one of the great democratic expressions of this century." Andrew Young, of the SCLC: "The march transformed what had been a Southern movement into a national movement," a movement that helped to achieve the Civil Rights Act of 1964 and the Voting Rights Act of 1965—those monuments not only to black protest activism but also to the social conscience of Lyndon Johnson's presidency.

Despite John Kennedy's belief, the immediate echo of the march did not seem to have moved congressional Washington. A day later, the *New York Times* observed that the demonstration "appeared to have left much of Congress untouched—physically, emotionally, and politically." Interpreting that immediate echo, James Reston wrote: "This whole movement for equality in American life will have to return to first principles before it will 'overcome' anything. And as moral principles preceded and inspired political principles in this country, as the Church preceded the Congress, so there will have to be a moral revulsion to the humiliation of the Negro before there can be significant relief." In November 1963, the spirit of the March on Washington was dealt a severe blow by the assassination of President Kennedy. It was the moral revulsion and political expertise of Lyndon Johnson, previously viewed as a racist southerner, that aroused and pushed Congress into legislating the progressive acts of 1964 and 1965.

August 28, 1963, was a glorious day in the life of A. Philip Randolph, the fulfillment of a dream he had had since the spring of 1941. As the thousands dispersed from the Lincoln Memorial, singing "We Shall Overcome," Rustin saw Randolph standing alone at a deserted end of the platform. He walked over and put an arm around the old man. "I could see he was tired," Rustin remembered. "I said to him, 'Mister Randolph, it seems that your dream has come true.' And when I looked into his eyes, tears were streaming down his cheeks. It was the one time I can recall that he could not hold back his feelings."

History, Roy Wilkins wrote some years later, "has attached the name of the Reverend King to the march, but I suspect it would be more accurate to call it Randolph's march—and Rustin's." James Farmer credited Rustin with "the successful fruition" of Randolph's idea. "Dr. King will go down in history as Lincoln did after the Gettysburg address," Charles Bloomstein said. "But if there had been violence that day the media would have seized upon it, and King's great speech would have been drowned out. Bayard's masterful planning of the march made King's speech both possible and meaningful."

Rustin was asked on a number of later occasions to organize marches similar to that of August 1963. He always resisted the idea. "If you bring off a good thing," he told a friend in England, "you shouldn't try to repeat it." That reflected not only his fine sense of political timing but also his eye for spontaneous moments in history that can seldom be successfully reorchestrated. "The march," he said in retrospect, "made Americans feel for the first time that we were capable of being truly a nation, that we were capable of moving beyond division and bigotry. I think it will be quite some time before there will be another such spiritual uprising in the hearts of people. The human spirit is like a flame. It flashes up and is gone. And you never know when that flame will come again."

Chapter 17

What Follows?

The March on Washington, Rustin wrote to a friend in London, "was the most exciting project I've ever worked on." In view of the celebrity it won him, it was his most rewarding as well. Widely acclaimed for his role in engineering the march, he began emerging as a political figure in his own right, not simply an intellectual factotum of the protest movement. He would continue functioning as a tactical and theoretical resource to the major black leadership, but he was now reinforced by the sense of independence and personal importance that national recognition had given him.

On September 6, 1963, a week after the demonstration in Washington, Rustin was featured on the cover of *Life*, standing alongside A. Philip Randolph, the senior statesman of civil rights. It was Rustin's first appearance in so glaring and flattering a spotlight. "No one was more surprised than I to find myself on the cover of *Life*," he told Sidney Aberman, a comrade at the War Resisters League. He added, with uncharacteristic or feigned modesty, "I don't know what to make of it, and I'm not sure that the sensation is entirely pleasurable." In later weeks and months, Rustin was showered with letters and editorial commentary, praising his genius at organizing broad and progressive coalitions on behalf of civil rights. "You are getting to be world-famous," John Nevin Sayre, his former colleague at the Fellowship of Reconciliation, wrote to him. Magazine headlines, reflecting his marginal but vital position with major black leadership, called him "The Strategist Without a Movement," "The Lone Wolf of Civil Rights," "The Socrates of the Civil Rights Movement."

But on Sunday morning, September 15, 1963, Rustin and the entire civil rights leadership had been shaken by one of the first replies to the optimistic March on Washington. Segregationists in Birmingham, Alabama, bombed a black church, killing four children and injuring many others. That event probably began to change the spirit of nonviolent goodwill resistance that had animated the protest movement since the Montgomery bus boycott of 1955–56. According to Stephen B. Oates, a biographer of Dr. Martin Luther King, the bombing in Birmingham was, to King, a symbol of "how sin and evil had blotted out the life of Christ."

One in a number of protest rallies around the country, a demonstration at Foley Square, in downtown Manhattan, attracted James Baldwin and Bayard Rustin, among other speakers. Baldwin urged a boycott of Christmas shopping, since the "ghastly" church bombing in Birmingham had "cost the nation the right to be called Christian." Rustin called upon blacks and whites to join in a national nonviolent uprising, to form "a mountain of creative social confusion, by sitting in the streets, by disrupting the ability of government finally to operate." A hint of desperation in both proposals suggested that the tactics of nonviolence were unequal to those employed by its enemies. But the mainstream of the civil rights movement had no honorable alternative to the principle of nonviolent resistance, the morality that had brought it into being and by which it lived. After the crime in Birmingham, it was the younger militants who began to feel that the ethic of nonviolence had outlived its usefulness, that it might well be necessary for blacks to take up arms in their own defense—an early omen of the cry for Black Power.

Rustin's new national importance also gained him the unwelcome recognition of J. Edgar Hoover and the FBI, an attention they had pre-viously lavished on Dr. King and other leaders of the black movement. On October 28, 1963, Hoover wrote to the attorney general, request-ing authority "to place a technical [listening] device at the residence of Bayard Rustin or any future residence to which he moves." Authority was granted, and on November 15 the FBI began tapping Rustin's tele-phone. He became aware of this when neighbors on West 28th Street began telling him of "telephone servicemen making checks at my apartment, when in fact no service had been requested." He also found that he was being trailed by FBI agents: "I would leave a building, notice someone apparently watching me, and then observe the same person when I arrived at my next destination."

He had resumed his close political alliance with Dr. King, which had been interrupted in the summer of 1960, and Hoover had a strong interest in Rustin's telephone conversations not only with King but also with other important aides of the SCLC leader—an interest he jus-tified by his belief that King and the civil rights leadership were secretly influenced by the American communist movement. The FBI stated in an internal memorandum:

> *Rustin is a very competent individual who is widely known in the civil rights field. He is personally familiar with numerous individuals with communist backgrounds. As one of Martin Luther King's closest advisers, he is in a position to wield considerable influence on King's activities.*
>
> *Technical coverage of Rustin is an important part of the overall coverage of King, who is the most prominent civil rights leader in the country today. Because of the influence being exerted on King by persons with subversive backgrounds, it is necessary for us to maintain coverage of individuals such as Rustin. In order to fulfill the Bureau's responsibilities to uncover communist influence in racial matters, it is recommended that technical coverage of Rustin be continued.*

Though Rustin's affair with communism had ended in June 1941, it was not his manner to break personal relationships for purely political reasons. Thus, he continued his social contacts with a number of communists he had known—one prominent example being Benjamin Davis, the Harvard-educated Harlem leftist who later became a leader of the American Communist Party. But Rustin retained those personal relationships even while—like A. Philip Randolph, his civil rights mentor and fellow democratic socialist—he became one of the nation's staunchest anticommunists.

Early in 1964, while Rustin was still pondering what form the next stage of the civil rights movement should take, and what role he would want to play in it, he was called to lead yet another project in mass action. From the Reverend Milton Galamison, a black Presbyterian minister in Brooklyn, chairman of the Citywide Committee for Integrated Schools, he accepted an invitation to organize a one-day protest against segregation in the New York public school system. That took the shape of a boycott; and on February 3, more than 450,000 students, nearly half of the citywide enrollment, stayed home from school. Rustin was applauded for another of his feats in mass organizing.

The accomplishment was to be tainted, however, by the communist history that kept clinging to him. On Tuesday morning, February 4, Rustin, who was scheduled to address a gathering at Syracuse University later that day, phoned the university to say that, exhausted by his efforts on February 3, he was unable to keep his speaking engagement. Whether or not he was as exhausted as he claimed, the *New York Times* did report that "Mr. Rustin stayed up all Sunday night [preceding the boycott] while younger persons slept." But on the evening of his canceled engagement at Syracuse University, Rustin, wearing a Russian fur hat, was seen entering the Soviet Embassy, on the East Side of Manhattan, to attend a cocktail party. His Syracuse hosts were incensed, as were critics who continued to suspect that he harbored communist sympathies.

Under a blaring front-page headline (BOYCOTT CHIEF SOVIETS'

GUEST), the *New York Daily News* reported: "Fresh from his labors of the day before, in directing a citywide school boycott, Bayard Rustin last night attended a private cocktail party, tossed by Nikolai Federenko, the Soviet UN ambassador." This gave the impression that Rustin's leadership of the school boycott had been endorsed and encouraged by the Soviet Union.

What was the truth? "I am not surprised," Rustin told the *New York Times,* "that the *Daily News* should attempt a Red smear of the school boycott." In an editorial titled "Who's Smearing Whom?" the *News* replied: "It was not the *News* that smeared Rustin. It was Rustin who smeared his own civil rights and integration cause by hobnobbing with a mess of Commies at the Tuesday evening cocktail party." Coming to Rustin's defense, James Wechsler, of the *New York Post,* wrote in his column: "It was almost inevitable that the *News* would try to portray the school boycott as the product of a communist conspiracy. Yet one still feels a certain surprise when the job is done so crudely and cynically."

The facts had no connection with communist influence. After Rustin and A. J. Muste helped to organize the San Francisco–Moscow peace walk a few years earlier, as a form of protest against the building of nuclear weapons, Muste had invited a Soviet peace group to pay a return visit to the United States. They arrived at the beginning of February 1964; Federenko threw a cocktail party to welcome them; and Muste persuaded Rustin, despite his exhaustion from organizing the school boycott, to attend. Upon arriving at the Soviet Mission, Rustin explained to reporters: "I am here as a member of the peace committee which hopes to put an end to nuclear and other weapons." But that was not how sections of the press understood or interpreted his visit.

How had the *Daily News* and other hostile arms of the press learned of the private cocktail party? And why had they singled out Rustin— one among nearly two hundred invited guests—to be interviewed and photographed as he entered the Soviet Mission? The FBI, in its surveillance of Rustin, had received this and other dispatches from an unidentified informant in New York:

XXXX advised at 1.30 p.m. today {February 4} that Bayard Rustin was contacted by a party identified only as "A.J." {This was A. J. Muste, overheard in a phone conversation with Rustin.} The party inquired whether Rustin was coming this afternoon to the reception at the Soviet Embassy. The caller reminded Rustin that the reception was at 5 p.m., whereupon Rustin replied that he would be there. . . .

I telephoned Inspector J. A. Sizoo at the Bureau and informed him of this information, and recommended that the Bureau authorize a discreet release of this information to cooperative news sources, to publicize Rustin's visit to the Soviet UN Mission. Rustin is of particular news interest in New York City at the present time, since he served as executive director and principal organizer for the school boycott . . . on 2/3/64, and has received extensive local publicity. . . .

At 3.20 p.m., Assistant Director XXXXX called from the Bureau and said he has just given this information to Mr. XXXX, of the New York Journal American *newspaper, who said he would have a photographer and a reporter at the scene, to get a picture of Rustin entering the Soviet UN Mission, and would give the matter good publicity. Mr. DeLoach said that XXXX had requested that an FBI agent who could identify Rustin accompany the reporter and photographer to assist them in identifying Rustin. Pursuant to Mr. DeLoach's instructions, I telephoned XXXX at the* Journal American, *and immediately thereafter sent SAS XXXX and XXXX to meet Mr. XXXX at the* Journal American, *to handle the matter.*

On February 7, an FBI memorandum noted proudly: "news reporters were present at the Soviet Mission . . . the night of 2/4/64 when Bayard Rustin arrived to attend a reception there. . . . Very effective coverage, from our standpoint, was given Rustin's connection to the Soviets." It was clearly part of J. Edgar Hoover's campaign to discredit the civil rights movement by linking it to the communist conspiracy.

• • •

Rustin's growing prominence as a public figure led to the allegation, in 1964, that he and Norman Hill, one of his trusted political advisers, plotted to seize leadership of the Congress of Racial Equality. Hill was the program officer of CORE, and according to James Farmer, its national director, the failed conspiracy was meant "to replace me with Bayard Rustin." "Norman Hill was known as Bayard's man in CORE," its general counsel, Carl Rachlin, said. "And I remember that at a CORE convention Norman and his wife, Velma Hill, played a role in trying to win leadership for Bayard in the organization."

Rustin's close personal and political associate was to give a somewhat different account. "Bayard felt at one stage," Tom Kahn said, "that if CORE went the way it was going, it would surely go down the drain, which it eventually did. And so he sent Norman Hill to work with CORE, in the hope of saving it from disaster. I was then a director of the League for Industrial Democracy, and Bayard also wanted to send me into CORE. But James Farmer said I was too bookish. I didn't know whether I should be flattered to learn that I was considered an intellectual or to be hurt because I was considered an intellectual." According to August Meier, the historian of CORE, "Farmer rejected Kahn's appointment because he did not want to strengthen Hill's 'Socialist bloc.' . . . Hill was personally disloyal and was building a machine to bring in Rustin as national director."

Norman Hill's own recollection: "Jim Farmer always knew that I and my wife, Velma, were close to Bayard Rustin and his political analyses, particularly where those concerned strategies and tactics of the civil rights movement. When the question came up about the direction CORE was taking, someone suggested that Bayard be invited to join the staff, not to replace Jim Farmer as national director. That was never mine or Velma's motive. We saw that CORE was about to be taken over by a black nationalist wing—which later occurred—and we were pressing for a broader programmatic emphasis. After all, I was the program director. It was never my aim to unseat Jim Farmer. I and a number of others merely wanted to bring Rustin into a closer working relationship with CORE. But Jim, who had always been somewhat at odds with Bayard, saw it all as a personal challenge to his leadership."

Despite the coolness that marked their political relationship (ever since the early 1940s, when they were competitors in the Fellowship of Reconciliation), Rustin and Farmer continued collaborating in civil rights protest activism.

In April 1964, Rustin and an interracial group of fellow socialists joined the pro-Farmer wing of CORE in a daylong demonstration at the opening of the New York World's Fair. In doing so, Rustin was helping to shore up Farmer's position against the nationalist faction in CORE, which had become disaffected with what they saw as his moderate leadership. That faction had vowed to stop the opening by a tactic of "stall-ins"—blocking all roads and bridges leading to the fair's grounds, in Flushing, Queens, and to other parts of New York City. Municipal authorities were alarmed by what Mayor Robert Wagner called "a gun to the heart of the city." And Queens District Attorney Frank O'Connor obtained a court order barring the planned stall-ins, on grounds that they "would constitute not civil but criminal disobedience."

Rustin thought the stall-ins would be counterproductive. Because the disruption of traffic entailed the dumping of garbage on the Triborough Bridge, he felt that the tactic would be an unjust inconvenience to ordinary citizens making their way to work and would also alienate potential allies of the civil rights movement. "I want to make it clear that I oppose the World's Fair stall-ins," he wrote to the *New York Times*. "Such a tie-up of traffic, I am convinced, will not prove to be an effective protest." On April 22, the fair's opening day, the proposed stall-ins collapsed. But, owing to the planned intimidation, only about ninety thousand people showed up at the fair, less than half of the two hundred thousand that had been expected.

The pro-Farmer faction of CORE, which Rustin and his political colleagues supported, picketed various exhibits on the fairgrounds. More than three hundred demonstrators were arrested that day. Farmer and Rustin—together with Michael Harrington, Ernest Green, James

Peck, Tom Kahn, Rachelle Horowitz, and the Reverend Donald Harrington—were seized for blocking the main entrance to the New York City pavilion. "We sat down in the mud, linking arms," the clergyman recalled. "Bayard was on my left and Michael Harrington on my right. I felt myself in distinguished company."

"When the police came to arrest us," Horowitz said later, "we remembered that Jim Farmer had suggested we should all go limp. They lifted us off the ground and dragged us to a paddy wagon. Farmer was so heavy that the cops could hardly carry him. They asked his cooperation, and Jim, on all fours, crawled into the wagon, looking like Toulouse-Lautrec. But Bayard had not gone limp, had not followed Farmer's suggestion. Through a window of the wagon, we saw him being escorted by the police, marching majestically with his head held high. When he entered the wagon, I said, 'Bayard, why didn't you go limp?' He replied, with one of his roguish smiles, 'My dear, Gandhi taught us that when courting arrest you should never go limp.' At that moment, I could understand some of the reasons he and Farmer had their differences. I think Farmer felt that Bayard was always trying to upstage him."

Rustin's return to Dr. King's inner council, early in 1964, was owed largely to the national recognition he had gained for organizing the March on Washington. In September 1963, not long after Rustin appeared on the cover of *Life,* an FBI wiretap picked up a conversation between two of King's political associates. "It is always a source of conflict to me," one of them said, "whether Rustin should have been dumped along the way [in 1960]. It has caused many problems. . . . I knew this thing [the Washington march] was going to come up. . . . He is extraordinarily talented. . . . At crucial points he gave [the SCLC] a lot of moxie." A few months later, another wiretap recorded King, in a talk with one of his aides, wondering "whether it would be possible for Rustin to come back into the civil rights movement, inasmuch as he has now received good press publicity as a result of the March on Washington."

Not everyone in the upper echelons of the SCLC favored Rustin's return to a formal relationship with the organization. A number of King's colleagues resurrected the old matter of Rustin's sex life. At the very least, they suggested, discussion of his renewed role in the SCLC should be postponed until after passage of the 1964 Civil Rights Act, to avoid risking a filibuster on Capitol Hill. Objecting to his return on other grounds as well, they argued that his wide-ranging political affiliations rendered him incapable of the concentrated attention that SCLC affairs required. There was also the question of the Reverend Wyatt T. Walker, pastor of Harlem's Canaan Baptist Church, who was slated to take over the SCLC's office in New York. Almost no one who knew Walker and Rustin could imagine their formidable egos coexisting harmoniously.

But Rustin did become one of the important members of an advisory group around King, formed in the spring of 1964. The Research Committee, as it was called, included Stanley Levison; the attorneys Harry Wachtel and Clarence Jones; the trade unionists Ralph Helstein and Cleveland Robinson; SCLC activists Andrew Young, L. D. Reddick, and James Bevel. According to Adam Fairclough, an SCLC historian, the Research Committee came into being when Wachtel and Jones felt that King was "badly informed on current events, especially in the North, and in danger of becoming intellectually stale. . . . At Wachtel's suggestion, King agreed to meet with a small group of advisers every two or three weeks in New York, with a view to exposing himself to new ideas, and deepening his knowledge of contemporary issues, especially politics and economics."

Partly because certain of its members were in competition for King's favor, the Research Committee did not always function as smoothly as the SCLC leader had hoped it would. As Harry Wachtel saw, King's southern-based advisers "had a feeling against" Rustin; and King's renewed interest in Rustin's political judgment was among the sources of this intellectual sibling jealousy. "Bayard and I spoke more candidly to King than did most others in the Research Committee," Wachtel said. "We just didn't say what we thought

Rustin helping to prepare ground for a self-help housing project in Dar-es-Salaam, Tanzania, 1962, while undertaking a mission of nonviolent education with Julius Nyerere's Tanzania African National Union. (Courtesy Bayard Rustin Estate)

Rustin and A. Philip Randolph announce plans for the 1963 March on Washington. (Photo Associated Press/Wide World)

The March on Washington,
August 28, 1963.
(Photo Wide World)

Rustin during plans for co-
ordinating the New York
City School Boycott, 1964.
(Photo Wide World)

With Dr. Martin Luther
King, Jr., 1965. (Courtesy
Bayard Rustin Estate)

Life acknowledges Randolph and Rustin as architects of the March on Washington.
(Photo *Life* magazine)

Norman Hill, Rachelle Horowitz, and Rustin at dinner for the A. Philip Randolph Institute, 1970 (Courtesy Bayard Rustin Estate)

Rustin confers with Max Shachtman at a meeting of Social Democrats USA. (Courtesy Bayard Rustin Estate)

A coalition of democratic socialism, labor, and civil rights: Michael Harrington, Cesar Chavez, and Bayard Rustin. (Courtesy Bayard Rustin Estate)

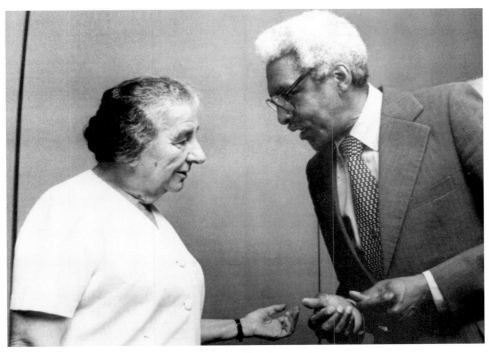

With Golda Meir in Israel. (Courtesy Bayard Rustin Estate)

Charles Bloomstein, Bishop Desmond Tutu, and
Rustin in South Africa, 1983. (Photo Walter Naegle)

Liv Ullmann (far left) and Rustin (right) on a mission of the International Rescue Committee in Southeast Asia. (Courtesy Bayard Rustin Estate)

Leo Cherne, Liv Ullmann, Rustin, and an unidentified local official planning the March for Survival to the Cambodian border. (Courtesy Bayard Rustin Estate)

With Joyce Mertz Gilmore in the early 1970s.
(Courtesy Bayard Rustin Estate)

Rustin with a collection of his antique canes at his
"museum" apartment, 1972. (Photo *New York Times*)

"Father" and "Son": Rustin visiting
with the retired A. Philip Randolph at
Randolph's apartment in the late 1970s.
(Courtesy Bayard Rustin Estate)

King wanted to hear. Bayard was a very strong presenter of his point of view, an innovative and challenging policy adviser. He was an intellectual guy, politically savvy, and King had a very high regard for him."

In December 1964, when King traveled to Norway to accept the Nobel Prize for Peace, he invited Rustin to join his entourage and coordinate its itinerary. Rustin flew to London on November 12 to plan a program of activities for King before the SCLC leader proceeded to Scandinavia. He would address a large fund-raising event on behalf of Britain's antinuclear movement. Rustin tried, but failed, to arrange a meeting between King and Prime Minister Harold Wilson. He was more successful in scheduling meetings with the lord chancellor, members of Parliament, and India's prime minister, Lal Shastri. Most impressive of all, he persuaded Canon L. J. Collins, of Saint Paul's, to present King in a sermon at the cathedral.

Dr. King and his delegation—family members, political associates, staff secretaries—arrived in London on December 5. Rustin told his friend Harry Wachtel, a member of the group, that the delegation, numbering twenty-six, was larger than necessary. He thought it was something of a circus. Wachtel, who sat next to King on the flight to London, remembered listening sympathetically as King mused about his problems with J. Edgar Hoover and the FBI—whose phone taps had gathered a mass of disturbing material about his personal and political life. Assuring King that his national and international position was much too strong to be damaged by Hoover's disclosures, Wachtel then shared a few concerns of his own, though they were trivial in comparison with King's. Not only was he a relative newcomer to King's advisory circle but he and his wife were the only whites in the Nobel Prize delegation. King quickly relieved him of those concerns; and in London as well as in Norway he made a point of always presenting Wachtel as an important counselor and one of the most prominent attorneys in New York. "Each new introduction gave me more status," Wachtel recalled.

The highlight of their three-day stay in London was King's sermon at Saint Paul's, on a Sunday afternoon. Wachtel remembered an "amusing" prelude to the event: "Martin and Coretta took a long time getting dressed, and they were late for their appearance at this high temple of Anglicanism. We were riding in the same car, and Bayard began griping that we were already ten minutes late. Martin got angry. 'Listen, Bayard,' he said, 'you can get out right here, make a telephone call, and tell them to get another speaker.' That was out of the question, of course." The patient thousands at the cathedral were to be rewarded with what Wachtel called "a magnificent sermon."

Addressing the gathering at Oslo University a few days later, King said, in part, "I accept the Nobel Prize for Peace at a moment when twenty-two million Negroes in the United States . . . are engaged in a creative battle to end the long night of racial injustice. I accept the award on behalf of a civil rights movement which is moving with determination and a majestic scorn for risk and danger to establish a reign of freedom and a rule of justice."

According to Wachtel, he and Rustin had helped in drafting King's remarks. "Martin," he recalled, "hadn't found time to write the acceptance speech, and his secretary, Dora McDonald, told Bayard and me that he wanted us to prepare a draft. We got to work and crafted a draft, indicating where Martin should insert remarks of his own. He delivered the acceptance speech much as we had written it, adding his own thoughts and oratorical flourishes." The following day, King delivered the much longer and more formal Nobel Lecture. "I don't know who, if anyone, helped him to write the Nobel Lecture," Wachtel said. "Perhaps Stanley Levison and Clarence Jones had a hand in it. King showed Bayard and me a copy of the lecture. We didn't like everything in it, but we concluded that those were his views, that they shouldn't be altered, except to correct factual errors."

King's delegation returned to New York on December 16. His biographer Stephen B. Oates records: "Fireboats saluted him in the East River, the city awarded him a medallion of honor, and 10,000 people cheered him lustily on 'Martin Luther King Night' in the Harlem

Armory." Rustin "did a heroic job," Wachtel said, recalling the journey to Europe and back.

"If the March on Washington represented the high point in the era of protest," Rustin wrote in retrospect, "then the [August] 1964 Democratic National Convention [at Atlantic City] marked its symbolic conclusion." It also marked the virtual end of the popularity Rustin had once enjoyed among young militants of the protest movement.

The main issue at Atlantic City stemmed from a fight between two rival delegations from Mississippi—the regular all-white party delegation and a group of insurgents representing the newly formed Freedom Democratic Party. Organized partly by activists in SNCC, the Freedom Democrats insisted on their right, as a democratically elected group, to be seated in place of the racist Mississippi regulars. The liberal attorney Joseph Rauh argued the FDP's challenge before the convention's credentials committee and received a sympathetic hearing.

But seating the predominantly black FDP was unacceptable to Lyndon Johnson, who was seeking to retain the presidency. Johnson feared that an expulsion of the Mississippi regulars would alienate white votes across the South and probably cost him the White House. Thus, he called in Walter Reuther and his running mate, Hubert Humphrey, and urged them to propose a compromise: two seats to the FDP delegation. Bayard Rustin, after a talk with Humphrey, endorsed the proposal, both men feeling that if the Mississippi regulars then walked out of the convention, it would be an automatic victory for the Freedom Democrats. But Joe Rauh was not immediately in favor of that plan. His proposed compromise was that both delegations be seated. In the fierce arm twisting that followed, Rauh, the general counsel for Reuther's United Automobile Warkers, was overpowered by the White House. "The only thing [Johnson] could think of," Rauh said later, "was muscle. Johnson's idea was, 'Every man has a price.' So what does he do to neutralize me? He gets my biggest client, Walter Reuther, to call me." But Rauh was not overpowered morally, for, he said, his conscience was not for sale. He had been defeated politically, however, for he soon realized that Johnson's compromise was the best he would get.

Rauh therefore presented it to the Freedom Democrats and recommended its acceptance. Leading civil rights figures who had endorsed Rauh's own compromise—the seating of both delegations—capitulated to political reality as well. The black leaders (Dr. King, Roy Wilkins, James Farmer, and, of course, Bayard Rustin) joined Rauh in urging the FDP delegates to accept Johnson's offer of two seats. It later seemed to Senator Walter Mondale that the issue "had to be compromised in the way we did it. And it was inevitable that some people would be unhappy."

Unhappy, indeed, the Freedom Democrats, led by Robert Moses and Fannie Lou Hamer, adamantly rejected Johnson's compromise. "If the Freedom Democratic Party is not seated now, I question America," Hamer had cried out during the convention. Moral purists, the Freedom Democrats abhorred the negotiating and deal making of politics-as-usual. Rauh remembered Robert Moses saying in Atlantic City, "You cannot trust the system. I will have nothing to do with the political system any longer." "SNCC and the FDP," the historian Howard Zinn noted, "were born in struggles for 'the impossible.' The politics of the FDP was not traditional politics, and its members were not politicians."

In Michael Thelwell's description, "The Freedom Party was an improbable collection of local people, predominantly black, with a youthful band of organizers who had entered Mississippi three years earlier. Their presence at Atlantic City represented the culmination of an organizing effort in the face of violence; mass evictions; the bombing of homes and churches; the kidnaping and murder of young freedom fighters like Michael Schwerner, James Cheyney, and Andrew Goodman. We owed nothing to the regular political system." Stokely Carmichael stated: "The Freedom Democrats went to Atlantic City to replace the racist Mississippi Party, not to join it. In effect, the 'compromise' called upon the MFDP to stand with the regular party, which meant to emulate its racist politics. This was an impossible contradiction."

Leaders of the frustrated Freedom Democrats, especially those active in SNCC, were more displeased with Rustin than with the other civil rights leaders who had urged acceptance of Johnson's compromise. They were particularly hurt by Rustin's saying they had snatched defeat from the jaws of victory. Although their disaffection with him had begun during preparations for the March on Washington, a number of SNCC activists still regarded him as one of their early intellectual heroes. Moreover, since he had helped in planning their challenge to the regular Mississippi Democrats, they had expected him to make a more resolute stand on their behalf.

But like Rauh, Rustin recognized that Johnson was unlikely to improve the terms of the compromise he offered. Bayard therefore recommended its acceptance as something better than nothing at all— surely as the beginning of a pragmatic political alliance he envisioned between the evolving civil rights movement and the liberal mainstream of the Democratic Party.

Rustin extended that analysis in *Strategies for Freedom,* a book he wrote some years later:

> We rather envisioned a [Democratic] party dominated by a coalition consisting of the labor movement, the minorities, and the liberals. We felt that such an alliance had the potential to win a majority, simply because its various components possessed an ideological commitment to social change and a personal relationship to working people.
>
> For some blacks, though, particularly those residing in the South, acquiring political power was of more urgency than building a coalition. . . . Thus the civil rights movement had to confront both immediate and long-range goals.
>
> At Atlantic City, we hoped to begin the long and difficult process of securing a leadership role within the political system . . . to feel that we were making headway, even if, in realistic terms, our gains were largely token.
>
> Seen in this context, I believe that the decision of the

Freedom Democrats to spurn the compromise settlement was a strategic error. A victory of unprecedented scale had in fact been achieved. Not only were racist delegations dealt a setback but, of more consequence, racial discrimination was outlawed for future conventions. This arrangement would, in turn, set in motion a process that would open the party machinery in state after state, would encourage more blacks to seek and win office, and would contribute to the eventual moderation of racial politics that had dominated the South for a century. . . .

The guiding force of the MFDP was the Student Nonviolent Coordinating Committee. A few years after the 1964 convention, SNCC collapsed. Its grand design for transforming Southern politics had failed. It found it could not build a political movement consisting exclusively of poor people. . . .

In pointing this out, I do not mean to appear overcritical of SNCC. Among its membership were some of the most intelligent and fearless political activists this nation has ever seen. That so many of them have dropped out of the racial struggle is one of the tragic consequences of our failure to resolve the problems which confronted the movement during its transition.

Part V

Chapter 18

"From Protest to Politics"

U p to three months before Rustin attended the Democratic Party convention in Atlantic City, he was not yet convinced that the era of militant civil rights protest had come to an end. "The Negro must stay in the streets," he told the *New York Times*'s Gertrude Samuels in May 1964. "American society is traditionally moved in response to action in the streets, what I call social dislocation."

But he couldn't have been as confident as he sounded; for in view of earlier remarks he had made, the gradual obsolescence of street action seems already to have occurred to him. In December 1963, he expressed to a *Times* reporter a feeling that the protest movement may have gone as far as it could "with its original approach," that it now risked "degenerating into a sterile sectarianism." At a symposium sponsored by Irving Howe and *Dissent,* in April 1964, Rustin (then a member of the magazine's editorial board) declared: "A tactic which just ties up everybody is wrong. . . . In social change, there is always alienation. But if you are trying to win allies, then you want to reduce alienation to an irreducible minimum." In his interview with Gertrude Samuels, he had even suggested the possibility of a struggle that went beyond segregation and discrimination—becoming part of a progressive alliance on behalf of all deprived Americans. If a rising tide lifted all boats, he seemed to say, then a unified social struggle would surely advance the cause of blacks on all fronts.

But much or all of this clearly contradicted his opening statement to Samuels: that there remained a need for militant black protest in the streets. Not surprisingly, a number of his critics charged him with being either disingenuous or confused. But closer to the truth, he may simply have been torn by a conflict between his tactical attachment to protest activism and his underlying belief in a broad strategy and program for social reform. Rustin appears to have resolved that conflict only during or after the Democratic convention in 1964, when he recognized that pure and simple protest militancy would contribute little to the remaining agenda of black social and economic progress. This reflected a philosophy he shared with A. Philip Randolph, the only other social democratic ideologue in the civil rights leadership.

In February 1965, the journal *Commentary,* edited by Norman Podhoretz, published a major article of that decade. Titled "From Protest to Politics," it was written by Rustin and attempted to chart a new course for the civil rights movement. One of its main premises was that militant street action had outlived its usefulness. The tactic had been designed to shatter the legal foundation of segregation and discrimination, especially in the South; and with the passage of civil rights and voting rights legislation, its objective had been achieved. The remaining problems were chiefly social and economic, so deeply rooted in the general structure of American life that they could not be solved by protest marches in the streets. Nor could American society be expected to support the passage of social and economic legislation designed for blacks alone. As Rustin said, some time after his *Commentary* piece appeared, "There can be no such thing as an exclusive Negro economic program, for that would counterpose the interests of a little more than ten per cent of the society to those of the overwhelming majority."

Therefore the time had come for protest activism to transform itself into a social movement, in an alliance with liberal and trade union organizations whose programs were aimed at alleviating the structural economic problems in American life. "We need allies," Rustin wrote in *Commentary.* "The future of the Negro struggle depends on whether the contradictions of this society can be resolved in a coalition of progressive forces which becomes the effective political majority in the United States. I speak of a coalition . . . [of] Negroes, trade unionists, liberal, and religious groups. . . . The labor movement, despite its obvious faults, has been the largest single organized force in this country pushing for progressive social legislation."

Rustin's coalition strategy garnered a mixed reception, being more warmly applauded by the liberal and trade union communities than by the black protest movement. Stokely Carmichael was among those who accused Rustin of abandoning his militant past. He found it "difficult to understand the motivating force which could cause Rustin to discredit publicly his own early work." A graduate student in California complained to Rustin that she now found herself in the strange position of "defending your activities against attacks by those who claim you are much too conservative." "I do not consider myself a 'conservative' by any stretch of the imagination," Rustin replied. "My basic belief in coalitions and alliances is that it is the only way to transform this country." James Farmer was to say: "Bayard has no credibility in the black community. [His] commitment is to labor, not to the black man. His belief that the black man's problem is economic, not racist, runs counter to black community thinking."

Support for Rustin's evolving position was reflected in this letter to the monthly *New Leader:* "Rustin has taken his stand and is prepared to lose influence over the activists until they are brought to their senses by the political realities which he is holding up to them. The real test of a political leader is that he is prepared to be isolated rather than go along with the crowd when the mass takes the wrong positions." A reader of "From Protest to Politics" wrote to him: "Your intellectual contribution to the movement has always been worthwhile, but you have come to display a largeness of vision, combined with a grasp of the facts and issues, which is rare in the movement today, with its sectarian trends and personality cults."

Rustin's argument in *Commentary* was influenced partly by his colleagues in the democratic socialist movement, including Tom Kahn, Michael Harrington, and Max Shachtman. "Max was crucial to the analysis in 'From Protest to Politics,' Kahn said later. "He felt that the socialist movement ought to reorient itself to the mainstream of the labor movement. And he supplied a similar analysis concerning the civil rights movement, which by itself could not go very far in meeting the deep economic obstacles to racial equality. Shachtman and A. Philip Randolph played key roles in helping us to understand why it was necessary to have a coalition of liberals, trade unions, and other progressive democratic elements."

But there were to be problems in such an alliance, Kahn conceded. "Coalition politics isn't sexy politics. It doesn't bring out a visceral response in people, because no one's political or personal agenda is fully satisfied. It didn't entirely fail, however. To a considerable extent, it won intellectually. It is represented, to a degree, in Jesse Jackson's Rainbow Coalition. Rustin's article in *Commentary*—emphasizing that issues were becoming less and less a matter of race and more and more a matter of economics—expressed a controversial view. Many people didn't want to hear it. But I think it became accepted dogma. Although it won intellectually, it was destroyed politically. And what destroyed it politically was the war in Vietnam."

The organization in which Rustin served the aims of coalition politics was the A. Philip Randolph Institute. Founded in the spring of 1965, the Institute was also conceived to provide Rustin with a formal leadership position in the civil rights movement, something his political colleagues felt he deserved, particularly after his staging of the acclaimed March on Washington. "Bayard's experience with the March," Charles Bloomstein recalled, "had given him a high and unprecedented visibility, but he had no official civil rights status. And he hardly had an income, save the small weekly stipend he received from the War

Resisters League. At a meeting with Bayard, Robert Gilmore, and Don Slaiman, of the AFL-CIO, I drew up the first budget for the Randolph Institute. When we came to the matter of salaries, Bayard said he would be satisfied with $5,000 a year. I told him that was ridiculous. Who was going to respect a national organization whose leader was so poorly paid? I insisted that he accept $10,000 a year and we left it at that. I might add that Bayard eventually overcame his objection to a living wage, and learned to be quite comfortable with an ever higher salary. But there is no question that he could have earned three or four times as much had he offered himself to the highest bidder. He was so talented."

Launched with a founding grant from the AFL-CIO and the promise of an annual subsidy, the Institute established headquarters at 217 West 125th Street, the building occupied by the Brotherhood of Sleeping Car Porters; and the proximity strengthened the relationship between Rustin and Randolph, the Brotherhood's leader.

In the early 1970s, the widowed and aging Randolph moved from Harlem, where he had lived since 1911, and resettled next door to Rustin in the Chelsea district downtown. There, in the closing years of Randolph's life, Rustin was to be his most solicitous friend and guardian. Not long before Randolph died, in 1979, at the age of ninety, Arnold Aronson, of the Leadership Conference on Civil Rights, joined both men at dinner. "It was a moving thing to see," Aronson remembered. "Bayard was encouraging Randolph to eat, as if Randolph was the child and Bayard the parent. Bayard would cut the meat and feed Randolph bits of it, with such tenderness and caring. It reinforced my old feeling that Randolph was the father Bayard never had, and that Bayard was the son Randolph never had."

Among its many activities, the Randolph Institute conducted nationwide voter registration campaigns; presented pro-labor testimony before committees of Congress; supported the election of liberal Democrats; offered tactical advice to those civil rights leaders who wanted it; sponsored conferences on a wide range of social and economic issues. Rustin, its executive director, traveled throughout the country, addressing liberal, religious, and trade union groups. Together with

Rowland Watts, of the Workers Defense League, the Randolph Educational Fund (the Institute's tax-exempt arm) organized the Joint Apprenticeship Program, later renamed the Recruitment and Training Program. The RTP was headed by Ernest Green, among the first blacks to graduate from Little Rock's Central High School and subsequently an assistant secretary of labor in the Carter administration. The main purpose of the training program Green supervised was to tutor hundreds of young African Americans and Hispanics for admission into the building construction unions, most of which had previously barred nonwhites. The RTP was to be the most successful program of its kind—until the early 1980s, when funds it had been receiving from the federal government were cut off by the Reagan administration. "What the Randolph Institute also did," said the AFL-CIO's Don Slaiman, "was to bring the overwhelming majority of trade unions into direct contact with civil rights leaders."

At least one of those leaders, James Farmer, may not have been so comfortable with the direct contact. Although Farmer had himself worked briefly for a trade union—and served temporarily on the Institute's national board—he had little or no fondness for the mainstream of the AFL-CIO and its president, George Meany. Nor could Farmer understand "how Bayard could go to the length he did in saying that the fight against race problems was now secondary to the fight against economic problems." Herbert Hill, the NAACP's labor secretary, also looked coldly upon Rustin's cooperation with the AFL-CIO, regarding it as a betrayal of the black protest movement.

Michael Thelwell, the former activist in SNCC, did not share that view. "I would never say that Bayard moved into betrayal. He was always at the liberal-socialist left of the black protest movement. There was a certain logic to his position, and I don't think his politics changed that much over the years. I first met him during a period when he was the most articulate and sensible spokesman for civil rights. He had no base at all. He was an itinerant but positive influence in the movement. He brought to civil rights protest the values of democratic socialism as well as his experiences with nonviolent pacifism and political organizing. As a socialist, he always had a sense that the labor movement was a logical ally of the black movement. In intellectual terms, that was true. In terms of reality, that wasn't necessarily correct. But that was Rustin's consistent position, and there was nothing false about it. So I wasn't surprised that a point came when the labor movement recognized him as an ally.

"As director of the Randolph Institute, he did take certain positions that were to the right of the black movement, such as his passionate support of Israel and his initial opposition to the establishing of Black Studies programs. I didn't agree with some of his positions, but I don't rush to any judgments about him. Rustin never changed the integrationist and social democratic ideas he had when we young militants first met him in the late nineteen fifties and early sixties."

The Randolph Institute's chief instrument of economic policy was the Freedom Budget for All Americans, proposing the expenditure of $100 billion toward the eradication of poverty in ten years. Announced in 1966, and drafted mainly by Leon H. Keyserling, who had been chairman of President Truman's Council of Economic Advisers, it represented the Randolph-Rustin belief that American society was more likely to support an economic program for the many than one for the few.

The Institute's national campaign for the Freedom Budget envisioned its endorsement and implementation by the Johnson administration. Liberal and religious organizations applauded its aims; the legislative machinery of organized labor lobbied on its behalf; and Roy Wilkins wrote in the *American Federationist,* a journal of the AFL-CIO: "United effort behind the Freedom Budget will almost certainly be a prime element in the programs of the NAACP and other groups in the foreseeable future."

But it was all to no avail. As Rustin recalled, the Freedom Budget "didn't sell"—not under the Lyndon Johnson presidency and surely not under that of his conservative successor, Richard Nixon. Johnson was preoccupied with the war in Vietnam. And Nixon had made his position clear while running for the White House in 1968: "The demand for a Freedom Budget, amounting to billions of dollars for the poor, is not the road to bring people out of poverty into the sunshine of self-respect and human dignity."

Keyserling, the proud architect of the program, was bitterly disappointed by its failure. The Budget "faded from the landscape, not because it was rejected but because it was abandoned," he complained to Rustin in 1971. "I am not interested in the strategic or tactical reasons why this was done." In fact, the Budget was both rejected and abandoned. "Unfortunately," Rustin explained to a correspondent, "the election of a conservative President and Congress, and the division which took place around the war in Vietnam, made it very difficult to continue to push for the Budget legislatively."

The war and its consequences were damaging not only to the social and economic hopes Rustin had invested in coalition politics but also to his position as a leading spokesman for that alliance. From then on, his unyielding attachment to the values and goals of the liberal coalition he advocated was to alienate him from a considerable number of his former admirers on the militant left, black and white. "The Freedom Budget and the earlier issues surrounding the Mississippi Freedom Democratic Party," recalled Rachelle Horowitz, Rustin's chief administrative assistant at the Randolph Institute, "represent important turning points, politically, for Bayard. The militants in the MFDP couldn't make the transition into real politics, by accepting the compromise Bayard and others advised them to. The Freedom Budget was opposed by two groups: fiscal conservatives and, sadly, peaceniks in the anti–Vietnam War movement who argued that you couldn't have both guns and butter."

Chapter 19

Guns and Butter and Vietnam

Soon after Rustin began leading the A. Philip Randolph Institute, he resigned from the War Resisters League; retired from his coeditorship of *Liberation,* an offspring of the League; and dropped out of the Committee for Non-Violent Action, a radical pacifist organization. His new civil rights responsibilities, he explained, left him little or no time for active participation in the peace movement.

Rustin's resignation, or the reason he gave, came as a surprise to Roy Finch, one of his great admirers in the WRL. "I would have thought," Finch wrote to him, "that in terms of your particular prophetic role, the civil rights movement is over." And because "prophets" were now sorely needed in the pacifist field, Finch said—referring no doubt to the growing campaign against the war in Vietnam—he had hoped that Rustin would keep faith with the pacifist struggle, leaving "others to carry the efforts of the civil rights movement." Finch's surprise was understandable, for Rustin had not disclosed an additional reason for his decision: He had become increasingly troubled by his philosophical differences with the radical wing of the antiwar movement. His new role in the building of coalition politics had helped him to recognize that absolute pacifism was no longer politically effective.

Some years after the Vietnam War ended, Rustin would explain, more fully, his changed views on the radical pacifism with which he had once been closely identified. "Whereas I used to believe that pacifism had a political value," he told an interviewer, "I no longer believe that. I believe that pacifism is a personal witness to the truth as one sees it. I do not believe that pacifism can be politically organized. I do not believe you can organize a society in which men will refuse to fight, until they have a proven alternative to war. Therefore I'm a pacifist to this extent: I believe that the first and most important thing we can do is to discover the means of defending freedom that men can use. It is ridiculous, in my view, to talk only about peace. There is something which is more valuable to people than peace. And that is freedom. So we have to find a peaceful way to defend democratic freedom."

Rustin did not sever his informal ties to such moderate pacifist groups as the Center for War-Peace Studies, Turn Toward Peace, and the World Without War Council. For a time, he even continued a relationship with SANE (the Committee for a Sane Nuclear Policy), before it adopted what he regarded as a radical stance toward the Vietnam War. In June 1965, when he addressed SANE's Rally to End the War in Vietnam, held at Madison Square Garden, Rustin gave equal emphasis to two imperatives: ending the war and continuing the fight against poverty at home. A member of the audience later wrote to him: "Your speech . . . brought sharply into focus the connections between the struggle for civil rights and the need for an end to militarist actions abroad." But, Rustin discovered, the radical peace movement placed a much greater emphasis upon opposing the war than on aiding the fight against poverty at home.

His leaning toward the moderate sector of the pacifist movement indicated the degree of opposition he considered appropriate to the war. The radical pacifists demanded an immediate and unconditional American withdrawal from Indochina. The moderates, including a number of Rustin's colleagues in the democratic socialist movement, urged an immediate negotiated settlement of the conflict.

These divergent approaches led to bitter political recriminations. Radical pacifists like David Dellinger regarded moderates like Rustin as hard-line anticommunists, insensitive to the North Vietnamese struggle for national liberation and therefore in tacit agreement with the anticommunist aims of Lyndon Johnson's war policy. They saw Rustin, moreover, as an early hero of radical pacifism who, in order to advance the causes of coalition politics and antipoverty legislation, had deserted the movement he once helped to inspire. Rustin was, to be sure, a lapsed apostle of radical pacifism, and that was indeed partly because of his anticommunism. According to Ernest Lefever, one of his former comrades in the Fellowship of Reconciliation, "Bayard, like me, was a pacifist. But as the reality of the larger world impinged on us in later years, we both moved away from our earlier utopian views, and embraced a morally concerned realist position. He became convinced, as I was, that the Soviet Union represented a serious threat to justice, freedom, and peace; and he was committed to an intelligent and thoughtful anti-communist posture."

Thus, in their turn, Rustin and the moderate pacifists viewed the peace radicals of the mid-1960s as hoping for a communist victory in Vietnam; as being one-sided in their criticism; as deploring only what they regarded as America's "unjust" and "immoral" foreign policy, while ignoring the tragedy of warfare itself—in short, as being more anti-American than antiwar.

Explaining his own position in 1967, Rustin said in a letter to the *New York Times* that no "effective" and "enduring" peace movement "can be built, or win influence with the American people, which becomes publicly identified with groups that want not peace but a Viet Cong victory." That year, he also told the author James Finn, a historian of pacifism: "I believe the great majority of the American people want to get out of Vietnam. The question, therefore, for them is: How do we get out? . . . I think that many groups in the peace movement fail to provide a step-by-step method by which the US can get out and still have national pride. Now it may be that they are right and I am wrong, that there is no way to gradually educate people for a way out. I happen to believe, however, that there is, and therefore I call for sitting down with everybody involved."

In Rustin's moderate opposition to the war his radical critics also saw a reluctance to offend the Johnson administration, an offense that would jeopardize prospects for the antipoverty legislation he wanted. That was not wholly his motive, but it must surely have been an important factor in his reasoning. After all, high on Rustin's domestic agenda was the Freedom Budget for All Americans; and the chances for its adoption, slim as they already were, would probably have vanished earlier than they did had Rustin openly attacked Johnson's prosecution of the war.

When the President began escalating America's role in that conflict, Rustin and the mainstream of the civil rights movement feared that Johnson would divert to the war effort resources that were needed for social investments at home. That fear was not loudly expressed, however, perhaps because the sound might have borne too close a resemblance to radical antiwar criticism. In fact, when Martin Luther King openly attacked the war in 1967, he was instantly linked with the radical and "anti-American" elements of the peace movement.

Rustin believed that it was possible to continue urging passage of antipoverty legislation even while the war lasted. "I think that one cannot take the view that we must wait until the war is over before we can have a Freedom Budget," he told James Finn. "We have to go out and propagandize and work for it in the same way that one works for peace in the midst of war." That reflected his conviction that the American economy was robust enough to provide butter at home while supplying guns abroad.

But as Michael Harrington asked some time later, "Was it possible simultaneously to give priority to both the tragedy in Indo-China and the fight for a decent America?" Whether that was possible or not, domestic projects like Rustin's Freedom Budget received no significant attention. "When the war took over," Harrington recalled, "the talent, the passion, the political power that had been mobilized for the fight against poverty had been diverted to Vietnam."

• • •

Leaders of government aside, perhaps no one in American politics was so maligned by radicals in the peace movement as Bayard Rustin. That animosity boiled to one of its higher points in the spring and summer of 1965, after Rustin questioned the ideological makeup of the April 17 March on Washington to End the War in Vietnam. Two days before the march, he had joined a gathering at the Greenwich Village town house of his friend and fellow Quaker Robert Gilmore; and he was among the signers of a statement that emerged from the meeting. While endorsing the general aim of the march, the statement also criticized "particular positions expressed by some [of its] elements" and went on to emphasize the need for a peace movement that was neither attached to any form of totalitarianism "nor drawing inspiration or direction from the foreign policy of any government." That was provocative enough to the radical sponsorship of the march. But the *New York Post,* which obtained a copy of the document, added fuel to the fire when it said in an editorial: "On the eve of this weekend's 'peace march' on Washington, several leaders of the peace movement have taken clear note of attempts to convert the event into a pro-Communist production."

The several leaders in question included Rustin and Gilmore; A. J. Muste and Norman Thomas; Alfred Hassler, of the Fellowship of Reconciliation; Professor H. Stuart Hughes, of Harvard; and Charles Bloomstein, a disenchanted member of the War Resisters League. But it was Rustin whom the radicals singled out for the brunt of their counterattack. Staughton Lynd (a professor of history at Yale and a cosponsor of the Washington march) wrote and circulated "An Open Letter to Bayard Rustin," which said in part:

> I was distressed that you took part in Red-baiting the march. . . . What I think it means is that you do not believe in an independent peace movement. You believe in a peace movement [that is] dependent on the Johnson administration. . . .
>
> Why, Bayard? You must know in your heart that your position betrays your essential moralism over the years. The lesson

of your apostasy on Vietnam appears to be that the gains for American Negroes you advise them to seek through coalition within the Democratic Party come only at a price. The price is to become a "national civil rights leader" who delivers his constituency. The price is to urge "jobs and freedom" for Americans only. . . . The price is to make our brothers in Vietnam a burnt offering on the altar of political expediency.

Why, of all those who had conferred at the Greenwich Village town house, had Lynd singled out Rustin for radical censure? It was because, he later explained, Rustin "has been a leading advocate of the strategy of working within the Democratic Party," a strategy requiring "implicit acceptance or muted criticism of the administration's barbarous foreign policy." But "most of all," Lynd added, it was because "Bayard has for so long inspired myself and others of my generation as a passionate practitioner of radical civil disobedience and nonviolent revolution." Troubled by the "Open Letter," A. J. Muste wrote to Lynd: "You should be aware of the fact that Bayard is undergoing a very grave inward struggle. . . . It is by no means one which affects only Bayard. . . . It is one which the civil rights movement is going through; and what happens to that movement may, for the time being, be more momentous than what happens to the so-called peace movement."

Nevertheless, Lynd resumed his attack in the June–July 1965 issue of *Liberation,* describing Rustin as "a labor lieutenant of capitalism," in "coalition with the marines" Lyndon Johnson was dispatching to Vietnam. From a former comrade and political admirer, that may have been the unkindest cut of all—surely the most stinging of the anti-Rustin rebukes that appeared in *Liberation.*

Rustin declined invitations from the magazine to defend himself in its pages. Although he had resigned his active coeditorship earlier in 1965, he had allowed the magazine to continue listing him as an associate editor; and in return, he might have expected the courtesy of being allowed to read the polemics against him before they appeared in print. Now that he had been attacked by associate editors like Lynd and

David Dellinger, he simply asked that his name be dropped from the masthead. Writing to Muste, Norman Thomas upheld Staughton Lynd's right to criticize Rustin. Still, he deplored "the tone and language employed," finding them inappropriate to "a family quarrel." Nineteen intellectuals, a number of them Rustin's associates, signed a letter to *Liberation,* bemoaning his "character assassination" in "a magazine to which he devoted many years of service—and without a hint of demur from any of its editors."

There was to be more than a hint of demur from David McReynolds, one of the associate editors. Writing at length in the magazine, McReynolds disclosed that he was "stunned" when he first saw the manuscript of Lynd's attack on Rustin; that he had "begged" Dellinger not to publish it; that he "asked whether *Liberation* had declared open season on Rustin." After stating that he did not consider Rustin to be above criticism, McReynolds added:

> I am both angered and ashamed that material appeared in *Liberation* in which one associate editor charges another with being a labor lieutenant of capitalism. . . . To suggest that Rustin raised questions about the [antiwar] March on Washington because he feared that the march would rock the Johnson troop ship is shocking. . . . Lynd charges that Rustin advocates coalition politics. Which is true. Lynd further charges that coalition politics means implicit acceptance of the US role in Vietnam. . . . Is Lynd aware that . . . Rustin signed the "Declaration of Conscience," urging young men to refuse service in the armed forces? . . .
>
> Politics always and everywhere involves compromise, accommodation, adjustment—and coalition. Dellinger and Lynd attack Rustin because he is in, or seeks to be in, a coalition with the trade union movement and the liberals. I myself have questions about the way Rustin is carrying out his strategy. But neither Dellinger nor Lynd realizes that once you enter politics you have only a choice of which coalition you will join.

Years after all that dust had settled, an even more eloquent defense came from Robert Pickus, among the anticommunist intellectuals in the moderate wing of the peace movement:

> Many of those on the left who turned against Rustin are part of the radical tradition that measures virtue by how much of an arm's length you keep from power and privilege in America. That's not a bad measure. But it's a dumb way to test whether you've remained true to your goals. A number of radical pacifists felt that if Rustin moved around with people in the AFL-CIO, and if they were supporting America's military program, then that proves that Bayard was not true to his goals.
>
> Bayard's mind did change on certain issues. But, my God, if you can grow from 18 to 70 without changing your mind, then that, too, can be a problem. Rustin was bound up with practical tasks, and with whether those tasks could be advanced or not. Did he change his goals and commitments? I think not. Did he change his strategy and analysis? I think he changed a little in his strategy and a lot in his analysis, because he had gained so much experience along the way. To me, it is proof that he was thinking all his life.
>
> For certain people in the peace movement, pacifism was mixed up with a half-Marxist opposition to the evil of America. So that they adopted Hanoi's view of the war and criticized only American militarism. That wasn't Rustin's trip. A number of others believed that pacifists should be above politics. They said that when you witness to truth, to goodness, to love, and to peace, you will have done your job. But I don't think the job is just to witness. The job, as Martin Buber said, is to drive the ploughshare of normative principle into the hard soil of politics. That's what I believe, and that's what Bayard Rustin believed.

Chapter 20

Advice and Dissent

As one of the advisers to Dr. King, Bayard Rustin argued against any linkage between antiwar activism and the civil rights struggle. Their separate objectives should be pursued separately, he believed, as did most other black leaders. But Dr. King—preeminent among those leaders—appeared to recognize no such separation when, in the spring of 1967, he not only identified himself with militant peace activism but also made his strongest attack upon America's escalation of the war in Vietnam.

In a controversial speech at Riverside Church, in Manhattan, King, on April 4, denounced "my own government" as "the greatest purveyor of violence in the world today"; declared that the war against "the suffering poor in Vietnam" had eviscerated the program against poverty at home; and called for "a unilateral ceasefire" by the United States. Almost a fortnight later, on April 15, he helped to lead a militant antiwar rally in New York City, some of whose participants openly advocated a communist victory in Vietnam.

All of this not only seemed to place King squarely within the ranks of anti-American peace activism—as many then called it—but also subjected him to harsh criticism for lending his status in civil rights leadership to a cause the black mainstream did not require him to represent. The *New York Times,* a devoted friend of civil rights, chided King for "fusing two public problems that are distinct and separate" and for doing "a disservice to both." *Life* described his speech at Riverside Church as an "abject surrender in Vietnam" and as "a demagogic slander that sounded like a script for Radio Hanoi." John P. Roche, a special assistant in Lyndon Johnson's White House, wrote this memorandum to the President: "King . . . has thrown in with the communists" and "is destroying his reputation as a Negro leader." Black leaders joined the firestorm of criticism. The NAACP's Roy Wilkins charged King with placing "the anti-war effort above all other efforts." Whitney Young, of the National Urban League, emphasized that the "urgent domestic programs of civil rights and the issue of war should be kept separate." Ralph Bunche, the highest-ranking black American in the United Nations secretariat, advised: "Dr. King should positively and publicly give up one role for the other."

Rustin could not have been surprised by that reaction. It confirmed both his fear that King's civil rights leadership would be compromised by a close alliance with the radical peace movement and his belief that different causes ought to be advocated under separate umbrellas. That belief preceded the dispute over Vietnam. Adam Roberts, one of his British political colleagues, recalled: "I once heard Bayard at a meeting in London, where the question was whether the campaign against thermonuclear weapons should be linked organically to some other objective. He opposed any such connection. He said that when we were finished dealing with one issue we should take off our caps, put them back on at a forty-five-degree angle, and stand up again for a different issue."

But when the storm of criticism erupted around Dr. King, Rustin's detractors identified him as the main opponent of King's decision to denounce America's role in the war—though Rustin's views on that issue carried no greater weight or prestige than those of the *Times,* Roy Wilkins, Whitney Young, and Ralph Bunche. "Most surprising was the attitude of Bayard Rustin," wrote one civil rights historian, who could not have been familiar with the history of Rustin's thinking on the subject.

Addressing a religious gathering in Chicago on April 14, 1967, Rustin further clarified his position. "Dr. King as a Negro leader," he said, "has the right to discuss Vietnam, just as every Negro and every white person as citizens have not only the right but also the duty to vote and discuss internal and foreign policy. But Negroes should not try to express their position on peace through the Boy Scout organization, the Red Feather campaign, or civil rights organizations. They should do this through established peace organizations, and not place civil rights organizations in double jeopardy." He underscored that point a week later, in an article for the New York *Amsterdam News:* "I would consider the involvement of civil rights organizations as such in peace activities distinctly unprofitable and perhaps even suicidal."

But that was among the few public stances that A. Philip Randolph did not share with Rustin. Randolph, the only major civil rights leader who concurred with King on the issue of Vietnam, said some time later:

> I have always been opposed to wars in principle—though, as in the case of World War II, I am able to support those that are vital to the survival of our democratic institutions. Vietnam does not seem to me to be such a war. It represents, as far as I can see, no defense of our vital national interests. The moral commitment of the American government went beyond the reaches of liberal concern for our own problems, in the sense that it committed an enormous and costly amount of the nation's resources to Vietnam—in terms of both money and human life. This, as I see it, is a great moral loss and a weakening of the country's moral fiber. As for Dr. King's decision to oppose the war, I cannot say I regard it as any great moral contradiction. He was, after all, one of the moral leaders of the country. Opposing wars and fighting for civil rights have natural and complementary motivations.

The question of Bayard Rustin's role in that whole issue would continue to be raised until 1986, the year before he died, when he said his last word on the subject. In a letter to the biographer William McFeely, he sought "to set the record straight" by refuting "what has been written elsewhere to the effect that I tried to get Martin to abandon his effort to end the war in Vietnam." His difference with King, he explained, was not a "division in principle between a concern for human rights abroad and those at home" but a division "on tactics," mostly. "I argued that he had a moral obligation to oppose the war in Vietnam and . . . that he should do so by becoming active in Clergy and Laity Concerned; but that his notion that he could combine the civil rights and peace struggles was an error." Of course, earlier in his career, Rustin had combined civil rights and peace activism. But if that had been pointed out to him later, he might have said that, unlike Dr. King, he wore membership caps in both movements and was the principal leader of none.

The issue of Vietnam was not the first disagreement on tactics that Rustin had had with King, nor would it be the last. Like a number of his other advisers, King was sometimes annoyed by the independence of Rustin's judgments, though he would continue to regard Bayard as a shrewd and knowledgeable counselor. "Rustin was a very brilliant presenter of ideas, an intellectually savvy guy," recalled Harry Wachtel, of King's advisory Research Committee. "Martin had a high regard for him, thought he had a penetrating mind. And that didn't endear Bayard to certain members of the Research Committee. They felt a kind of sibling jealousy toward him. The ones from the South also felt that Bayard was too friendly with Roy Wilkins, Whitney Young, and liberals in the North. They didn't feel a similar resentment of his close relationship with A. Philip Randolph, though some of them believed that Bayard quoted Randolph's scripture as if it were his own. He did do that. But it isn't uncommon to carry a respected sceptre while you're attempting to influence policy." At any rate, Rustin regarded most of his critics on the Research Committee as jesters in King's court, or as sycophants who told King whatever they thought he wanted to hear.

Especially after the 1963 March on Washington—when there was a mending of the rupture that occurred in the summer of 1960—King displayed a strong and steady interest in Rustin's tactical advice, even when he couldn't or didn't accept it. He invited Rustin to almost all major deliberations of the Southern Christian Leadership Conference. In September 1964, King urged Rustin to attend that year's SCLC convention and help in "drawing together a clear presentation of insight and sentiment on the pressing issue of our civil rights struggle." He wrote again to Rustin, in May of 1965: "I am counting on your presence" at a special meeting to discuss "the feasibility of the SCLC becoming a national organization." And in August 1967—not long after the national uproar over his antiwar speech at Riverside Church—King considered it "a must" for Rustin to attend the SCLC's tenth-anniversary convention.

Like bad and good news, the occasions on which King rejected Rustin's tactical advice were more widely publicized than the occasions on which he accepted it. And when the rejections led to one disastrous outcome or another, Rustin was almost never credited for his political foresight. On the contrary, he was usually blamed for the failure of initiatives he had advised against—as if his endorsement would have made all the difference.

In the summer of 1965, when the Watts community of Los Angeles erupted in one of the worst urban riots of the decade, King invited Rustin to join him on a peacemaking tour of the scene. Considering such a mission to be politically futile, Rustin tried to dissuade King from undertaking it. He suspected that it would be as unwelcome to the powers in Los Angeles as was King's attempt to help cool the Harlem riot of 1964, when, as Rustin remembered, Adam Clayton Powell, Jr., told the SCLC leader, "Get the hell out of Harlem, this is my territory." He felt that it would be enough for King to issue a national statement, deploring not only the violence in Watts but also the long-festering social and economic problems that produced the explosion. That advice was rejected, however; and despite his reservations, he accompanied King's delegation to Los Angeles.

The outcome was quite what Rustin had feared it would be: the local "powers" wanted nothing to do with King and his peacemaking retinue. As he recalled, the young militants in Watts heckled King and his entourage, calling them "bourgeois blacks" who had "made it." They believed that their own "manifesto of violence" had won, if only because it succeeded in gaining the attention of the black and white establishments. Then there was King's meeting with the municipal powers of Los Angeles. "The biggest confrontation I've ever seen with King was in Mayor [Sam] Yorty's office," Rustin later told Harry Wachtel. "He ordered us to 'get the hell out.' Who were we to come to Watts?"

Later that summer, a number of friends and civil rights activists met with King in the South to discuss the future of the movement: "Where do we go from here?" Northerners at the meeting, held in the home of Andrew Young, included Velma Hill, Norman Hill, Don Slaiman, and Bayard Rustin. "The living room at Young's house was crowded and warm," Velma Hill recalled. "Some of us sat on the floor—including King, in his shirtsleeves, with his legs folded beneath him. He said he had given the subject of the meeting a great deal of thought, had agonized over how to proceed, had consulted with friends and prayed to the Lord for guidance. He had decided, he said, to organize a new phase of the movement in the North, beginning with a campaign against sub-standard housing in Chicago. Bayard argued eloquently against the decision. He pointed out that King's leadership and the base of the nonviolent movement were Southern in character, dependent upon the black church and King's understanding of Southern black culture. Moreover, Bayard explained, with voter registration and the end of segregation, there was the prospect of realigning the Democratic Party in the South and electing more blacks to public office."

Rustin felt also that Dr. King, buoyed by his triumphs in the streets of the South, misunderstood the character of political action in the urban North, where entrenched machines—like Mayor Richard Daley's in Chicago—yielded not to moral suasion but to clout at the ballot box. Harry Wachtel agreed with Rustin: Chicago "was not the place to go; it would be wiser for the SCLC to consolidate the gains of the 1965 Voting Rights Act, a major piece of legislation that nonviolent activism had won." But King had not been moved. "He was determined to go into Chicago," Velma Hill said. "He had prayed, and he felt a call to Chicago. He was irrevocably committed to that phase of the northern strategy."

The Chicago effort was to be a fiasco, worn down in part by the indifference and intransigence of municipal machine politics. It was another vindication of Rustin's advice, another negative victory in which he could take no great pleasure. "The whole Chicago experience left [King] depressed," his biographer Stephen B. Oates wrote later. "He didn't know where he was going from here."

Of the tactical differences between Rustin and King, the most publicized occurred around the Poor People's Campaign. In December 1967, King announced that an aggregation of the poor would descend upon Washington in the coming April and would remain encamped in the city until they moved the conscience of Congress. On one of his visits to New York, King sought Rustin's "strategic thinking" on the Poor People's Campaign. And after considering the project, Rustin wrote a memorandum, which he presented at a meeting of King's Research Committee, on January 29, 1968. He did not, in that document, explicitly oppose the Poor People's Campaign; but he raised enough questions to suggest his serious reservations about the project. He felt that the announced demands of the campaign were too broad to be achievable; and that a massive disruption of Washington could, at that stage in American politics, lead to "further backlash and repression." The campaign, he said, might "not only fail to attract persons dedicated to nonviolence but also attract elements that cannot be controlled." Rustin's coolness toward the campaign may also have stemmed in part from his feeling that street protests were no longer the best modes of pursuing black economic progress. At all events, his advice was ignored. And whether or not he felt hurt by the rejection, he later told a reporter in Washington, "I seriously question the efficacy of Dr. King's plans for the April march." King and others in his Research

Committee were shocked, feeling that Rustin's public airing of a private disagreement constituted a breach of organizational ethics.

It even led to a rift between Rustin and Harry Wachtel, which was not healed until seventeen years later, when Wachtel wrote to him:

> *I did know from Martin, first-hand, and from Coretta and others, second-hand . . . that Martin was stung by your public views about the Poor People's Campaign. For you were on the inside when that was being planned and developed. . . . It was this act on your part, in the spring of 1968, which made Martin feel so badly. He felt let down because he held you up so high. . . . Having said that, let me say, from a place distant from the battle, that your service in the movement was tremendous. Your role was unique and irreplaceable. It was that ingredient—"irreplaceable"—that added salt to Martin's wound.*

In his criticism of the proposed campaign, Rustin was not alone among King's cohort. Jesse Jackson's dissent caused King to suspect that Jackson was competing with him for leadership of the SCLC. "It may be that you want to carve your own niche in society," he told Jackson at one point. And the wife of the prominent black physician Arthur Logan wrote to King from her home on the Upper West Side of Manhattan. Marian Logan, a board member of the SCLC and a close friend of its leader, questioned the wisdom of the Poor People's Campaign and urged its cancellation. King was deeply wounded by her letter, partly because he discerned in it the influence of Rustin, who was himself a close friend of the Logans.

Rustin did not think he had been indiscreet in going public with his criticism. He believed it was his right to raise questions, in private or in public, "on matters that were to affect profoundly" the cause of civil rights. While he understood the anguish King suffered "when his judgment was sometimes questioned by those he felt ought to be closest to him," Rustin also believed that open "disagreements over strategies and tactics should bring an element of strength, not weakness, to any movement." Moreover, he no longer saw himself as just an intellectual aide to black leadership. As executive director of the A. Philip Randolph Institute, he had acquired a measure of formal leadership, which entitled him to speak independently on matters of concern to the movement.

Neither Rustin nor King was to take part in the Poor People's Campaign. On April 4, 1968, King was murdered in Memphis, where he had gone to lead a demonstration in support of striking sanitation workers.

That evening, President Johnson, fearing an outbreak of urban violence, summoned civil rights leaders to a meeting at the White House. When his special assistant John P. Roche suggested that Rustin be included, the President, hesitant at first, brought up the question of Rustin's sexuality. "I've known him for twenty-five years," Roche said, "but we're not talking now about sexuality. We're talking about one of the most serious problems we now face in politics. We'll have to keep a lid on rioting and racial tensions, and he's one of the ablest people I know."

Rustin was on a plane to Memphis when the pilot announced that he had been instructed to return to Washington for an emergency landing at Dulles Airport. Told by a flight attendant that he was the passenger wanted at the White House, Rustin, as startled as he was flattered, immediately assumed a starched ceremonial bearing. "In all his majesty," Roche recalled, "Bayard marched down the airliner's stairway, set up especially for him, and stepped into the waiting limousine. Tall and distinguished, with graying hair, he had a great gravitas about him." When Rustin flew back to New York after the White House meeting, the outbreak of violence President Johnson feared had already begun. "Up in the air," he recalled, "I saw the first flames of smoke circling Washington."

Rustin resumed his journey to Memphis on the morning of April 5, "to mastermind" (as the *Washington Post* put it) the nonviolent march King had planned to lead on April 8. "On learning of King's death," he

said, "I determined that this second march [an earlier one had been dis-
rupted by violence] must be held and must be successful." It was. The
New York Times called it a massive, orderly, silent march.

Rustin's old friend William Sutherland wrote to him from East
Africa: "If you decide to step into his [King's] shoes, it would be one of
the few reasons I would return to the States—to work with you." It was
a great compliment—for Sutherland was then working with Julius
Nyerere, the president of Tanzania—but Rustin's resourceful imagination had conceived nothing so improbable as stepping into King's
shoes. The murder in Memphis, he replied to Sutherland, left "a fantastic vacuum" that no one or any combination of persons could fill.
"Perhaps only once in a century," he wrote to a magazine some weeks
later, "do the ideas of a man and the needs of his time meet in such a
dramatic way."

But the question of Rustin's role, if any, in the planned Poor People's
Campaign was yet to be resolved. Led by King's senior associates in the
SCLC, the campaign opened on May 12, 1968, when contingents of the
poor, mainly from the South, began pitching their tents in the vicinity
of the Lincoln Memorial. Resurrection City, as the encampment was
called, could not have been more inaptly named: settled during a period
of heavy rains, it was soon bogged down in mud and rotting refuse.
These gloomy conditions impaired the planning of the campaign's
major public event, a Solidarity Day mobilization, scheduled for May
30. Ralph Abernathy, who inherited King's leadership of the SCLC,
later admitted: "We had to face the fact that the on-site leaders could
not operate Resurrection City and lead demonstrations on Capitol
Hill."

It was then that Abernathy telephoned Bayard Rustin in New
York, inviting him to assume all responsibilities for organizing and
coordinating the Solidarity Day demonstration. Rustin was reluctant.
Knowing how unpopular he was with certain elements of the SCLC, he
feared that his involvement with the project might stir a rebellion,
which Abernathy—so soon after succeeding King—could not then

afford. But when Abernathy insisted, promising full cooperation by the SCLC, Rustin agreed to meet with him in Washington on May 19. At the conference, he listed fourteen conditions under which he would be willing to organize Solidarity Day—none more important than that he should have "full authority." After accepting all fourteen points, Abernathy flew to New York, where he announced Rustin's appointment and declared that the Solidarity Day event had been re-scheduled for June 19.

Reassured by the key role Rustin would be playing, the NAACP and the National Urban League instructed their network of branches across the country to cooperate fully with his efforts. Funds to aid the operation began flowing in from those branches as well as from friendly trade unions. Walter Reuther's United Automobile Workers, with its large black membership, contributed $25,000. On June 2, Rustin issued an official "Call to Americans of Goodwill to Join a National Mobilization in Support of the Poor People's Campaign," containing a revised outline of tactics and objectives. The *Washington Post* applauded Rustin's "Call," for giving the campaign "a focus, the lack of which" had made its purposes "seem quixotic and unrealizable."

But the anti-Rustin faction in the SCLC did not share the *Post*'s view. At a Washington press conference on June 4, Hosea Williams denounced the Call as "a bunch of jazz and foolishness." It was "completely out of order," he said, adding that Rustin had exceeded his limited mandate. Apparently caving in under the rebellion, Abernathy now announced that he had neither authorized nor issued the Call. Of course, he had not: he had granted Rustin "full authority."

Feeling that Abernathy had lost faith in their original pact, Rustin ceased his organizing activities in New York, pending Abernathy's reaffirmation of their fourteen-point agreement. "I have repeatedly sought meaningful clarification of this agreement," he wrote to Abernathy on June 8. "These efforts having failed, I am left with no choice but to withdraw as national coordinator of the Mobilization."

Those facts could not have been known to the irate correspondent who wrote to Rustin, charging him with the "absolutely reprehensible"

act of "torpedoing the Poor People's March." Nor was the march torpe-
doed. It was to take place under a leadership more acceptable to Hosea
Williams and, no doubt, Abernathy as well.

Rustin surely had no hand in the fate that befell Resurrection City. Its
population, *Time* reported on June 14, 1968, "shrank to a minimum
estimate of five hundred. Violence was rising, vituperative militance
was alienating liberals, who are Abernathy's only real source of support;
and the pretender to the role of Martin Luther King was letting the
Poor People's Campaign wallow in disorder, disintegration, and self-
defeat." On June 24, the Washington police moved in, dismantled
Resurrection City, and evicted the remnants of its population. "In a
sense," the SCLC's Andrew Young told the *New York Times,* "whoever it
was who ran us out of there maybe did us a real favor."

Part VI

Chapter 21

Standing Fast: Against Separatism

"It is possible," said the *Washington Daily News* in April 1969, "that Bayard Rustin, the man who put together the 1963 March on Washington, does not speak for the new militant black or the new militant white, and that six short years have blunted the memory of that extraordinarily powerful display of unity and brotherhood." Almost all of that was true. New militant voices were indeed challenging Rustin's; and though the 1963 march remained sharp in sectors of American memory, its "powerful display of unity and brotherhood" was no longer so widely celebrated, certainly not by the young ideologues who arrived upon the national stage. The emergence of Black Power and the New Left; the assassination of political leaders in whom the young had invested their public ideals; the acrimonious and divisive debate over the war in Vietnam; the formation of a disillusioned counterculture— all of this conspired to shatter the social and racial optimism the March on Washington had helped to engender.

The resulting strains and polarizations reduced Rustin's standing as one of the major spokesmen for a liberal and civil rights consensus. "Mr. Rustin is himself a remarkable Negro leader," the *Washington News* went on to say, "one who withstood, by virtue of his unassailable reputation for intellectual integrity, assaults upon his personal life that would have destroyed a lesser man. As one of the chief architects of the civil rights movement of the sixties, he must be listened to. What is he saying?" He was saying essentially what he had always said: He was still advocating political cooperation, interracial tolerance, nonviolence and democracy, programs for economic advancement, the integration of American opportunity.

But his message had lost a portion of its earlier audience. Once an intellectually creative influence upon young activists, he now found himself, in the new climate of militancy, upholding "old" public values against the insurgent and irreverent demands of many who were his political children. It was a remarkable tribute to his integrity that he stood his ground—that throughout the rest of his life he made a courageous and principled defense of his social convictions, no matter how unfashionable his critics saw them to be.

Among those critics was his former protégé Stokely Carmichael, the SNCC firebrand who helped to introduce one of the fashionable ideologies of the late sixties. "What we are going to start saying is Black Power," he declared in June 1966, while addressing a rally in Greenwood, Mississippi. Carmichael then led his audience through a chant of "Black Power! Black Power!"—an incantation that was to begin echoing in provinces of separatist feeling across the United States. "We had made a victory," he said later. "They could not bring back Freedom Now [the civil rights slogan]. It was over. From now on it was Black Power."

Alarmed by the visceral appeal and potential spread of Carmichael's message, the Freedom Now movement reiterated its own. At Rustin's suggestion, A. Philip Randolph and a number of civil rights leaders signed and issued a statement, titled "Crisis and Commitment." "We are committed to the attainment of racial justice by the democratic process," it said. "We repudiate any strategies of violence, reprisal, or vigilantism, and we condemn both rioting and the demagoguery that feeds it. . . . We are committed to integration, by which we mean an end to every barrier which segregation and other forms of discrimination have raised against the enjoyment by Negro Americans of their human and constitutional rights." In a sense, the battle between old and new was joined. And in an article for *Commentary,* in September 1966, Rustin added to the crossfire: "I would contend that 'black power' not only lacks any real value for the civil rights movement but that its propagation is positively harmful. It diverts the movement from a meaningful debate over strategy and tactics, it isolates the Negro community, and it encourages the growth of anti-Negro forces."

Conspicuously absent from "Crisis and Commitment" was the signature of Dr. King. He had declined to sign the statement, not because he disagreed with its affirmations but because he was reluctant to drive too hard a wedge between himself and the militants of Black Power. He did not wish to encourage the impression "that one wing of the civil rights movement sought to destroy another wing." That was either good politics or good manners. In any case, Stokely Carmichael did not appear at all worried that Black Power might be seen as seeking to destroy that wing of the movement to which King belonged.

On his speaking tours, Rustin relentlessly attacked Black Power and its tendency, he felt, to substitute radical rhetoric for complex social and economic analyses—such as his promotion of coalition politics required. Rustin was often heckled by Black Power student groups, which had no interest in his programmatic prescriptions for racial progress. And as they used one method or another to disrupt him, so did he develop his own stratagems for neutralizing them. Eric Lee, a graduate of Cornell University, recalled an appearance Rustin made on campus in the late sixties: "Bayard spoke forcefully on the issue of separatism, discussing it as a world-wide trend, which he called 'tribalism.' When it came time for questions, a number of black separatists in the audience tried to disrupt with hostile shouts. But Bayard insisted that he would answer no one who didn't come to the microphone. One of the black students who had been quick to shout his objections then meekly walked up to the microphone. But before he could begin to speak, Bayard further disoriented him by insisting that he give his name. By this time militancy had turned to respect. It was an example of the courageous and unpopular activities Bayard engaged in during the declining years of the civil rights movement." Raymond Mack, a former provost of Northwestern University, remembered a meeting in the New York office of the National Urban League at which "two agitated young black men made vigorous statements" about the importance of black pride. "When they finished, Bayard Rustin said, softly and respectfully, 'Young gentlemen, I agree with you about the importance of pride in being black, but being black is not a program.' I thought that was the essence of Rustin."

To admirers of both Rustin and Carmichael, the rupture of their political relationship was one of the more regrettable casualties of the battle over Black Power. Their mutual intellectual admiration had begun in the early sixties at Howard University, where Rustin sometimes addressed the Nonviolent Action Group (many of whose members were to become active in SNCC). To the young activists at Howard, Rustin gave a glimpse of "radicalism that had status and prestige behind it," Tom Kahn recalled. After his break with Rustin, Carmichael—like a number of student radicals in the mid and late sixties—adopted such new nationalist and revolutionary heroes as Malcolm X, Frantz Fanon, Mao Tse-tung, and Ho Chi Minh.

Late in 1966, a rabbi in Princeton, New Jersey, was so saddened by the schism between Carmichael and Rustin that he wrote them a joint letter. "In a profound sense," he said, "the two of you and the late Malcolm X express the spirit of a people in a remarkably similar fashion, whatever the verbal differences may be. How frustrating and tragic, then, that a hang-up over a slogan [Black Power] has split the two of you. Each of you is impoverished by the split, for each of you is by it alienated from a part of himself. And all of us are deprived of the great leadership you could offer by virtue of your basic temperaments— if only you were reunited." Had that ideological rift not occurred, Carmichael might indeed have become Rustin's intellectual heir apparent in the civil rights movement.

But though they were never to be reunited politically, they retained a strong personal regard for each other: like a warring father and son, neither could forget the terms and spirit of their early bonding. Rustin had replied to the rabbi in Princeton: "I've known Stokely for many years, and was fond of him at the first meeting. He is so essentially a humanist, terribly bright, and always willing to put his body on the line. I, too, am very upset about the split; but, frankly, I don't know what more I can do about it. I am afraid that our political differences could only be mended if one of us changed his ideology." But there could now be no rational exit; neither could now change the ideology that defined him in the public consciousness of the black movement. "Nevertheless," Rustin added, "we are personally friendly; and I know that if I were in deep trouble he would come to my aid as I would help him if he needed it." By the late 1970s, after the collapse of SNCC and the Black Power movement, Carmichael had expatriated his revolutionary passion to Guinea, in West Africa, returning occasionally to the United States. Norman Hill, Rustin's deputy at the A. Philip Randolph Institute, would recall one of Carmichael's visits: "He came to the office, looking rather disheveled. He was seeking financial help from Bayard, and I accompanied them to a coffee shop nearby. There Bayard gave Stokely five hundred dollars, making it clear that the money was for his personal use, not to subsidize his revolutionary activities."

In October 1966, the *Village Voice* photographed Rustin and Carmichael exchanging effusive greetings on Harlem's West 125th Street. That was an expression of the personal regard they would always share. Two months later, they were locking political horns at New York's Hunter College, in one of their clashes over Black Power. Here are two characteristic passages from that confrontation, before a partisan audience of more than a thousand.

Rustin led off, with an analysis that underscored his catholic approach to social reconstruction: "Slogans like Black Power or demands for control of the ghetto won't provide jobs for the masses of the black unemployed, nor housing and schools. Nor will such rhetoric frighten white people into giving us what we need. Only a majority movement for democratic and radical social change can solve the deep-rooted problems of the Negro community. Negroes alone can't build such a movement. We need allies. And we must spur a coalition into existence, built not merely on sentiment but on common economic interests in such programs as full employment. Black Power, as it is defined rather vaguely by SNCC, is an attempt to provide psychological solutions to problems that are profoundly economic."

From his own abilities at thoughtful articulation, Carmichael replied on behalf of the new black zeitgeist: "We have repeatedly seen that political alliances based on appeals to conscience and decency are chancy things . . . because institutions and political organizations have no conscience outside their own special interests. The political and social rights of Negroes have been and always will be negotiable and expendable the moment they conflict with the interests of our allies. . . . The single aspect of the Black Power program that has encountered most criticism is this concept of independent organization. . . . If such a program is developed it will not have the effect of isolating the Negro community, but the reverse. When the Negro community is able to control local office and negotiate with other groups from a position of strength, the possibility for meaningful political alliances on specific issues will be increased. That is a rule of politics, and there is no reason why it should not operate here. The only difference is that we shall have the power to define the terms of these alliances."

It was one of the instructive debates at that stage of the black movement and among the last public exchanges between Carmichael and Rustin. The Black Power crusade did not survive. Nor did an important segment of its leadership. "Yes," Carmichael told the writer Milton Viorst during the 1970s, "SNCC worked for Black Power, and Black Power killed SNCC."

The movement for Black Studies, an offspring of Black Power agitation, survived and prospered as its progenitor did not. But in its ideologically belligerent infancy—before respected academic programs were developed at some of the major universities—Black Studies had no harsher critic than Bayard Rustin. According to the historian C. Vann Woodward, himself an early critic of the movement, Rustin viewed the inception of all-black curricula as a surrender to the demands "for black autonomy, separatism, and politicalization of academic life"; he believed that Black Studies "permitted or encouraged" its young partisans to evade the challenge of rigorous academic training in favor of "soul courses" and a "soothing, comfortable" campus experience. Such an experience, Vann Woodward added—stating a point of view he shared with Rustin—provided a "symbolic victory" where a "real" victory was difficult to achieve.

In 1969, the A. Philip Randolph Institute published *Black Studies: Myths and Realities,* a collection of critical essays edited by Rustin. Its contributors included Vann Woodward, along with others like the psychologist Kenneth B. Clark; the NAACP's Roy Wilkins; the political economist Thomas Sowell; Rustin's deputy, Norman Hill; Andrew Brimmer, of the Federal Reserve Board; and Martin Kilson, a professor of government at Harvard. They represented a cross section of intellectuals who concurred with Rustin's disparaging view of Black Studies and its campus militancy.

Part of what Rustin deplored about the movement was demonstrated on a morning in April 1969 when national newspapers carried the startling photograph of black students, armed with rifles, emerging from Cornell University's Willard Straight Hall. They had occupied the building for thirty-six hours, to enforce their demand for separate black facilities on campus. The photograph and its significance struck Rustin as one of "the extremes in absurdity," coming so soon after the epic civil rights struggle for desegregated public accommodations in American life. In speeches and news interviews, Rustin attacked college administrators for capitulating to demagogic separatists, a surrender suggesting their readiness to buy campus peace at any cost. In his view, it also reflected the administrators' belief in black intellectual inferiority.

Rustin elaborated upon the theme when, accepting the Stanley M. Isaacs Human Relations Award that month, he told a large gathering at New York's Plaza Hotel: "We are living in a time when everybody is proposing what will make them feel good, instead of what will solve the problem. . . . It is very cheap to turn to young Negroes, who are in internal agony . . . and give them the hopes of Black Studies that they can easily pass. . . . I will say also that a multiple society cannot exist where one element in that society, out of its own sense of guilt and masochism, permits another segment to hold guns at their heads, in the name of justice." Gunnar Myrdal, author of *An American Dilemma,* a classic study of race relations, wrote from Sweden to congratulate Rustin on his speech—"for being one of the very few who have the courage" and "knowledge" regarding a problem "I am deeply concerned with."

Militant commentators, on and off the campuses, were not so congratulatory. Their general response was to dismiss Rustin as an Uncle Tom—than which there is no more decisive closing of a debate on black social issues. "I don't think he made that statement to enlighten anyone," said the director of a Black Studies program in California, "just to accommodate the system that so long has paid Bayard Rustin's salary."

At the beginning of his campaign against Black Studies programs, Rustin seems to have ignored the possibility that a number of them were staffed by qualified teachers, not only by opportunistic ideologues. Hence he had unintentionally offended competent members of the growing black professorial class, much of it excluded previously from appointments on prestigious national campuses. The black academics' acerbic responses to Rustin's criticism reflected not only their resentment but also their obligation to defend an innovation that had widened their opportunities for employment and professional advancement.

Recognizing his original oversight, Rustin gradually modified his criticism by acknowledging the need for excellent professors in an important area of American education. "The study of the black experience in the United States," he later told a graduating class at Tuskegee University, "is so vital to an understanding of our country and our people that it must attract scholars of the very highest intellectual eminence. We must not permit this promising area of study to become a refuge for charlatans, more skilled at intellectual intimidation than at investigation." But, significantly, what he had once condemned outright he now called a "promising area of study."

Were he still alive, he would also be obliged to concede that Black Studies matured along the lines of excellence he advocated. Especially at major institutions like Harvard, Princeton, Yale, the University of Massachusetts—to name only a few—African American Studies not only designed and developed distinguished academic programs but also attracted black scholars of "the very highest intellectual eminence."

Chapter 22

Standing Fast:
For Labor and Jewry

R̲ustin's early popularity as a pacifist and civil rights activist had been built upon what admirers perceived as his visionary radicalism. That he was a tough-minded pragmatist as well began to be noticed only in the mid-sixties and early seventies, when certain unfashionable positions he took lost him the applause of many who once regarded him as a radical hero.

It was mostly his former admirers who then accused him of cashing in his militant credentials for a place within the community of conservative opinion—of working more closely with white institutions and causes than with the black civil rights struggle. "After the mid-sixties," James Farmer said, "Bayard seemed to move toward the right. He became more closely allied with what I would call the conservative wing of organized labor. It was not the force that a younger Bayard Rustin would have sided with." It did Rustin little good to plead, as he did, that he was being politically and socially pragmatic, not ideologically conservative. Even so, Farmer's charge overlooked the likelihood that Rustin had been siding quietly with organized labor ever since 1941, when he first joined the mass movement led by A. Philip Randolph, who was then the only black vice president of the American

Federation of Labor (later the merged AFL-CIO). It was a fact, however, that after the mid-sixties no civil rights spokesman paid the high price in public criticism Rustin did—for his attachment to organized trade unionism and for his personal stand against all forms of anti-Semitism.

Yet in both of those stances he saw himself as serving the cause of the black struggle: The first represented his belief that a strong and integrated labor movement was indispensable to the fight for economic progress among the black working classes; the second signified his abhorrence of bigotry and his hope that the black struggle would not dishonor itself by participating in the denigration of any other ethnic group. He had come to feel that the terms "us" and "them" constituted one of the cruder lines of division in human relationships—especially since "us" had seldom failed to justify the hatred and persecution of "them." None of Rustin's principled stances exonerated him in the eyes of his radical critics. But those positions, as C. Vann Woodward said, were definitive aspects of his world view, his imagination of humane and democratic reform.

If Rustin grew tired of defending himself against the charge of ideological conservatism, a few of his long-standing intellectual colleagues did not. John P. Roche was to say, "Bayard and I stood for the same set of principles all our lives. When we were young activists, in the early forties, we wanted to change the world immediately. We and our friends felt that the world was made up of Play-Doh, that we could easily reshape it to a form of our desire. We were wrong. Our hopes did not change the world in quite the way we wanted. But we remained progressive democrats. We saw that you weren't going to clean up everything by seven o'clock tomorrow morning; that you had to prepare for the long haul. This marked our common view when we reached maturity." Roche was to work as a special assistant to Lyndon Johnson and later as a professor of international relations at Brandeis and Tufts universities, in Massachusetts.

"We came to recognize," Roche added, "that one ought to work thoughtfully with institutions of power. Success wasn't possible without the help of other progressive forces. Ever since we adopted that long-range view, Bayard and I have been called conservative. But if our alliances on behalf of social progress make us conservative, then I guess that anyone with good common sense becomes a conservative."

In one of the weekly columns he contributed to black newspapers during the late sixties, Rustin, discussing a number of the political and social alliances for which he had been vilified, told his readers: "I have even, I understand, been listed by a prominent writer as one of those Americans who should not be spoken to in 1968." His critics were referring chiefly to his defense of the Johnson administration, his coalition with organized labor, and his close relationship with the liberal Jewish community.

While Rustin saw organized labor as the only national institution whose economic program was geared to the needs of black workers, his detractors viewed it as racist. The charge of racism echoed from an earlier period, when the constitutions of most craft unions (in the original American Federation of Labor) barred blacks from membership. But that exclusionary practice was now virtually extinct. A few craft unions still admitted only a token number of blacks, but by the 1960s almost none of them remained lily white. "During the 1940s," the labor historian Thomas R. Brooks observed, "there were twenty-six AFL affiliates whose constitutions barred Negroes from membership. In 1963, the Brotherhood of Locomotive Firemen and Enginemen, the last union to explicitly exclude Negroes, dropped the Jim Crow clause in its constitution." That progress was owed in large part to the unyielding campaign A. Philip Randolph had waged in the AFL since the late 1930s. Moreover, after 1955, when the racially conservative American Federation of Labor merged with the progressive Congress of Industrial Organizations, black membership in the AFL-CIO increased dramatically.

From 1966 to 1986, *Newsday* reported, the number of blacks in trade unions rose from 1,695,000 to 2,435,000, thus "increasing [their] influence and presence in the otherwise shrinking American labor movement." Rustin must have had much of that in mind when, replying to a critic of his ties with organized labor, he wrote: "It is rarely acknowledged that the trade union movement is probably the most integrated institution in American society: more so than the churches, the corporations, and the universities." Consequently, he felt, his racial position was in no way compromised by an alliance with the labor movement.

Addressing an AFL-CIO convention in October 1969, he directed his remarks not at the assembled delegates but at his radical critics out in the land—a ringing defense of his politics and the agenda of organized labor:

> We have heard your rhetoric. What is your program? What is your program for eradicating the causes of black rage and white fear? What is your program for expanding our economy so that all may share in its abundance? What is your program for giving every American a job, at wages that allow him to live in dignity? What is your program for tax reform, for closing the great gap between rich and poor? What is your program for tearing down the slums and rebuilding our cities? What is your program for guaranteeing quality education for young people? What is your program for giving health care to the elderly and the infirm? What is your program for cleaning our air and our waters? What is your program for building a new America? I believe that, of all the mass institutions in American life, only the labor movement has answers to these questions. And these are the key questions for the great mass of black Americans.

Perhaps he had saddled the labor movement with a greater burden of answers than it could bear. But if that was the feeling among the assembly of convention delegates, they drowned it out with a standing ovation. Don Slaiman, the AFL-CIO's civil rights director, regarded Rustin's speech as one of the best ever delivered at a meeting of the labor federation.

Reflecting some time later upon the range of Rustin's political alliances, the writer Moshe Decter said, "Bayard moved from the far left to somewhere else; and that somewhere else is not easy to define. But the common cause he made with institutions like the labor movement saved him from the worst excesses of ideological commitment, whether on the left or the right. He remained a social democrat, but it didn't matter to him what labels were. He was sensible to all the party lines. Very rarely do you get such a consummate tactician, organizer, and activist who is at the same time a brilliant intellectual analyst."

That rare concord of interests and abilities also led Rustin to make common cause with the liberal Jewish community, whose historic ties with the civil rights movement had been severely strained by the rise of black nationalist militancy. In 1966, he chaired the Committee on the Rights of Soviet Jewry, convened partly by Moshe Decter, and presided at the first hearing, in New York, to investigate the plight of Jews in the USSR. In 1972, after Arab terrorists had murdered Israeli athletes at the Olympic Games in Munich, he was the only black leader who attended a memorial service in Manhattan. According to one report, "some in the audience wept as Rustin's voice rang out" in the singing of a haunting spiritual. In 1981, at the invitation of Elie Wiesel ("your role is crucial"), he chaired the Committee on Conscience of the United States Holocaust Memorial Council. Four years later, he was among those who nominated Wiesel for the Nobel Peace Prize, citing Wiesel's "incalculable" role in "raising the world's consciousness to the horrors which unbridled prejudice can unleash."

Jewish organizations honored him for his deep involvement with their various concerns. In 1976, Hebrew University established a scholarship in his name. And awards came to him from the American Jewish Committee, the American Jewish Congress, the Anti-Defamation League, and the Jewish Community Relations Council. "I want you to know how deeply grateful I am for your sense of identification with my people," Rabbi Joachim Prinz, a leader of the American Jewish Congress, wrote to him in 1967. Some years later, Rustin heard from Howard Squadron, also of the Congress: "You have been so close to us here that we regard you as a member of the family.'"

So much so that on occasion, branches of the family took a compla-cent view of Rustin's predictable support. Irwin Suall, of the Anti-Defamation League, recalled, "During the planning of a rally to support Soviet Jewry, a staff member of the ADL came to me and said, 'We want a black spokesman on the program. Who do you think that might be?' I told him that there was nothing to discuss, that there was no better candidate than Bayard Rustin. 'Everybody knows where Rustin stands,' he said. 'Let's find someone else, some new person.' I was shocked. Then and there I could imagine people in the black community saying, 'Bayard Rustin has been penalized by the Jews because he's so faithful a supporter.' That was a hard pill for me to swallow."

Elements in the black community *were* critical of his close relation-ship with Jewish organizations. Irwin Suall recognized that while Rustin's "tremendous intellectual courage endeared him to many peo-ple, it also contributed to his controversial standing among blacks." Fran Lee, a consumer advocate in Manhattan, was moved by Rustin's commitment to causes beyond those of his racial community. "I some-times saw Bayard addressing meetings in the garment district. 'Look at that man,' I once said to myself, 'fighting for Jews, even when his own people are against him.' I don't think he ever got his due."

Rustin was neither unaware of his controversial standing among blacks nor untroubled by it. "He hears about it, and it hurts," Jacqueline Trescott, of the *Washington Post,* wrote in 1983. "Sometimes, he says, he cries." He told Trescott: "What people forget is that when I was raising money for Dr. King a great deal of that money came from the Jewish people. . . . I can't call on other people continuously to help me and mine, unless I give indication that I am willing to help other people in trouble. . . . The biggest hurt is to be called an Uncle Tom by your own people. On the door of my house a Star of David has been printed. I have been called a Jew lover. I don't mind that. What I mind is that the people I love most would misunderstand my motives. I have been accused of holding certain views because that's what the Jewish community wants me to hold. That hurts me."

In his solidarity with the Jewish community, Rustin was not only reciprocating its earlier support of the civil rights movement but also expressing his admiration for aspects of Jewish history and culture. "What Bayard liked about Jews," his old pacifist comrade Roy Finch said, "was how well organized and unified they were. He thought that Jews used every bit of the power and influence they had. And he wanted blacks to do the same, to exert influence as a unified people, in coalition with other forces." He was fond of citing the moral lessons he drew from ancient Hebrew prophets; and he often pointed out that a number of the moving spirituals in African American religious music derived their inspiration from Jewish experience in the Old Testament. "Bayard," one of his friends said, "sometimes conveyed a sense of the Old Testament prophet come into the modern world with the high mission to do that incredibly difficult task: to move the people, to change society."

Not surprisingly, he was appalled by anti-Semitism among blacks, a group only too familiar with the injustices of racial persecution. "It would be one of the great tragedies of Negro and Jewish experience in a hostile civilization," he wrote in 1967, "if either group begins using against the other the same weapon which the white majorities of the West used for centuries to crush and deny them their humanity." Feeling that the moral authority of the civil rights struggle drew strongly from the Constitution and the Declaration of Independence, Rustin denounced black anti-Semites for undermining "the moral and legal foundation of our demands," for "making a travesty of a movement that has been the conscience of this nation."

But in his appearances before Jewish gatherings he was equally firm in arguing that, beyond nationalists and political extremists, there were fewer anti-Semites in the black community than was generally supposed. The number had been overstated, he believed, "in part by blacks who want to exaggerate it, and in part by Jews who were slightly hysterical about it." His estimate of the low incidence of anti-Semitism among blacks was confirmed by a survey the Anti-Defamation League conducted in 1966. Reporting its findings, an official of the ADL wrote to him: "Negroes, when asked whether or not they would rather rent from, buy from, work for, or owe money to Jews or other white people, chose Jews by a very high percentage."

During a major speech to the ADL in May 1968, Rustin told his audience that it would be a mistake if Jews allowed a small minority of black anti-Semites to drive them from "the struggle for social justice and democracy." What Jews might interpret as anti-Semitism in an inner city like Harlem, he said, "was often an expression of social and economic frustration." He went on to explain: "If you happen to be an uneducated, poorly trained Negro living in the ghetto, then you see four kinds of white people. One is the policeman, the second is the businessman, the third is the teacher, and the fourth is the welfare worker." Excepting the police officer, he said, the others were likely to be Jews; and residents of the inner city tended to resent their dependence upon privileged outsiders, whatever their ethnic identity. Even black leaders were sometimes seen and denounced as middle-class symbols of success. Jews, then, ought not to abandon the fight against injustice "merely because two percent of Negroes in this country are engaging in anti-Semitism." He said that if all Jews told him to mind his own business, that they did not need his voice on the side of their cause, he would continue speaking out against anti-Semitism—for it was a moral imperative, and he "could do no other."

"What is truly at stake," Rustin concluded, "is whether we can band together in a great political movement, beyond party, to bring about the socialization of this nation . . . or whether we are going to permit the nation to be torn asunder in a race war, [one] in which people who don't want to be on either side may be forced to take sides. That is our problem. That is our challenge. And I hope the Jewish people . . . will continue to be part of the coalition of forces necessary to meet this challenge."

In one of the conspicuous demonstrations of his political courage, Rustin stood by the United Federation of Teachers during an unpopular series of strikes that shut down the New York public school system in parts of 1967 and 1968. They were unpopular partly because they were in violation of New York's Taylor Law, which barred strikes by public employees, and partly because of the racial tensions they helped to feed.

As the UFT was predominantly white in membership, the first strike—in the fall of 1967—had scarcely begun when segments of the black and Hispanic communities complained bitterly that their children were the chief victims. Unimpressed by the union's demands for improved working conditions and more effective educational programs, Charles Kenyatta, a militant nationalist spokesman in Harlem, told the *New York Post:* "Puerto Rican and black children are the ones this thing is aimed at, and it's not right. I'm for seizing the schools right now, and holding them at gunpoint." Bayard Rustin, the only active black leader who supported the UFT and its president, Albert Shanker (A. Philip Randolph, who did so as well, was in semiretirement), drew a torrent of abuse, attracting epithets like "Jew lover" and "Uncle Tom." But he had taken his principled stand on what he regarded as legitimate trade union issues and on behalf of his belief in a coalition with the organized labor movement.

"I, almost all of us, stayed strictly out of it," one civil rights spokesman said later, "and that was the only thing to do. Bayard should have done the same thing." His refusal to do so was at considerable cost to his image in the black community. But it was partly his involvement that saved the strike from being seen as a confrontation predominantly between blacks and whites.

On the evening of April 6, 1968, the UFT signified its admiration of his courage by honoring him with its John Dewey Award (previous recipients were Eleanor Roosevelt and Dr. Martin Luther King, Jr.). The union's admiration was not, of course, shared in the black and Hispanic neighborhoods. On April 2, the leader of a parent group in Harlem had written to Rustin: "We, the black and Puerto Rican communities . . . hereby officially ask you not to accept an award from the teachers union, which serves the cause of your people's oppression." And on April 6, activists picketed the New York Hilton, where Rustin was to receive the Dewey prize. He did not appear, however—though for a reason other than the one his critics had urged. He was in Memphis, organizing a memorial march for Dr. King, who had been killed in that city two days earlier.

An even more controversial school strike began in the spring of 1968; and Albert Shanker was later to explain the circumstances leading up to it: "In 1966, there had been a confrontation at Intermediate School 201 in Harlem, where parent groups had demanded the removal of a white principal in favor of a black one. The union was obliged to defend the incumbent principal, on grounds that a qualified administrator ought not to be removed for the reason alone of his color. We held discussions with A. Philip Randolph and Bayard Rustin—at Randolph's apartment in Harlem—in which they backed our position. After the confrontation at I.S. 201, we went to the Ford Foundation and asked them to fund an experiment in the local community control of schools. We wanted to find a place where we could work cooperatively with black and Hispanic community groups. An experimental board for community control was then established in the Ocean Hill–Brownsville district of Brooklyn. And Sandra Feldman, who was then our field representative [she was later to become the UFT's president], began working closely with the governing board to develop an experimental program. It wasn't until May 1968 that things blew up."

The blowup was triggered by the decision of Rhody McCoy, administrator of the governing board, to transfer a number of white teachers out of the predominantly black district. The UFT subsequently called a strike, charging that the arbitrary transfers violated the due process of an objective hearing. And for standing once more with the union, Rustin was accused of supporting the UFT in a move to neutralize an experiment in black and Hispanic self-determination. That strike, which spread to other school districts, would not be settled until November 1968. "We were fearful," Shanker said later, "that the creation of separate districts in the city [under the system of school decentralization advocated by Mayor John Lindsay] would cause . . . a fragmentation of teachers into many different organizations, each with its own salary schedule and personnel policies. And everything we had struggled for would have been broken up."

Rustin was credited with a role in bringing that strike to an end. At a meeting of trade union leaders—A. H. Raskin, the *New York Times*'s labor correspondent, reported—Shanker and Harry Van Arsdale, of the Central Labor Council, "listened attentively as Bayard Rustin pleaded with the UFT not to insist on a punitive settlement." He "put in poetic terms the need for reconciliation of the UFT and the parents in the ghetto districts." One participant said, after the meeting, "No one could listen to this man, who had been martyrized by his people for standing up for the legitimate rights of the union, without coming away tremendously impressed."

Of course, Rustin had no power to dictate terms of settlement. But the UFT leaders took his advice into account, for they knew the pressure he was under, the vilification he suffered for upholding the union's position. Had Rustin ever asked to be released from his pledge of support, Shanker would readily have understood. "I asked Bayard many times if he wished to continue with us," he recalled. "But Rustin never wavered. If he had doubted the wisdom of what we were fighting for, he would have left us, and he would have given me lessons and lectures in democratic principle. I was fascinated by the spirit in which he kept going, by his great vitality and humor—even when he feared that the course we adopted might lead to greater problems. He saw the immediate complexities, but he also had a long-range vision. He always said that if we kept things decently together, then, in the end—in the right set of future political circumstances—good sense might prevail."

In the spring of 1993, Mark Goldberg, an educational administrator, asked Shanker whether he had a "special hero or role model." Shanker named Rustin. "The great thing about Rustin," he said, "was that he didn't put up his finger to see which way the wind was blowing. He had the guts to say what he felt was right, no matter how unpopular it was."

Chapter 23

Turn to Human Rights Abroad

O n his retreats from Manhattan, especially in the summer and early autumn, Rustin often spent weekends at Scotland Farm—near Millerton, in upstate New York—the country home of his friends Joyce Mertz Gilmore and her husband, Robert. He had known them since the 1940s and had been best man at their wedding. With Joyce he shared an avid interest in the arts and international travel. Robert, a Quaker, was probably his closest political confidant. While visiting Scotland Farm in October 1971, Rustin, then five months short of his sixtieth birthday, suffered a heart attack and was rushed to a hospital in Sharon, Connecticut, some three miles away.

He was a difficult patient at first. No sooner was he admitted than he began refusing medical treatment, demanding that he be released immediately. The attending physician recognized this behavior as a form of "acute psychosis" or a "reactive excitation," not uncommon with patients who feared to acknowledge the seriousness of their condition. Moreover, Rustin had never been hospitalized before, had never been entirely at the mercy of a regimentation in which he had no hand—excepting, of course, the imprisonments he served during the 1940s and again in 1953.

"When the doctors and nurses tried to examine him," said a friend who visited Rustin at the hospital, "he would break into his imperious British accent, ordering them to go away. I think he was frightened. By using his commanding accent, he could imagine that he still had some control over his life." Against medical advice, he demanded to see newspapers, his mail, and the schedule of his speaking engagements. The refusal of such demands only made his detention more intolerable. Early one morning, after a patient had died in his room, Rustin got out of bed and announced that he was leaving the hospital. A nurse, who learned the name of his personal physician in Manhattan, made an emergency call to Dr. Arthur Logan, who was also Duke Ellington's friend and physician. Logan calmed Rustin, emphasized the seriousness of his illness, and advised the nursing staff to transfer him into a private room, where he would be spared the depressing sight of patients expiring around him.

His disposition then improved. Reconciled now to the potential consequence of his coronary incident, he established a friendly and cooperative relationship with his chief attending physician, Dr. Roger Moore. "We chatted a good deal," the doctor said later. "I enjoyed his talks about his Quaker beliefs; about his travels around the world"; about the important political personalities he had met at home and abroad; and—because Dr. Moore was a fan of short- and middle-distance running—about Rustin's accomplishments in track athletics during high school.

Discharged from the hospital on November 20, 1971, Rustin spent the next four weeks convalescing at the Gilmores' town house in Greenwich Village, before continuing his recovery in the Virgin Islands. At the Gilmores' in Manhattan, he received many letters praying for his return to political activism: from Ted Kennedy; from a young black activist in Brooklyn, Al Sharpton; from Hubert Humphrey, who was considering a run at the presidency in 1972. As a priority, Rustin had a personal fence to mend. On November 30, he wrote to Marion Chatfield, a nurse with whom he had had an unpleasant encounter at the Sharon hospital, praising her now as "a splendid nurse and a good friend." Dr. Moore saw this as Rustin's way of apologizing to Chatfield, to whom he had been most insulting while she "helped to hold him down when he once tried to get out of bed and ripped off his ECG electrodes and other appurtenances."

After completing his convalescence in the Virgin Islands, at the winter home of labor attorney Theodore Kheel, Rustin returned to New York in early February 1972. A dear friend and colleague was shocked by his immediate and oblivious resumption of beloved activities like drinking and smoking and dancing. She was reassured only when she heard this from Dr. Arthur Logan: "There are two kinds of heart attack victims. There is the hypochondriacal kind that pamper themselves; and there is the kind that deny they ever had a serious heart attack. The deniers tend to live longer." Rustin was to live another fifteen years; and he would die from an ailment not of the heart but of the appendix.

By early 1972, when he resumed his official duties, Rustin had for some time been wearying of civil rights work in America. Feeling that he had done as much as he could in that arena, he was developing a stronger interest in human rights issues abroad. Withdrawing from his active leadership of the Randolph Institute, in favor of Norman Hill, he became its honorary president—though he still helped to shape the organization's policies and programs.

"From the time I joined the Randolph Institute in 1971, Bayard did very little in the civil rights field," Arch Puddington, its former research director, said. "But he continued giving important tactical advice to Roy Wilkins and Vernon Jordan. When Wilkins had serious tactical problems at the NAACP, he would call Rustin. Jordan, the leader of the National Urban League [succeeding the deceased Whitney Young], would do the same. Certain elements in the Southern Christian Leadership Conference, who had always disliked Rustin, didn't want a public association with him. But when they were in a jam, they, too, called on him for advice. He spent many hours thinking through the problems of all those people. He even got calls from antagonists like Stokely Carmichael and Amiri Baraka, and he always responded positively to them. He was very forgiving. He may not have forgotten the attacks of his ideological enemies, but he almost never held anything against them."

Rustin also maintained a relationship with the Socialist Party. Although he was not a dues-paying member, when the party split in 1972 he was elected chairman of the majority faction, renamed Social Democrats USA. A minority faction, led by Michael Harrington, eventually became the Democratic Socialists of America. But as chairman of the larger group, Rustin was mostly a figurehead, "a front man," as Charles Bloomstein said. He attended meetings but took little or no part in policy debates and disputes, particularly the ones he considered too acrimonious. "Although Bayard shared the fundamental position of the Social Democrats," Puddington said, "he was more or less indifferent to its sectarian squabbles. He was never very interested in his chairman's duties. At convention time, he would make an opening speech and then would have nothing further to do with the proceedings. What he most enjoyed was attending meetings of the Socialist International abroad. There was a mutual exploitation between himself and the SD. He exploited it because its activists, mainly Carl Gershman and Rita Freedman, prepared his briefing papers at international meetings. In turn, the SD exploited him for his international prestige. He could be very impressive at those gatherings abroad, and he gave the SD a sense of world credibility it would not otherwise have had."

The split in the old Socialist Party had occurred partly over the war in Vietnam and partly over the presidential politics of 1972. Rustin's majority faction favored not only a negotiated settlement of the war but also the presidential candidacy of either Hubert Humphrey or Henry "Scoop" Jackson. Harrington's minority, calling for an immediate American withdrawal from Vietnam, advocated the candidacy of George McGovern.

That division ended a political alliance of more than twenty years between Rustin and Harrington. Their mutual personal regard remained intact, however. In the fall of 1976, when Harrington led a delegation of his DSA to Geneva, seeking membership in the Socialist

International, he formed the impression that SD lobbyists "were moving heaven and earth to keep us out." If so, it was without Rustin's knowledge. Harrington believed "my old friend Bayard Rustin" when he "assured me that he did not want to block our membership." As Puddington recalled, "Bayard always liked Mike Harrington. He respected Mike's intellectual abilities, and Mike always called Bayard to consult with him politically."

Despite his declining interest in the civil rights field, Rustin retained a concern for issues like affirmative action and quotas, favoring the general aims of affirmative action but opposing any specific provision for quotas. In September 1974, when he and Norman Hill testified before a committee of Congress, he made his clearest statement on both points:

> The A. Philip Randolph Institute believes the affirmative action concept to be a valid and essential contribution to an overall program designed to ameliorate the current effects of racial bias, and, ultimately, to achieve the long-sought goal of racial equality.
>
> We do not believe, however, that affirmative action can or should occupy the pivotal role in a strategy for racial progress. Affirmative action . . . can only succeed when combined with programs which have as their objective a much more fundamental economic transformation than affirmative action [alone] could bring about.
>
> We are, furthermore, unalterably opposed to the imposition of quotas or any other form of ratio hiring. . . . What the imposition of quotas, and the resulting furor they have generated, have accomplished is to exacerbate the differences between blacks and other racial and ethnic groups. And to the degree that these tensions and divisions have been provoked, the time when black people are accepted into American social and economic life as full and equal participants has been that much delayed. . . .

It seems painfully obvious that an affirmative action program cannot achieve its objectives peacefully and democratically if it must function within the context of scarcity. . . . And
we are particularly dismayed by the notion that opportunities
can be expanded for some groups at a time when the job market is shrinking for all. You simply cannot elevate significant
numbers of blacks or women into better-paying, higher-
skilled, and more satisfying jobs if those jobs do not exist.

It was also in 1974, as human rights issues abroad gained more and
more of his attention, that Rustin lost the ablest administrative assistant he ever had. Rachelle Horowitz, who had virtually run the
Randolph Institute since its founding in 1965—freeing Rustin to roam
as a spokesman-at-large—resigned and moved to Washington, where
she became political director of the American Federation of Teachers. A
lapsed English major, a conscientious dropout from Brooklyn College,
she had been one of the earliest student volunteers in the civil rights
projects Rustin began organizing in the late 1950s; and, with one brief
interruption, they had worked steadily together since then. She was
thus among the pioneering organizers of a movement that, having
passed the height of its fashion, was now in decline.

"I started working with Bayard when I was seventeen or eighteen,"
she said later, "and I stayed with him until I was thirty-five. So he sort
of brought me up, as he did a number of other young people, black and
white, who played important roles in the social and civil rights struggles. Just about the time he deepened his interest in problems of international human rights, I was ready to pursue domestic political objectives of my own. At the age of sixty-two, he now wanted to phase down
his American activities. I, at thirty-five, now wanted to become some-
body in my own right. It had never occurred to me that I wouldn't
always be working with Bayard, for I was so awed by his political talents. But he said that he wished to do other things that pleased him. He
said that if he saw injustice anywhere out in the world, then that's
where he wanted to be."

Rustin's involvement with the issues of international human rights had begun in 1970; and in view of his close relationship with American Jewry, it isn't surprising that he began with the cause of Israel. That June, he and the Randolph Institute invited more than fifty prominent blacks to sign a newspaper advertisement urging the United States to supply Israel with the jet aircraft and other matériel it needed for its defense. This appeal brought Rustin as much applause for his humanitarian leadership as rebuke for his hawkish initiative. The latter came chiefly from his dovish former comrades in the pacifist movement, one of whom wrote to him: "In the circles in which you move, jets and other weapons seem the logical situation. But couldn't you have made one last attempt to put your weight on the side of cease-fire and pressures for all weapons to be withheld from the area by all sides?" That was indeed a position Rustin might have taken at an earlier point in his career. But he now felt that, especially after the Holocaust, radical pacifism was not an option for a besieged Jewish people. Moreover, he told the *New York Times,* because Israel was "a democratic state, surrounded by essentially undemocratic states," all sworn to its destruction, "those interested in democracy everywhere must support Israel's existence."

A number of Rustin's acquaintances believed that his firm stand on Israel was influenced by a degree of pacifist guilt: the fact that he had chosen to be jailed as a conscientious objector during World War II. "I have a hunch," said Irwin Suall, of the Anti-Defamation League, "that when Bayard learned, after his imprisonment, what had occurred in the Holocaust, his commitment to the Jewish cause, to Israel in particular, was strengthened. He might not have become a conscientious objector had he anticipated the atrocities Hitler would unleash upon the Jewish people."

In September 1975, Rustin announced the formation of the Black Americans to Support Israel Committee, to which he recruited an impressive list of national cosponsors. But a number of other black Americans raised serious objections to the committee. Its name was too inclusive, they said, and it certainly didn't speak for them. "It is an insult to the collective intelligence of thirty-five million blacks," one of those critics wrote to a Jewish publication, "that one hundred 'leaders' use their good name to support Zionism." Of course, BASIC did not mean to imply that it represented a consensus. Underlying the objections was a view that Rustin's pro-Israel sympathies ignored the plight and grievances of stateless Palestinians. It was a point the psychologist Kenneth B. Clark made when he declined Rustin's invitation to join the sponsors of BASIC. "I felt," he explained later, "that the Palestinians were human beings too; and that we could not have peace in the Middle East until the Palestinian problem was solved."

Appearing on the televised talk program *Like It Is,* Stokely Carmichael accused Rustin of working for the cause of Zionism. To that, Rustin later replied that he had worked for many other causes as well: the anticolonial struggle in Africa; the campaign against weapons of mass destruction; fair play for American Indians; justice for Japanese Americans interned during World War II. He did not think the cause of Zionism had a less legitimate claim upon his support. Concerning the Palestinians, Rustin said that he could not endorse a movement pledged to the use of terrorism against innocent civilians. But, if only because of his belief in the survival of a Jewish homeland, Rustin was indeed a Zionist. And he was to be among those who condemned the United Nations resolution that equated Zionism with racism.

On several visits to the Middle East, Rustin formed a deep admiration for Israeli society, particularly its democratic political and trade union structures, and the biblical tone of its religious culture. Perhaps his unhappiest experience in Israel was a visit he made to Yad Vashem, the Holocaust memorial; he found the scenes so unbearable that he had to turn away.

Of the many Israeli leaders Rustin met, Golda Meir captivated him most. She, likewise, was enchanted by him. Once, when he came down with a cold, she invited him home and cooked him her favorite chicken soup. If he wasn't already a Zionist before their first meeting, then he must surely have become one during the long and animated political discussions they held in her office. "After that," one of his friends in New York said, "he would put up with no criticisms of Israel." Meir regarded him as "a great man," with a "remarkable talent" for expressing sympathy: "he simply goes out and does something about it." His voice in support of Israel was "good and loud," she said. When Meir died, in 1978, Rustin was away on a human rights mission to Southeast Asia and could not join the American delegation to her funeral. He wrote to President Carter, who had invited him: "I count it my good fortune to have been able to call Golda Meir teacher, friend, and colleague."

Though the accomplishments of Rustin's solidarity with Israel were mostly symbolic, Elie Wiesel was moved by them nonetheless. At a birthday occasion for Rustin in March 1987—the last Bayard would live to celebrate—Wiesel paid him this eloquent tribute: "So where have I met you? I think I met you somewhere in our respective exiles. That's when we decided, each with his own language and tradition, that victims of persecution and oppression must create their own community, their own fraternity. Our memory is filled with gratitude for what you have done for my people, the Jewish people. I see you as my magnificent, melodious friend, our friend."

In his work beyond the black movement at home, Rustin wished to demonstrate what his whole political life was essentially about—a struggle on behalf of democratic values. And as a delegate for Freedom House, monitoring elections and human rights procedures around the world, he traveled to countries like Chile, El Salvador, Grenada, Haiti, Poland, and Zimbabwe. "Bayard was an important catalyst in everything we did, after he began working with us in the late 1970s," said Leonard Sussman, chairman of Freedom House. "He was one of two or three people who could influence the course of this organization. And in our collaboration we put democratic principles at the heart of what Freedom House wished to see in the world."

But there were times when they saw only what they wished to see—such as in the first of the two elections that led to the independence of Zimbabwe. In 1979, when Bishop Muzorewa's minority party defeated other parties representing the black majority, Rustin and the Freedom House delegation were about the only observers who thought the elections were free and fair. Admittedly, their judgment was based on the evidence of their eyes: at the polling places, they had witnessed no egregious violations of the right to vote. What they did not know— and what popular nationalist leaders like Robert Mugabe and Joshua Nkomo did—was that arrangements for the elections had been rigged to prevent millions of nationalist voters from participating.

A year later, when those electoral wrongs were righted, Mugabe won an overwhelming victory; and this time, the Freedom House observers were correct in concluding that the elections had been free and fair. Still, Rustin could not fully applaud the victory, for Mugabe did not seem to him to be a genuine democrat. His Freedom House colleagues were also troubled by a potentially authoritarian strain they detected in Mugabe's politics. "When the votes were being counted," Leonard Sussman recalled, "Bayard and I went to see Mugabe. We thought he was going to win, and we told him, 'Please try and retain a pluralistic system. Don't let it go in a one-party direction.' That was our message. 'Don't worry, we'll take care of that after the elections,' he said. Later, Mugabe did go the route of a one-party system, though it hasn't turned out to be as bad as we feared it would be."

In the spring of 1981, Rustin, accompanied by Charles Bloomstein, visited Poland to address Lech Walesa's Solidarity movement on the techniques of democratic nonviolent resistance. At a meeting in Warsaw, Walesa, wearing faded blue jeans, commended Rustin on the purpose of his visit and explained the political aspirations of Solidarity. "You in the West, with your higher level of democratization," he said, "should help us and apprise us where to go." "How far can I go in criticizing the communist regime?" Rustin asked. "You can't possibly say anything worse than I've already said," Walesa replied.

"Bayard was the only black person I saw in Poland," Bloomstein would remember, "and he was certainly a curiosity. Wherever he went, people were always staring at him. And because of the ceremonial bearing he put on for their benefit, some of them thought he was some kind of African royalty."

Rustin's prescriptions for democratic social change were more readily accepted by Solidarity in Poland than by the anti-apartheid movement in South Africa, which he visited on three occasions from 1983 to 1986. Nor, unawed by the heroic status of the African National Congress, did he himself feel that the black leadership was yet temperamentally prepared for the complex challenges that democratic rule in South Africa would present. Although the ANC seemed "fairly democratic," he also saw that it remained "dedicated to guerrilla warfare," which "is not the democratic process." He thought that Mongosuthu Buthelezi, leader of the rival Inkatha Party, with whom he held talks, had "great leadership qualities." But, he also observed, Buthelezi, the Zulu chieftain—reared by standards of aristocratic privilege—was ill suited to "usher in democracy as we know it." Buthelezi was "a man who cannot stand any form of criticism."

One of the main differences between Rustin and the major black leadership in South Africa concerned the issue of international economic sanctions: to what degree would they be an effective means of bringing down the apartheid regime and facilitating the emergence of democratic government? Rustin disagreed with the call for total sanctions. Advocating limited sanctions instead, he felt they would be punitive enough to nudge the process of democratization toward the inevitable defeat of apartheid. Total sanctions, he believed, might so devastate the national economy as to paralyze the movement for a nonracial democracy.

Among the smaller liberal democratic organizations that endorsed Rustin's position was Black Sash, a woman's group. Joyce Harris, one of its leaders, was to say: "I spoke out against total sanctions at a time when it was unpopular to do so, and Bayard Rustin agreed with me. Perhaps his most significant contribution to the South African debate was that too much time was spent talking about the end of apartheid, and not enough about what would follow it. He feared that one form of dictatorship might be replaced by another; and he felt very strongly that South Africans should be educated for the post-apartheid era."

On one of his visits, Rustin dined with Helen Suzman, the aging and indefatigable liberal democrat, for many years a lonely anti-apartheid voice in the South African parliament. Suzman, reflecting the position of the ANC, did not concur with Rustin's proposal of limited economic sanctions. Neither did she share his belief that South Africans needed to be educated in the responsibilities of a post-apartheid democracy. But, she said later, "I admired his dedication and unswerving devotion to the cause of better race relations, his unemotional attitude towards the problem, and the fact that he carried no chip on his shoulder."

In 1986, Rustin designed a program called Project South Africa. Unique in the United States, its main purpose was to generate financial support for those grassroots social organizations in South Africa that believed in educating the masses in the demands of democratic decision making. "The fundamental issue in South Africa," Rustin said in 1986, "is not and cannot be apartheid. The fundamental issue is democracy. You could destroy apartheid without achieving democracy. Whenever it comes to the question of human rights, democracy is the place to begin."

As a vice chairman of the International Rescue Committee, Rustin undertook several missions to Southeast Asia, helping to alleviate the plight of refugees from Indochina. One of the more poignant of those missions took place in February 1980, when an IRC team including Rustin, Liv Ullmann, Elie Wiesel, and Joan Baez organized a March for Survival, to aid refugees in Cambodia. With truckloads of food and medicine and clothing, they set out from Bangkok, Thailand, planning to cross the border into Cambodia, where some of the most inhumane refugee camps were situated. But a detachment of Cambodian troops blocked their path at the border. Forced to retreat, they delivered a moral message instead. Aiming bullhorns across the border, Joan Baez sang freedom songs; Rustin sang spirituals; and Elie Wiesel recited Kaddish, the Jewish prayer for the dead.

Leo Cherne, chairman of the IRC, later praised Rustin for his crucial role in helping to liberalize American immigration policy toward the Vietnamese "boat people" and other refugees from Southeast Asia. "Because of Bayard's close association with the labor movement," Cherne said, "he and I were welcomed by Lane Kirkland and George Meany. And when we explained the horrible conditions under which the refugees lived, the AFL-CIO passed a resolution imploring the Carter administration to act immediately. The labor leaders assured Carter that the admission of more refugees would not add to the problem of unemployment, for they would be taking only jobs which most Americans did not want. Carter then issued an order increasing the number of Indochinese refugees who could enter the United States. I have no hesitation in saying that most of the credit belonged to Bayard."

Summarizing Rustin's influence within the IRC and his contributions to the human rights program, Cherne added, "One of the most difficult things to achieve is a democratic agreement on varying plans and programs because everyone is an expert on what he or she believes and insists on dominating the discussion. Bayard had a remarkable gift for injecting reason, for reconciling a group of people who were at each other's throats. When he worked within a group, he was not interested in satisfying his sense of political importance. He was concerned mainly with the practical and useful results of his work. That was a sign of his talent at welding coalitions. I have never known another human being who possessed that attribute to the degree that Rustin did. He had a tremendous influence on me. He was my conscience. I speak not of ritual but of the content of our different religious faiths when I say that I have never known a more thoroughgoing Christian or a better Jew."

Chapter 24

The Aesthete and Collector

After Rustin's illness in 1971, two striking changes occurred in his appearance. His heavy shock of hair, which had been graying since the early 1960s, turned wholly white, reminding him proudly of his beloved grandfather, Janifer. He also began dressing more stylishly and dramatically than in the past.

His plain business suits gave way to spectacular and youthful-looking outfits, some with ornate belts, colorful vests, and chic sports jackets. On a summer day, he could be seen in East Indian attire—bulgani shirts and cotton jodhpurs. At formal dinners, he wore a tuxedo, but he often set himself apart by adding gray gloves and a gold-knobbed swagger stick. Observers were mistaken in believing that he dressed expensively. "He bought cut-rate suits off the rack at Rothman's on Fifth Avenue," Arch Puddington remembered, "and had them altered by his tailor. His salary was much lower than that of a research director at the NAACP. He wore clothes beautifully because he had a good build. But I know he wasn't buying expensive clothes. The truth of the matter was that he was a cheapskate. Only in collecting art did he spend much money."

But on the streets and avenues, at home and abroad, Rustin's appearance was so elegant—and, with his crown of white hair, so distinguished—that he attracted far more attention than he had in his younger years. A number of his critics, particularly those who identified him with his bland old business suits, now referred to him as a dandy; but that was not how he regarded himself; he was simply enjoying his discovery of a new sense of style. Accompanying him on a walk through midtown Manhattan in 1986, Joyce Harris, from South Africa, was struck by how often "he turned heads," and she found herself "basking in his reflected glory." Something of a latent actor—or "a kind of poseur," as Liv Ullmann described him, admiringly—he was not at all unaware of the effect his appearance and style had upon onlookers. "He knew it with his cane and walking stick," Ullmann said, recalling some of Rustin's displays in Thailand. "He knew it with the white straw hat that he sometimes wore. He knew it when he strode majestically through a hotel lobby. He knew it, when he went shopping for art in the stores of Bangkok. And he certainly knew it with his cultivated British accent."

But the effect was not always quite the one he sought, as he discovered on a Sunday evening in January 1972. On his way to a movie house near Times Square—to see *The French Connection*—he had on one of his eye-catching outfits and stepped crisply with a cane. Nearing the theater, he attracted the attention of a police officer, who stopped him and asked to have a look at his cane. The officer's request was not motivated by admiration; he had some knowledge of the ulterior uses to which certain antique canes could be put; and inspecting the one in question, he found that it concealed a seventeen-inch sword. Rustin was placed under arrest and charged with the illegal possession of a dangerous weapon.

"Rachelle Horowitz telephoned and asked me to go down to the police precinct, to see what I could do to help," their mutual friend Richard Ravitch recalled. "When I arrived, I tried to get Bayard released. He had a heart condition, and I was concerned not only about his health but also about the indignity of his being taken to court next morning in a paddy wagon. But I was told he could not be released unless a judge came to the station and signed a document. I got in touch with Richard Kuh, an attorney and a political admirer of Rustin's. Kuh telephoned Judge Irving Lange, who came down and signed an order for Bayard's release." A few weeks later, with Kuh representing Rustin, a grand jury refused to indict. "Thanks to you," Rustin wrote the attorney, "I have my cane and my freedom." Kuh replied that "with some clients, their very personalities assure a good result."

It would be surprising if Rustin did not know that his cane concealed a sword. An expert on old canes, he had been appraising and collecting them for many years. He had acquired some of the more interesting ones during his visits to London. And two days after his arrest, the *New York Times* photographed him at his apartment, reclining around nearly a dozen antique walking sticks, selected from his collection of more than a hundred.

Rustin's apartment, one of his colleagues said, was a virtual museum, crammed with an extraordinary range of the art objects he had been acquiring for decades. The eclectic collection included lutes, a harpsichord, and other Baroque musical instruments; African carvings; Gothic paintings and prints; Krishna and Buddha figures; scores of antique clocks and fob watches; wall hangings from Latin America; Chinese vases and other porcelain from the Orient; old lamps and candelabra; modern and primitive jewelry (necklaces, bracelets, rings, bangles, beads); German and Italian Renaissance furniture; and a profusion of crucifixes and Madonna statuary, in metal, wood, and marble.

Referring to the apartment, his friend LuEsther Mertz wrote to him in 1966: "That place of order, and peace, and beauty, to which you can retreat from your work amidst the chaos of life, is some kind of comment on the person you are." In 1970, Susan Ginsburg, of *Auction* magazine, described Rustin's acquisitions as "an extended expression of the humanistic principles [he] has applied to the better known aspects of his life."

Rustin told Ginsburg how he built his collection:

> I started after World War II. I had a job then which took me to Europe two or three times a year. It was at that time that

I started frequenting the London auction galleries—Christie's and Sotheby's. Things were relatively inexpensive then, and I was able to acquire quite a collection of European musical instruments of the seventeenth and eighteenth centuries—harpsichords, violas, guitars, and lutes. I play the lute and the guitar myself. I later sold the instruments to various institutions, because they became too difficult to keep properly. I didn't have the space, and in the New York climate they would have been ruined, unless the air had been humidified. In any case, I think that people often collect one thing at one time of their lives, have an intense experience [with it], until it exhausts itself, and then go on to something else. The things I have change and they change me. . . . . It's a very reciprocal relationship.

A number of the pieces in his collection were gifts from dealers—notably Leon Medina, in Greenwich Village—in appreciation for the antiques he bought for them during his travels. Friends and dealers alike marveled at his "fine eye." Arnold Aronson, of the Leadership Conference on Civil Rights, recalled a day in Washington when "Bayard and I were walking along Constitution Avenue. Seeing some jewel boxes in a window, he went into the store. He judged the quality of things by touching them. He picked up an old ring, and talked more knowledgeably about it—what the stone was and where it came from—than the person who was selling it. He looked at pieces of African art and told the dealer what the different styles of carving were and what African country each piece came from."

On occasion, Rustin entered an antique shop—especially in New York, where he was well known to dealers—and made a beeline for the basement or to a deserted nook in which, his instinct told him, "junk" was stored. There he would sometimes salvage a rejected piece, rub the dust off, discover that it was an authentic eighteenth-century artifact, and purchase it for a pittance. Browsing in Greenwich Village one evening, he came upon an Oriental rug that instantly won his admiration. He couldn't make up his mind whether to buy it and decided to consider the matter overnight. Arriving the next morning to claim his prize, he found it had been snapped up by the artist Jacques Lipchitz. From then on, he was always to say, humorously, that Lipchitz had stolen an Oriental rug from him.

One of Rustin's favorite retreats, during or after his work hours, was Bernhardt Crystal's gallery and antique store on Union Square. He would go there not only to shop but also to relax among the art pieces. Because he was a good friend of Crystal's, he also gave buyers his best judgment of the artworks on display, making sales for the gallery. Crystal felt that Rustin could have been a major American art dealer, if such an enterprise had ever appealed to him. It was like his singing: almost everyone who heard him thought he would have had a brilliant career on the musical stage, if he had not been drawn more strongly to the fight against racial and social injustice.

Bernhardt Crystal could not help noticing the tactile test that Rustin employed in his appraisal of wood carvings, old and new. He always touched the pieces with reverence, polishing some of them with a combination of his spit and his fingers, trying to expose the original patina of the wood. When Rustin loved a piece of work, Crystal saw, he loved it with all his senses. "In my lifetime of selling art," Crystal said later, "I've known no one who appraised things as lovingly as Bayard did."

He added, "Bayard's taste in art went from one extreme to the other. His excitement was as much for an agate bead as for a twelfth-century Buddha. And he would get as much pleasure from a fifth-century Coptic cross as he would from a cross that had been made three weeks ago. The perfect execution of a piece was what he liked. How he felt about a piece had nothing to do with its monetary value or with the historical period in which it was produced. When he came into the gallery and saw something he liked, he would simply say, 'Oh, this is beautiful.' It made me feel that no gallery owner would have the heart to overcharge Bayard Rustin for anything he wanted to buy. I offered to give him a number of things, but he wouldn't accept them. He said my living depended upon what I sold."

Rustin had a special feeling for religious statuary. The day Crystal moved his gallery to Union Square from East Seventeenth Street, Rustin came in, took off his jacket, rolled up his sleeves, and helped his friend with the packing. Crystal had a large Christ figure, which he thought of putting on the truck. But to Rustin that was unthinkable. "Bayard put that figure on his shoulder," Crystal recalled, "and walked with it to this building. He felt the figure was too sensitive a piece to be loaded on a truck."

Yet despite Rustin's feeling for such statuary—and the abundance of Christ and Madonna figures in his collection—he was not, he once said, "a terribly religious person." Interested in religion as literature, he also felt that "truly magnificent art is very often bound to religion" and that great periods of art "often grow out of some centrally accepted idea." Nor, despite the knowledge he had acquired on the subject, did he cultivate a scholarly interest in art. "I depend a great deal on my eye," he said, "on what pleases me. Most of the works I own are unidentifiable by artist, specific date, or place of execution. In the late Gothic and early Renaissance periods, there was a different kind of egotism involved than exists today. What I am interested in is not the monetary value of the piece but the ultimate exchange between the object and myself."

As the political demands on his time increased, Rustin gave up his playing of musical instruments. In compensation, he listened to a great deal of recorded classical music. The favorites in his record collection included Bach's *Art of the Fugue,* B Minor Mass, and harpsichord concertos; Beethoven's *Missa Solemnis;* Brahms's *German Requiem;* Mahler's Ninth Symphony; and Mozart's "Coronation" Mass. He also loved Samuel Barber's Adagio for Strings, partly because he and the composer shared the honor of being the most famous graduates of West Chester High School.

Among other significant recordings in his collection were *The Art of Roland Hayes* (the great tenor, with whose voice Rustin's was once favorably compared) and two souvenir albums of Rustin's own

singing—Negro spirituals and Elizabethan art songs. The harpsichordist Margaret Davison, who accompanied him on the latter, was to
say, "Bayard could have had an excellent career in music, but he had
that political call, that driving prophetic mission." Rustin himself said,
late in his life, "Once in a while, when I hear the classical guitar,
Segovia or Bream, I wish I had kept on playing. Or when I hear some of
the old recordings I did, I wish I had kept on singing. But the feeling
passes in a few minutes."

In October 1978, Paul Downing, a writer for the *Portland* (Maine) *Press
Herald,* had one of the more surprising encounters of his career.
Assigned to interview Rustin, who was fulfilling a speaking engagement at Bowdoin College, he arranged for a meeting in the college's
Doggett Lounge. When Downing arrived, the lounge was unoccupied,
except for someone at the piano—"a man with a shock of wiry hair"—
playing a piece from Bach's *Anna Magdalena Notebook.* Supposing the
pianist to be a member of the school's music faculty, Downing
approached him and said, "I'm looking for Bayard Rustin." "I am he,"
the pianist replied, much to the writer's astonishment.

"He was smoking a cigarette-type cigar," Downing reported, "and
the ash trays were on an antique chest. . . . He ran his fingers over the
worn wood. . . . 'A lovely piece,' he said, 'but it has been allowed to go
into disrepair.

"'Spanish,' he continued. 'Probably late sixteenth century.'

"'Not Italian?'" I asked. . . .

"He fingered the ironwork, and lifted the ornate hasp. 'No, I think
it's Spanish.' He went on to give the reasons for his opinion, its proba-
ble use in the Great Hall of some noble house. Blankets or similar possessions—possibly books locked up for safe-keeping—were kept in
such chests; and they doubled as beds when accommodations for visitors were short."

Downing concluded, "It is a unique interview with a black civil
rights leader which begins with Bach and goes on into a discussion of
antique Spanish furniture before getting to the subject at hand."

Chapter 25

"Swing Low, Sweet Chariot"

Rustin was in high spirits on July 17, 1987, when he embarked upon his last human rights mission abroad, his last mission of any kind. With Bruce McColm, of Freedom House, he left for Haiti, to study the prospects for democratic elections in that despotic country. They were joined on the mission by Walter Naegle, Rustin's steady companion of ten years and his administrative assistant as well. Naegle had accompanied him on several of his visits to countries abroad, including England, India, and South Africa.

From the Holiday Inn in Port-au-Prince, the three-man team went forth daily for talks with the American ambassador, journalists and clergymen, officials of the Human Rights League, and leaders of the contending political factions. Those included Leslie Manigat, who was later elected president but was quickly toppled by a military junta.

In their week-long survey, Rustin and his delegation found that American authorities were insufficiently aroused by the local dictatorship; that "strategies for change [were] vague and ambivalent"; that few presidential candidates were represented by political parties; that the military was bent on suppressing the development of "a democratic infrastructure."

Rustin was also appalled by social and economic conditions in the country. "Bayard told me later," Arnold Aronson said, "that of all the poverty he had seen throughout the world, Haiti's was the worst. He just couldn't stand it. He said he made a point of leaving by the back door of his hotel, to avoid facing all those poor people, knowing that he was powerless to do anything for them."

He returned to New York on July 23, and not long after, he began feeling signs of what he believed to be dysentery. He wrote to a friend, on August 4, that he seemed to have "contracted a miserable stomach bug" in Haiti but hoped to leave for London the following day.

That was not to be. On August 5, he consulted a physician, who diagnosed an infection caused by tropical parasites and prescribed the appropriate treatment. But his condition worsened steadily. On August 11, he consulted another physician, who diagnosed a different intestinal infection and prescribed yet another form of medication. This was even less effective than the first, inducing stomach cramps, vomiting, and loss of appetite.

With all those discomforts, Rustin insisted on keeping his public engagements. "He had work to do to the very end," said Lawrence Templin, one of his former political colleagues. "His utter devotion to causes was marked by the use of his last ounce of talent, the driving urge to talk, to plan, to organize." It seemed to Walter Naegle that "he had a high tolerance for pain, because if I was suffering as he was, there's no way I could have done the things he did." When Rustin attended a board meeting at Freedom House, Leonard Sussman told him to go home—"he looked so sick." He didn't go home, and, Sussman recalled, "he was in a hospital three days later."

That was on August 21, when, his abdominal pain now unbearable, he entered Lenox Hill Hospital. There, exploratory surgery revealed that he was suffering not from any of the infections previously diagnosed but from a perforated appendix. "The misdiagnosis was a crying shame," his British friend Adam Roberts lamented.

On August 22, Rustin's postoperative condition seemed hopeful. But later that day he complained of chest pains; and near midnight of

August 23, he went into a cardiac arrest. All efforts to revive him failed. Aged seventy-five, he died early in the morning of August 24.

The *New York Times* said, in an editorial tribute: "He didn't lead so much as he influenced—through pragmatism, intellect, and foresight. Other civil rights leaders wielded power; Bayard Rustin wielded influence." To the *New York Post,* his death marked "the passing of the last great apostle of the creed of nonviolence." "Bayard had seemed ever young," said Velma Hill, who had worked with him through much of the nonviolent struggle. And to Liv Ullmann, who considered him "one of the more important human beings for our time," his death seemed strange, "because he was so tremendously alive."

Curtis B. Gans, a former peace activist, wrote to Norman Hill at the A. Philip Randolph Institute:

> I last met Bayard in 1965. It was in Harlem, on his fifty-third birthday. He was working in blue jeans, a cigarette dangling from his mouth, roaming from one déclassé office to another on West 125th Street. I had come for his counsel, because I was going to be in charge of organizing an anti-Vietnam march on Washington for SANE.
>
> He taught me a number of lessons: how to make sure that there were enough latrines, so that biological problems would not be social problems for the city of Washington; how the police could be brought in to cooperate, if you were committed to an orderly demonstration; how the American flag could be used to symbolize the legitimate right of dissent; how to show that while we may legitimately disagree about particular policies, we were all Americans. He also taught me that the object of any march was not simply to exercise itself but its message to an audience. If the message could be couched and presented in a way that was persuasive to ordinary Americans, then it did not matter who was marching. He taught me a number of other things: how to approach every political action like an artist, with a conception of the whole, while working on the several parts;

how to control a crowd and a meeting; how to measure progress by small steps while never losing sight of the larger picture.

While Bayard's life went through a few distinct phases, there were some constants to which everyone can fully repair: a reverence for the institutions of democracy; a belief in individual liberty; an abiding faith in reason and the intellectual process; a profound belief in the capacity of the individual citizen to better his or her condition; the concomitant willingness to acknowledge and accept the responsibility for one's ideas and actions.

On October 1, 1987, more than a thousand of Rustin's friends, acquaintances, and admirers gathered for a memorial service at the Community Church in Manhattan. They included former comrades who had become political antagonists. Despite the profound disagreements that had shattered their relationship with Rustin, they retained an affection and admiration for him. "Many of us who felt out of touch with Bayard and his political views after he left the peace movement," the radical pacifist Larry Gara said, "feel, nevertheless, a deep personal loss at his death. We must never forget the tremendous contributions he made to the nonviolent movement for peace and justice."

Among speakers at the service were the Reverend Donald Harrington, pastor of the Community Church; Charles Bloomstein, probably Rustin's most steadfast political ally since 1942; Phiroshaw Camay, a trade unionist from South Africa; DeWitt Luff, a member of the Rustin family; Vernon Jordan, a former leader of the National Urban League; Norman Hill, Rustin's successor at the A. Philip Randolph Institute; Lane Kirkland, president of the AFL-CIO; the Reverend Thomas Kilgore, from whose church hall in Harlem Rustin organized the 1963 March on Washington; Liv Ullmann, of the International Rescue Committee; Rabbi Marc Tanenbaum, representing the American Jewish Committee. The principal eulogists were Kirkland, Tanenbaum, and Jordan.

Kirkland said: "Bayard had many adversaries and opponents, but I never heard him speak of an enemy. No matter how intense the conflict, he never lost his sense of the human bond on which the resolution of conflict rests. Although he gave his whole heart and mind to the causes he fought for, no cause could ever limit or define him. Only on issues of right and wrong did he ever take sides. He defended Israel against those who said that her people had no right to exist, although he was not a Jew. He defended the people of Indochina, although he was neither Indochinese nor Asian. It was in the cause of right that he defended black workers in South Africa and marched on countless picket lines with American trade unionists. He traveled the world on behalf of the helpless, the homeless, the poor, the exploited. He understood and he taught that human freedom was a seamless fabric that all of us have to repair whenever or wherever it is torn."

Rabbi Tanenbaum: "Bayard had a very profound moral and spiritual bond with, of all people, the first-century rabbi named Hillel. Whenever Rustin and I were together, he would ask me to recite, in Hebrew, Hillel's core philosophy: 'If I am not for myself, then who will be for me? And if I am only for myself, then what am I?' We [at the American Jewish Committee] felt a great trust in the honesty and truthfulness of this natural aristocrat of compassion."

Vernon Jordan: "Bayard was the consummate adviser to the entire civil rights leadership. We counted on him for intellectual firepower, for strategic thinking, for long-range planning, for pragmatic idealism. He was chairman of the ideas committee for us all. He captured the spirit of heated internal debate and wrapped it in sound and sensible statements of compromise and consensus. We each sought him out privately, to ask his thoughts on our organizational agendas. He was our intellectual bank, where we all had unlimited accounts. In the 1963 March on Washington, he demonstrated capacities some of us never knew he had. He proved to us and the nation that he was a first-class organizer, logician, tactician, mobilizer, peacemaker, strategist, and coalition builder, as he led the civil rights movement to one of its finest hours. His lifetime of devotion to the causes of civil rights and human rights invokes the words of Oliver Wendell Holmes, who wrote that, as life is action and passion, it is required of a man to share the action and passion of his time or risk being judged not to have lived. Bayard Rustin truly lived."

The memorial service ended with Rustin's recorded voice, singing, in a lively and limpid tenor, one of the spirituals he loved:

Now won't you sit down, sit down?
I can't sit down.
Just got to Heaven,
Got to move around.

On Memorial Day weekend of 1988, Rustin's cremated remains were interred at Scotland Farm, the country residence of his friends Robert and Joyce Gilmore as well as Robert's third wife, Elizabeth. He had spent some of his happier weekend hours at the fourteen-hundred-acre farm. It was where, taught by the farm's overseer, Charles Flint, he had learned to drive the 1965 Morgan sports car he acquired in 1972. In Manhattan, during the mid-1950s, he had given up in disgust when a friend tried to teach him the precise meshing of gearshift and clutch on a Volkswagen beetle. "Though he was skillful and adroit in most areas of physical movement," the friend said, "he was not mechanically inclined. He lacked sympathy with machines. He felt ashamed, put down, by his body's lack of coordination. He hated not being able to do things well." But Rustin took more readily to Charles Flint's tutelage and was soon chauffeuring himself through the small towns and villages around Scotland Farm. Alex, one of Charles Bloomstein's sons, sometimes drove around with Rustin, sharing a joint of marijuana. "All heads would turn and stare at this striking and majestic black man, impeccably dressed, driving this antique Morgan roadster," young Bloomstein said. "No one knew what to make of Rustin's flamboyant apparition." But Scotland Farm also held a few unpleasant memories for Rustin. It was where he had suffered his near-fatal heart attack in 1971;

and where, in a pine forest, he had helped to dig Joyce Gilmore's grave in 1974.

"We decided," Walter Naegle said, "that Scotland Farm was the most appropriate place to bury Bayard's ashes. They fit perfectly in one of the antique vases, an Indian brass container, from his art collection." The twenty friends or so at Rustin's burial included Naegle, Charles Bloomstein, his sons, Steven and Alex; LuEsther Mertz, Joyce Gilmore's mother; Charlie Flint and his wife, Lori. "We held a Quaker ceremony," Naegle remembered. "We stood around mostly in silence, broken occasionally by someone who felt moved to speak. After that, I put the brass container into the ground, near Joyce's grave. Everyone took turns filling the hole with earth. I threw in the last handful or two. We all joined to drape pine needles around the spot. Then we went back into the house and had a meal. It was a beautiful day. The weather was gorgeous. We couldn't have asked for a nicer day."

Notes

The Rustin papers (BR papers) are now catalogued by the Library of Congress. However, the author consulted them before they were deposited with the Library. Thus no box numbers are listed here. Other abbreviations used in these notes are FOR for Fellowship of Reconciliation, NYPL for New York Public Library, SCPC for Swarthmore College Peace Collection and WRL for War Resisters League.

Chapter 1

page

5   "both wholesale and retail": Charles Bloomstein to the author, 8/5/95.

5   "He was all-absorbing": Rachelle Horowitz to the author, 8/10/95.

5   "essential qualities": Charles Bloomstein, "Bayard Rustin," *Dissent*, Winter 1988.

5   "Bayard seemed to envelop people": Worth Randle to the author, 10/6/88.

5   "a thoroughly self-emancipated person": William Hefner to the author, 8/5/88.

5   "wide vocabulary and extraordinary intelligence": Interview with Larry Gara, 9/2/88.

5   "I don't know what Rustin's IQ was": Robert Horton to the author, 8/6/88.

5   "Using that knowledge": Charles Bloomstein, "Bayard Rustin," *Dissent*, Winter 1988.

5   "Things that happened to him": Interview with Larry Gara, 9/2/88. In that interview, Gara described Rustin as "one of the genuine pacifists I had met."

6   a gourmet who loved pig knuckles: Thomas R. Brooks, "A Strategist Without a Movement," *New York Times Magazine*, 2/16/69.

6   "a remarkably cheerful character": Charles Bloomstein to the author, 8/5/95.

7   "He was full of life": Interview with Anna Luff, 10/31/87. Luff added in that interview: "At first my mother said . . ."

8   "extremely touching": Interview with Liv Ullmann, 10/11/88.

8   "Seeing your name and picture": Mrs. Bayard W. Allmond, Jr., to Rustin; undated, but evidently in spring 1969, in BR Papers.

8   "One of my aunts was studying French": Rustin to B. W. Allmond, 5/27/69, in BR Papers.

9   "I think it significant": Conrad W. Wilson to Rustin, 10/26/76, in BR Papers.

9   "As a child, Bayard used to say": Interview with Anna Luff, 10/31/87.

9   "Very few of the black leaders": James Farmer, at memorial service for Rustin in Media, Pa., 11/15/87.

10   it wasn't "theatrical": Interview with Liv Ullmann, 10/11/88.

10   Dellinger called him a liar: Interview with Dellinger, 1/11/91.

10   "Bayard's sense of drama": Interview with Igal Roodenko, 8/10/88.

11   "a brilliant tactician": Paul Goodman, Letter to the Editor, *Liberation*, Nov. 1965.

11   "sharp political mind": Michael Randle to the author, 7/3/89.

11   "the primary and secondary bullshit index": Charles Bloomstein to the author, 5/8/95.

11   "Bayard could sometimes be a bullshit artist": Interview with Ralph DiGia, 6/6/88.

11   "total command of an audience": Interview with Igal Roodenko, 8/10/88.

12   "This is the first time": "Rights Leader Sparks Some Sharp Criticism," *Newark Star-Ledger*, 1/20/67.

12   "He was an excellent soap-box performer": Robert Bone to the author, 9/16/88.

12   "On one of Bayard's national tours": Glenn Smiley to the author, 11/9/88.

14   "People were astounded": Stephen Trachtenberg to Rustin, 5/23/79, in BR Papers.

14   "Bayard stood out": Interview with Stephen Cary, 4/4/89.

14   "I fought for many years": Martin Mayer, "The Lone Wolf of Civil Rights," *Saturday Evening Post*, 7/11/64.

14   "his iconoclastic delight": Michael Randle to the author, 7/3/89.

14   "At dinner parties": Steven Bloomstein to the author, 6/7/89.

15   "Baldwin bawled me out": Jim Forrest to Charles Bloomstein, 4/4/89, in Bloomstein's personal files.

15   "I had just graduated from college": Alex Bloomstein to the author, 11/28/88.

16   "a handsome man": Robert Penn Warren, *Who Speaks for the Negro?* (New York: Random House, 1965), pp. 236–37.

16   "fine and finished quality": Interview with Jonathan Brice, 6/9/88.

17   "an incredible piece of drawing": Interview with Roy Finch, 11/1/88.

17   "Bayard is not a Negro leader": Whitney Young, quoted in Martin Mayer, "The Lone Wolf of Civil Rights," Saturday Evening Post, July 11, 1964.

17   "One of the qualities I have admired": Whitney Young to Rustin, 7/20/64, in BR Papers.

18   "total commitment": Interview with John Lewis, 10/25/89.

18   Rustin's gift at coalition building: Interview with Adam Roberts, 1/31/90.

19   "active concern for races": C. Vann Woodward, in Rustin's *Down the Line* (Chicago: Quadrangle Books, 1971), p. x. See also Warren, *Who Speaks for the Negro?* p. 237.

19   "My activism did not spring": Rustin to Joseph Beam, 4/21/86, in BR Papers.

Chapter 2

20   West Chester's "wealth" and "cultivation": Margaret Berwind Schiffer, *Survey of Chester County Pennsylvania Architecture* (Exton, Pa.: Schiffer Publishing Co., 1976), p. 9.

20   Marking its centenary: *West Chester Centennial Souvenir*, 1899. Available at Chester County Historical Society, West Chester.

21   Among the works describing the first Quaker encounter with blacks in Pennsylvania: Thomas F. Drake, *Quakers and Slavery in America* (New Haven: Yale University Press, 1950).

21   Quaker influence among Delaware Indians: See Albert C. Applegate, *Quakers in Pennsylvania* (Baltimore: Johns Hopkins University Press, 1892).

21   Quaker Meetings were lily white: Interview with Stephen Cary, 4/4/89.

22   "At no period in history": George Cadbury, "Negro Membership in the Society of Friends," *Journal of Negro History* 21, 1936.

23   "They were a fine family": Nicholas J. Tavani to the author, 2/25/89.

23   "a member of the Black Stars Social Club": Interview with Robert Spence, 1/24/89.

24   "We were told that we should never discuss": Rustin interview with Caroline Moorehead, 12/6/85, in BR Papers.

24   "Other than Bayard's Quaker grandmother": Interview with Charles Porter, 4/3/89.

25   "Bayard started coming on": Ibid.

26   "She not only stimulated": Rustin's prepared address to the United Federation of Teachers ("Integration Within Decentralization"), April 1968; accepting the UFT's John Dewey Award.

26   "In the 1920s and '30s": Interview with Oliver Patterson, 10/31/87.

26   "Bayard had no equal in academic subjects": John Rodgers, at Rustin memorial meeting in Media, Pa., 11/15/87.

26   "'Pin-Head' was an excellent tennis player": Interview with John Melton, 1/25/89. Rustin later said that he liked the people who pronounced his first name properly—not *Bay*ard, but *Bye*ard.

27   "He never came out for a substitute": John Rodgers, at Rustin memorial meeting, 11/15/87.

28   "They were hands-off . . . types": Interview with Charles Porter, 4/3/89.

29   "Mr. Hart was an enthusiast": Rustin interview with Carrol Buchanan, 2/5/85, in BR Papers.

30   Mencken's ranking of Hergesheimer: Allen Churchill, *The Literary Decade*, (Englewood Cliffs, N.J.: Prentice-Hall, 1971), p. 50.

31   "I don't think any of us": Interview with Robert Spence, 1/24/89.

31   "I got not one penny": "Rustin Warns Against Lag in Education," West Chester *Daily Local News*, 8/27/65.

32 "Many regard the purchase of Wilberforce": George A. Singleton, *The Romance of African Methodism* (New York: Exposition Press, 1952), pp. 91–2.

32 "the greatest social institution": W. E. B. Du Bois, *The Autobiography of W. E. B. Du Bois* (New York: International Publishers, 1968), pp. 185–87.

33 "I had never known southern blacks": Rustin interview with Carrol Buchanan, 2/5/85.

33 "Rustin had excellent training": George Hall interview with Carrol Buchanan; cited by Buchanan in his interview with the author, 6/9/88.

34 "At the end of our performances": Rustin interview with Carrol Buchanan, 2/5/85. All of Rustin's further recollections of his life at Wilberforce are quoted from his interview with Buchanan, in BR Papers.

35 "I tasted the food a few times": Interview with John M. Royall, Jr., 10/12/90.

36 "He was a marvelous orator": Interview with Rosamond Nelson, 7/23/88.

38 "Dr. Hill wanted Stokowski to hear me sing": Rustin interview with Carrol Buchanan, 2/5/85.

38 "I ran into some difficulties at Cheyney": Ibid.

38 "In some sense": Rustin to Leslie Pinckney Hill, 4/18/51, in BR Papers.

38 "a rich white lady": Interview with Rosamond Nelson, 7/23/88.

39 "to be single-eyed": Helen MacKinlay, *Angel Mo' and Her Son Roland Hayes* (Boston: Little, Brown, 1945), p. 91.

39 "singing wasn't the principal medium": Interview with James R. Dumpson, 6/7/88.

39 "simply a political animal": Interview with William Sutherland, 7/3/88.

Chapter 3

40 Harold Chance's requirements of young peace activists: "Enlist for Peace," *Fellowship,* June 1937.

41 "a very small and very ordinary town": Interview with Carl Rachlin, 9/11/89. All further comments by Rachlin in this chapter are quoted from the same interview.

43 "I have often wondered": Robert Bilheimer to the author, 8/8/88.

44 "My father was then the business manager": Ibid.

46 "utterly bewildered Negroes": Irving Howe and Lewis Coser, The *American Communist Party* (New York: Praeger, 1962), p. 213.

46 "He came down the stairs one day": Interview with Anna Luff, 10/31/87.

47 "I first encountered communists": Rustin, *Strategies for Freedom* (New York: Columbia University Press, 1976), p. 9.

47 "there were five or six of us": Interview with Howard Wallace, 5/10/89.

48 "a vital and dynamic community": Interview with Rustin, 6/10/80.

48   "Each Thursday night": Ibid.

50   "he taught some kind of modern dance": Interview with Lorvelle Henry, 6/8/90.

50   DePaur had heard him sing: Interview with Leonard DePaur, 5/27/88.

50   Reviews of *John Henry*: In the *Herald Tribune* ("Plays from Down South"), 2/25/40; the *New York Post* ("John Henry Is Nice to Listen To"), 1/11/40; the *New York Times* ("The Play"), 1/11/40.

50   "I was absolutely taken with him": Rustin interview with Martin Duberman, 2/25/83, in BR Papers.

51   "I wanted a club": Whitney Balliett, "Night Clubs," The New Yorker, 10/9/71.

51   "Though Bayard and his young friends": Interview with Charles Bloomstein, 1/9/89.

52   "From the early '30s on": Mark Naison, *Communists in Harlem During the Depression* (Urbana: University of Illinois Press, 1983), p. xvii.

52   "The democratic revolution had come to Harlem": George Chaney, *A Long Journey* (Chicago: Quadrangle Books, 1968), pp. 91–2.

52   "In the alcoves it was dark": Meyer Liben, "CCNY–A Memoir," *Commentary*, Sept. 1965.

53   "As the Depression deepened": Howe and Coser, The American Communist Party, pp. 198–99.

53   "was visiting the basement one evening": Interview with Milton Kramer, 11/15/88.

54   "I used to follow Bayard": Interview with Howard Wallace, 5/10/89.

55   "Bayard knew the best soups and pâtés": Interview with Milton Kramer, 11/15/88.

55   "the Norman Thomas socialists": Rustin interview with Columbia University Oral History Project, 11/14/84. Decades earlier, Eugene Debs, leader of the American Socialist Party, had said that it was the party of the whole working class, that it could not make separate appeals to all races. See, e.g., I. M. Rubinow, "The Negro and Socialism," *New York Call*, 5/19/12.

56   "No longer was President Roosevelt a warmonger": Wilson Record, *The Negro and the Communist Party* (Chapel Hill: University of North Carolina Press, 1951), pp. 210–12.

56   "the communists' primary concern": Rustin, *Strategies for Freedom*, pp. 9–10.

Chapter 4

58   "This man of great dignity": Rustin, "A. Philip Randolph," *The Yale Review*, Spring 1987.

61   "lecture on the nature and strategy of mass movements": The revolt of Randolph's March on Washington Youth Division and his public reprimand are drawn from Herbert Garfinkel, *When Negroes March* (Glencoe, Ill.: Free Press, 1959), pp. 67–9.

61   "the symbolic inauguration of the modern civil rights movement": Rustin, *Strategies for Freedom* (New York: Columbia University Press, 1976), pp. 14–15.

62   Fellowship of Reconciliation had been conceived: Richard Deats, "The Rebel Passion," *Fellowship*, Dec. 1980.

62   "One must choose": Muriel Lester, *It Occurred to Me*, cited in *Fellowship*, July/Aug. 1990.

62   "Through all the years": John Nevin Sayre, "How the Fellowship Began," Fellowship, Jan. 1943.

62   American branch of the FOR was inaugurated: Jessie Wallace Hughan, "The Beginnings of War Resistance" (New York: War Resisters League, 1936). See also Hughan's "25th Anniversary Reminiscences," Fellowship, Nov. 1940.

63   a future that seemed most unlikely: Muste's journey from pacifism to Trotskyism and back is well recorded in Nat Hentoff, Peace *Agitator* (New York: Muste Memorial Institute, 1982).

63   "When he became a revolutionary Marxist": Sidney Hook, *Out of Step* (New York: Harper & Row, 1987), p. 199.

64   "I surmise that not a few": Nat Hentoff, ed., *The Essays of A. J. Muste* (New York: Bobbs-Merrill, 1967), p. 136.

64   "The Fellowship controversy has revealed": Reinhold Niebuhr, "Why I Leave the FOR," *The Christian Century*, 1/3/34.

65   "We could not conceive of God": Muriel Lester, *Entertaining Gandhi*, (London: Nicholson & Watson, 1932), p. 3.

65   "If I can't love Hitler": Milton Mayer, "The Christer," *Fellowship*, Jan. 1952.

65   "The Unitarians have always admired": "The Churches and the War," *Time*, 12/22/41.

65   "Some seventeenth sense told me": Milton Mayer, "The Christer," *Fellowship*, January 1952. All later quotations from Mayer on the subject of Muste in this chapter are from "The Christer."

66   "I learned more about nonviolence": Hentoff, *Peace Agitator*, pp. 113–14.

67   "very detailed and comprehensive report": Rustin to Muste, 8/5/41; Muste to Rustin, 8/14/41; in BR Papers.

68   "the most significant and historic": "The Lakeside Conference and After," *Fellowship*, Oct. 1941.

68   "I was a product of the 1930s": George Houser, *No One Can Stop the Rain* (New York: Pilgrim Press, 1989), p. 6.

69   "the most important explication": Hentoff, *Peace Agitator*, pp. 190–91.

69   "Shridharani's book became our gospel": Rustin interview with S. Kapur, 4/9/87, in BR Papers.

69   "the most significant event": Glenn Smiley, "A Pebble Thrown into the Pond," *Fellowship*, June 1989.

70   "Why do you come out here": "What They Said and Did at March on Washington Confab," (Baltimore) *Afro-American*, 7/10/43.

70   "the gathering place of absolute pacifists": Conrad Lynn, *There Is a Fountain*, (Westport, Conn.: Lawrence Hill, 1979), p. 86.

70   "vivid memory": Interview with John P. Roche, 9/10/89.

70   "dark and dingy": James Farmer, *Lay Bare the Heart*, (New York: New American Library, 1985), pp. 149–50.

72   "maybe just a notch up from shabby": Marion Bromley to the author, 10/17/88.

72   "obviously minimum": Minutes, FOR National Committee Meeting, 11/28/41. FOR Files, Document Group 13, SCPC.

72   "Take-home pay": Constance Muste, "Fellowship and the Paycheck," *Fellowship*, June 1948.

72   "the FOR staff was truly a family"; "Bayard was certainly the star": Marion Bromley to the author, 10/17/88.

73   "advanced knowledge and judgment": Ernest Bromley to the author, 10/18/88.

73   "In the street we met a woman": Catharine Raymond to the author, 10/3/88.

74   "When Bayard and A. J. took positions": Interview with William Sutherland, 7/3/88.

74   "a very talented person": John Swomley to the author, 9/12/88.

75   "Bayard told me about things": Interview with Milton Kramer, 11/15/88.

75   "a persuasive and powerful speaker": John Swomley, "The Coming of World War II," *Fellowship*, June 1990.

75   "the infighting was fierce": Farmer, *Lay Bare the Heart*, p. 84.

75   "Bayard and Jim Farmer": Interview with George Houser, 11/11/88.

75   "To be perfectly candid": Interview with Farmer, 9/3/89.

76   "That's when I met Rustin": Interview with John P. Roche, 9/10/89.

76   "Bayard particularly liked a song"; "Whenever Bayard came": Interview with Charles Bloomstein, 10/21/87.

Chapter 5

81   "to present an unpopular point of view": Rustin to Edward Hudson, 10/24/49. FOR Files, Rustin Box, SCPC.

81   "delighted in ideas and tactics": Interview with William Sutherland, 7/3/88.

81   "spread the message"; "stimulate the organization": "FOR and Other Organizations . . . ," memorandum by Muste, Dec. 1948. FOR Files, Box 3, SCPC.

82   "While he emphasized": "Speaker Condemns Acts of Racial Discrimination," *Dayton Journal*, 6/15/43.

83   "Why fight and die abroad": Orval Etter, "Remembering Bayard Rustin," *Fellowship*, Jan./Feb. 1988.

83   "I have heard many say": "Report of Youth Secretary—Bayard Rustin," 9/12/42. FOR Files, Box 3, SCPC.

84   "Somewhere between the mass meetings": Garfinkel, *When Negroes March*, p. 143.

85   "A. Philip Randolph is guilty": *Pittsburgh Courier*, 1/23/43.

85   "the vision, intelligence, and courage": Muste to Randolph, 1/11/43. FOR Files, Box 10, SCPC.

85   "[Randolph] spoke in a way": Rustin to Muste, 2/22/43. Ibid.

86   "Muste and Randolph had been elated": Farmer, Lay Bare the Heart, p. 156.

86   "There was something about the conference": J. Holmes Smith to Muste, 7/8/43. FOR Files, Box 21, SCPC.

86   "The great wartime upsurge": Garfinkel, *When Negroes March*, p. 144.

87   "a stimulating one-man crusade": Houser, *No One Can Stop the Rain*, p. 8.

87   "An effective technique": Rustin, "Lesson Plan in Nonviolent Action." FOR Files, Box 21, SCPC. See also Rustin, "The Negro and Nonviolence," *Fellowship*, October 1942.

87   Rustin raised such an issue in Indianapolis: Rustin, "Nonviolence Works Again," *Fellowship*, May 1942.

88   Rustin was brutally beaten: "Rustin vs. Jim Crow," *Fellowship*, July 1942.

88   "Bayard was always determined to test": Wilfred Gamble to the author, 7/26/88.

89   "I was interested in nonviolence": Interview with Wallace Nelson, 8/9/88.

89   "never forget that man": Carolyn Lindquist to the author, 11/13/88.

89   "Someone told me": Gay Morenus Hammerman to the author, 8/28/88.

90   "When the meeting began": John Mecartney, "Bayard Rustin and Nonviolent Defense," unpublished manuscript in Mecartney's personal files.

90   "Rustin was totally different": Interview with Denny Wilcher, 11/10/89.

91   "Bayard Rustin has been here": Margaret McCulloch to Muste, 7/4/72. This controversial exchange was continued in Muste to McCulloch, 7/8/42; McCulloch to Muste, 7/20/42; Muste to McCulloch, 8/5/42. FOR Files, Box 15, SCPC.

92   "I do think that in many ways": Muste to Bernard Junker, 7/16/42. Ibid.

93   "Bayard impressed me": Interview with Farmer, 9/3/89.

93   "Peace was number one": Farmer, *Lay Bare the Heart*, p. 86.

94   "Rustin sat impassively": Ibid., pp. 102–11.

94   "Rusty and I compared notes": J. Holmes Smith to Muste, 7/8/43. FOR Files, Box 21, SCPC.

94   "Bayard is very angry": John Swomley to Muste, 7/7/43. Ibid., Box 11.

95   "I am convinced that we must effect": Swomley to Muste, 7/11/43. Ibid.

95   "Muste called me into his office": Farmer, *Lay Bare the Heart*, p. 160. Farmer's resignation was also discussed in Muste to Swomley, Nevin Sayre, et al., 5/7/45; Muste to Farmer, 5/11/45; Farmer to Muste, 5/16/45. FOR Files, Box 7, SCPC.

95   "I don't think anybody could make a better speech": Rustin interview with Columbia University Oral History Project, 2/28/85.

Chapter 6

97   "I condemn it with my whole being": Evan Thomas to Muste, 1/7/43. FOR Files, Box 11, SCPC. See also Thomas, "Why We Oppose Military Conscription," New York, War Resisters League, 1944.

97   "It is a pity": John Haynes Holmes, "From My Standpoint," *Fellowship*, May 1942.

98   "I cannot voluntarily submit": Rustin to Local Draft Board No. 63, 11/16/43, in BR Papers.

98   "I didn't think my automatic exemption": John Mecartney to the author, 12/15/89.

99   "The place is somber": Doris Grotewhol to Rustin, 2/9/44, in BR Papers.

99   "It is hard to think of you in prison": Muste to Rustin, 3/1/44, in BR Papers.

99   "must be a rare woman": John Nevin Sayre to Julia Rustin, 3/9/94.

99   "Bayard's birthday is March 17": Julia Rustin to Sayre, 3/15/44. FOR Files, Box 1, SCPC.

100   "the young men to whom I felt most akin": Hentoff, ed., *The Essays of A. J. Muste*, pp. 6–7.

100   "Both morally and practically": Rustin, "Letter to Warden of Ashland Federal Prison," May 1944, in William Hefner's personal files.

101   "I go to prison with high hopes": Rustin to Peggy Deuel, 2/25/44, in BR Papers.

101   "I am convinced that Dr. Hagerman": Muste, "Memorandum on Visit to Ashland Federal Correctional Institution," 7/27/44. FOR Files, Rustin Box, SCPC.

101   to help "effect attitudes for the better": "Letter to Warden of Ashland Federal Prison."

102   "Being taught by a Negro": Rustin to Davis Platt, 5/5/44, in Platt's personal files.

102 "The fellows here": Rustin to Davis Platt, 8/17/44, in Platt's personal files.

102 "He drove us nuts": Interview with Larry Gara, 9/2/88.

102 "It was the guards": William Hefner to the author, 12/9/88.

102 "When you're dealing with people": Martin Mayer, "The Lone Wolf of Civil Rights," *Saturday Evening Post,* July 11, 1964.

103 "He has trouble getting letters out": Bronson P. Clark, in *Prison Newsletter,* July 1944.

103 "I should have known": Rustin to Davis Platt, 5/12/44, in Platt's personal files.

104 "kicked up a fuss": Bronson P. Clark, in *Prison Newsletter,* July 1944.

104 "I came to respect Santayana": Rustin to Davis Platt, 3/16/45, in Platt's personal files.

105 "Beecham is conducting": Doris Grotewhol to Rustin, 2/22/44, in BR Papers.

106 "I was amazed to find": Doris Grotewhol to Rustin, 6/25/44, in BR Papers.

106 "your grandfather's fear": Grotewhol to Rustin, 8/23/44, in BR Papers.

106 "God knows ever more": Rustin to Davis Platt, 4/20/45, in Platt's personal files.

107 "Huddleston went to the utility room": Quoted by Eleanor Clark to Doris Grotewhol, 5/3/44, in BR Papers.

107 "As you know": Rustin to Doris Grotewhol, 5/5/44, in BR Papers.

108 "Perhaps this will force you": Doris Grotewhol to Rustin, 5/24/44, in BR Papers.

108 "Lewisburg was a rough and dangerous place": Interview with Larry Gara, 9/2/88.

108 "They simply washed their hands": Rustin interview with Columbia University Oral History Project, 2/28/85.

109 "Still, what is oppressive": Rustin interview with Columbia University Oral History Project, 1/2/85.

109 "to discover the amount of money": Rustin, "To Mr. Gillet, U.S. Penitentiary," 5/19/46, in BR Papers.

110 "Bayard came out of penitentiary": Interview with Howard Wallace, 5/10/89.

110 "There are tremendous and pressing demands": Muste to Rustin, 2/23/46, in BR Papers.

Chapter 7

112 "I am surprised the university"; "consists in the nonviolent": *St. Paul Recorder,* 1/24/47 ("Passive Resistance Method Scores"; "Minneapolis NAACP Hears Rustin Explain . . . Technique").

112 "I got into a series of conferences": Rustin interview with Columbia University Oral History Project, 2/28/85. .

113 "Wanting to drive us from the cafeteria": Interview with A. C. Thompson, 10/4/88. See also "The Interracial Workshop," typescript FOR Files, Rustin Box, SCPC.

113 Irene Morgan versus Virginia: Roger Goldman and David Gallen, *Thurgood Marshall* (New York: Carrol and Graf, 1992), pp. 61–2; Pauli Murray, *Pauli Murray: The Autobiography of a Black Activist, Feminist, Lawyer* (Knoxville: University of Tennessee Press, 1989), pp. 237–38; Catherine Barnes, *A Journey from Jim Crow* (New York: Columbia University Press, 1983), pp. 45–47; "Jim Crow Barred in Interstate Buses," *New York Times*, 6/4/46. See also "The Case of Irene Morgan, *The New Republic*, 9/15/47.

114 "The Journey was not meant": Homer Jack, "The Journey of Reconciliation," undated article in BR Papers.

114 "disobedience movement": "Negroes Cautioned on Resistance Idea," *New York Times*, 11/23/46.

115 "I am sure that Marshall": "Our Guest Column: Beyond the Courts," *Louisiana Weekly*, 1/4/47.

116 "If you are Negro": Pamphlet by Rustin and George Houser, "You Don't Have to Ride Jim Crow," in BR Papers. Rustin and Houser also collaborated in writing this song (sung to the tune "No Hidin' Place Down Here"):

> *You don't have to ride Jim Crow.*
> *You don't have to ride Jim Crow.*
> *On June 3rd*
> *The High Court said*
> *When you ride interstate*
> *Jim Crow is dead,*
> *You don't have to ride Jim Crow.*

See Houser, *No One Can Stop the Rain*, p. 8.

117 "We had meetings every night": Interview with Wallace Nelson, 8/9/88.

117 "People on the bus": Lynn, *There Is a Fountain*, pp. 109–11.

118 "Whenever they emerge": James Peck, *Freedom Ride* (New York: Simon & Schuster, 1962), pp. 19–20. See also Rustin and Houser's account of the Journey of Reconciliation, "We Challenged Jim Crow," reprinted in Rustin, *Down the Line* (Chicago: Quadrangle Books, 1971), pp. 13–25.

118 "White cab drivers": Peck, *Freedom Ride,* pp. 22–3.

119 "Get the niggers out of town": Dorcas Jones to the author, 4/19/91.

120 "When we went into the buses": Rustin to Beverly White, 5/3/50, in BR Papers.

120 "Chapel Hill was as idyllic": Gay Morenus Hammerman to the author, 8/22/88.

121 "If interracial collaborators": "North Carolina Can Take it," *Greensboro Daily News*, 4/16/47.

122 "He said to me": Rustin interview with Columbia University Oral History Project, 9/12/86. See also "Chapel Hill Judge Sentences Rustin and Roodenko," *Fellowship*, July 1947.

123 "Our conviction, unfortunately": "Negro Acclaimed at Home and Abroad Sentenced to North Carolina Road Gang," press release, 3/9/49. FOR Files, Rustin Box, SCPC.

123 "Bayard was radiantly elated": Worth Randle to the author, 10/6/88.

124 "not only to devise techniques": "Civil Disobedience, Jim Crow, and the Armed Forces," in Rustin, *Down the Line*, 1971, p. 50.

124 "became convinced that it was possible": John Swomley, "FOR's Early Efforts for Racial Equality," *Fellowship*, July/August 1990.

125 Exchange with Senator Morse: *Congressional Record*, 80th Congress, Second Session, Senate, April 12, 1948, pp. 4416–18.

126 "The draft bill has run head-on": "Crisis in the Making: US Negroes Tussle with Issue," *Newsweek*, 6/7/48.

126 "Sincerity demands that you veto": Randolph to Truman, 6/21/48, Harry S. Truman Presidential Library.

127 "You should not register": "Speaker Requests Defiance of Draft," *New York Times*, 7/18/48; "Randolph Invites Arrest," *Pittsburgh Courier*, 8/24/48.

127 "On that fateful afternoon": Farmer, *Lay Bare the Heart*, pp. 159–60.

127 "there shall be equality": "Truman Orders End of Bias in Forces and Federal Jobs," *New York Times*, 7/27/48.

128 "to split the movement": "Randolph Withdraws from Anti-Jim Crow League," *Fellowship*, Oct. 1948.

128 "morally bound to continue": "Youthful Followers Declare They Will Carry on Campaign," *Philadelphia Tribune*, 8/28/48.

128 "It was nearly three years": Rustin interview with Columbia University Oral History Project, 2/28/85.

128 "We in the nonviolent movement": Jervis Anderson, *A. Philip Randolph: A Biographical Portrait* (New York: Harcourt Brace Jovanovich, 1972), pp. 281–82.

Chapter 8

130 "As you know, I have been interested": Rustin to Charles S. Johnson, 12/26/46; Johnson to Rustin, 12/28/46; in Johnson Papers, Amistad Research Center, New Orleans. Rustin's "Statement of Plan of Work," submitted to the Rosenwald Fund, emphasized his intention "to study the psychology underlying nonviolent resistance with Gandhi at his ashram." Copy in the Library of Fisk University.

131 "inner authority" and "great prophetic voice": Rustin interview with Caroline Moorehead, 12/6/85, in BR Papers.

131 "Muriel and I have been taken care of": Rustin to John Nevin Sayre, 12/5/48. Sayre Files, Box 14, SCPC.

131 "He met us and gave us some idea": Interview with Devi Prasad, 7/18/88.

131 "in an inflammatory manner": FBI Rustin File, No. 100-158700-91.

132 "receiving a warm welcome": FOR press release, "Negro Acclaimed at Home and Abroad." FOR Files, Rustin Box, SCPC.

132 "Nothing makes the Indians quite as happy": Rustin to George L. Paine, 10/27/49. FOR Files, Box 1, SCPC. Rustin explained his adjustment to other forms of Indian culture in the same letter.

132 "three times as much": Muriel Lester to Muste and John Nevin Sayre, 12/26/48. FOR Files, Rustin Box, SCPC.

133 "I cannot say too strongly": Richard Keithan to Sayre, 12/26/48. Sayre Files, Box 14, SCPC.

133 "Bayard's qualities are such that": Muste to Lester, 1/4/49. Ibid.

134 "nonviolent in means": Minutes, FOR national committee meeting, May 19–21, 1949. FOR Files, Box 3, SCPC.

134 "He came back from India": Catharine Raymond to the author, 10/3/88.

134 "My feeling is that he should arrange": Swomley memorandum to Muste, 3/9/49. FOR Files, Rustin Box, SCPC.

135 "We had chains on us": Rustin interview with Columbia University Oral History Project, 9/12/85.

135 "Twenty-Two Days on a Chain Gang": *New York Post*, Aug. 1949; reprinted in Rustin, *Down the Line*, pp. 26–49.

135 "a creative response": John Nevin Sayre memorandum to Rustin, 5/25/49. Sayre Files, Box 14, SCPC.

135 "spellbinding exposé": Joseph Felmet to Rustin, 6/4/49. FOR Files, Rustin Box, SCPC.

135 "that the present convict system": Brooks to Rustin, 9/29/49. FOR Files, Rustin Box, SCPC.

136 "so that we are completely without a military": "Speaker Says U.S. Heading Toward Own Destruction," *Lancaster Intelligencer Journal*, 3/10/50.

136 "crackpot" idea: George Houser, Roy Kepler, Alfred Hassler, and other prominent members of the Peacemakers were appalled by Rustin's call for a renouncing of citizenship as a radical act of pacifist protest against the building of nuclear weapons.

136 "The important thing": "Support Grows for Fast for Peace," undated press release, in BR Papers.

137 "there I met Bayard Rustin": Michael Harrington, *Fragments of the Century* (New York: Saturday Review Press, 1973), p. 68.

137 rally in Times Square: Interview with David Dellinger, 1/11/91;

Harrington, *Fragments of the Century*, pp. 68–9; "Poster Walk and Street Meeting Report," typescript in BR Papers.

138 "This means that a person": George Houser, "Nonviolently Speaking," *Equality*, May 1945.

Chapter 9

140 "But we never got there": Interview with William Sutherland, 7/5/88.

141 "I double-crossed them, however": Ibid.

141 "My introduction to the African liberation struggle": Houser, *No One Can Stop the Rain*, p. 10.

142 "The Committee [on Africa] had no money": Ibid., p. xi.

143 "It was I who brought home from London": Interview with Sutherland, 7/5/88.

143 "Bayard, Norman Whitney, and I": Interview with Stephen Cary, 4/4/89.

144 "Let us join together": "To Men Everywhere," *Nippo*, 8/22/88; letters to the editor, *Nippo*, 8/23/88; copies in Cary's personal files.

144 "I first met Bayard there": Godric Bader to the author, 6/6/90.

144 "held in such respect": Rustin, "Nkrumah, Man of Ghana and God," unpublished manuscript. WRL Files, Box 18, SCPC.

145 "poor struggling student": Peter Abrahams, "The Blacks," in Langston Hughes, ed., *An African Treasury* (New York: Pyramid Books, 1961), pp. 50–62.

145 "calm and quiet deliberation": Rustin, "Nkrumah, Man of Ghana and God."

146 "sculpture in wood and stone"; "a system of decentralized democracy": Rustin, "Negro American: Inspiration to Africa," unpublished manuscript. WRL Files, Box 18, SCPC.

146 "The communities live under a government": Onyenaekeya Udeagu, "Ibos as They Are," in Hughes, ed., *An African Treasury*, pp. 26–9.

147 talks with Nnamdi Azikiwe: Rustin, "Nnamdi Azikiwe: Nehru of Nigeria," unpublished manuscript. WRL Files, Box 18, SCPC.

147 "The admiration of the West African": Rustin, "Negro American: Inspiration to Africa."

148 "ought to concentrate"; "some special attention": John Nevin Sayre to Percy Bartlett, 1/15/53, Sayre Papers, Box 14, SCPC. Minutes of FOR executive committee meeting, 1/5/53, FOR Files, Box 4, SCPC.

148 "the proposition we discussed": Azikiwe to Rustin, 4/2/53, in BR Papers.

Chapter 10

153 Rustin's arrest and jailing in California: "Lecturer Jailed on Morals Charge," *Los Angeles Times*, 1/22/53; "Lecturer Sentenced to Jail," Ibid., 1/2/53.

154 "Bayard told me . . . he had been framed": Interview with David McReynolds, 10/4/89.

154 "Bayard was in tears": Glenn Smiley to the author, 11/9/88.

155 "I never said, 'You know, I'm gay'": "Time on Two Crosses," interview with Rustin by George Chauncey and Lisa Kennedy, *Village Voice*, 6/30/87.

155 "I never heard the word 'gay'": Charles Porter to the author, 4/18/89.

155 "Bayard told me that he didn't take it easily": Interview with William Sutherland, 7/5/88.

156 "It was in college that I came to understand": "An Interview with Bayard Rustin," *Open Hands*, Spring 1987.

156 "In the black aristocracy": Rustin interview with Mark Bowman, in BR Papers.

157 "I got to know Locke very well": Open Hands, Spring 1987.

157 "danced with all the women": Interview with Carl Rachlin, 9/11/89.

157 "Bayard was charming with women": Interview with Dr. A., 9/22/88.

158 "Physically, sexually": Gay Morenus Hammerman to the author, 8/28/88.

158 "When I was having sexual problems": Interview with Milton Kramer, 11/15/88.

158 "He was a very sensual person": Ibid.

158 "He had broad musical tastes"; "Bayard was a mentor": Interview with David Platt, 10/26/90.

159 "complaining that Bayard had led their sons astray": Interview with James Farmer, 9/3/89.

159 "Other episodes were reported": John Swomley, letter to the editor of *Fellowship*, Jan./Feb. 1988.

160 "Muste was one of the wisest persons": Interview with Milton Kramer, 11/15/88.

160 "During the . . . conversation": Muste to Rustin, 10/22/44, in BR Papers.

161 "I sense that I have betrayed you"; "I have not seen completely to the bottom": Rustin to Davis Platt, 11/3/44, 4/5/45, in Platt's personal files.

161 "To hold a philosophy of nonviolence": Rustin to Steve Smith, 12/18/52, in BR Papers.

161 "I must tell you what a real blow": John Swomley to Rustin, 1/27/53. Rustin Folder, Document Group 13, SCPC.

162 "I'm with you all the way": David McReynolds to Rustin, 2/3/53. McReynolds Files, Box 1, SCPC.

162 "In some ways, your letter meant": Rustin to John Swomley, 3/8/53. Rustin Folder, Document Group 13, SCPC.

163 "My father had reluctantly told the family": John Muste to the author, 5/13/91.

164 "Rustin had been thought of as Muste's successor": Interview with Larry Gara, 9/2/88.

164 "His sexual life was something he had to follow": Interview with David McReynolds, 10/4/89.

165 "Bayard's abilities were apparently boundless": Catharine Raymond to the author, 10/3/88.

Chapter 11

166 FOR had cut him off, penniless: See Dean Russell, "Unfinished Business," letter to the editor, *Fellowship,* Oct./Nov. 1987.

166 "all we can to help Bayard": FOR executive committee statement, 1/28/53. FOR Files, Rustin Box, SCPC.

166 "was always living on the financial edge"; "it would have been completely out of character": John Swomley, "Dear Friends," letter to the editor, *Fellowship*, Jan./Feb. 1988.

166 "As I understand it, the sum of $15": Muste to Dr. A., 3/27/53, in BR Papers.

167 "The tone of your letter": Dr. A. to Muste, 5/27/53, in BR Papers.

167 "Coming back to New York": Interview with Dr. A., 9/22/88.

169 "Bayard and I were in Zimbabwe": Interview with William Sutherland, 7/3/88.

169 "Bayard was not ashamed of his homosexuality": Interview with Tom Kahn, 10/27/89.

170 "It was a time when Bayard": Interviews with Sutherland, 7/3/88.

170 "Bayard's apartment had the look of a museum": Interview with Ralph DiGia, 6/6/88.

171 "Bayard made me feel that being white": Interview with Sally Sullivan, 11/9/89.

171 "Bayard was then in urgent need": Interview with Igal Roodenko, 8/10/88.

172 "Bayard was the most valuable man": Interview with Roy Finch, 11/1/88.

172 "the most creative nonviolent activist": Interview with David Dellinger, 11/1/91. See also an interview with Roodenko and DiGia by Susan Pines, in *The Nonviolent Activist* (War Resisters League publication), Dec. 1987.

172 "I greatly admired A. J.": Abraham Kaufman to the author, 8/29/89.

173 "Muste was one of those rare people": Interview with David McReynolds, 10/4/89.

174 "People at the AFSC urged me": Interview with Stephen Cary, 4/4/89.

174 "the most sophisticated and widely read": Lawrence S. Wittner, *Rebels Against War* (New York: Columbia University Press, 1969), p. 230.

174 "*Speak Truth to Power* marks the first attempt": Robert Pickus, "Speak Truth to Power—a Revolutionary Approach in the Search for Peace," *The Progressive*, Oct. 1955.

175 "It was a great week that we all had": Interview with Stephen Cary, 4/4/89.

176 "Bayard had still not fully recovered": Interview with one of Rustin's former live-in companions, who asked that he not be identified.

Chapter 12

185 "Lillian Smith had once traveled with me": Howell Raines, *My Soul Is Rested* (New York: Penguin Books, 1977), p. 53.

185 "I had merely an intellectual understanding": King, *Stride Toward Freedom* (New York: Harper & Bros., 1958), p. 101.

186 "Bayard was too talented": Interview with David McReynolds, 10/4/89.

186 "They can bomb us out": Rustin, "Montgomery Diary," *Liberation*, April 1956; reprinted in Rustin, *Down the Line*, pp. 55–61. In this chapter, much of Rustin's account of his role in the bus boycott is based on his "Montgomery Diary."

187 "I know you, Mr. Rustin": Coretta Scott King, *My Life with Martin Luther King, Jr.* (New York: Holt, Rinehart & Winston, 1969), pp. 137–38.

187 "should not be hated": David Garrow, *Bearing the Cross* (New York: Morrow, 1986), p. 67.

188 gun resting on an armchair: Rustin, "Montgomery Diary," April 1956; Raines, *My Soul Is Rested*, p. 52.

188 "If in the heat and flow of battle": Rustin interview with Columbia University Oral History Project, 4/3/85.

188 "King had read about Gandhi": Rustin interview with Thomas Mikelson, 6/4/84, in BR Papers.

188 "Christ furnished the spirit": Martin Luther King, Jr., "Pilgrimage to Nonviolence," *The Christian Century*, 4/13/60.

189 "If the job of nonviolent education": Rustin to "Dear Arthur and Ralph," 2/25/56. Group CDG-A, Rustin Files, SCPC.

189 "Boycott . . . a desire to hurt economically": Ibid.

190 "I have been followed by police cars": Ibid.

191 "My principal inspirations have come": Glenn Smiley, *Nonviolence: The Gentle Persuader* (Nyack, N.Y.: Fellowship Publications, 1991), foreword.

191 "Bayard has had a good influence on King": Glenn Smiley to John Swomley, 2/29/56. FOR Files, "Southern Work, 1955–58," SCPC.

191 "I would teach him everything": Smiley, *Nonviolence*, pp. 4–5.

191 "I've just had one of the most glorious": Glenn Smiley to Muriel Lester, 2/28/56. Ibid.

192 "most of the credit": Garrow, *Bearing the Cross*, p. 94.

192 "Even the shrewd and intelligent help": Harris Wofford, *Of Kennedys and Kings* (New York: Farrar Straus Giroux, 1980), p. 115.

192   "I'll never forget that Dr. King": Raines, *My Soul Is Rested*, p. 55. "For the record": Rustin to King, 3/8/56. King Papers, Box 5, Mugar Library, Boston University.

193   "especially effective in counseling": Homer Jack, "To Those Interested in the Nonviolent Aspects of Montgomery," undated typescript in Norman Thomas Papers, Reel 30, NYPL.

193   "The leadership in general": Rustin, "Report on Montgomery, Alabama," 3/21/56, in BR Papers.

194   "Our Struggle": Reprinted in Paul Goodman, ed., *Seeds of Liberation* (New York: George Braziller, 1964), pp. 262–69.

194   Formation of Committee for Nonviolent Integration: Minutes of the WRL executive committee meeting, 4/23/56. WRL Files, Box 1, SCPC.

194   Though finances were "holding up well": King to Rustin, 9/20/56. FOR Files, "Montgomery 1956–61," SCPC.

195   Formation of In Friendship: "In Friendship for Welfare Aid to Victims of Racism," 11/4/56, in Norman Thomas Papers, Reel 31, NYPL. Other correspondence in the Thomas Papers describe the effort to organize In Friendship. See also Stanley Levison interview with James Mosby, 2/14/70, in Civil Rights Documentation Project, Moorland-Spingarn Collection, Howard University.

195   "Mike Harrington had known Bayard": Interview with Rachelle Horowitz, 6/7/89.

196   "the story of Montgomery": King, *My Life with Martin Luther King, Jr.*, p. 144.

196   "Tomorrow I want to be paid": Smiley, *Nonviolence*, pp. 19–20.

196   "I rode the first integrated bus": King, *Stride Toward Freedom*, p. 173.

196   "a post-Gandhian contribution": Rustin, "Montgomery, Alabama," *The War Resister*, Fourth Quarter 1957.

Chapter 13

197   "As an aide to Dr. King": Rustin, *Strategies for Freedom,* pp. 38–9.

197   SCLC was a needed counterbalance; dawn of black protest activism: Ella Baker interview with John Britton, 6/19/68; Stanley Levison interview with James Mosby, 2/14/70; in Civil Rights Documentation Project, Moorland-Spingarn Collection, Howard University.

197   "I can show you how to do it": Rustin interview with Columbia University Oral History Project, 4/3/85. Copies of the seven working documents that led to the founding of SCLC are in BR Papers.

198   "spoke movingly on the power of nonviolence": Rustin, "Even in the Face of Death," *Liberation*, Feb. 1957. See also "A Statement to the South and Nation," by the Southern Leaders Conference on Transportation and

Nonviolent Integration, Jan. 10–11, 1957, in BR Papers.

198   "helped to place King at the head": Adam Fairclough, *To Redeem the Soul of America* (Athens: University of Georgia Press, 1957), pp. 2, 23.

199   "I had known that there would never be any role": Ella Baker interview with John Britton, in Civil Rights Documentation Project, Moorland-Spingarn Collection.

200   "Ella Baker was very tough on Martin": Rustin interview with Taylor Branch, 6/24/84, in BR Papers.

200   "In the absence of some early": Telegram sent at 3 P.M., copy in BR Papers.

201   "Dr. Gideonse was an authoritarian figure": Interview with Rachelle Horowitz, 6/7/89.

202   "impartial observers": See Albert Blumherg telegram to Rustin, 2/8/57, in BR Papers; John Swomley, "Dialogue with Communist Party Leaders," *Fellowship*, March 1990; Roy Finch, "The Communist Convention," *Liberation*, March 1957; Nat Hentoff, *Peace Agitator*, pp. 160–68; Howe and Coser, *The American Communist Party*, pp. 490–98; Muste to J. Edgar Hoover, 4/2/57, in WRL Files, Box 12, SCPC.

203   Robeson . . . concert did not take place: Minutes, FOR executive committee meeting, 10/27/50. FOR Files, Box 4, SCPC.

203   "study and untrammeled discussion": Press release, "American Forum," 5/13/57. WRL Files, Box 12, SCPC. For an account of the Forum's origin and decline, see Maurice Isserman, *If I Had a Hammer* (New York: Basic Books, 1987), pp. 174–80.

203   "The communists don't belong in jail"; "romantic nonsense": Hentoff, *Peace Agitator*, pp. 165–66.

204   "I've always tried to keep communication open": Ibid., p. 251.

204   "After the Hungarian revolution": Interview with Tom Kahn, 10/27/89. Rustin resigned from the American Forum in a letter to Muste, 5/20/57, in BR Papers.

205   Robeson "was ignored": Martin B. Duberman, *Paul Robeson* (New York: Knopf, 1988), pp. 447–48.

206   "The program was . . . too long": Michael Harrington, *Fragments of the Century* (New York: Saturday Review Press, 1973), p. 104.

206   Rustin suggested certain changes: Dated 5/10/57, in BR Papers.

207   "Our most urgent request": King's address to the Pilgrimage, 5/17/57, in BR Papers.

207   "an orator in the black Baptist mode": Harrington, *Fragments of the Century*, pp. 104–5.

207   "I learned from the occasion": Rustin interview with Sandra Cleary, 8/20/86, in BR Papers.

207   "the crowd was on its feet": Dan Wakefield, *The Nation*, 6/1/57.

207 "the number one leader": James L. Hicks, "King Emerges as Top Negro Leader," New York *Amsterdam News*, June 1, 1957.

208 "with the direct hope that the march would fail": Hicks, *Amsterdam News*, ibid.

208 "Including mailings and telegrams": Roy Wilkins to C. B. Powell, 6/4/57, in A. Philip Randolph Papers, Box 30, Library of Congress.

208 "But Bayard was the mastermind": Interview with Thomas Kilgore, 12/10/89.

209 "Much of the new movement": Rustin to King, 4/15/60. King Papers, Box 5, Mugar Library, Boston University.

209 "The emphasis should be": Rustin to King, 5/19/60. King Papers, Box 72, Mugar Library.

209 "King wrote his books": Rustin interview with Thomas Mikelson, 6/4/84, in BR Papers.

209 "any additional suggestions" and names: King to Rustin, 2/20/58, 3/22/58. King Papers, Box 5, Mugar Library.

210 "In regard to King's book": Rustin to "Dear Yone," 11/14/58, in BR Papers.

210 "central and dominant purposes": Excerpts from Randolph's address, in BR Papers.

211 "As my time to speak approached": Curtis B. Gans to Norman Hill, 9/25/87, in Hill's personal files.

212 "Our country had become intimidated": Interview with Rachelle Horowitz, 6/7/89.

Chapter 14

213 "Bayard was always flying off": Interview with Igal Roodenko, 9/1/88.

214 twenty-nine pacifists . . . arrested: William D. Miller, *A Harsh and Dreadful Love* (New York: Liveright, 1973), pp. 283–86.

214 "Because of an international conference": Rustin to King, 6/19/57. King Papers, Box 64, Mugar Library, Boston University.

214 not been "an estimable or adventurous period": Michael Foot, *Aneurin Bevan: A Biography* (New York: Atheneum, 1974), pp. 599–600.

215 "There must be unilateral [disarmament]": "Remarks by Bayard Rustin at Trafalgar Square," in BR Papers.

215 "the limpid beauty" of Russell's speech in Foot, *Aneurin Bevan*, pp. 599–600.

215 "Bayard Rustin delivered": Michael Randle to the author, 7/3/89.

216 march from Trafalgar Square: See also "A Wide Alliance on the March to Aldermaston," *Times* (London), 4/5/58; Richard Taylor, *Against the Bomb* (Oxford: Clarendon Press, 1988), pp. 115–89; Kathleen Tynan, *The Life of*

Kenneth Tynan (New York: Morrow, 1987), pp. 193–94.

216 Rebuffed in their attempts: "Five Americans on H-Bomb Protest," London *Daily Telegraph*, 4/17/58; Rustin to Muste, 4/8/58, in BR Papers.

216 "Bayard was a lively person": Interview with Marvin Gewirtz, 9/2/89.

217 "One sunny afternoon": Godric Bader to the author, 1/24/89.

218 "Bayard's evident fascination": Tony Smythe to the author, 1/16/90.

218 "beautiful rendering of English": Interview with Adam Roberts, 4/31/90.

218 "charming and extremely intelligent": April Carter to the author, 7/8/89.

218 "I think Bayard was attracted": Michael Randle to the author, 2/6/90.

219 "It was something that should never have happened": Michael Randle to the author, 7/3/89.

219 new form of European colonialism: April Carter, "The Sahara Protest Team," in *Liberation Without Violence*, ed. A. Paul Hare and Herbert H. Blumberg (London: Rex Collins, 1977), p. 126.

220 "I don't see how the Sahara Project": George Willoughby to Rustin, 10/25/59, in BR Papers.

220 "Bayard was a brilliant organizer": Michael Randle to the author, 7/3/89.

221 "was shocked by your departure": Tom Kahn to Rustin, 10/29/59, in BR Papers.

222 "What is happening here": Rustin to Randolph, 11/5/59. Papers of the Brotherhood of Sleeping Car Porters, Box 25, Library of Congress.

222 "I imagine you are pretty essential": Ralph DiGia to Rustin, 11/13/59, in BR Papers.

222 "We are categorically convinced": Tom Kahn to Rustin, 11/11/59, in BR Papers.

223 "One of the reasons you are so valuable": Stanley Levison to Rustin, 11/1/59, in BR Papers.

223 "People are going to make trouble": Tom Kahn to Rustin, 11/16/59, in BR Papers.

Chapter 15

224 "We do not wish Bayard Rustin's relationship": Edward Gottlieb to Randolph, 3/2/60, in BR Papers.

225 controversial advertisement: "Heed Their Rising Voices" appeared in the *New York Times*, 3/29/60.

226 "The attack upon Bayard": Interview with Rachelle Horowitz, 6/9/89.

226 "the vicious attack": L. D. Reddick to Randolph, 4/15/60.

227 *Times* v. *Sullivan*: See Anthony Lewis, *Make No Law: The Sullivan Case and the First Amendment* (New York: Random House, 1991), pp. 5–35; 160; 283.

227 "Early in May": Interview with Paul Barnes, 8/22/88.

229 "the white Southerner's ability": David Garrow, *Bearing the Cross* (New York: Morrow, 1986), pp. 136–37.

229 memorandum to Dr. King: Rustin to King, 6/15/60. King Papers, Box 5, Mugar Library, Boston University.

230 he quietly resigned: "Bayard Rustin Resigns as Aide to Rev. King," *New York Citizen Call*, 7/2/60. Rustin interview with Columbia University Oral History Project, 5/30/85. Garrow, *Bearing the Cross*, pp. 139–40. Taylor Branch, *Parting the Waters* (New York: Simon & Schuster, 1988), pp. 314–16.

230 "I cannot permit a situation to endure": "Rustin Resignation Fires up Powell vs. King, Randolph Rift," *New York Courier*, 7/9/60.

231 "lost much moral credit": James Baldwin, "The Dangerous Road Before Martin Luther King," *Harper's*, Feb. 1961.

231 "Levison, Bayard's great friend": Interview with Rachelle Horowitz, 8/5/95.

231 "pushed . . . to the sidelines": Harrington, *Fragments of the Century*, pp. 107–17.

232 "Bayard was easily the most effective speaker": Interview with Devi Prasad, 7/18/88.

232 A peace "walk": See Bradford Lyttle, *You Come with Naked Hands* (Manchester, N.H.: Greenleaf Books, 1972), p. 58.

233 "surprise at how far": April Carter to the author, 10/19/88.

234 World Peace Brigade in Africa: Charles C. Walker, "Nonviolence in Eastern Africa 1962–4: The World Peace Brigade and Zambian Independence," in *Liberation Without Violence*, ed. Hare and Blumberg, pp. 157–77.

234 Peace Brigade in Tanzania: Rustin interview with Columbia University Oral History Project, 4/3/85. Interview with William Sutherland, 7/5/88.

234 "The project is built around us": Rustin to Muste, 2/22/62. Muste Files, Reel 89.16, SCPC.

235 "heartened," Kaunda said: Walker, "Nonviolence in Eastern Africa . . . ," in *Liberation Without Violence*.

236 "inestimable help to us": Jane Stembridge to David McReynolds, 8/9/60. WRL Files, Box 14, SCPC.

236 Moses . . . Jane Stembridge: Howard Zinn, *SNCC: The New Abolitionists* (Boston: Beacon Press, 1964), pp. 7, 35.

237 "Tom represented a socialist collaboration": Interview with Michael Thelwell, 7/29/90. All further statements by Thelwell in this chapter are from the same interview.

237 "I told Malcolm": Rustin interview with Columbia University Oral History Project, 5/8/85.

238 "Bayard was one of the first": Milton Viorst, *Fire in the Streets* (New York: Touchstone Books, 1979), p. 350.

238 "I think Bayard's influence": Interview with Tom Kahn, 10/27/89.

Chapter 16

240 outline of the Emancipation March: Rustin memorandum to Randolph, 1/3/63, in BR Papers.

241 Whitney Young told Randolph: See Nancy J. Weiss, *Whitney M. Young, Jr., and the Struggle for Civil Rights* (Princeton, N.J.: Princeton University Press, 1989), p. 103. Roy Wilkins told Randolph: Interview with Rachelle Horowitz, 6/9/89; Tom Kahn, 10/27/89.

242 "a canker that never healed": Mary King, *Freedom Song* (New York: Morrow, 1987), p. 182.

242 "then a crisis might have been forced": Michael Thelwell, *Duties, Pleasures and Conflicts* (Amherst: University of Massachusetts Press, 1987), pp. xi, xii.

242 "I regarded the compromise": Interview with Horowitz, 6/9/89.

243 "stormy" from the beginning: James Forman, *The Making of Black Revolutionaries* (New York: Macmillan, 1972), pp. 361–62.

243 "When Medgar Evers was murdered": Rustin interview with Columbia University Oral History Project, 9/12/85.

243 "joint chiefs of staff": Farmer, *Lay Bare the Heart*, p. 215.

243 "neither feels hostility": Murray Kempton, "A. Philip Randolph," *New Republic*, 7/6/63.

244 "Birmingham was one of television's finest hours": Rustin, undated discussion with unidentified interviewer, in BR Papers.

244 "We face a moral crisis": See Theodore Sorensen, *Kennedy* (New York: Harper & Row, 1965), pp. 495–96.

244 "as gifted and impressive a group": Arthur Schlesinger, Jr., *A Thousand Days* (Boston: Houghton Mifflin, 1965), pp. 968–73.

246 "Dr. King, who had no legislative experience": Roy Wilkins, *Standing Fast* (New York; Viking, 1982), p. 291.

246 "At one meeting Wilkins leaned": Farmer, *Lay Bare the Heart*, p. 218.

246 "Martin simply couldn't in-fight": Rustin interview with Columbia Oral History Project, 10/31/85.

246 At the July 2 meeting: Interview with John Lewis, 10/25/89; interview with James Farmer, 9/3/89; Farmer, *Lay Bare the Heart*, p. 239; Rustin interview with Columbia University Oral History Project, 5/8/85.

248 "Bayard had a high respect": Interview with Tom Kahn, 10/27/89.

249 "How do you move [that] many people": "Negroes Wrestle Huge Planning Problems," *National Guardian*, 8/5/63.

249 "I am a technician": "Technician for March on Washington," *Philadelphia Sunday Bulletin*, 8/18/63.

250 "bent on demonstrating": "Marchers Widen March Demands," *New York Times*, 8/21/63.

250 "just like they were getting ready for D-Day": "Marchers' Master Plan," *Life*, 8/23/63.

250 "Merely contemplating the possibilities": Ibid.

250 *Wall Street Journal*: "Most Whites . . . Say They Oppose Rights Demonstration," 8/28/63.

250 "Tempers are bound to flare": "Negroes Warned on Capital March," *New York Times*, 7/8/63.

250 "If Negro leaders persist": "The March Should be Stopped," *New York Herald Tribune*, 6/25/63.

250 William Jennings Bryan Dorn: (His remarks and those of other invited legislators) are in the BR Papers.

251 Thurmond launched a blistering attack: "Thurmond Assails a Leader of the March," *New York Herald Tribune*, 8/14/63.

251 To an irate member of the NAACP: Frank Walker to Roy Wilkins, 8/21/63; Wilkins to Walker, 8/23/63, in NAACP Papers, Box A-228, Library of Congress.

251 a statement prepared for the press: 8/16/63; in BR Papers.

251 In letters and telephone calls: Emergency preparations and instructions for the day of the march were reported in Organizing Manual No. 2, issued by Rustin's staff; "Negro Policemen to Guide March," *New York Times*, 8/23/63; "The March Day," New York Herald Tribune, 8/23/63; "80,000 Lunches Made Here . . . for Washington Marchers," New York Times, 8/28/63; "Notes of MOW Committee Meeting," 8/17/63, and "Medical Committee for Civil Rights to Bayard Rustin," 7/22/63 (both in BR Papers); "Marchers' Master Plan," *Life*, 8/23/63. The account also draws upon interviews with Seymour Posner, 9/16/88; Rachelle Horowitz, 6/7/89; and Tom Kahn, 10/27/89.

252 "the most elaborately nurse-maided demonstration": Mary McGrory, "Randolph's Eloquence," *New York Post*, 8/11/63.

252 "It was my theory": Rustin interview with Columbia University Oral History Project, 5/8/85.

253 "We were ecstatic" Interview with Rachelle Horowitz, 6/7/89.

253 It was Malcolm X: Based on an account by Ossie Davis, in *Voices of Freedom*, ed. Henry Hampton and Steve Fayer (New York: Bantam Books, 1990), p. 162.

254 "The city was so empty": Marya Mannes, "A Mounting Tide . . . ," *Washington Post*, 8/29/63.

254 "Washington politicians were scared to death": Burke Marshall, in V*oices of Freedom*, p. 161.

254 "There has been no protest": Peregrine Worsthorne, London Sunday *Telegraph*, 8/25/63.

255 "Mr. Rustin, it is past six o'clock": Interview with Rachelle Horowitz, 6/7/89.

255 "subdued and saddened": Coretta Scott King, *My Life with Martin Luther King, Jr.*, pp. 236–37.

255 "great crush of humanity": "Traffic Control Works Smoothly in Capital," *New York Times*, 8/29/63.

256 "that whole vast concourse": King, *My Life with Martin Luther King, Jr.*, p. 237.

256 "We will march because we recognize": Charlton Heston, quoted in *Washington Star*, 8/1/63.

256 "Tens of thousands of these petitioning Negroes": "Marching into History," *New York Herald Tribune*, 8/29/63.

256 "the greatest assembly": "200,000 March for Civil Rights," *New York Times*, 8/29/63.

257 "I went crazy with that figure": Interview with Seymour Posner, 9/16/88.

258 "Like their white political brethren": James Reston, "I Have a Dream," *New York Times*, 8/29/63. Excerpts from the day's major speeches were printed in the *Times*, 8/29/63. In his address, Roy Wilkins made the dramatic announcement that W. E. B. Du Bois, the father of progressive civil rights activism in the twentieth century, had died in Ghana the previous day.

259 "I have been increasingly perturbed": Pauli Murray to Randolph, 8/21/63, in BR Papers.

260 Lewis's text was unsparing: The original text of John Lewis's controversial speech was published in *Liberation*, Sept. 1963. The revised and expurgated version is collected in "Speeches by the Leaders," a recording by the NAACP, transcribed and published late in 1963.

260 "Lewis was denouncing": Wilkins, *Standing Fast*, p. 293.

260 "I didn't think it was necessary": *Voices of Freedom*, p. 166.

260 "a dynamite speech": Forman, *The Making of Black Revolutionaries*, p. 333.

260 "So we had this hurried conference": Interview with John Lewis, 10/25/89.

261 "an anguished echo": Reston, "I Have a Dream," *New York Times*, 8/29/63.

261 "evoked the spirit of America": Ned O'Gorman, "The Freedom March, *Jubilee*, Oct. 1963.

261 "by divine inspiration": Farmer, *Lay Bare the Heart*, p. 245.

262 "One cannot help but be impressed": President Kennedy's public statement, issued 8/28/63, appeared in *New York Times*, 8/29/63.

262 "If one was an American": Kay Boyle, "No Other Place to Be," *Liberation*, Sept. 1963.

262 "Who ever heard of angry revolutionists": *The Autobiography of Malcolm X* (New York: Grove Press, 1964), pp. 280–81.

262 "The day was important in itself": James Baldwin, quoted in Reston, "I Have a Dream," *New York Times*, 8/29/63.

262 "a day of public disgrace": David Lawrence, "Freedom March Described . . . ," *Richmond News Leader*, 8/29/63.

263   "It was a wonderful and immensely important": Marya Mannes, "A Mounting Tide . . . ," *Washington Post*, 8/29/63.

263   "The march transformed": Andrew Young, "Remembering the March on Washington," quoted in an undated newsletter of the A. Philip Randolph Institute, in BR Papers. See also Doris D. Saunders, *The Day They Marched* (Chicago: Johnson Publications, 1963).

263   "I could see he was tired": Jervis Anderson, *A. Philip Randolph: A Biographical Portrait* (New York: Harcourt Brace Jovanovich, 1972), pp. 331–32.

264   History "has attached the name": Roy Wilkins, *Standing Fast*, p. 239.

264   "Dr. King will go down in history": Charles Bloomstein to the author, 8/5/95.

Chapter 17

265   "was the most exciting project": Rustin to Godric Bader, 9/16/63, in BR Papers.

265   "No one was more surprised": Rustin to Sidney Aberman, 12/12/63, in BR Papers.

266   "You are getting to be world-famous": John Nevin Sayre to Rustin, 3/25/64, in BR Papers.

266   "how sin and evil had blotted out": Stephen B. Oates, *Let the Trumpet Sound* (New York: New American Library, 1985), pp. 260–62.

266   "cost the nation the right": "Rallies in Nation Protest Killing . . . in Alabama," *New York Times*, 9/23/63.

266   "a mountain of creative social confusion": Ibid.

267   "to place a technical [listening] device": Memorandum for the attorney general, 10/28/63, in Rustin FBI Files.

267   "telephone servicemen making checks"; "I would leave a building": Rustin to Douglas Lee, 8/14/73, in BR Papers.

267   "Rustin is a very competent individual": U.S. Government memorandum, 1/25/66, from Rustin surveillance in FBI Files.

268   organize a one-day protest: "Boycott Cripples City Schools," *New York Times*, 2/4/64.

268   "Mr. Rustin stayed up": "Picket Line Organizer," ibid.

268   His Syracuse hosts were incensed: "Rustin's Absence Angers University," *New York Times*, 2/6/64. BOYCOTT CHIEF SOVIETS' GUEST: *New York Daily News*, 2/5/64.

269   "I am not surprised": "Rustin Attends Party at Soviet Mission," *New York Times*, 2/5/64.

269   "Who's Smearing Whom?": *New York Daily News* (editorial), 2/6/64.

269   "It was almost inevitable": James Wechsler, "News Story," *New York Post*, 2/6/64.

269 "I am here as a member": "Just Red Guest—Not Red, Boycott Chief Says," *New York Journal-American*, 2/5/64.

270 "XXXX advised at 1.30 p.m.": U.S. Government memorandum, 2/4/64, New York; subject Bayard Rustin (N.Y. 100-158790), in Rustin FBI Files.

270 "news reporters were present": U.S. Government memorandum, 2/7/64, ibid.

271 "Norman Hill was known": Interview with Carl Rachlin, 9/11/89.

271 "Bayard felt at one stage": Interview with Tom Kahn, 10/27/79.

271 "Farmer rejected Kahn's appointment": August Meier and Elliot Rudwick, *CORE: A Study in the Civil Rights Movement* (New York: Oxford University Press, 1973), pp. 322–23.

271 "Jim Farmer always knew": Interview with Norman Hill, 5/12/88.

272 "a gun to the heart of the city": "Mayor Says Stall-In Holds Gun to the Heart of the City," *New York Times*, 4/21/64.

272 "would constitute": "The Stall-In," *New York Times* (editorial), 4/21/64.

272 "I want to make it clear": Rustin, letter to *New York Times*, 4/21/64.

273 "We sat down in the mud": Donald Harrington to the author, 4/26/89.

273 "When the police came": Interview with Rachelle Horowitz, 6/7/89.

273 "It is always a source of conflict": In Rustin FBI Files, 9/30/63, SAC New York, 100-73250.

273 "whether it would be possible": U.S. Department of Justice, New York, 3/4/64, in Rustin FBI Files.

274 King was "badly informed": Fairclough, *To Redeem the Soul of America*, p. 170.

274 "Bayard and I spoke": Interview with Harry Wachtel, 9/18/89. Discussion of King's Nobel Prize mission to Europe is based on the same interview.

276 "Fireboats saluted him": Oates, *Let the Trumpet Sound*, p. 313.

277 "If the March on Washington represented": Rustin, *Strategies for Freedom*, pp. 50–1.

277 "The only thing [Johnson] could think of": Fred Powledge, *Free at Last* (Boston: Little, Brown, 1991), p. 598.

278 "If the Freedom Democratic Party": Clayborne Carson, *In Struggle* (Cambridge, Mass.: Harvard University Press, 1981), p. 125.

278 "You cannot trust the system": Quoted in *Voices of Freedom*, p. 202.

278 "The Freedom Party was an improbable collection": Interview with Michael Thelwell, 8/6/93.

278 "The Freedom Democrats went to Atlantic City": Stokely Carmichael and Charles Hamilton, *Black Power* (New York: Vintage Books, 1967), pp. 92, 96.

279 "We rather envisioned": Rustin, *Strategies for Freedom*, pp. 51–4.

Chapter 18

283 "The Negro must stay in the streets": Gertrude Samuels, "Five Angry Men Speak Their Minds," *New York Times Magazine,* 5/17/64.

283 "with its original approach": "Rights Leader Advises Negroes to Shift Tactics . . . ," *New York Times,* 12/2/63.

283 "A tactic which just ties up everybody": "The Negro Movement: Where Shall It Go Now?" *Dissent,* Summer 1964.

284 "There can be no such thing": "Negroes Can't Go It Alone," *Manhattan Tribune,* 12/21/68.

285 "We need allies": Rustin, "From Protest to Politics," *Commentary,* Feb. 1965.

285 "difficult to understand": Kwame Turé (formerly Stokely Carmichael) to the author, 6/25/93.

285 "defending your activities": Susan Neuhauser Atlee to Rustin, 4/6/71, in BR Papers.

285 "I do not consider myself": Rustin to Atlee, 6/23/71, in BR Papers.

285 "Bayard has no credibility": James Farmer, quoted in "Bayard Rustin Is Dead at 75," *New York Times,* 8/25/87.

285 "Rustin has taken his stand": Felix Morrow to *New Leader,* typescript dated 9/21/64, in BR Papers.

285 "Your intellectual contribution": William Miller to Rustin, 7/16/65, in BR Papers.

286 "Max was crucial": Interview with Tom Kahn, 10/27/89. For a critique of the realignment analysis see Ronald Radosh, "From Protest to Black Power: the Failure of Coalition Politics," in *The Great Society Reader,* ed. Marvin E. Gettleman and David Mermelstein (New York: Random House, 1967).

286 "Bayard's experience with the March": Charles Bloomstein to the author, 5/2/95.

287 "It was a moving thing to see": Interview with Arnold Aronson, 10/26/89.

288 "What the Randolph Institute also did": Interview with Donald Slaiman, 9/12/89.

288 "how Bayard could go"; Herbert Hill. . . . looked coldly: Interviews with Farmer, 9/3/89, and Hill, 10/5/88. When an admirer wrote to inform him of a speech Hill had made against him in the Middle West, Rustin replied, "Herb Hill isn't one of my favorite people. He does spit and snort a lot." (To Dorothy Knoke, 2/9/68, in BR Papers.)

288 "I would never say that Bayard moved into betrayal": Interview with Michael Thelwell by Jewel Greshak, 1980, in Thelwell's personal files.

289 "United effort behind the Freedom Budget": Roy Wilkins, "The NAACP and the New Strategy," *American Federationist,* Nov. 1966.

290 "The demand for a Freedom Budget": "Freedom Budget Opposed by Nixon," *New York Times*, 5/15/68.

290 "faded from the landscape": Leon Keyserling to Rustin, 12/2/71, in BR Papers.

290 "Unfortunately, the election": Rustin to Gar Alperovitz, 10/18/71, in BR Papers.

290 "The Freedom Budget and the earlier issues": Rachelle Horowitz to the author, 5/2/95.

Chapter 19

291 he resigned . . . organization: Rustin to Edward Gottlieb, 1/28/65; to A. J. Muste, 1/28/65; to Neil Haworth, 11/17/65; in BR Papers.

291 "I would have thought": Roy Finch to Rustin, 2/9/65, in BR Papers.

292 "Whereas I used to believe that pacifism had a political value. . . .": Rustin interview with Walter Naegle, 4/21/83, in BR Papers.

292 "Your speech . . . brought sharply into focus": Michael Tobin to Rustin, 6/10/65, in BR Papers.

293 "Bayard, like me, was a pacifist": Lefever to the author, 8/5/88.

293 "I believe the great majority": James Finn, *Protest: Pacifism and Politics* (New York: Vintage Books, 1968), p. 330.

294 "I think that one cannot take the view": Ibid., p. 338.

294 "Was it possible simultaneously": Harrington, *Fragments of the Century*, p. 204.

294 "When the war took over . . . ": Ibid., p. 204.

295 "particular positions expressed": "Statement on Student March in Washington," 4/16/65. Muste Papers, Reel 89.29, SCPC.

295 "On the eve of this weekend's 'peace march'": "Memorandum for a March," *New York Post* (editorial), 4/17/65.

295 "I was distressed that you took part": Staughton Lynd, "An Open Letter to Bayard Rustin," 4/19/65, in BR Papers.

296 "has been a leading advocate": "Letters," *Liberation*, Oct. 1965.

296 "You should be aware": Muste to Staughton Lynd, 4/20/65. Muste Papers, Reel 89.29, SCPC.

296 "a labor lieutenant of capitalism": Lynd, "Coalition Politics or Nonviolent Revolution?" *Liberation*, June/July 1965. See also David Dellinger, "The March on Washington and Its Critics," *Liberation*, May 1965.

297 McReynolds disclosed that he was "stunned": David McReynolds, "Transition: Personal and Political Notes," *Liberation*, Aug. 1965.

298 "Many of those on the left": Interview with Robert Pickus, 12/12/88.

Chapter 20

299   denounced "my own government": "Beyond Vietnam," in *Dr. King . . .
      Speak on the War in Vietnam,* booklet produced by Clergy and Laymen
      Concerned About Vietnam, 1967, pp. 10–17.

300   "fusing two public problems": "Dr. King's Error," editorial, 4/7/67.

300   "abject surrender in Vietnam": Quoted in Fairclough, *To Redeem the Soul of
      America,* p. 338.

300   "King . . . has thrown in": John P. Roche, "Memorandum for the
      President," 4/5/67, in LBJ Presidential Library.

300   "the anti-war effort above all other efforts": Roy Wilkins, "Dr. King's New
      Role," *New York Post,* 4/15/67.

300   "urgent domestic programs": "Jewish Veterans Attack Dr. King's Stand on
      War," *New York Times,* 4/6/67.

300   "Dr. King should positively": Undated and untitled news clipping in BR
      Papers.

300   "I once heard Bayard": Interview with Adam Roberts, 4/3/90.

300   "Most surprising was the attitude": Fairclough, *To Redeem the Soul of
      America,* p. 338.

301   "Dr. King as a Negro leader": "Rustin Urges Making Jobs Top Target of
      Rights Drive," *Chicago Sun-Times,* 4/15/67.

301   "I would consider the involvement": Rustin, "Dr. King's Painful
      Dilemma," New York *Amsterdam News,* 4/22/67; reprinted in Rustin,
      Down the Line (Chicago: Quadrangle Books, 1971), p. 169.

301   "I have always been opposed": Jervis Anderson, *A. Philip Randolph: A
      Biographical Portrait* (New York: Harcourt Brace Jovanovich, 1972), p. 331.

302   "to set the record straight": Rustin to William S. McFeely, 12/29/86, in
      BR Papers.

302   "Rustin was a very brilliant presenter": Interview with Harry Wachtel,
      9/18/89.

303   "drawing together a clear presentation": King to Rustin, 9/18/64, in BR
      Papers.

303   "I am counting on your presence": King to Rustin, 5/20/65, in BR Papers.
      King considered it a must for Rustin to attend: Carol Hoover to Rustin,
      8/5/67, in BR Papers.

303   "Get the hell out of Harlem": Rustin interview with Columbia University
      Oral History Project, 2/28/85.

304   "bourgeois blacks": Rustin, "The Watts Manifesto and the McCone
      Report," *Commentary,* March 1966.

304   "The biggest confrontation": Rustin conversation with Harry Wachtel,
      10/31/85, transcript in BR Papers.

304   "The living room at Young's house": Velma Hill to the author, 3/5/96.

304 Chicago "was not the place": Interview with Wachtel, 9/18/89.

305 "He was determined to go": Velma Hill to the author, 3/5/96.

305 "The whole Chicago experience": Oates, *Let the Trumpet Sound*, p. 405.

305 King sought Rustin's "strategic thinking": "On Bayard Rustin—
Harrington vs. Newfield," *Village Voice*, 4/18/68.

305 Rustin wrote a memorandum: "Memo on the Spring Protest in
Washington," 1/29/68, in BR Papers; reprinted in Rustin, *Down the Line*,
pp. 202–5.

305 "I seriously question the efficacy": Report by Jack Nelson in *Washington
Post* and *New York Post*, 2/26/68.

306 "I did know from Martin": Harry Wachtel to Rustin, 9/25/85, in BR Papers.

306 Marion Logan . . . questioned: See Gerold Frank, *An American Death*, (New
York: Doubleday, 1972), pp. 39–40.

306 "on matters that were to affect profoundly": Rustin, "Ally to the End in
King's Philosophy . . . ," letter to *New York Times*, 9/25/85.

307 "I've known him for twenty-five years": Interview with John P. Roche,
9/10/89.

307 "Up in the air": Rustin interview with Columbia Oral History Project,
4/3/85.

307 "On learning of King's death": Rustin, "Ally to the End . . . ," letter to
New York Times, 9/25/85.

308 massive, orderly, silent march: "Mrs. King Asks 'Peaceful Society' After
Orderly Memphis March," *New York Times*, 4/9/68.

308 "If you decide to step": William Sutherland to Rustin, 4/7/68, in BR
Papers.

308 "a fantastic vacuum": Rustin to Sutherland, 5/1/68, in BR Papers.

308 "Perhaps only once in a century": Rustin, "A Silent Tragedy," *Fellowship*,
May 1968.

308 "We had to face the fact": Ralph Abernathy, *And the Walls Came Tumbling
Down* (New York: Harper & Row, 1989), p. 522.

308 Knowing how unpopular he was: In an article for the *New York Times* ("A
Realist Is Called to Save a Dream"), 6/2/68, Ben Franklin wrote that
Rustin was "regarded by some of the SCLC leaders as a moderating and
even somewhat villainous agent of the establishment." See also Tom Kahn,
"Why the Poor People's Campaign Failed," *Commentary*, Sept. 1968.

309 United Automobile Workers . . . contributed $25,000: Walter Reuther to
Rustin, 5/29/68, in BR Papers.

309 *Post* applauded Rustin's "Call": "Goals for the Poor," *Washington Post* (editorial), 6/5/68.

309 "a bunch of jazz and foolishness": "Williams Blasts Rustin on Goals of the
Poor," *Washington Evening Star*, 6/4/68. See also "Abernathy Denies Rustin
Authority," ibid., 6/5/68.

309   "I have repeatedly sought": "Rustin Quits March," *New York Times*, 6/8/68.
309   "absolutely reprehensible" act: Olly Leeds to Rustin, 6/7/68, in BR Papers.
310   "shrank to a minimum estimate": *Time*, 6/14/68.
310   "In a sense, whoever it was": "City of the Poor Shuts Peacefully," *New York Times*, 6/25/68.

Chapter 21

313   "It is possible that Bayard Rustin": "Rustin on Campus Chaos," *Washington Daily News,* 4/29/69.
314   "What we are going to start saying": Oates, *Let the Trumpet Sound*, p. 386.
314   "We had made a victory": Carmichael in *Voices of Freedom*, p. 291.
314   "We are committed": "Crisis and Commitment" (advertisement), *New York Times*, 10/14/66.
315   "I would contend that 'black power'": Rustin, "Black Power and Coalition Politics," *Commentary*, Sept. 1966.
315   "that one wing of the civil rights movement": Garrow, *Bearing the Cross*, pp. 533–34.
315   "Bayard spoke forcefully": Eric Lee to the author, 8/10/88.
316   "two agitated young black men": Raymond Mack to the author, 7/26/88.
316   "In a profound sense": Rabbi Everett Gendler to Rustin, 11/3/66, in BR Papers.
317   "I've known Stokely for many years": Rustin to Rabbi Gendler, 11/11/66, in BR Papers.
317   "He came to the office": Interview with Norman Hill, 5/12/88.
317   locking political horns at . . . Hunter College: "Exchange of Views Between Rustin and Carmichael," LID (League for Industrial Democracy) *News Bulletin*, Fall 1966/Winter 1967.
318   "SNCC worked for Black Power": Viorst, *Fire in the Streets*, p. 376.
319   demands "for black autonomy": Rustin, *Down the Line*, pp. xiv–xv.
319   "the extremes in absurdity": Ibid., p. 300.
319   "We are living in a time": "Notable and Quotable," *Wall Street Journal*, 5/6/69.
320   "for being one of the very few": Gunnar Myrdal to Rustin, 5/5/69, in BR Papers.
320   "I don't think he made that statement": "Black Studies Program Criticism Scored by Valley Street Official," *Los Angeles Times*, 4/30/69.
320   "The study of the black experience": Rustin, "Word to Black Students," reprinted in *Down the Line*, pp. 327–34.

Chapter 22

322 "After the mid-sixties": Interview with James Farmer, 9/3/89.

323 "Bayard and I stood": Interview with John P. Roche, 9/10/89.

324 "During the 1940s": Thomas R. Brooks, *Toil and Trouble* (New York: Delta Books, 1964), p. 245.

324 "increasing [their] influence": "Blacks Wield More Clout in Unions Despite Bias," *Newsday*, 9/7/87.

325 "It is rarely acknowledged": Rustin to Dan Golenpaul, 10/8/70, in BR Papers.

325 "We have heard your rhetoric": "Conflict or Coalition," reprint of Rustin's address, 10/3/69, to the AFL-CIO convention, transcript in BR Papers.

326 "Bayard moved from the far left": Interview with Moshe Decter, 10/24/89.

326 "some in the audience wept": "We'll Burn Candles Here, Too," *New York Daily News*, 9/7/72.

326 "your role is crucial": Elie Wiesel to Rustin, 1/30/81, in BR Papers. Wiesel's "incalculable" role: Rustin to Nobel Prize Committee, 1/21/85, in BR Papers.

326 "I want you to know": Rabbi Joachim Prinz to Rustin, 6/12/67, in BR Papers.

326 "You have been so close to us here": Howard Squadron to Rustin, 9/28/78, in BR Papers.

327 "During the planning of a rally": Interview with Irwin Suall, 7/3/88.

327 "I sometimes saw Bayard addressing meetings": Interview with Fran Lee, 12/19/90.

327 "He hears about it": Jacqueline Trescott, "The March," *Washington Post*, 8/21/83.

328 "What Bayard liked about Jews": Interview with Roy Finch, 11/1/88.

328 "Bayard sometimes conveyed": Interview with a friend of Rustin who requested that he not be identified, 11/8/89.

328 "It would be one of the great tragedies": Rustin, "Premise of the Stereotype," New York *Amsterdam News*, 4/8/67.

328 "in part by blacks who want to exaggerate it": Rustin, quoted in "Jews and Blacks," *Midstream*, Jan. 1974.

329 "Negroes, when asked": Anti-Defamation League to Rustin, 4/13/66, in BR Papers.

329 major speech to the ADL: "The Anatomy of Frustration," delivered 5/6/68; transcript in BR Papers.

330 "Puerto Rican and black children": "The View from the Ghetto," *New York Post*, 9/14/67.

330 "I, almost all of us": "Negroes Can't Do it Alone," *Manhattan Tribune*, 12/21/68.

330 "We, the black and Puerto Rican communities": Ralph K. Poynter to Rustin, 4/2/68, in BR Papers.

331 "In 1966, there had been": Interview with Albert Shanker, 10/23/89.

331 "We were fearful": "Schools in an Uproar," *New York*, 4/11/88.

332 "listened attentively as Bayard Rustin": A. H. Raskin, "Race Meant More Than a Union Card," *New York Times*, 11/24/68.

332 "I asked Bayard many times": Interview with Albert Shanker, 10/23/89.

332 "The great thing about Rustin": Mark Goldberg, "A Portrait of Albert Shanker," *Educational Leadership*, March 1993.

Chapter 23

333 "acute psychosis": Dr. Roger Moore to the author, 11/16/89.

334 "When the doctors and nurses tried": Interview with Rachelle Horowitz, 8/9/89.

334 "We chatted a good deal": Dr. Roger Moore to the author, 11/16/89.

334 "a splendid nurse": Rustin to Marion Chatfield, 11/30/71, in BR Papers.

335 "There are two kinds": Interview with Rachelle Horowitz, 8/9/89.

335 "From the time I joined": Interview with Arch Puddington, 5/7/89.

336 "a front man": Interviews with Charles Bloomstein, 10/18/87; Arch Puddington, 5/7/89.

337 "were moving heaven and earth": Michael Harrington, *The Long-Distance Runner* (New York: Henry Holt, 1988), p. 200.

337 "The A. Philip Randolph Institute believes": "Affirmative Action in an Economy of Scarcity," Testimony of Bayard Rustin and Norman Hill, 9/17/74, to the Special Subcommittee on Education, U.S. House of Representatives.

338 "I started working with Bayard": Interview with Rachelle Horowitz, 6/9/89.

339 "In the circles in which you move": Ann Davidon to Rustin, 10/26/73, in BR Papers.

339 "a democratic state": "Blacks and Jews Viewed as Drawing Closer Again," *New York Times*, 4/14/75.

339 "I have a hunch": Interview with Irwin Suall, 7/3/88.

339 "It is an insult": "Let Us Decide," letter to the editor, *Jewish Exponent*, 11/14/75.

340 "I felt that the Palestinians": Interview with Kenneth B. Clark, 2/9/89.

340 *Like it Is*: Rustin was invited to rebut Carmichael on 7/11/76, transcript in BR Papers.

341 "a great man": Undated statement by Meir, in Walter Naegle's personal files.

341 "I count it my good fortune": Rustin to President Carter, 12/12/78, in BR Papers.

341 "So where have I met you?": Elie Wiesel at Birthday Tribute to Rustin, 3/18/87, transcript in BR Papers.

341 "Bayard was an important catalyst": Interview with Leonard Sussman, 10/5/89. The account of Rustin's and Freedom House's monitoring of the Zimbabwe elections is based on the same interview.

342 At a meeting in Warsaw: Interview with Charles Bloomstein, 9/11/89.

343 "fairly democratic" . . . "great leadership qualities": Rustin interview with Columbia University Oral History Project, 2/6/86.

343 Advocating limited sanctions: Rustin, "The Need for Democracy," *Friends Journal*, 2/15/87. See also "South Africa: Is Peaceful Change Possible?" by Rustin, Charles Bloomstein, and Walter Naegle, published by New York Friends Group, Inc., 1984.

343 "I spoke out against total sanctions": Joyce Harris to the author, 8/22/88.

344 "I admired his dedication": Helen Suzman to the author, 2/28/89.

344 "The fundamental issue in South Africa": Rustin interview with Columbia University Oral History Project, 9/12/85.

344 March for Survival: "The Fancies and the Fact," *Time*, 2/18/80. Also interview with Liv Ullmann, 10/11/88.

345 "Because of Bayard's close association": Interview with Leo Cherne, 8/4/90. Cherne's other tributes to Rustin were expressed in the same interview.

Chapter 24

346 "He bought cut-rate suits": Interview with Arch Puddington, 12/27/88.

347 "he turned heads": Joyce Harris to the author, 8/22/88.

347 "a kind of poseur": Interview with Liv Ullmann, 10/11/88.

347 charged with the illegal possession: "Nab Rustin on Sword-Cane Charge," *New York Daily News*, 1/31/72.

347 "Rachelle Horowitz telephoned": Interview with Richard Ravitch, 7/21/88.

348 "Thanks to you": Rustin to Richard Kuh, 3/24/72. "with some clients": Kuh to Rustin, 5/15/72; in BR Papers. See also "Indictment of Rustin Barred," *New York Times*, 3/3/72.

348 "That place of order": LuEsther Mertz to Rustin, 12/8/66, in BR Papers.

348 "an extended expression": Susan Ginsburg, "Portrait as a Collector," *Auction*, May 1970.

348 "I started after World War II," ibid.

349 "Bayard and I were walking": Interview with Arnold Aronson, 10/26/89.

350 "In my lifetime of selling art"; "Bayard's taste in art": Interview with Bernhardt Crystal, 7/15/88. All later remarks by Crystal were made in the same interview.

352 "Bayard could have had an excellent career": Interview with Margaret Davison, 11/8/89.

352 "Once in a while": Rustin interview with Peg Byron, *Washington Blade*, 2/5/86.

352 the college's Doggett Lounge: *Portland Press Herald*, 10/7/78.

Chapter 25

353 he left for Haiti: "Report on Haiti Trip," undated manuscript in BR Papers. Also interview with Walter Naegle, 10/26/87.

354 "Bayard told me later": Interview with Arnold Aronson, 10/26/89.

354 "contracted a miserable stomach bug": Rustin to M. Moran Weston, 8/4/87, in BR Papers.

354 "He had work to do to the very end": Lawrence Templin to the author, 6/10/89.

354 "he had a high tolerance for pain": Interview with Walter Naegle, 10/26/87.

354 "he looked so sick": Interview with Leonard Sussman, 10/5/89.

354 "The misdiagnosis was a crying shame": Interview with Adam Roberts, 4/31/90.

355 "He didn't lead so much as he influenced": "How Bayard Rustin Led," *New York Times* (editorial), 8/26/87.

355 "the passing of the last great apostle": "Bayard Rustin: 1912–1987," *New York Post* (editorial), 8/25/87.

355 "Bayard had seemed ever young": Velma Hill to the author, 3/5/96.

355 "one of the more important human beings": Interview with Liv Ullmann, 10/11/88.

355 "I last met Bayard in 1965": Curtis B. Gans to Norman Hill, 9/25/87, in Hill's personal files.

356 "Many of us who felt out of touch": Larry Gara, quoted in *The Nonviolent Activist*, Jan./Feb. 1988.

356 Among speakers at the service: Speeches at Rustin's memorial service are from the author's recording of the event.

358 "Though he was skillful": Interview with a former companion of Rustin, 11/8/89.

358 "All heads would turn and stare": Alex Bloomstein to the author, 8/6/89.

359 "We decided that Scotland Farm": Interview with Walter Naegle, 6/28/88.

Index